Chuck,

TRUTHS TO LIVE BY

This was my Father's last book before he went home to heaven. I hope you enjoy some of the material. In many ways you remind me of him in your leadership style. I wish he could have met you. Thank you for the opportunity to work for you.

Your friend,

Joe

TRUTHS
TO LIVE BY

LIFE APPLICATIONS BY PASTOR JOE ARMINIO

by Joseph V. Arminio

Total Fusion Press
Strasburg, Ohio

Truths To Live By: Life Applications By Pastor Joe Arminio
Published by Total Fusion Press
PO Box 123, Strasburg, OH 44680
www.totalfusionpress.com

ISBN (paperback): 978-1-943496-10-5
ISBN (hardback): 978-1-943496-11-2

Library of Congress Control Number: 2016959755

Cover Design by Joy Arminio and Jonathan Vinci
Interior Design by Kara Starcher
Edited by Kristin Arminio

Published in Association with Total Fusion Ministries, Strasburg, OH.
www.totalfusionministries.org

24 23 22 21 20 19 18 17   2 3 4 5 6

Dedication

To my precious mom, who never served in the military, but was the strongest soldier I ever knew. Only standing about 4' 10", she was a giant in her faith, tenacity, will and determination. Mom, thanks for teaching me endurance, and a spirit of never give up. I dedicate this book, and the completion of it, to you. I love and miss you greatly, but I will see you again. Keep on enjoying Jesus and Heaven.

And to my precious congregation at Abundant Life of Whippany, New Jersey, thank you for your love, support, prayers and participation in the Gospel of our Lord Jesus Christ. It has been a great joy serving you these past 25 years and I look forward to our future years together as we touch our world for Christ and His Kingdom. Truly, you have taught me more than I have ever imparted to you. I love and appreciate you all tremendously. You all are the best!

Table of Contents

Acknowledgments

To my beloved wife, Debbi, my high school sweetheart and my help-meet for over 38 years. God has blessed us with five children, five grand-children and counting. You are a woman that is committed as a Christian, wife, mother, grandmother and friend. Thank you for all of your love and support, especially during the most difficult season of my life. You have been a tremendous life partner and co-laborer.

To Bishop Peter Bruno, who taught me how to love God and love His people. Bishop, you saw in me what I did not. You are one of the greatest examples to me of tenacity, perseverance and a "no quit" constitution.

To Kristin, for her endless hours on this project. For the inputting on the computer, the grammatical corrections, the editing, proofreading and being the overall project manager, thank you dear.

To Joy and John, thank you for your contribution and creation of the cover of this book.

To Christine, Deanna and Maria, thank you for your labor in proof-reading the manuscript.

To my precious family, thank you for being my greatest support over the years. Debbi, Faith, Q, Joseph, Kristin, Joy, Alexandra, Benjamin, Chloe, Nicoletta and Raegan. You are my loves and my legacy.

Introduction

I wrote Truths to Live By with a three-fold purpose. It is a day-by-day devotional, a read through the Bible in a year, and a unique Bible trivia book.

First, it is my earnest desire and prayer that these daily devotionals, which were birthed out of my personal devotions, sermons and revelations from the Holy Ghost, would be a prophetic word to you in season and a source of tremendous encouragement on your journey with Jesus.

Second, to help you read through the Bible from Genesis to Revelation in one year, which will be a great accomplishment. Just follow the scripture readings for the designated day. (You can separate the scripture readings by morning and evening reading.) Go for it, you can do it!

Third, through the Bible trivia questions and answers (produced in the back of the book), you will increase your Bible knowledge.

So let's go on quite possibly the most exciting odyssey of your journey with Jesus, and God bless you with revelation and truths to live by.

~Pastor Joe Arminio

January

January 1

"Ripe Fruit"

1 John 4:16-19 — And we have known and believed the love that God hath to us. God is love; and he that dwelleth in love dwelleth in God, and God in him. Herein is our love made perfect, that we may have boldness in the day of judgment: because as he is, so are we in this world. There is no fear in love; but perfect love casteth out fear: because fear hath torment. He that feareth is not made perfect in love. We love him, because he first loved us.

As we embark on a new year, it seems fitting to reflect and meditate on the awesome, unfailing, immutable love that God has for us. So many people are troubled and even tormented by the spirit of fear. But we see through Scripture, as we develop, mature and are perfected in God's love; His love will cast out, (or throw away in a violent or intense manner, as the original Greek implies) all fear. As the people of God, we need to be perfected in God's love. That word perfect does not mean errorless or flawless or even sinless. The word means develop or to come to a place of maturity. We need to develop and come into the full maturity and completeness in God's love.

The Bible lists in Galatians 5:22, nine fruits of the Spirit; the first is love. God has put in all of our hearts, what is called seed love. Like all seed, it must be watered and cared for if there is going to be a harvest (fruit). The seed of love must be watered by the Word of God in our hearts and lives if we are going to see the maturity and the development of that seed. No luscious fruit starts out in a mature state; it has an origin. It begins with a seed. God is love, and He put His "Love Seed" into our spirits. We then have to water that seed with His Word so the seed will grow and mature into the "perfect" fruit of love. It is this love that throws fear out and away from our lives.

Allow God's love to mature in you so that you will be fearless and bold in your walk with God and before men. If there are still fears in your life, the Holy Spirit is challenging you to go deeper into God and allow His love to be perfected in you.

Scripture Reading: Genesis 1, 2; Matthew 1

Trivia Question: Which is the first commandment with a promise?

January 2

"Too Heavy to Bear"

Psalm 3:3 — But thou, O Lord art a shield for me, my glory, and the lifter up of mine head.

Life has a way of putting pressure on us; circumstances try to weigh us down. The Psalmist says that the Lord is our shield or protector and our glory. The Hebrew word for glory means, heavy or weighty, to bear the burden or carry the weight. In the natural realm, if you are carrying an extremely heavy item on your shoulders, it will weigh you down, causing your head to be in a downward position. The Psalmist says that the Lord is the lifter up of mine head. The only way we allow God to be the lifter up of our heads is if we make Him our Glory first and foremost. Remember, He is our heavy burden bearer. When we allow Him to carry the heavy load of life's trials and circumstances, He lifts the load, so we in turn do not have to carry it any longer. We allow Him to be the lifter up of our heads. We can only lift our heads when He takes the load off our lives. He is our glory—our burden bearer.

Psalms 55:22 says, "Cast thy burden upon the Lord, and He shall sustain thee: He shall never allow the righteous to be moved (or slip or fall)." Let God be your burden bearer so that you can lift up your head, and also "lift up your eyes unto the hills, from whence cometh your help, your help cometh from the Lord." (Psalms 121:1, 2) If your head is down, your eyes look down, but if you allow the Lord to be your burden bearer, He will also be the lifter up of your head. Your eyes will be lifted and focused on the one that can always help—the Lord. The prophet wrote, "The government shall be upon His shoulders." If He can carry the government, He can carry your problem and the weight of your trials. Give it all to Him today!

Scripture Reading: Genesis 3, 4, 5; Matthew 2

January 3

"The Perfect Storm"

Matthew 14:30-31 — But when he saw the wind boisterous, he was afraid;
and beginning to sink, he cried, saying, Lord, save me.
And immediately Jesus stretched forth his hand, and caught him,
and said unto him, O thou of little faith, wherefore didst thou doubt?

Like Peter, there are times when our lives reflect some sort of storm. In Peter's case, it was a literal storm and tempest that arose on the Sea of Galilee as he and his friends were traveling to the other side by boat. We have heard many sermons on why Peter started to "sink." Obviously, he took his eyes off Jesus and put them where they didn't belong – on his crisis and storm. Many times as believers we do the same and allow the circumstances to get the best of us. We allow our emotions to get our eyes off the "promise" and we only see the "problem." It's so easy to allow our emotions to get us out of faith and into fear. Such was the case with the apostle Peter.

I want to draw your attention to how Jesus responded to Peter after the apostle took his eyes off of the Lord, got into fear and started to drown. The passage says, *immediately* Jesus reached out His hand and pulled him up and out of the water as Peter cried out, "Lord save me."

When we allow life's storms to distract us, so that we take our eyes off the one we call "Prince of peace" and we begin to sink; all we need to do is what Peter did, cry out "Lord save me." The Lord will not reprimand you; first He will rescue you. He will not scold you; He will save you! After he rescues and saves, He then will correct and deal with the real issue, "O thou of little faith, why did you doubt?" The Lord will always correct us if need be, but aren't you glad He saves us and rescues us first? Are you in a situation where you have taken your eyes off Christ and put them on your crisis, or looked away from the promise and started focusing on the problem? If your faith is starting to sink and falter, then cry out to Jesus. He will reach out His saving hand, and pull you out of unbelief and doubt, and bring you into trust and faith once again. "Behold, The Lord's hand is not shortened that it cannot save, neither His ear heavy that it cannot hear." (Isaiah 59:1)

Scripture Reading: Genesis 6, 7, 8; Matthew 3

January 4

"Your Daddy"

Matthew 11:27 — All things are delivered unto me by my Father, and no man knoweth the Son, but the Father, neither knoweth any man the Father except the Son, and he to whomsoever the Son will reveal Him.

It is so important to get a revelation of Father. Out of a revelation of who our heavenly Father is, we will get a revelation of relationship. God our Father desires relationship with us, His children. Jesus came to reveal the Father to us. Jesus reveals the Father's love, nature, character, personality, mercy, grace and wisdom to His people. If we want a revelation of God our Father and a relationship with Him, we need to look to Jesus who reveals the Father to us. Jesus said to the apostle Philip, "If you had known me, you should have known my Father also, and from henceforth you know Him, and have seen Him…he that hath seen me hath seen the Father." (John 14:7-9)

As we intimately get to know the Son, He reveals to us the Father. As we get to know Jesus through His Word, through meditation on the Word and through prayer and fellowship with Him, He so graciously reveals the Father to us. We can have the same relationship with the Father as Jesus the Son has with the Father.

Whatever God has called us to do, or whatever and to whomever He calls us to minister, our fervor, fire and passion must come forth as a direct result of our relationship with the Father. Jesus ministered with such intensity because of His relationship with His Father. We must do the same.

Scripture Reading: Genesis 9, 10, 11; Matthew 4

Trivia Question: Who said of God that He is "of purer eyes than to behold evil," and that He cannot look on iniquity?

January 5

"Emancipation Proclamation"

John 8:32 — And you shall know the truth,
and the truth shall make you free.

It is everyone's desire to search and find truth. True Christians know truth when they surrender their lives to the one who declared, "I am The Way, The TRUTH, and the Life, The Lord Jesus Christ." The Apostle John wrote in one of his epistles (1 John 5:7), "For there are three that bear record in Heaven, The Father, the Word, and the Holy Spirit…" Jesus is called the Word. When we received the Lord Jesus into our hearts, we received the Word of God, which is the absolute truth of God. In His High Priestly intercessory prayer, Jesus prays to the Father, "sanctify them through thy truth, thy Word is truth."(John 17:17)

The truth of God is the Word of God. You cannot separate Jesus from His Word, for He is the Word of God. Likewise, you cannot separate the Word of God from the truth because "thy word is truth." When we need liberty in our lives, it is the truth (the Word) that brings emancipation. We must come to a place as Christians where we intimately embrace the truth of His Word so we can live at liberty in all areas of our lives. We must stand fast in the liberty with which Christ has made us free, and not be entangled again with the yoke of bondage. The truth will make us free and keep us free. Sin and sinful habits put a yoke around our necks and bring oppression and bondage, but the truth, which is the Word of God, makes us free and allows us to walk in liberty. He that the Son sets free is free indeed.

Do not allow sin to put you in spiritual prison, incarcerated by the shackles of darkness. Renew your mind in the Word of God daily to enjoy a life in Christ of freedom, liberty and blessing!

Scripture Reading: Genesis 12, 13, 14; Matthew 5:1-26

Trivia Question: Of whom did Christ say that they loved "the uppermost seats in the synagogues?"

———————————————

January 6

"Facing Your Giants"

1 Samuel 17:48 — And it came to pass, when the Philistine (Goliath) arose, and came and drew near to meet David, that David hastened, and ran toward the army to meet the Philistine.

There are many giants surrounding our lives that challenge our faith and confidence we have in the Lord. As the giant Goliath from Gath approached the armies of Israel and challenged the army of God, so the *giants* of our day rise up against us. They challenge the integrity of God's Word and the faith that is in our hearts toward our God.

As David, the adolescent shepherd boy, rose up and ran *toward* his enemy, he was an example for us to teach us to rise up in the faith of God and run toward the giants that challenge our lives.

Fear is a giant that tries to intimidate, permeate and debilitate our lives. We cannot allow fear to gain the upper hand. We must confront it and run toward this giant to slay it once and for all. The Bible says fear brings torment. Just as Goliath tormented the armies of Israel through fear and paralyzed them to the point where they could not express their faith in God; so the spirit of fear will try to do the same to you. You must do with fear as David did, run toward it, attack it, and eventually knock it down and cut off its head (so it cannot rise again). God has not given us the spirit of fear, but of power, love and a sound mind. Do not allow fear to intimidate or torment you. Run toward the giant and slay it with the Word of God!

Scripture Reading: Genesis 15, 16, 17; Matthew 5:27-48

Trivia Question: To whom did God say, "The Lord searcheth all hearts?"

January 7

"One Big, Happy Family"

Isaiah 43:25 — I, even I, am he that blotteth out thy transgressions for mine own sake, and will not remember thy sins.

When God takes out His big "eraser" and wipes away your sin, you can be assured that it is gone—forever! What great truths to meditate on this day; that ALL your sins have been blotted out by Almighty God. Jesus as the Lamb of God that takes away the sin of the world has become your propitiation (appeasement or substitute for your sins). God the Father took your sin and laid on Him (Jesus) the iniquity of us all.

Notice that God blots out our sin for His own sake. Our God is a Father, and always desired a huge family. God our Father is a Holy God and can never look upon sin, so He sent His Son to become our sin substitute. When you received Jesus Christ into your life and by faith allowed His blood to cleanse you, your life changed and you became a child of God. You were elevated from a wretched sinner to a sanctified saint. Now you can approach a Holy God and be accepted. That affects the Father as much as it affects you. Now the Father can fellowship and commune with a righteous people and call us sons and daughters (for His own sake). Oh, that we will fellowship and commune with our Father, through His Son and by the Holy Spirit.

He blots out our transgressions, He calls us into His family for intimate fellowship and He has no recollection of our sin. He has subdued our iniquities and has cast our sins into the depths of the sea. Today, reflect on the awesome love and mercy that He has toward you.

Scripture Reading: Genesis 18, 19; Matthew 6

Trivia Question: Who said, "Behold the handmaid of the Lord, be it unto me according to thy word?"

January 8

"Love the Law of Love"

James 2:8 — If ye fulfil the royal law according to the scripture, Thou shalt love thy neighbour as thyself, ye do well.

The Bible states that those that have been born again have been delivered from the power of darkness, and have been translated into the Kingdom of God's dear Son. Jesus Christ is the King of God's Kingdom. He is the majestic authority that governs this wonderful, divine kingdom. The Kingdom of God, governed by King Jesus, is very different from the kingdoms of this world. Jesus, who is the Royal Majesty on HIGH, has a governing *Royal Law* that His people must walk in and live by. This is the *Royal Law* of love. If we walk in and fulfill this law, which is to love our neighbors as ourselves, we will do well and be well!

One of the scribes asked King Jesus, "Which is the first and greatest commandment of all?" Jesus responded by saying, "Love the Lord your God with all your heart, mind, soul and strength and love your neighbor as you love yourself, there is no other commandment greater than this." (Mark 12:28-31)

Love is the *Royal Law* or commandment that governs the Kingdom of God where Jesus reigns as King. If we want to be a part of His Kingdom, and do well as servants of His Kingdom, we must walk in and fulfill this *Royal Law*—Love. "By this shall all men know that you are my disciples, if you have LOVE one to another." (John 13:35)

Scripture Reading: Genesis 20, 21, 22; Matthew 7

Trivia Question: Finish Paul's saying "the natural man receives not _____."

January 9

"Divided We Fall"

Ephesians 4:3 — Endeavoring to keep the unity of the Spirit in the bond of peace.

Jesus Christ desires a strong body. The church is the Body of Christ. You are a part of His Body. When the Body of Christ is in unity, it results in strength. Unity brings strength. That is why Paul admonishes us to endeavor and strive for unity and harmony. Paul knew a united body is a strong body.

In the natural realm, we take certain vitamins and supplements (like protein) to build up our muscle mass and strength. There are certain foods vital to the human body that we need to eat if we are going to have strong bodies. Unity and harmony are vital "ingredients" to the spiritual body of Christ. Unity will build *spiritual muscle,* and when Christians are in harmony, it results in strength.

One year we had a massive blizzard that produced two and a half feet of snow at the site of our church office. The snow had stopped and that night I decided to go to work on some things in the office. The church parking lot was plowed, however the entryway was completely plowed in with snow. I underestimated how much snow was there and upon my entry got stuck. There I was, my van half in and half out of the snow. I waived a man down as he drove by in his plow truck and asked if he would sit in my van while I pushed ... and pushed ... and pushed ... to no avail. He left me a shovel and went on his way. I shoveled for a while, but the snow was definitely prevailing. I sat in my van and prayed, "Lord, send me some people to help me." After a few minutes, what seemed like forever, out of nowhere appeared three young men with shovels resting on their shoulders and they walked right up to me. I asked if they could push me out and they very happily agreed. Within two minutes, these young men unified their energies and drove me out. I told them they were an answer to my prayer and I blessed them in the name of the Lord. Alone, I could not do it, but with the help of those young men coming to my aid, the job got done. Unity brings strength.

This day protect unity at any cost; guard unity and harmony with a bloody sword. Allow nothing or no one to interrupt the *flow of unity*. Remember that unity brings strength, and strength will result in deliverance and victory!

Scripture Reading: Genesis 23, 24; Matthew 8

Trivia Question: What is the first part of the verse, which ends, "and into His courts with praise?"

January 10

"Deep Roots"

Psalms 92:13 — Those that be planted in the house of the Lord shall flourish in the courts of our God.

God the Father wants all His children to be productive—fruit bearing Christians. The Bible refers to believers as "Trees of Righteousness, the planting of the Lord that He might be glorified." (Isaiah 61:3)

If we do not allow God to root and plant us, then we will not blossom for God. So many Christians go from local church to local church. What they are really doing is constantly uprooting and re-planting somewhere else. Any professional landscaper or those in the horticulture field will tell us, if we keep on uprooting and re-planting a tree, the productivity of that tree at best will be threatened, and at worst, the tree will die.

We must allow God to plant us in a local body of believers. It is there where our spiritual roots start to grow and go deep in God. As Christians allow the Five Fold Ministry Gifts that are in the church, (Apostles, Prophets, Evangelists, Pastors and Teachers) to mature them, they become rooted in the House of God and will eventually start bearing fruit. It is

9

impossible to flourish or bloom in God if we are not first planted in the House of God. Let us ask God to plant us so we can bloom, become productive fruit bearing trees for His Kingdom; and let our fruit remain that the Lord will be glorified! "In this is my Father glorified, that you bear much fruit, so shall you be my disciples." (John 15:8)

Scripture Reading: Genesis 25, 26; Matthew 9:1-17

Trivia Question: Of whom was it asked in astonishment whether he also was among the prophets?

January 11

"Nothing is too Hard for Me!"

Jeremiah 32:27 — Behold, I am the Lord, the God of all flesh, is there anything too hard for me?

Perhaps you are confronted with a great trial, or maybe you are going through the hardest time of your life. Our Lord is proposing this question to you, "Is there anything too hard for me?" Only you can answer this question with the conviction that God has put in your heart. The Bible says, "Faith comes by hearing and hearing by the Word of God." As you study and meditate on God's Word and seek to engraft God's promises into your spirit, the faith of God within you rises up in response to this question and says, NO! There is nothing too hard for the Lord.

There is a silent Amen in your spirit that says there will be a calm in the midst of the storm. There will be a way in the wilderness; there will be rivers in the desert, because God is not a man that he should lie, neither the Son of man that He should change His mind. Has He said it and shall He not do it? Or has He spoken and shall He not make it good?

God's Word promises you victory in the midst of your trial and you can believe that He is faithful to bring you through! There is nothing too hard for the Lord. Beloved, keep on believing and trusting and cleaving to the Lord and His Word, and He will bring you absolute victory.

Scripture Reading: Genesis 27, 28; Matthew 9:18-38

Trivia Question: What did Naomi re-name herself?

January 12

"The Power of Prayer"

Hebrews 7:25 — Wherefore He is able also to save them to the uttermost that come unto God, by Him, seeing He ever lives to make intercession for them.

What a wonderful truth is revealed! Jesus as our High Priest is always praying and interceding for us. One of the duties and responsibilities of a priest in the Old Testament was to intercede for, or pray on behalf of, the people. The priest represented man to God. The priest was the go-between, the mediator. Jesus, the mediator of the new covenant, is our intercessor before our heavenly Father. Jesus said in John 14:6, "I am the Way, the Truth and the Life, no man comes unto the Father but by Me." When we become born again, we are given a wonderful privilege in prayer; that is, we can come to the Father in Jesus name. Jesus, as our High Priest, is our mediator, and makes Heaven and all of its rich resources available to us!

The Bible teaches us that Jesus ever lives to pray for us. Some people would have us believe that Jesus is sitting idle on the right hand of the Father. The truth is He is praying and interceding for you and me. You may be asking, "What is the Lord praying about for me?" Perhaps what Jesus said to Peter a long time ago will give us some insight as to how our High Priest is interceding for us. Jesus told Peter that the devil desired (the word desired in the Greek means to demand for trial) to have him, even to sift him as wheat. Jesus comforted Peter by telling him, "But I have prayed for you, that your faith would not fail." Beloved, Jesus, who ever lives to make intercession for us, is praying that our faith will not fail. With that kind of prayer support, you can believe that you will have victory over all your trials and tribulations in Jesus mighty name!

Scripture Reading: Genesis 29, 30; Matthew 10:1-23

Trivia Question: How many wives did Abraham have?

January 13

"Fly like an Eagle"

Isaiah 40:31a — But they that wait upon the Lord shall renew their strength; they shall mount up with wings like eagles;

they shall run and not be weary; and they shall walk, and not faint.

The Bible likens born again believers to eagles. Can you imagine that? Eagles are incredible birds with some amazing characteristics including wingspans of sometimes up to eight feet. One of the most outstanding things about an eagle is its ability to mount up and fly high above the turbulence and storm. The eagle's strong, majestic wings enable him to fly high and above any obstacles in his path.

What about Christians that have had their spiritual *wings* broken? There are so many wounded "eagles" in the body of Christ. If our wings are broken, then we are unable to mount up above our problems and the storms of life. Some people think when a wing is broken you just endure all the storms that come and hope you will survive. I have good news for all those with broken wings- you will FLY HIGH again!

The Psalmist wrote in Psalms 147:3, "He heals the broken in heart and binds up their wounds (wings)." Allow the great physician Jesus Christ to heal and mend any broken, wounded areas in your life, so that you can fly high and above all that life brings your way. You are an eagle and you were created to mount up and soar above all the storms of life.

Scripture Reading: Genesis 31, 32; Matthew 10:24-42

Trivia Question: Who was the brother-in-law of Moses?

January 14

"Don't Drive in Reverse"

Philippians 3:13 — But I do concentrate on this: I forget all that lies behind me and with hands outstretched to whatever lies ahead I go straight for the goal. (Phillips)

It is imperative that we forget those things that are behind and go forward in the things of the Lord. We must forget our past, so that we can embrace our future. God desires us to always go forward and not backward. It was said in Jeremiah 7:23-24 that God's people did not obey His voice and did not hearken unto Him. They walked in the counsel and the imaginations of their evil hearts; consequently they went backward and not forward.

We need to walk in all of God's ways, obey His voice so that we can go forward, and progress in God. We must forget the former things, and consider not the things of old. Many people live in their past and it hinders them from receiving what the Lord has for them in the present and eventually the future. Let this coming year be the best year yet, as you let go of the past to lay hold of your future. Your destiny in God depends on it. "Behold, I will do a new thing, now it shall spring forth, shall you not know (see) it? I will even make a way in the wilderness, and rivers in the desert." (Isaiah 43:19)

Scripture Reading: Genesis 33, 34, 35; Matthew 11

Trivia Question: Who was the oldest person in the Bible?

January 15

"The Healing Balm"

Isaiah 53:4 — Surely He has borne our griefs and carried our sorrows: yet we did esteem him stricken, smitten of God and afflicted.

The Hebrew word for sorrows is makob, pronounced (mak-o-baw), meaning pains. The many messianic prophecies concerning the Messiah who was to come, said He would carry the pains of the human race. Pain comes in all shapes and sizes, both externally and internally. Jesus the Messiah bore our sin, sickness and pain in His own body.

Many people experience some sort of emotional pain in their lives. Emotional pain sometimes hurts more than physical pain and comes as a result of a broken relationship, a hurtful experience, someone slandering your good name, or a host of other things. Christians must not focus on the hurt and who or where it came from, but focus on the one who carried the pain for us.

Jeremiah 30:17 declares, "I will restore health unto you and I will heal you of your wounds saith the Lord…" Some wounds go deep and are very painful, but the Lord has provided total deliverance and healing. He is the true balm of Gilead. Purpose in your heart to receive healing from the Lord so your wounds will go away, causing the pain to leave your life. Remember, if Jesus carried your pain, then you do not have to carry it any longer.

Scripture Reading: Genesis 36, 37; Matthew 12:1-21

Trivia Question: What was King Solomon's other name?

January 16

"Slip and Slide"

Psalm 37:31 — The law of his God is in his heart, none of his steps shall slide.

It is so important that we hide God's Word in our hearts. David wrote, "Thy word have I hid in my heart, that I might not sin against thee." The less we sin, the less we slide. As Christians, we need to feast on the Word of God, engraving God's Holy Word into our spirits. The Bible records the history of Israel, when she constantly did not hearken to the voice of the Lord. Many times she fell into apostasy or a "backslidden" state. When God's people fail to obey His Voice and reject the Word of God, eventually sin will dominate their walk. When we yield to sin, we "slide" back or backslide away from God.

The promise the Psalmist gives us is, if we give first place to the Word of God and meditate on God's holy writ, hiding it in the depths of our being, then not one of our steps shall slide. We cannot and will not fall away or slide away from God and His glorious presence. Beloved, allow God's Word to live big on the inside of you. Like David of old, meditate on the Word day and night. Be like Joshua and take heed to His exhortation, "This book of the Law, (Word of God), shall not depart out of thy mouth, but thou shalt meditate therein day and night, that thou mayest observe to do according to all that is written therein, for then thou shalt make thy way prosperous, and then thou shalt have good success." (Joshua 1:8)

Scripture Reading: Genesis 38, 39, 40; Matthew 12:22-50

Trivia Question: How many kings were conquered by Moses and Joshua?

January 17

"Whose Report will You Receive?

Psalms 112:7 — He shall not be afraid of evil tidings, his heart is fixed, trusting in the Lord.

The prophet Isaiah exhorts us under the inspiration of the Holy Spirit, "Who has believed our report?" There are going to be different "reports" that come to us in our lives. There is the "natural" report and then there is the "super-natural" report. We must make a choice as to which one will influence our lives. We cannot be afraid when an evil report comes our way. We must have our hearts fixed and established in the Lord and His Word. The Word of God is God's report.

When the twelve spies came back to Moses and the congregation of Israel after spying out the land, ten brought back an evil report based on what they saw in the natural realm. Two of the men, however, Caleb and Joshua, saw the same opposition and saw the same giants, but chose to believe the report of the Lord. God said it was their inheritance, no matter what they saw or how they felt. The Bible says the ten spies brought back an evil report which caused the people to fear and cry and weep all night. Caleb was the one that spoke up and said, "Let us go up at once and possess it, for we are well able to overcome it." Caleb made a choice to believe and receive God's report. We must overcome an evil report with God's report— The Word of God. When God's Word has total influence over our lives, we will rise up like Caleb and not be afraid of evil tidings.

Scripture Reading: Genesis 41; Matthew 13:1-32

Trivia Question: How old was Caleb when he received his inheritance of the land?

January 18

"Building Blocks"

Psalms 127:1 — Except the Lord build the house, they labour in vain that build it: except the Lord keep the city, the watchman waketh but in vain.

Many of God's people, because of their background and the dysfunction in their lives, have taken on a "role and performance" personality. This type of personality has the perception that if I "do" then I will please God and gain His favor and love. Nothing we can ever do or accomplish will gain God's love for us. God loves us no matter what we do or do not do. God is love and loves us with a never-ending love. He loves us unconditionally, without reservation, with no strings attached. Even if we do not love Him back, He still loves us with His perfect love.

We must allow the Lord to build our houses, whatever it is in our lives that needs building; our spiritual structure, our character, our integrity, our homes and our lives. If we think we must do the building ourselves, we will labor, and labor in vain. We must yield and surrender to Christ allowing Him to do the necessary building in our lives. Jesus is the master builder and will do in us what He says he will do. Paul says, "For it is God who worketh in you both to will and to do of His good pleasure." (Philippians 2:13)

Let God do the work, allow Him to do the building as we yield to His expert craftsmanship. He will undoubtedly make something beautiful out of our lives. "For we are His workmanship created in Christ Jesus..." (Ephesians 2:10)

Stop saying, "I'm trying to live my life for Christ," rather say, *"I'm going to let Christ live His life in me."*

Scripture Reading: Genesis 42, 43; Matthew 13:33-58

Trivia Question: What Jewish tribe was Paul from?

January 19

"A Friend in the Flames"

Isaiah 43:2 — When thou passest through the waters, I will be with thee; and through the rivers, they shall not overflow thee; when thou walkest through the fire, thou shalt not be burned; neither shall the flame kindle upon thee.

We have a promise that the Lord will never leave us nor forsake us, and no matter what we go through in life, He will be there to bring us through. When we pass through the waters, His promise is that He will be right there with us. The Israelites of old, when going through the waters of the Red Sea, were assured of God's awesome presence in their midst. As they looked on either side of them and saw those "water walls," in the natural it was a frightening sight. But they had a promise from Moses that God would go with them and not forsake them!

Even when we go through deep waters (rivers), the Lord says we will not drown. In Matthew's Gospel, the account of Peter walking on the water to Jesus is an amazing story. Jesus bids Peter to come out of the endangered boat to walk to Him on the water. Peter responds in faith but takes his eyes off Jesus and starts to drown. Immediately, the Master reaches His hands out to Peter and saves him from the deep waters!

When we walk through the fire, Jesus will be there. The three young Hebrew boys were thrown into the fiery furnace, which was turned up seven times hotter. They were bound hand and foot and tossed into the flames, but the Lord was with them. When King Nebuchadnezzar looked into the furnace, he saw four men walking in the midst of the fire! Jesus was there and protected those boys from the flames. Hallelujah!

If you are passing through the waters, going through deep waters or even walking through the fire, be encouraged; you will not drown, you will not burn, for the Lord will never leave you nor forsake you. He will deliver you!

Scripture Reading: Genesis 44, 45; Matthew 14:1-21

Trivia Question: What were the Hebrew names of Shadrach, Meshach and Abednego?

January 20

"But this, But that"

Luke 9:62 — And Jesus said unto him, no man having put his hand to the plow, and looking back is fit for the Kingdom of God.

This was the Lord's response to a man who said, "I will follow you, *but* let me first go bid farewell who are at home, at my house." (Luke 9:61) When we really examine this portion of Scripture we see that Jesus was dealing with the conjunction *but*. Jesus knew the man's heart and went past the *but* and knew that this was a mere excuse not to follow the Lord.

In our mind's eye, we see a man behind a plow making a furrow. If that man constantly looks back, he will get off course and his furrow will not be straight, but zigzagged. Jesus was dealing with the *but* and the excuse of this man. The Lord knew if he went home, he probably would not return to Jesus. The Lord was trying to reinforce the importance of putting God first. We cannot allow family or friends to influence our commitment to Christ in any way. The Greek word for fit means ready for use. If we constantly look back, we will not be ready for the use and service of the Master. We must put our past behind us, lay hold of the plow (whatever God is calling us to do), and focus straight ahead looking unto Jesus, the Author and Finisher of our faith.

Scripture Reading: Genesis 46, 47, 48; Matthew 14:22-36

Trivia Question: What was Luke's occupation?

January 21

"Burning Fire"

*Luke 9:56 — For the Son of man is not come
to destroy men's lives, but to save them.*

Jesus said this in response to James and John when they foolishly asked Him if He wanted them to call down fire to consume the Samaritan people. Jewish history tells us that the Orthodox Jews from Judea hated the people from the region of Samaria (Samaritans). They felt they had many reasons to feel this way about each other, but it all developed from prejudice, racism and sin! James and John, (the sons of thunder), thought their noble solution to the problem of the Samaritans not receiving the messenger that Jesus sent would please Christ, but on the contrary, Jesus rebuked them.

We see that the fire of God is two-fold, when God manifests His fire it can be for "consuming" or it can be for "consecration." When Elijah called God's fire down, it was to consume the sacrifice. On the other hand, when God manifested His fire at the burning bush with Moses, the bush was not consumed. This fire was the call of "consecration." God was calling Moses to be set apart for a specific purpose, to deliver His people from Egyptian bondage. John the Baptist told us that Jesus would baptize us with the Holy Spirit and fire. This fire is not to consume us, but to *consecrate* us. The fire of God will purge and purify us so that we will be set apart for the plan and purpose of God. Let Jesus baptize you in the Holy Spirit fire this day and He will burn out the chaff and dross and consecrate you for the service of your King.

Scripture Reading: Genesis 49, 50; Matthew 15:1-20

Trivia Question: Who was the father of James and John?

January 22

"Open the Gift"

*Ephesians 4:12 — For the perfecting of the saints, for the work of
the ministry, for the edifying of the body of Christ.*

The Lord is so good. "When he ascended up on high, he led captivity captive, and gave gifts unto men." (Ephesians 4:8) Jesus gave going away gifts to His body, the church. When people go away they usually receive the gifts, but our Lord is so wonderful that He gave the gifts to us. There are many special gifts that Jesus blessed us with when He ascended on high. Five of them are very special because they help mature and build up the body of Christ. These gifts are: Apostles, Prophets, Evangelists, Pastors and Teachers, commonly referred to as the Five-Fold Ministry Gifts.

These sacred offices are held by those called by God, and are used by the Holy Spirit to mature and develop the church. The term perfecting of the saints simply means the maturity of the Christians. When the Five-Fold Ministry Gifts are in manifestation and they are teaching and preaching the Gospel of the Kingdom, the Word will always bring the church to maturity. When the church comes to maturity and starts growing in grace, then the church steps out and does the "work of the ministry."

One man has not been called to do it all or minister to every need. For example, the Pastor's responsibility is to preach and teach the word of God to his flock so that they will develop and grow and do the work of the ministry. When the church understands this principle, then the body of Christ is edified and built up. The Five-Fold Ministry teaches, that when Christians are matured, the work of the ministry is accomplished and the whole body of Christ is built up! Thank God for His Divine Order.

Scripture Reading: Exodus 1, 2, 3; Matthew 15:21-39

Trivia Question: How long did Paul stay in Corinth on his second missionary journey?

January 23

"A Victorious Body"

Ephesians 2:6 — And hath raised us up together, and made us sit together in heavenly places in Christ Jesus.

When Jesus was raised from the dead, His body was raised too; the head and the body were raised together. Jesus is the Head and His body is the church. This is a tremendous truth to meditate on this day. You have been raised with Christ to sit with Him in heavenly places. Paul writes in the first chapter of Ephesians that this lofty position is "far above all principality, and power, and might, and dominion, and every name that is named, not only in this world but also in that which is to come." (Ephesians 1:21)

Jesus Christ was raised from the dead victoriously conquering sin, Satan, sickness and disease. Because born again believers have identified themselves with Christ through regeneration and new birth, Christians also have been raised in victory. The Bible says that "all things" have been put under the feet of Jesus. Satan, his cohorts, all of Hell and the regions of darkness are under the feet of the Master. Remember, the church is the body of Christ, which means that the kingdom of darkness is under us. We reign over sin, Satan, sickness and also disease! The head and the body were raised together.

Jesus sits at the right hand of the Father and His body takes on that same position in heavenly places (spiritually speaking). From our Father's lofty vantage point all our *problems* seem so minute. If you are in a plane and looking out the window from 35,000 feet, everything on the ground looks very small. So when we look down from our heavenly position, all of our problems, concerns and trials seem so small! Be mindful today that you have been raised with Christ far above all principality, power, might and dominion. From your position with Christ even the biggest problems look trivial. The head and the body have been raised together.

Scripture Reading: Exodus 4, 5, 6; Matthew 16

Trivia Question: How many prayers did Paul pray in the book of Ephesians?

January 24

"Painful Pruning, Flourishing Fruit"

John 15:2 — Every branch in me that beareth not fruit he taketh away: and every branch that beareth fruit, he purgeth it, that it may bring forth more fruit.

Let it be known that God desires His children to be productive. We have been called to bear "fruit." The fruit we are called to produce varies; it could be the fruits of the Spirit that we read about in Galatians, it could be winning souls to the Lord, it could be producing the fruits of righteousness, and so on. Whatever the case, one thing is certain, we as Christians need to be fruit-bearing.

Jesus said if we are already bearing fruit, He will from time to time, prune our lives so that we will continue to be fruit-bearing to the glory of God. Many of God's people resist and reject the pruning process of the

Lord, and consequently do not produce the fruit they are capable of. Jesus said that the Father is glorified when we bear much fruit. (John 15:8) If the Lord is pruning your life in any way, cutting things back if you will, there are two things to note. One, He sees you prune-worthy, which means you are producing fruit, because He only prunes branches that are already bearing fruit. Two, He sees your great potential to bear more fruit. That is awesome to think about. So do not despise or reject the pruning process, or the cutting away of some areas of your life. The process is not always pleasant, but afterwards, you will bear precious fruit. "Now, no *correcting* for the present seems to be joyous, but grievous, but nevertheless afterward it yields the peaceable *fruit* of righteousness unto them who are exercised by it." (Hebrews 12:11)

Scripture Reading: Exodus 7, 8; Matthew 17

Trivia Question: What were the names of Moses's parents?

January 25

"Cry Out"

Psalms 138:3 — In the day when I cried thou answeredst me, and strengthenedst me with strength in my soul.

We serve the living God this day and can be assured that He not only hears our cry, but responds to our prayers. "For the eyes of the Lord are over the righteous (all those that are born again), and His ears are open to their prayers. . ." (1 Peter 3:12)

God is our heavenly Father, and as a Father He is touched with the feelings of our weaknesses. As children of God, like a natural child, sometimes we get ourselves in trouble or just become overwhelmed by life's circumstances and trials. It is reassuring to know we can cry to the Lord in our time of need, and be confident that our Father hears us and responds to our hearts cry. The psalmist wrote in Psalms 20:9, "Save, Lord, let the King hear us when we call...and He does!"

Our Father will always give us an answer to our dilemma, if we will just inquire of Him. When we cry to Him, even in a desperate situation, His promise is that He will give us an answer and a remedy to the problem. He also promises to strengthen our souls. The soul is the emotional part of us that at times, especially during tests and trials, has a tendency to get out of control. When we call on the Lord, He will answer us and bring strength and stability to our emotions. Beloved, are you going through a difficult time in your life? Just cry to the Lord, He will hear, He will answer and He will bring strength and stability to you. He is a present help in your time of trouble!

Scripture Reading: Exodus 9, 10; Matthew 18:1-20

Trivia Question: What is the longest Psalm in the book of Psalms?

January 26

"Fear vs. Faith"

Mark 5:36 — As soon as Jesus heard the word that was spoken, he saith unto the ruler of the synagogue, Be not afraid, only believe.

Let me explain why Jesus responded with these comforting words to the ruler (Jairus). It was Jairus who came to Jesus with an urgent request for his very sick daughter. The need was great, the request simple: could you please come and heal her? Jesus responded in the affirmative and started His journey to Jairus' home. Aren't you glad the Lord responds to our needs and says, YES! I will come and deliver you.

As He made His way to the bedside of that sick twelve-year-old girl, He was interrupted by a woman who had an urgent need of her own. This woman's menstrual cycle was irregular and caused bleeding for twelve long years. Jewish law forbade a woman with this kind of disorder to be out in public, so we know that her life was in shambles for that certain period of time. She heard Jesus was coming through and said, "If I could just touch Him, I would be healed." (Matthew 9:21) She did touch Him, and her faith healed her.

Some valuable time passed by as Jesus was detained. Eventually someone met them on the way, who came from Jairus' home, and had very bad news, "Your daughter is dead, no need for Jesus to come." You can imagine how Jairus' heart sank within him as fear and anxiety started to grip his life. Jairus must have thought, in that split moment of time, "If Jesus wasn't delayed with this woman, He would have been able to get to my little girl in time." But beloved, know this... delay is not denial! As soon as Jesus heard the negative report He turned to Jairus and said, "Don't fear, only believe." (Luke 8:50) In other words, Jesus was saying that He promised to

22

come and heal the girl and that was exactly what He was going to do. He told Jairus not to allow fear to choke out the promises of God – just believe.

Beloved, do not allow fear or anxiety to choke out God's precious promises to you. Regardless of what you see or hear, continue to believe and trust in what the Lord has told you. Jesus went to Jairus' house and raised that girl from the dead! Jesus will resurrect your dead situation too, if you will cast out fear and believe God's Word!

Scripture Reading: Exodus 11, 12 Matthew 18:21-35

Trivia Question: What does the Aramaic term Talithacumi mean?

January 27

"A Work for the Lord"

Luke 10:2 — The harvest truly is great, but the laborers are few, pray ye, therefore the Lord of the harvest, that He would send forth laborers into His harvest.

In John's Gospel, Jesus invited us "to look on the fields, for they are already white unto harvest." (John 4:35) We are living in some of the most exciting days ever recorded in the history of man. We are living in the days when God is pouring out His Spirit upon all flesh.

The greatest mandate from the Messiah is to go and preach the Gospel to all flesh. We have a great commission from the Lord and that must be fulfilled by our generation. Lost people and hurting individuals are all around us just waiting for a word of hope and a touch of love. Will you be a laborer in the harvest? In the early 90's, I believe the church needed to *repent,* and many of God's people did indeed do that. In the mid-90's, God sent a *refreshing* to His church—wonderful times of refreshing in His presence. I perceive in the latter years of the 90's, the repentance that led to refreshing continued to spread, even up to the present day, and that in the years ahead, will bring us to *revival.* To me, revival is wielding the spiritual sickle and reaping the harvest. Beloved, it takes workers to reap the harvest. It takes laborers to go into the harvest field and reap for the Lord.

Our prayer this day needs to be, "Lord, send laborers into your harvest field, but Lord send me also, for I am available."

Scripture Reading: Exodus 13, 14, 15; Matthew 19:1-15

January 28

"A Humble King"

John 4:49 — The nobleman saith unto Him, Sir come down ere my child die.

This high-ranking royal official came to Jesus one day with an urgent request. Jesus was holding one of His miracle "crusades" in the city of Cana in the region of Galilee. Jesus traveled from Judea into His hometown region of Galilee (about 90 miles); and when the royal official heard that Jesus was in Cana (the place where Jesus performed His first miracle, turning the water into wine), the nobleman caught up with Jesus. He beseeched Him to turn his situation around. The nobleman's son was sick unto death and he knew Jesus, the miracle man from Galilee, was his only hope.

What is so interesting about this story is that the nobleman lived in Capernaum, about six miles "northeast" of Cana. Yet when he asked the Lord to come and heal his son, he asked Jesus to "COME DOWN." Geographically speaking, you had to travel "UP" to go to Capernaum from Cana.

I believe the man recognized Jesus and his lofty position as King as much higher than his own position, even though he was a man of high-ranking royal status himself. The nobleman knew that He was making a request to someone much more royal and that Jesus would have to "condescend" to heal his son.

Aren't you so glad today that the Lord was willing to come down from all the glory and splendor of Heaven to become our sin substitute on Calvary's cross? Imagine a king descending to come to that place. "He humbled Himself and became obedient unto death." (Philippians 2:8) We serve a great King today who is touched with the feelings of our weaknesses. He is willing to meet us on our level, wherever we are spiritually and emotionally, and to minister to our need; even the urgent needs that demand a supernatural intervention by God!

Scripture Reading: Exodus 16, 17, 18; Matthew 19:16-30

Trivia Question: What was the Apostle Matthew's occupation?

January 29

"True Joy"

Nehemiah 8:10b — For the joy of the Lord is your strength.

There is such a drastic difference between joy and happiness. The two words are not synonymous. Happiness is many times a result of happenings. For example, if you get a pay raise or a job promotion, or just have a great day, you become happy. Take the raise or promotion away and you experience a real bummer of a day; you are unhappy. Again, happiness is derived from happenings. We have, however, been called to real, unadulterated, genuine JOY! Jesus said in John 15:11, "These things have I spoken unto you, that MY JOY might remain in you..." This fruit of the spirit in our lives is manifested because Jesus, by His Spirit, imparted His joy to us and in us, not because it results in a good day or a bad day. As matter of fact, the joy of Jesus is manifested even when things are not going so well. His Joy has been implanted in us to produce something – STRENGTH!

The joy of the Lord is our strength. We need God's supernatural strength (spiritual and otherwise) to have His spiritual energy and effort within us to do what He has called us to do. That is why the devil works so hard to come and try to steal our joy. If Satan succeeds in robbing our joy, he also gets our strength. The devil is not ignorant of the Scriptures, he knows joy leads to strength and strength leads to productivity for the Kingdom. That's why you hear much about God's people experiencing "burn out." Somewhere along the way, the devil robbed someone's joy! Put a garrison over your "joy tank," keep it filled and you will be strong and do great exploits for Jesus. Do not allow the enemy to rob you in this area. Remember, you do not have to manufacture this joy; this is HIS joy in you. Praise God forevermore!

Scripture Reading: Exodus 19, 20, 21; Matthew 20:1-16

Trivia Question: Name the four degrees of fruit bearing.

January 30

"No Turning Back"

Luke 9:62 — And Jesus said unto him, No man, having put his hand to the plough, and looking back, is fit for the Kingdom of God.

This hard saying that Jesus spoke in response to the man's excuse to the Lord's request to "Follow Me," is very significant to all of us. In the natural, if we are plowing a field and constantly looking back, two things will happen. First, we take our eyes off the focal point that is out ahead of us. To plow a straight furrow, a good farmer needs to pick a focal point out ahead of him and focus on it, keeping his eyes on that object. Second, if the farmer constantly looks back over his shoulder, he will plow a zigzag field that will not be as productive as it could have been. Beloved, we as God's precious sons and daughters are called to look to Jesus, keeping our eyes fastened on Him, for He is the "author and finisher of our faith." (Hebrews 12:2)

As believers, we are instructed not to look back once we have entered into our walk with the Master. We must let go of past victories, past failures, and past memories that bring us down, so that we can embrace our present and look forward to our future in Christ. We do not want to take our eyes off the Lord, for surely our walk and experience in God will become quite zigzagged, up and down or in and out. We need not look back in these areas because the Lord has forgiven and forgotten our past and has given us a brand new fresh start in Him. So beloved, put your hands to the plow, keep your eyes looking ahead, fixed on Jesus and do all that God has called you to do. Be all that God has called you to be. All to the Glory of God! Remember, the "best is yet to come" and the future looks very bright for the believers because Jesus is Lord!

Scripture Reading: Exodus 22, 23, 24; Matthew 20:17-34

Trivia Question: Can you name the three sons of Noah?

January 31

"Deeper and Dirty"

Luke 13:7-8 — Then said he unto the dresser of his vineyard, Behold, these three years I come seeking fruit on this fig tree, and find none: cut it down; why cumbereth it the ground? And he answering said unto him, Lord, let it alone this year also, till I shall dig about it, and dung it.

In the parable, Jesus is teaching on the importance of bearing fruit for the Kingdom of God. The man who owned the vineyard was frustrated because for three long years he was looking for figs and at every examination of the tree it was the same old story – no fruit! In his exasperation, he told the dresser of the vineyard to cut it down, for it was only taking up space and very unproductive. The dresser pleaded with the owner and said that he would "dig" about it and "dung" it.

As Christians, we are called "Trees of Righteousness," the planting of the Lord that God would be glorified in and through or lives. We must allow God by His Spirit to go down deeper within us allowing Him to dig, especially in those sensitive areas of our lives. If we want to bear fruit, then the Holy Spirit must dig about us, taking away all the weeds and dead dry leaves, so the water of the Word will be poured deeply within us. It's the Word in us that eventually will cause us to bear fruit.

We also need to be willing to get "dunged on" every now and then. What I mean is the willingness to get dirty for God. Jesus was willing to go anywhere and speak to anyone to bear fruit. Some of the places He went and the people He ministered to were considered undesirable. Jesus got dirty when He ministered to people. He was willing to love and minister to all people, like the woman caught in adultery, the man with leprosy, the demoniac from Gadara, and the crooked tax collector named Zacchaeus; the list goes on and on.

When we are willing to let God, by His Spirit and through His Word, go deeper in our lives and if we are willing to get spiritually dirty in the ministry, we will then bear fruit to the Glory of God the Father. Are you willing to go deeper in God? Are you willing to go anywhere and talk to anyone and share with him/her the Gospel story? Say yes, and bear fruit for God and the Kingdom!

Scripture Reading: Exodus 25, 26; Matthew 21:1-22

Trivia Question: How many lepers did Jesus heal in Luke 17?

February

February 1

"See Him Flee"

James 4:7 — Submit yourselves therefore to God.
Resist the devil and he will flee from you.

Most Christians can quote by heart, that latter end of James 4:7, "… resist the devil and he will flee from you." The entire verse needs to be examined. Only by living in the former part of the verse can the latter part come to pass.

"Submit yourself to God," not many words, but how important they are for believers. If we want to see Satan, Hell and all the powers of darkness run from us, we must know our authority in Jesus Christ and more importantly live a life of total submission to the Lordship of Jesus.

James 4:7 is a promise, and like all the promises of God it is conditional, meaning if we do our part then God will do His and follow up His Word to perform it. The problem is that many Christians are resisting and rebuking the devil and nothing is happening. The devil is not fleeing! When we live an un-submissive life we really live in rebellion, and rebellion is sin, and sin will give place to the devil. In other words, rebellion will give legal right for Satan to hang around. Rebellion is as the sin of witchcraft. The Bible declares "neither give place to the devil." When we will not submit ourselves to God in every area of our lives, then we yield to sin, which gives place to the devil and Satan adheres to sin. If you want to see the devil flee (one that runs in terror), know your authority in Christ; but more importantly live a life of submission to God!

Scripture Reading: Exodus 27, 28; Matthew 21:23-46

Trivia Question: What was Hosea, the prophet's, wife's name?

29

February 2

"Faithful and Free"

*Matthew 10:8 — Heal the sick, cleanse the lepers, raise the dead,
cast out devils: freely ye have received, freely give.*

The Lord has abundantly blessed His people. He is so good to His children. As a child of God, you have been blessed in so many ways. God blesses His own with the understanding that His people will in turn bless others. In other words, God blesses us so that we can be a blessing to others.

The Scriptures teach us through the parable of the talents, to invest or sow what God has graciously given to us. The man with the five talents invested them and received five talents more. The man that was blessed with two talents invested them and was blessed with two more. The man who was given one talent buried it out of fear and was reprimanded sharply by the Master. When we give out of our blessing and give back what God has given to us, we are blessed even more! Whatever God has put on the inside of you, gifts, talents, abilities or anointing; whatever it is, you must be willing to sow or freely give it away. When you are faithful over a little, God makes you ruler over much. It is required of stewards that they are found faithful!

To whom much is given, much is required. Count your blessings this day and look to the Lord to show you how you can freely give what you have abundantly received from Him. He will bless you even more!

Scripture Reading: Exodus 29, 30; Matthew 22:1-22

Trivia Question: Where does it say we will be given a new name?

February 3

"The Medicinal Word"

*Proverbs 4:20-22 — My Son, attend to my words, incline your ear
to my sayings, let them not depart from your eyes, keep them
in the midst of your heart. For they are life to those that find them
and health to all their flesh.*

We as Christians have been called to give first place to the Word of God. We must give full attention to God's Word. Our spiritual ears must always be open. Our eyes must be fastened upon the Word of the Lord, and the Word of God must be the very core of our experience in God, as we keep His Word in the midst of our hearts. It is always the Word of God that will bring us out of defeat and into victory, out of discouragement and into encouragement, out of despair and into hope, out of sickness and into health. This portion of Scripture says that His Word is life to those that find them. Jesus said, "The Words that I speak to you, they are spirit and they are life." (John 6:63)

This word of life we receive from the Lord also brings health to all of our flesh. Yes, the Word of God will quicken our physical bodies and heal and restore them to wholeness. The Hebrew word for health means medicine. The Word of God acts like medicine to our bodies. Allow the Word of God, as you give attention to it, to open up your ears and eyes to keep it in the center of your heart. Let it become your life and health, spiritual medicine that will keep you healthy spiritually, physically and emotionally all the days of your life.

Scripture Reading: Exodus 31, 32, 33; Matthew 22:23-46

Trivia Question: What happens if man tries to cover and conceal his sin?

February 4

"H E A R T"

John 10:4 — And when he putteth forth his own sheep, he goeth before them, and the sheep follow him: for they know his voice.

Jesus is the good shepherd, and as our shepherd He speaks to us every day. We are the sheep of His pasture. The sheep of the good shepherd hear His voice, know His voice and follow His voice.

The way the Lord speaks to us is in our spirits. Man is a spirit being who possesses a soul and lives in a body. The way we communicate with God and the way He dialogues with us is within our hearts. The way we hear the voice of God is in our hearts. "You see, our heart can HEAR because it has an ear." If you take the word HEART and drop the letter T, you have the word *hear*. If you drop the letter H, you have the word *ear*. You see, our heart can hear because it has an ear. Are you listening to the voice of the Lord? What is He saying to you? There are so many voices today that try to influence you, but the voice of the Lord, always in harmony with His

Word, will guide you and lead you. The good shepherd guides His precious sheep into green pastures and beside the still waters. Allow the ear of your heart to hear the voice of the good shepherd and follow Him wherever He leads you!

Scripture Reading: Exodus 34, 35, 36; Matthew 23:1-22

Trivia Question: Where were Mary and Martha from?

February 5

"Gone for Good"

Deuteronomy 10:16 — Circumcise therefore the foreskin of your heart, and be no more stiff-necked.

God cut a covenant with the patriarch Abraham that was established through circumcision. We see in the 17th chapter of Genesis where God instructs Abraham to circumcise all the male children in his house at eight days old. The covenant of circumcision was for Abraham's seed and throughout every generation. Circumcision was the cutting away of the foreskin.

Spiritually speaking, we are called to *cut away* anything from our hearts that will hinder our lives from being totally committed to Christ. Moses said circumcise the foreskin of your heart. We all need to examine our hearts to see if there is anything that we recognize that could keep us back from going all the way for Jesus. We need to *cut away* pride, wrong attitudes, bitterness, unforgiveness, anger or anything that should not be a part of our lives and in our hearts. We need a fresh circumcision of our hearts before God to allow the sword of the Spirit, which is the Word of God, to *cut away* anything and everything that doesn't have spiritual value and could cause us to be spiritually unhealthy.

Scripture Reading: Exodus 37, 38; Matthew 23:23-39

Trivia Question: How many spies went to spy out the Promised Land?

February 6

"Stress Remedy"

John 11:25 — Jesus said unto her, I am the resurrection, and the life, he that believeth in me, though he were dead, yet shall he live.

Jesus said this to Martha when she tried to make Jesus feel guilty for arriving late to Bethany. Martha's brother Lazarus was sick unto death and she sent word to Jesus. He remained where he was for two days, and a total of four days elapsed before Jesus arrived at Bethany. Jesus, always led by the Spirit of God, never panicked or felt pressure concerning this urgent request. The Father revealed to Him, "that the Son of God might be glorified by it." (John 11:4) Jesus moved in power, dealt with the doubt and unbelief of the people and told them, if they would believe, they would see the Glory of God. Jesus commanded the stone be rolled away from the tomb where Lazarus lay dead, and demanded Lazarus to come forth. Lazarus came forth, was loosed and let go!

In the busy, anxiety packed, stressful world we live in, we must learn from Jesus that we should not panic or feel pressure even when stressful news comes to our ears. We need to listen to the voice of the Holy Spirit and be led exclusively by Him and respond accordingly. Do not be led by stress, but by the Spirit. Jesus can and will resurrect even a dead situation.

Scripture Reading: Exodus 39, 40; Matthew 24:1-22

Trivia Question: Why did the chief priests want Lazarus dead?

February 7

"Take Root for Fruit"

Jeremiah 4:3 — For thus saith the Lord to the men of Judah and Jerusalem, break up your fallow ground, and sow not among the thorns.

God's Word is likened unto precious seed, and He desires to sow His Word into our hearts so that the seed of the Word will germinate and take root in order to produce a harvest.

Jesus many times used the laws of agriculture to teach a spiritual meaning to His people. Jeremiah picks up on this concept in the Old Testament, when he said we must break up the fallow (hard) ground. He was not talking about our gardens, but the ground of our hearts. See, in the natural, if seed is sown on hard ground or cement, nothing will produce because the seed does not have a chance to be rooted. Without the root, we cannot bear fruit!

The Lord is deeply concerned about the soil of our hearts. Do we have good, fertile soil in our hearts, or are there hardness and thorns on the inside of us? We can't sow seed on fallow ground or among thorns. We must prepare our hearts as fertile soil to have the seed of the Word of God sown and rooted deep on the inside of us. If there is anything causing hardness in your heart, get it right before the Lord so you can be prepared for His precious seed to be sown.

Scripture Reading: Leviticus 1, 2, 3; Matthew 24:23-51

Trivia Question: What was the name of the woman with whom David sinned?

February 8

"Be Thou Healed"

Mark 1:41 — And Jesus, moved with compassion, put forth his hand, and touched him, and saith unto him, I will; be thou clean.

There was a leper who came to Jesus one day with an age-old question, "Is it your will to heal me?" (Matthew 8:2) When you look at this portion of Scripture, you see that the leper, like many people today, recognized that Jesus had the power and the ability to heal, but his question was if Jesus was willing to heal him. "I know you can make me whole, but are you willing?"

Beloved, we must look at the response of Jesus and settle this question once and for all in our hearts. His Word is forever settled in Heaven, but we must settle it in our hearts. Jesus said "I WILL, BE THOU HEALED!" It is God's will for you to be whole, sound and healed – spirit, soul and body. We can never really express faith in God to be healed if we are not sure that it is His absolute will. There will be reluctance and a hesitation in our expression of faith. It is like cashing a check with your name on it, but not knowing where it came from or who sent it. There is a hesitation, even though it belongs to you and is yours to use any way that you choose. Healing belongs to you, Jesus paid the price to provide and secure healing for your heart, mind and body. His response to the leper is still ringing out today, "It is my will, be thou healed!"

Scripture Reading: Leviticus 4, 5, 6; Matthew 25:1-30

Trivia Question: Whose daughter was raised from the dead by Jesus?

February 9

"Speak Out"

*Isaiah 55:11 — So shall my word be that goeth forth out of my mouth,
it shall not return unto me void, but it shall accomplish that which I please,
and it shall prosper in the thing whereto I sent it."*

Just as the rain and snow comes down from Heaven and cannot go back up or be reversed, and it waters the earth for a purpose, gives seed to the sower, and bread to the eater; so in the spiritual sense the Word of God will never return to Him void. When God's Word is spoken, it will always accomplish something and fulfill His purpose.

God has entrusted His Word to His people. The Christian is to speak God's Word with the awareness that it will fulfill and accomplish the will of God and destiny in his or her life. When Jesus spoke the Word, Heaven came to attention, Hell shook and people's lives were never the same. Jesus knew the authority of His Father's Word and knew that as He spoke the Word of God that it would not return void, but would accomplish that which the Father willed and it would prosper in the thing where it was sent. Jesus used the Word of God to hit the *bull's-eye* of people' hearts. Jesus spoke the Word of God with conviction and authority, the same way that you and I can speak it today. As you believe in the Word, you must speak the Word expecting the same results that Jesus received during His earthly ministry two thousand years ago.

Scripture Reading: Leviticus 7, 8, 9; Matthew 25:31-46

Trivia Question: Who holds the keys of Hell and death?

February 10

"Seek and Prosper"

*2 Chronicles 26:5 — And he sought God in the days of Zechariah,
who had understanding in the visions of God:*

and as long as he sought the Lord, God made him to prosper.

This was spoken about one of the kings of the southern kingdom of Judah named Uzziah, whose name means, "my strength is from Jehovah." Uzziah was a king who had a wonderful beginning, but a tragic ending to his life.

Uzziah was only sixteen years old when he began to reign, and this young man had a hold on God. He sought the Lord, and because of his genuine commitment to Jehovah, the Lord strengthened and prospered him. Uzziah had towers, wells, much cattle, husbandmen, vinedressers (he loved farming and agriculture), a mighty army that was fully arrayed in the best armor and was on the cutting edge of technological warfare. God caused him to prosper and to be strong as long as he sought the Lord. Ironically, Uzziah's heart became prideful and he forgot the one that really caused him to prosper. He decided to operate outside of his anointing and office as king. He did so by presumptuously intruding into the priest's office. He was rebuked by Azariah, the priest, became leprous and died as a lonely man full of leprosy.

Beloved, this is a sad story, but we can learn that there is no place in our lives for pride and haughtiness. We must always know who has blessed us and keep our hearts humble before the Lord. I believe that God still wants to abundantly bless His people as we put him first and foremost in our lives! "Beloved, I wish above all things that you may PROSPER and be in health, even as your soul prospers." (3 John 1:2)

Scripture Reading: Leviticus 10, 11, 12; Matthew 26:1-19

Trivia Question: Who was Uzziah's father?

February 11

"Lift Him High"

John 12:32 — And I, if I be lifted up from the earth, will draw all men unto me.

Jesus spoke these words both practically and prophetically. Obviously, in the practical when His followers sought to lift Him up in praise, worship and reverence it caused others to see Him as the highly exalted Son of God. Prophetically, Jesus was also speaking of His death by crucifixion that was to come. As He would be lifted up on Calvary's cross, people would truly

36

get the revelation that He was whom He said He was. We see in the life of the centurion, as he watched Jesus "lifted up," he cried out, "Truly, this was the Son of God." (Matthew 27:54)

Jesus prophesied in John 3:14, "and as Moses lifted up the serpent in the wilderness, even so must the Son of man be lifted up."

Beloved, Jesus still needs to be lifted up because people still need to be drawn to Him. Now there are different ways we can, as New Testament believers, lift up Jesus. We can lift Him up through high praises and worship, we can speak out in godliness on great issues of our day and give our Christian perspective; there are so many different ways.

One way that I want you to consider this day as a born again believer, God wants to give you favor and good understanding with God and man. In other words, we need as believers, to believe and expect God to elevate and promote His church on the earth. Some may think that this is haughty or prideful, but the Scriptures teach that if we humble ourselves, God Himself will exalt us. You see, if the church is exalted and promoted, so is Christ lifted up once again. Now we are quick to give Jesus all the glory and honor for all that He does in our lives, the blessings, the benefits and all promotions. Jesus knows that if His body is exalted then He will be lifted up as the head, and we the church will be sure to point to Him so that they are drawn to the Son of God.

Believe God for favor and promotion in all areas of your life so that you are elevated on the job, academically, financially, or socially; you will be quick to give Christ all of the honor and glory. That, my friend, will lift Him up and people will be drawn to Him like those lost at sea are drawn to the beacon of a lighthouse!

Scripture Reading: Leviticus 13; Matthew 26:20-54

Trivia Question: Where was Phillip the apostle from?

February 12

"What's in the Name"

John 14:14 — If you ask anything in my name, I will do it.

What an absolute privilege we have as believers in prayer. Jesus cleans away our sin by the shedding of His precious blood, and then enables us to go to the Father in His name. When we pray to our heavenly Father in the name of Jesus, we are afforded all the special benefits and bold access that the Father gave to Jesus.

Jesus said in John 16:24, "up to now have you asked nothing in my name, ask, and you shall receive, that your joy may be full." As long as Jesus was physically walking with the disciples on earth, they didn't need to ask the Father anything in Jesus' name. All they had to do was just turn to Jesus and ask HIM. Jesus was saying that there was going to come a day soon, (after His death, burial, resurrection and ascension) that He would not physically be next to them, but now they could approach a Holy Father and use His Name. Imagine just as Jesus prayed to His Father with power and passion, we too can approach the throne of grace boldly to find grace to help in time of need, as long as we come in the name of Jesus. Call on your heavenly Father this day and make your request known to Him, always coming to Him in the Name of His precious Son, Jesus Christ. Ask and you shall receive!

Scripture Reading: Leviticus 14; Matthew 26:55-75

Trivia Question: Who is the Apostle and High Priest of our profession?

February 13

"Scared of a Shadow?"

Psalms 23:4 — Yea, though I walk through the valley of the shadow of death, I will fear no evil: for thou art with me; thy rod and thy staff they comfort me.

"Precious in the sight of the Lord is the death of His saints." (Psalm 116:15) To the Christian who is born again of the Spirit of God, nothing can separate him from the Love of God! No, not even death. The Bible says in Hebrews 2:15, that people are in lifelong bondage to this inevitable dreaded event, but to the Christian, even death has no power. To be absent from this body is to be present with the Lord!

You see, David by inspiration of the Holy Spirit, calls it the "shadow of death." Now let me ask you a question, is there any real fear when it comes to seeing somebody's shadow? A shadow cannot hurt or harm you, it cannot defeat you, and it cannot rise up victorious over you. That's what death is to a born again believer, it does not defeat us, it is only the "shadow of death." That is why there is no sting in death, but victory over the grave. Jesus Christ defeated sin, Satan, sickness and death. He holds the keys to Hell and death. So when a Christian fulfills his or her mission on earth and leaves this temporal place to live at home in Heaven for eternity, he only has to pass through the "shadow of death"—from this life into the next. Glory to God! Death has been defeated and its shadow is powerless over a child of God. Beloved, live victoriously over everything that has been defeated by our Lord and Savior and enjoy all the benefits He left for us this day and every day.

Scripture Reading: Leviticus 15, 16, 17; Matthew 27:1-31

Trivia Question: What were the four major sins of the people of Sodom?

February 14

"Broadway Lights"

Proverbs 14:12 — There is a way that seemeth right to a man,
but the end thereof are the ways of death.

There are two roads (or ways) that are before all of mankind according to Jesus. In Matthew 7:13-14, Jesus describes both of them. One He calls the "broad way", and on this road there are many traveling. This road is wide and broad and appears quite glamorous to the natural sight. Jesus said the end of this road leads to destruction and death.

The second road is called the straight-way (straight street), and that is a very narrow road. There are not many that have chosen to walk down this road. At times, it is bumpy and full of tests and trials and, quite simply, it is a HARD way to travel. Jesus said that at the end of this road is Everlasting Life.

Beloved, the choice is up to us. We must choose which road we will travel on, *Broadway* or *Straight Street*. *Broadway*, although it looks good and many are travelling on it, leads to destruction. *Straight Street* does not have many travelers and is a hard journey, but it leads to life. Choose the right way and live. Remember, just because the crowd is saying one thing, and the crowd is going a certain way, does not necessarily mean that it is the right way. Follow the way of the Lord, that is the straight and narrow way that leads to blessings, benefits and life!

Scripture Reading: Leviticus 18, 19; Matthew 27:32-66

Trivia Question: Who lived on a street literally called Straight Street?

February 15

"He Cares for your Cares"

1 Peter 5:7 — Casting all your care upon Him, for He careth for you.

We are called as God's people to hurl or throw all of our cares, worries and frets on the Lord Jesus Christ. He is stronger than we are and has big shoulders to carry all that we cast upon Him. The Bible says in Isaiah 9:6, "the government shall be upon His shoulders." If He can carry the weight of the government of the church on His shoulders, He can carry my problem!

The word casting, in the Greek language, means to hurl or throw. The word care, in the Greek language, means anxiety or to be drawn in different directions (like the proverbial chicken without a head). We are called to cast, hurl or throw anything and everything that will bring anxiety into our lives on Him, because He cares for us. Anxiety brings stress and stress brings fear and fear will choke your faith and cause you to be spiritually paralyzed. When you can't move you cannot throw, and it is imperative that we continually cast all of our cares upon Him.

Paul writes in Philippians 4-7, "be anxious for nothing, but in everything, by prayer and supplication with thanksgiving, let your requests be made known unto God, and the peace of God that passes all understanding shall keep your hearts and minds through Christ Jesus."

Scripture Reading: Leviticus 20, 21; Matthew 28:1-20

Trivia Question: How many years did God add to Hezekiah's life?

February 16

"Conform vs. Transform"

*Romans 12:2 — And be not conformed to this world, but be ye transformed
by the renewing of the mind, that you may prove what is the good,
and acceptable and perfect will of God.*

One translation says, "do not be poured into the world's mold, but be transformed by the renewing of your mind." We are called as Christians not to fit in the world's mold or be conformed to the world's system. It is so important for us to renew our minds as we meditate on the Word of God. The Word of God will literally change and transform us. When we allow

God's Word to transform our hearts and cause our thinking to be in line with God and His plan for us, then we can prove what is the good, acceptable and perfect will of God.

I have a conviction in my heart that says, more of the Word and less of the world will bring definition and clarity for us to know the will of God in our lives. I need to know the perfect will of God, not just the good or acceptable, but the perfect will of God.

Don't try to fit in to the world's mold, but get into the Word of God and allow God to bring transformation into your life and reveal to you by His Spirit and through His Word what His perfect will is for your life!

Scripture Reading: Leviticus 22, 23; Mark 1:1-22

Trivia Question: What are the two greatest commandments?

February 17

"A Big Thank You"

1 Peter 2:5 — Ye also, as lively stones, are built up a spiritual house, an holy priesthood, to offer up spiritual sacrifices, acceptable to God by Jesus Christ.

We as believers/priests are referred to as "living stones." It almost seems like a paradoxical term, how could a stone be alive? Paul writes in Romans 12:1 that we are to present our bodies a "living sacrifice." How can a sacrifice be alive? In the Old Testament, the animal was killed and offered as a sacrifice to the Lord. In the new covenant, God is looking for stones that are living and sacrifices that are alive. Beloved, you are the sacrifice that God is looking for. To the believer or priest, it is a two-fold sacrifice, the sacrifice of SELF and the sacrifice of SERVICE.

The sacrifice of self is where the Christian offers up the spiritual sacrifices of praise to God. "Let us offer the sacrifice of praise to God continually, that is, the fruit of our lips giving thanks to His Name." (Hebrews 13:15) We must be a living thank you card to the Lord, constantly expressing our appreciation for all that He has done through praise.

The sacrifice of service is when we present our bodies as living sacrifices that are Holy, so He may accept them and perform His perfect will in our lives. When we give our services to the Lord, we are offering spiritual sacrifices to God so that His perfect will may be accomplished in and through us to the Glory of His Name.

Will you offer up spiritual sacrifices to God as a living stone, the sacrifice of self and the sacrifice of service, so that you may live a life of praise and power to the glory of our Lord and Savior, Jesus Christ?

Scripture Reading: Leviticus 24, 25; Mark 1:23-45

Trivia Question: What is the name of the last battle in the Bible?

February 18

"Break Every Chain"

*Exodus 20:5 — Thou shalt not bow down thyself to them,
nor serve them: for I the Lord thy God am a jealous God,
visiting the iniquity of the fathers upon the children unto the third
and fourth generation of them that hate me.*

The Bible teaches, in many cases, that sin is spiritually hereditary. The sins of the fathers are passed down from generation to generation. We see this in many families today. A great-grandfather could have been involved in some wicked thing, and he passed it down spiritually to his son, then his son's son, and so forth.

We do not have to receive or succumb to that kind of diabolical plan to destroy our lives and our families. Jesus Christ, and His Blood with His Word will absolutely break that flow of paternity. We can stop any passing down of sin, iniquity and wickedness by applying the Blood of Christ to the situation (we overcome the devil by the Blood of the Lamb, Revelation 12:11) and by speaking God's Word over the situation (you shall know the truth and the truth shall make you free, John 8:32).

There was a king in the Bible named Hezekiah who had a terrible example for a father (Ahaz). Ahaz sacrificed to false gods, cut to pieces the vessels of the house of God, and closed the doors of the temple. Ahaz was a wicked king who eventually died, and because of his wickedness, he didn't even get an honorable burial place with the former kings of Israel.

You might think, like father, like son." No, not in this case. Ahaz's son Hezekiah started to reign in his stead. As a young man of twenty-five years, Hezekiah decided to break that flow of paternity. Early in his reign, in the first year of the first month, he repaired the doors of the house of the Lord and eventually restored worship back to the temple. Hezekiah refused to let the sin of his father be passed down to him and he did something about it.

Christian, if this story in the Word of God applies to you in any way, do as the righteous king did, take care of it early or right away in your Christian walk. Apply the Blood and the Word to break that spiritual hereditary disease called iniquity!

Scripture Reading: Leviticus 26, 27; Mark 2

Trivia Question: What leper in the Bible was told to dip in the Jordan River seven times and would be healed?

February 19

"Complete Surrender"

Luke 9:23 — And he said to them all, If any man will come after me, let him deny himself, and take up his cross daily, and follow me.

The principles in the Kingdom of God are very different from the world's teachings, philosophies and principles (what little they have). We are governed by a different kingdom and ruled by a Majestic King, Jesus Christ the Lord.

In this kingdom, King Jesus teaches that the way to get ahead is to get behind. The way to be elevated is to become lowered first. The way to gain is to be willing to lose. We have been given a different set of principles for a very unique kingdom, ruled by a very special king.

Beloved, as Christians we must first be willing to deny ourselves, if we want to follow Jesus. The Amplified Version says that denying oneself means to forget, lose sight of himself and his own interest and give up himself. We must take up our cross daily. This cross that we take up and carry daily is our surrendered will that we offer up to God everyday of our lives. "Not my will but thy will be done," is our continual, perpetual, everyday prayer. If we are not willing to lay aside our will, our goals, our objectives and our motives, then we actually wrestle against God and His will for our lives. The cross will then become extremely heavy and burdensome. He says that His yoke is easy and His burden is light. Let's learn how to deny our flesh when it cries out for pampering and comfort, yield to the spirit in all things and lay our lives and our will down before God and pick up our cross and follow Him.

Scripture Reading: Numbers 1, 2; Mark 3:1-21

Trivia Question: Who had an excellent spirit?

February 20

"You are Called"

Galatians 1:15 — But when it pleased God, who separated me
from my mother's womb, and called me by His grace.

The Apostle Paul received the revelation that the call on his life went beyond his Damascus road experience. Paul realized, although his spiritual eyes were not open prior to that experience, in the providence and sovereignty of God, the call on his life was ordained much earlier. Paul understood like Jeremiah, "Before I formed you in the womb, I knew you, and before you came forth out of the womb, I sanctified (separated) you, and I ordained you a prophet unto the nations." (Jeremiah 1:5) Paul knew by the Spirit of God that there was a sovereign separation when he was born to fulfill God's call on his life.

There are too many Christians that do not understand that they have been sanctified and called by His grace to fulfill His purpose and plan. Christians walk around not knowing what the will of God is for their lives. We cannot be ignorant of what the will of the Lord is for our lives. Beloved, know this day that God has called you before the foundations of the world and has separated you to fulfill a divine purpose with a divine plan. (Ephesians 1:4) In Jesus' name, GO FOR IT!

Scripture Reading: Numbers 3, 4; Mark 3:22-35

Trivia Question: Who was the youngest king to reign over Jerusalem?

February 21

"Deliverance is Here"

2 Corinthians 1:10 — Who delivered us from so great a death,
and does deliver, in whom we trust that He will deliver us.

We serve a God of deliverance. Joel prophesied in Joel 2:32, "and all those that call on the name of the Lord shall be delivered." He's a God that has delivered us, delivers us today and will deliver us tomorrow. Past, present and future deliverance belongs to the child of God.

God sent forth His son, Jesus, to set the captive free. A beautiful picture of Jesus' deliverance is portrayed in his crucifixion and resurrection. In

Matthew 27, when Jesus died on the cross and yielded up His Spirit to the Father, it is said that the veil in the temple was ripped in two and the Old Testament saints were raised from their graves (past deliverance).

The Centurion, whose servant was paralyzed and suffering, asked Jesus for help, "…Lord, I do not deserve to have you come under my roof. But just say the word, and my servant will be healed. (Matthew 8:5-13) The Centurion recognized that Jesus really was the Son of God and made a public confession of Christ, thus setting his soul free (present deliverance).

A few days after the resurrection, Jesus appeared to the eleven disciples causing them to be liberated from all their doubts and fears, and told them, "Lo I am with you always, even unto the end of the age," (future deliverance). (Matthew 28:20)

God has delivered you, will deliver you now, if need be, and will be there to deliver you in the future!

Scripture Reading: Numbers 5, 6; Mark 4:1-20

Trivia Question: What does Eli, Eli, lama sabachthani mean?

February 22

"Power from On High"

Luke 10:19 — Behold I give unto you power to tread upon serpents and scorpions and over all power of the enemy, and nothing by any means shall hurt you.

Because of the blood covenant we have with the Father God, through the Son, Jesus Christ and sealed by the Holy Spirit, we have been given full authority over Satan, demons, and all of the forces of darkness.

We have been called to walk on and trample over the diabolical influences of Hell. Jesus had complete authority over Satan, and when He rose again He gave us that mandate because the Christians are His body. The enemy has power, but God has so much more, and has transferred that power (or authority) to the church. We have complete authority over the powers of darkness. That is why Jesus said, "…and nothing shall hurt you." The child of God is protected, preserved and provided for by his/her heavenly Father. Beloved, you do not have to fret or be afraid this day, or any other day, because you walk in the light of your redemption and the power (authority) you possess in Jesus' Name. Walk as more than conquerors this day and shake up the kingdom of darkness!

45

Scripture Reading: Numbers 7; Mark 4:21-41

Trivia Question: How many days did it take God to create the world?

February 23

"Faith not to Faint"

Galatians 6:9 — And let us not be weary in well doing,
for in due season we shall reap if we faint not.

Scriptures teach us that if we faint in the day of adversity, our strength is small (Proverbs 24:10). We must draw from His strength each and every day, especially in the midst of tribulation. Satan tries to wear us down and cause us to quit, but God's promise is that if we keep on we shall reap. Daniel 7:25 talks about the devil trying to wear out the saints of the most High God. We are not ignorant of Satan's devices, whether it is temptation, lust of the flesh, lust of the eyes or the pride of life. Many of God's people have victory in all of these areas, but allow the enemy to bring stress and frustration into their lives and eventually it wears them out.

Are you believing God for something in your life? Don't stop believing, don't stop trusting, and don't stop laying hold of God's promises. When we stay in faith, we are doing well. His promise states that if we do not give in to the flesh and keep doing well (remaining in faith), in due season we shall reap and receive an answer to our prayer. Beloved, do not faint! Don't allow the enemy to wear you out and cause you to faint under the load. Remember, the Word teaches us, "But those that wait upon the Lord shall renew their strength, they shall mount up with wings like eagles, they shall run and not be weary, they shall WALK and not FAINT." (Isaiah 40:31)

Scripture Reading: Numbers 8, 9, 10; Mark 5:1-20

Trivia Question: What Southern king restored worship back into the temple?

February 24

"Go as the Good Samaritan"

Luke 10:37 — And he said, He that shewed mercy on him.

Then said Jesus unto him, Go, and do thou likewise.

The story of the Good Samaritan has been shared from the beginning of New Testament times. Jesus shared how a certain man was mugged by thieves, and was stripped, wounded and left for dead. The priest and Levite saw the man by the roadside, but chose to ignore the need and passed by on the other side of the road. The good Samaritan also saw the need, but was moved with compassion, and bound up his wounds, poured in the oil and the wine, set him on his own beast and brought him to an inn, where he spent the night helping him to recover from his wounds. Jesus asked the question, who was a real neighbor to the man who was mugged? The obvious answer was the Samaritan. Jesus said, "Go and do thou likewise."

Scripture teaches us to be willing to go and touch people with the life and love of God. We are not to pray that God will send unbelievers to us, but we should be praying that God would help us to be willing to go to the unsaved and share the Gospel of Christ. There are so many people that are emotionally stripped, wounded and dying spiritually who need a compassionate Christian to minister healing and the Gospel to them. Are you willing to go?

Scripture Reading: Numbers 11, 12, 13; Mark 5:21-43

Trivia Question: Who did Jesus cast seven demons out of?

February 25

"Peace in the Midst..."

Mark 4:35 — And the same day, when the even was come, he saith unto them, Let us pass over unto the other side.

Jesus gave a promise to His disciples that they were to go over the Sea of Galilee to the country of the Gadarenes. A tremendous storm came out of nowhere and threatened the disciples as they were in the boat in the middle of the sea. Their lives were in danger as the waves beat against the boat and water poured into the vessel threatening to sink it. It was a very scary predicament, but Jesus was in the boat too! Jesus, who was sleeping in the stern of the boat, not because He was being insensitive or oblivious to the problem, was simply "resting" on the Word of God.

The Word of the Father that Jesus received, He in turn gave to His disciples, "Let us pass over to the other side." Jesus knew the Word of God would come to pass no matter what challenge came His way. He was confident in the Word of the Father.

Has God given you a promise? Has all *hell* broken loose in your life since the promise was given? Are you engaged in a spiritual storm enroute to seeing the promise fulfilled in your life? Beloved, know this one thing – Jesus is in your boat (He is in the midst of your situation). He forcefully speaks and says, "Peace be still!" (Mark 4:39) There will be a calm in your storm. There will be peace in your trial. Jesus is in your boat with a promise that you will make it to the other side, in spite of any storm or challenge that will come your way. The Word of God is true and will come to pass in your life, as you trust in Him.

Scripture Reading: Numbers 14, 15; Mark 6:1-32

Trivia Question: What were the names of Jesus' biological brothers?

February 26

"Don't Hesitate, Meditate"

Psalms 119:97 — Oh, how I love thy law! It is my meditation all the day.

We have been exhorted through Scripture to do more than just read or even study God's Word. We have been called to meditate upon the Word of God. Meditation is different than just memorizing Scripture. Where memorization has to do with your mind, meditation of the Word deals with engrafting God's Word into your spirit (heart). It is important to memorize God's Word, but even more important to meditate on the Word of God.

The word meditate, means to speak repeatedly or to mutter. When we meditate upon a certain area of the Bible, we are taking a verse or verses and speaking them out of our mouth. We first study the verse, then we mutter it from our lips over and over again. The process will literally engraft the verse into our heart. David said, "Thy word have I hidden in my heart, that I might not sin against thee." David learned to meditate on the Word. David loved the Word of God and meditated day and night on it. (Psalm 1:2)

When we engraft God's Word into our spirit, it is very difficult to be shaken because we are rooting His Word deep down on the inside of us. In the natural, the deeper the roots go down for a tree, the less likely it will be blown over during storms and high winds. The deeper the Word is in our hearts (through meditation), the less likely we will be moved when tests, trials, and the storms of life come and the spiritual winds blow.

Meditate on and in the Word of God, and let it be rooted deeply in your heart today. "This book of the law shall not depart out of your mouth, but you shall meditate therein day and night, that you may observe to do according to all that is written therein, for then you shall make your way prosperous, and you shall have good success." (Joshua 1:8)

Scripture Reading: Numbers 16, 17; Mark 6:33-56

Trivia Question: What was Joshua's famous declaration for himself and his family?

_____

February 27

"Beauty on the Wheel"

Isaiah 64:8 — But now, O Lord, thou art our father; we are the clay, a nd thou our potter; and we all are the work of thy hand.

What a great truth to know that God is our heavenly Father. We who God formed from the dust of the ground are the clay. God is the Master Potter and we are the very work of His hands.

As a potter puts a lump of clay on his potter's wheel to work it and form it into a useable, beautiful vessel, so our heavenly Father works on us, to fashion and form us into a vessel of honor, fit for His service. God has not forgotten how to form something out of the dust or clay of the ground. He did it once in the Garden of Eden, and He is still doing it today as we allow Him to place His hands on us to form something beautiful out of our lives.

The first vessel, Adam, was a beautiful sight to behold. He was perfect in every way. So it is in our lives, as we remain on the potter's wheel, God our Father and our Potter works on us, shaping and forming us into beautiful vessels for Him. The only thing that caused Adam, God's first vessel, to break and become unusable was sin; and sin eventually caused him to return to the ground, "for dust you are and to dust shall you return." (Genesis 3:19) Don't allow disobedience and sin to cause you to come off the potter's wheel. If you come off the wheel, the potter's hands cannot continue to mold you and you will become a broken vessel, unusable for the Lord. Stay on the wheel and allow your Father/Potter to make something beautiful out of your life – for His Honor and Glory!

49

Scripture Reading: Numbers 18, 19, 20; Mark 7:1-13

Trivia Question: What was Cain's occupation?

February 28

"Good as New"

Jeremiah 30:17 — For I will restore health unto thee, and I will heal thee of thy wounds, saith the Lord; because they called thee an Outcast, saying, This is Zion, whom no man seeketh after.

God is in the restoration business. No matter how beat up, damaged, or just old and worn, God can and will restore your life.

In the natural, if you knew how and were skilled in restoring furniture, and if you took time to work on a piece and gave it a lot of tender care, it would be turned into a picture of beauty. As a matter of fact, the value of the piece would be greater after the restoring process.

Well, that is what God does for us, He RESTORES us in every way, spiritually, physically, emotionally, financially, maritally, parentally and in every aspect of our lives. He will even heal the deepest wound caused by the greatest hurt in your life. The good news is that God will restore you if you allow Him to do it. When He does, you come out more valuable and more beautiful than ever. There is a worth that accompanies your life because the touch of the Master has restored you to perfection.

Scripture Reading: Numbers 21, 22; Mark 7:14-37

Trivia Question: What prophet was shut up in prison during King Zedekiah's reign?

February 29

"Let there be Light"

Genesis 1:4 — And God saw the light, that it was good, and God divided the light from the darkness.

From the beginning of time, God separated the light from the darkness. God is light, and in Him there is no darkness. Light will always expel darkness. Darkness cannot overcome light. It does not matter how dark a room is, just one little match or light will be immediately noticed and the light gets the attention. In Him (Jesus) was life, and the life was the light of men, and the light shines in darkness and the darkness overcame it not." (John 1:5)

Light represents righteousness and darkness represents sin. Light represents good and darkness represents Satan. The problem with man, according to Jesus, is that man loved darkness rather than light. You may ask why would men choose darkness over light, why would human beings prefer darkness rather than light? The answer is found in John 3:19-21, "men love darkness rather than light because their deeds are evil." Jesus said, "For everyone that does evil hates the light, neither comes to the light, lest his deeds should be reproved. But he that loves truth, comes to the light, that his deeds may be manifested, that they are wrought in God." It's rather simple, if man chooses to remain in a sinful status, he will remain in darkness because he does not want his evil deeds to be seen.

Beloved, choose light, choose God and let His light shine through you, that He may be glorified. "Let your light (which is really God's light shining through you) so shine before men, that they may see your good works and glorify your Father in Heaven." (Matthew 5:16) Beloved, confess any sin in your life and walk in His divine light this day!

Scripture Reading: Numbers 23, 24, 25; Mark 8:1-21

Trivia Question: Who had an argument over a man by the name John Mark?

March

March 1

"The Big Test"

Acts 14:22 — Confirming the souls of the disciples, and exhorting them to continue in the faith, and that we must through much tribulation enter into the Kingdom of God.

Jesus never preached that the Christian walk would be easy. On the contrary, He said at times it would be quite hard. Jesus said in John 16:33, "In the world you shall have tribulation, but be of good cheer, I have overcome the world." The Bible teaches that Christians are in the world but not of the world. Because we are in the world, we are going to go through tests, trials, and tribulations. The good news is this, that Jesus overcame every trial and tribulation and as He is, so are we in this world. The Apostle Paul taught that tribulation works patience. (Romans 5:3)

Trials and tribulations should not cause us to retreat from the battle, they should thrust us into rest. Patience is rest. When we are in patience, we are resting. Jesus said, "In your patience possess ye your souls." (Luke 21:19) We must have full control over our emotions during the tribulations of life. The test can either drive you into panic or direct you into peace. When you were in school, it was very important to pass all the tests during the school year. Promotion to the next grade was dependent upon it.

Beloved, stand on God's Word during tests, trials, and tribulations, rest in and on His Word for perfect peace and have full control of your emotions so that you may pass the test and allow God to promote you. If you pass the test, He really will promote you!

Scripture Reading: Numbers 26, 27; Mark 8:22-38

Trivia Question: In what Book is the Lamb's Book of Life mentioned?

March 2

"Just a Taste"

Psalms 107:1 — Oh give thanks unto the Lord, for He is good,
for His mercy endureth forever.

The Lord is so good; at times it boggles the mind and is beyond our comprehension. Paul wrote about the riches of His goodness. God is abundant in goodness. Heaven never runs out of stock of God's goodness. The shelves of Heaven are full of God's goodness because Heaven is full of God. God is good.

Paul said in Romans 2:4 that it was "the goodness of God that led us to repentance." When you get a revelation of how good God really is and how bad sin is, it causes you to repent and turn away from all unrighteousness and taste of the goodness of God. The Psalmist wrote, "Oh, taste and see that the Lord is good." (Psalm 34:8) When we understand the goodness of God, it causes us to repent and turn to him, that we might taste and be a partaker of His goodness. In the natural, when you taste a food that is good, it probably will not be the last time you eat it. You will go back for more, most likely very often. When we taste of the Lord and see that He is good, it causes us to go back to Him for more, and more, and more. Let His goodness cause you to give thanks to Him this day.

Scripture Reading: Numbers 28, 29; Mark 9:1-29

Trivia Question: What did Jesus say no man could tame?

March 3

"Troubled Waters"

Psalms 32:6 — For this shall every one that is godly pray unto thee
in a time when thou mayest be found: surely in the floods
of great waters they shall not come nigh unto him.

Beloved, are you going through some hard times? Have the storms of life beat up on you lately? Do you feel like you are in some deep waters and it is starting to make you feel insecure? Listen, the promise of God states that even when we go through tough times, "The Lord will not leave us, nor forsake us." (Hebrews 13:5)

We must believe no matter how bad or contrary the situation looks, the Lord has promised to bring us through. God promises His children that the floods will not come near us. We must believe, receive and thank Him for that promise. Isaiah 43:2 says, "When you pass through the waters, I will be with you, and through the rivers (deeper waters or tougher times), they shall not overflow you (you are not going to drown), even when you walk through the fire, you shall not be burned, neither shall the flame kindle upon thee." What an absolute, glorious promise from God. Whatever you are facing today beloved, remember God is facing it with you too, and He says that you will pass through without drowning, burning or being devastated. Hallelujah to the Lord! Keep His promise living big in your heart and you will have security when you go through the deep waters and floods of life!

Scripture Reading: Numbers 30, 31; Mark 9:30-50

Trivia Question: The saying, "Many waters cannot quench love" is found in what book of the Bible?

March 4

"The Beautiful Breakdown"

Ecclesiastes 3:3 — ....a time to break down, and a time to build up.

The wise King Solomon said, "There is a time and a season for everything." (Ecclesiastes 3:1) There is a time to break down, and then a time to build up. Now we are not talking about a nervous breakdown, but a time when we allow the Lord, by His Spirit, to break up the fallow ground of our hearts in order for us to build up for His honor and glory. It is essential that we put this in perspective and in proper order. First comes breaking, and then comes building.

To a weight lifter or bodybuilder this concept is very much understood. When a bodybuilder works out with weights doing reps and sets, what he/she is doing is forcing more blood and oxygen into that particular muscle. The body seems like it is pumping or working out, but in actuality the muscle tissue is fatiguing or breaking down. The workout is a time of breaking down but through proper rest and nutrition (muscle needs protein to build up and get bigger), the muscle will grow.

Many Christians want to build up before they break down. This will not work. People that long to see growth in their lives MUST be willing to allow God, by His Spirit to break them down. Psalms 51:17-18 says,"The sacrifices of God are a broken and a contrite heart....Build thou the walls of Jerusalem." Beloved, let God break any and every area that needs to be broken in your life and then watch how He starts to build you up and cause you to grow in abundant grace for His honor and glory. Remember, break down, then build up.

Scripture Reading: Numbers 32, 33; Mark 10:1-31

Trivia Question: Who has said in his heart, "There is no God"?

March 5

"Overcome the Surf"

James 1:8 — A double-minded man is unstable in all ways.

We are exhorted in the Word of God, not to be double-minded. You may ask, what is meant by the term double-minded? In an obvious sense, it means do not have two minds or two thoughts. In a theological sense it takes on a deeper meaning. In the verses prior to this text (the rules of Hermeneutics teach us to interpret a verse in context), we see James talking about temptation, trials, patience and wisdom. In order to overcome temptation, endure trials, walk in patience and receive God's wisdom, we must express our faith in God. James says in James 6:1, "But let him ask in faith, nothing wavering...." We cannot waver in our faith. Waves of the sea are subject to wind and the elements. The wind drives the wave and it is tossed. The wave also swells up and down.

Christians are not to be driven by the elements, environments or events of life. Christians are not to be up one day and down another day with their faith. Christians are not to be double-minded. We are called to renew our minds (Romans 12:2), hear the Word of God (Romans 10:17), meditate on the Scriptures (Joshua 1:8), and hide God's Word in our hearts (Psalms 119:11). All of this will produce faith. If we fail to address these four areas or do them in a hit or miss fashion, we can become double-minded. This will bring instability in our lives. If we are between two opinions as in the days of Elijah and the nation of Israel (1 Kings 18:21), and we waver like the waves of the sea in our faith, we shall not receive anything from the Lord (James 1:7). Let us put on the mind of Christ and become one with

56

Him and His Word, and receive by faith all that we need from our Father in Heaven!

Scripture Reading: Numbers 34, 35, 36; Mark 10:32-52

Trivia Question: When is man tempted?

March 6

"Watch the Performance"

Jeremiah 1:12 — Then said the Lord unto me, Thou hast well seen: for I will hasten my word to perform it.

The word, hasten in the Hebrew means to be alert, sleepless, to lookout, to watch for.

God is watching, looking out and over His Word to perform it in our lives. It is so important that we believe and speak God's Word over our lives and circumstances. The Bible teaches, "For the eyes of the Lord run to and fro throughout the whole earth, to show Himself strong in the behalf of them whose heart is perfect toward Him." (2 Chronicles 16:9) The Lord desires to show Himself strong on your behalf, He desires to manifest His power to you. HE is ever watching over His Word to perform it. As His eyes run to and fro, and He beholds a believer embracing and speaking His Word, that draws His attention and His power and presence into the situation. He is ever alert, does not slumber or sleep; He is looking out and watching over His Word. When someone is standing on His Word, it is at that point where God will back up His Word to perform it in their life. We must be fully persuaded, what God has promised, He is able to perform. Beloved, trust in the Word of God, embrace it in your heart and confess it with your mouth, and see how God will hasten His Word to perform it!

Scripture Reading: Deuteronomy 1, 2; Mark 11:1-19

Trivia Questions: What King had riches and honor in abundance?

March 7

"Lay it Down"

Psalms 55:22 — Cast thy burden upon the Lord, and he shall sustain thee:

he shall never suffer the righteous to be moved.

Don't carry around the weight of sin, guilt, pressure or anxiety. You must cast it all on the Lord. When we obey this Scripture and cast our burdens on Him, then He gets mightily involved and comes to our aid to sustain and hold us up. Think about it, He can carry our burden (when we give it to Him), and at the same time hold us up. The Lord wants to hold us up so we stay in place. He does not want us to be moved! We should be standing in our right position – on the Word and promises of God. David wrote, "He called me out of the horrible pit, out of the miry clay, set my feet upon a rock and established my goings." (Psalm 40:2-3)

We need to have our feet planted solidly on the rock of His Word, and to be established in Him. When we cast our burden upon Him, He will truly sustain us and never allow you or I to be moved. Psalms 62:2 says, "He only is my rock and my salvation, He is my defense, I shall not be greatly moved."

Scripture Reading: Deuteronomy 3, 4; Mark 11:20-33

Trivia Question: Who said, "Blessed are the pure in heart, for they shall see God."

March 8

"Praise Power"

Psalms 68:35 — O God, thou art terrible out of thy holy places: the God of Israel is he that giveth strength and power unto his people. Blessed be God.

There is much data and information today on how to increase our strength, muscle mass, cardiovascular condition and overall physical health and well-being. I believe people perform better in life when they are in good physical condition.

It is much more important however, that people get into spiritual condition, developing a strong relationship with the Lord. The Bible says that God gives strength and power. This strength and power is not for building physical muscle mass to win a bodybuilding contest. This is spiritual strength and power that God gives to perform spiritually in the Kingdom of God.

Two ways to receive God's strength and power is to pray and praise. There's something about prayer and praise that brings the manifested strength and power of God into our lives. There were two men in Acts 16 by the names of Paul and Silas. They were thrown into jail with their hands and feet in stocks and shackles. At midnight, Paul and Silas prayed and praised and God's strength and power manifested as they burst loose from their iron bonds. Now that is power and strength. This day seek God in prayer and start to praise Him, even if you feel incarcerated in any way. Watch and see how your shackles will be loosed and fall off and how God will bring strength and power to your life to set you free from anything that has a hold on you. Truly the Lord is your strength and power!

Scripture Reading: Deuteronomy 5, 6, 7; Mark 12:1-27

Trivia Question: Who got saved as a result of Paul and Silas's ministry and dramatic "Jail House Rock?"

March 9

"Four-Fold Blessing"

1 Chronicles 4:10 — And Jabez called on the God of Israel, saying, Oh that thou wouldest bless me indeed, and enlarge my coast, and that thine hand might be with me, and that thou wouldest keep me from evil, that it may not grieve me! And God granted him that which he requested.

The Lord answered the prayer of a man in the Bible by the name of Jabez. Jabez, whose name means sorrow or pain, prayed a four-fold prayer. Jabez asked God: to bless him, to enlarge his borders, that God's hand would be upon him, and that God would keep him from evil. A four-fold prayer would invoke a four-fold blessing.

I believe we can learn from this man's prayer how to invoke God's blessing on us. Remember, Jabez means pain. It is said of Jabez that he was more honorable than his brother. Even when we experience pain and sorrow, as Christians we must maintain an honorable and upright attitude before God. The Lord will withhold no good thing to them who walk uprightly. We need to cry out to God in the midst of our pain to bless us, enlarge and stretch us, keep His hand on us and allow no evil to come near us. Instead of complaining in our pain, we must call on the Lord. As we honor God with our behavior and attitude, I believe He will grant our request as He did for Jabez.

Scripture Reading: Deuteronomy 8, 9, 10; Mark 12:28-44

Trivia Question: Who referred to believers as salt of the Earth?

March 10

"Supernatural Wisdom"

James 1:5 — If any of you lack wisdom, let him ask of God, that giveth to all men liberally, and upbraideth not; and it shall be given him.

We are living in a time where we need God's wisdom daily in our lives. There is a natural wisdom that comes from textbooks, education, and the intellect of our day. Natural wisdom will suffice for natural matters, but only the wisdom from God will get the job done for spiritual problems and circumstances.

This verse of Scripture teaches us that if we are in need of this divine wisdom, we can truly ask the Lord. The Scripture teaches that God will give us a full supply of His wisdom and will not scold us for asking. Jesus taught us to ask and it shall be given unto you. We must ask in faith when we are petitioning the Lord for wisdom or for anything else.

Solomon could have had anything he wanted; riches, fame, power or whatever his heart desired. When asked by God "Ask what I shall give?" Solomon responded by saying, "Give me now, wisdom and knowledge that I may go out and come in before this people, for who can judge this, thy people who are so great?" (2 Chronicles 1:10) God was so pleased with Solomon's reply to His question that He blessed him with wisdom. He also attained riches, wealth, honor and power. Beloved, are you in need of wisdom today? Ask God, He will give it to you!

Scripture Reading: Deuteronomy 11, 12, 13; Mark 13:1-13

Trivia Question: How many songs did Solomon write?

March 11

"Firm Foundation"

1 Corinthians 3:11 — For other foundations can no man lay, than that is laid, which is Jesus Christ.

We have a sure foundation as believers in this life. Scriptures teach us that Jesus Christ is our foundation. The Bible says, "as lively stones, are built up a spiritual house...." We are spiritual houses for the Lord and need a strong foundation to stand on. In the natural, the foundation of the house or building is the most important part of the edifice. With a strong, deep foundation you can build tall and high. Even though the foundation cannot be seen, without it the house will crumble and fall.

Jesus is our rock and foundation. He and His Word are the very platform that we build our lives on. David wrote in Psalms 119:89 "Forever, Oh Lord, your Word is settled in Heaven." Think about it, the Word of God is the very foundation that Heaven stands on. Like cement, when poured and allowed to dry to make a strong foundation, the Word settled in Heaven becomes its foundation. When we settle God's Word in our hearts, it becomes our strong foundation. We shall not be moved! Glory to God! Beloved, allow Jesus and His Word to be your foundation today.

Scripture Reading: Deuteronomy 14, 15, 16; Mark 13:14-37

Trivia Question: Who was the man from Caesarea, a centurion of the Italian band?

March 12

"Prepared Protection"

Jonah 1:17 — Now the Lord had prepared a great fish to swallow up Jonah. And Jonah was in the belly of the fish three days and three nights.

We all know the story of Jonah and how he rebelled against God. He wanted to do his own thing, and eventually ran away from the call and the will of God. As he was on a ship going to Tarnish, after he paid the fare, (there will always be a price to pay when we run from the call of God), a storm came endangering all the passenger's lives. The Bible says that God prepared a great fish to swallow up Jonah. If you are like most people (including myself), we view the great fish as being sent by God to punish Jonah for all of his wrongdoing, rebellion and iniquity. Truly, Jonah deserved to be punished.

How about looking at it in this light? The great fish was sent by God to protect Jonah from drowning in the raging sea! Obviously, if the whale had not come to swallow Jonah, he would have eventually become tired from fighting the angry waves, he would have had stopped treading water and eventually drowned. Granted, the smelly belly of the whale was not like a three-day, three-night stay at a luxury hotel, but it kept him safe and secure until he made right with God and repented for his sin.

Beloved, I believe God sends us a big fish every now and then to protect us from being overwhelmed and overcome by life's situations. These big fish sent by God may come in the form of other people, circumstances or just a good sermon from the pulpit. Though it may be unpleasant and uncomfortable for a season, the whole intent is to keep you safe and protected until you get things right with God and to keep you from drowning! "Now, no chastening for the present seems to be joyous, but grievous: nevertheless afterward it yields the peaceable fruit of righteous unto them who are exercised by it." (Hebrews 12:11)

Scripture Reading: Deuteronomy 17, 18, 19; Mark 14:1-25

Trivia Questions: What does the Bible say about "respect of persons?"

March 13

"A Constant"

Hebrews 13:8 — Jesus Christ, the same yesterday, and today, and forever.

In an ever-changing world, where seasons, styles, sensations and structures come and go, we have a continual constant in the Lord Jesus Christ. The same Jesus who walked the shores of Galilee is the same Jesus who lives today, and will manifest His power tomorrow and forever.

Some believe and teach, (they do not get it from the Scriptures), that the power of God and the miraculous ended when Jesus ascended back to the right hand of the Father. If that were true, why did Jesus talk so much about the Holy Spirit and that the people of God would be endowed with great power for ministry and service. "Verily, Verily, I say unto you, He that believes on me, the works that I do shall you do also, and greater works than these shall you do, because I go to my Father." (John 14:12) "I will pray the Father, and He shall give you another comforter that He (Holy Spirit) may abide with you forever." (John 14:16)

Jesus Christ is truly the same yesterday, today and forever because Christ's Spirit is working on the Earth today. What Jesus did in the Bible days for human kind, He will do for you today, and we have the promise that

He will do it tomorrow and forever. Trust the Lord today for your miracle!

Scripture Reading: Deuteronomy 20, 21, 22; Mark 14:26-50

Trivia Question: How many died in the battle at Ai because of Achan's sin?

March 14

"Live Life Transparent"

Joshua 7:1 — But the children of Israel committed a trespass in the accursed thing: for Achan, the son of Carmi, the son of Zabdi, the son of Zerah, of the tribe of Judah, took of the accursed thing: and the anger of the Lord was kindled against the children of Israel.

God told Joshua to tell the people when they conquered Jericho that the city would be accursed and to keep themselves away from the spoils of Jericho. God told them that if they tried to bring the spoils back with them, the camp of Israel would become a curse. Everyone obeyed, but Achan, he wanted to do his own thing. Achan took some garments, silver and gold and hid them in his tent. Because of one man's sin and disobedience, the entire camp of Israel paid the price. Joshua and his army had to defeat the people of Ai in order to progress to the promise land. Word came back after they viewed the country that only two or three thousand soldiers would be needed for this battle. Because of Achan's hidden sin the army of Israel became powerless and three things happened. First, the people of Ai pursued the army and thirty-six men died. Second, they could not stand up before their enemies, for they lost their authority. Third, they lost the presence of God in their lives.

Scripture teaches us in Proverbs 28:13, "He that covers his sins shall not prosper." Hidden sin brings visible trouble! When we allow sin to come into our lives, and fail to acknowledge and repent of it, and try to make believe nothing is wrong as we cover up, we will give place to the devil. Instead of having the devil on the run, Satan will be chasing after us. We relinquish our God given authority and seemingly God's presence becomes light at best. Never allow sin to go on in your life, repent of it and confess to obtain the mercy of God. If we try to hide our sin, eventually it will be exposed! "But if you will not do so, behold you have sinned against the Lord, and be sure your sin will find you out." (Numbers 32:23)

Scripture Reading: Deuteronomy 23, 24, 25; Mark 14:51-72

Trivia Question: What year was proclaimed the year of Jubilee?

March 15

"Covering Sin, Covering Skin"

Psalms 32:1 — Blessed is he whose transgression is forgiven, whose sin is covered.

What a contrast between God covering our sin and man covering his own skin. The only substance that can cover sin is the blood of the Lamb, Jesus Christ. When someone repents of his/her sin and calls out to God, Jesus responds by appropriating His efficacious blood to that individual and his/her sins are covered.

Man's best attempts to cover his sin were fig leaves. Remember Adam in the garden, when his eyes were opened after Eve was deceived and he transgressed against the Lord. The man and woman knew they were naked and knew they sinned, so they tried to cover themselves with fig leaves.

When man tries to cover his sins, he will not prosper (Proverbs 28:13). When we fall short of God's mark, we need to ask God to forgive us and allow the blood of Christ to cover and cleanse us from all unrighteousness. When our transgression is forgiven and our sin covered by the Lamb's blood, we will walk in peace, comfort and assurance!

Scripture Reading: Deuteronomy 26, 27; Mark 15:1-26

Trivia Question: Who was the king in Babylon that saw the finger of God writing on the wall?

March 16

"True Salvation"

Psalms 3:8 — Salvation belongeth unto the Lord: thy blessing is upon thy people.

In both the Hebrew and the Greek (the Old Testament was written in Hebrew and the New Testament was written in Greek) the word salvation implies the ideas of deliverance, preservation, safety, healing, health, soundness of the mind and victory. Salvation belongs to the Lord, He is the one who possesses it, and He offers this wonderful gift to whosoever.

The prophecy of the coming Messiah in Zechariah 9:9 says, "The king comes, he is just and having salvation." Jesus of Nazareth came two thousand years ago bringing the gift of salvation."

In a day where occultism is rampant, and false Christs and self-proclaiming messiahs are springing up everywhere, we need to remember that only Jesus the Christ, the only wise God, the King Eternal offers deliverance, healing, safety, preservation, victory and life. Salvation does not belong to false leaders and teachers of our day – it belongs to the Lord. Only Jesus can bring deliverance and healing. Only Jesus can bring true peace and safety. Only Jesus can bring healing to the hurting. This day reach out to Him, the one to whom salvation belongs!

Scripture Reading: Deuteronomy 28; Mark 15:27-47

Trivia Question: What Gospel records Jesus riding on a donkey and colt?

March 17

"Water that Never Runs Dry"

*Psalms 42:1 — As the hart panteth after the water brooks,
so panteth my soul after thee, O God.*

They tell us that the deer can smell water up to seven miles away. When a deer is extremely thirsty, he becomes very focused on one thing—the brook of water. The deer pants after the water and desire causes the deer to run to the brook. The male deer knows only the brook of water can satisfy him during his time of thirst.

The Psalmist likens that kind of desire, satisfaction and extremism to his soul going after God. David said, like a deer that pants for water, so does his own soul pant after God. David knew God as his all sufficiency, the only one that can satisfy his hungry heart and quench his thirsty soul. The word pant in the Hebrew (Aw-Rag) means, to long for. David longed after God. When you long for someone or something, it's like nothing else matters. Nothing else can satisfy; you embrace that which you are longing for. David longed after God, like a thirsty deer longed after water.

Jesus is the fresh water that will satisfy your every desire and need. He is our all in all! Are you panting after and longing for Him? Everything and every one else just will not satisfy the desire that's in your soul, only Jesus can do that.

Scripture Reading: Deuteronomy 29, 30; Mark 16

Trivia Question: What was one of the names given to David?

March 18

"Keys of Victory"

*Revelation 1:18 — I am he that liveth, and was dead; and, behold,
I am alive for evermore, Amen; and have the keys of hell and of death.*

When Jesus died He had to descend into the lower parts of the Earth. Ephesians 4:9 "....but that He also descended first into the lower parts of the Earth." There was a two-fold purpose of the dissension into Hell by our Lord. First, the Bible teaches the wages of sin is death. Jesus took upon Himself the sin of the entire human race. He who knew no sin became sin; Jesus had to pay the penalty for sin. He had to descend to Hell and pay the price for you and me. I am sure Satan and his cohorts finally thought that they had the Son of God bound forever. I am sure that Satan was dangling the key ring with the keys of Hell and death on it.

Jesus descended for a second purpose, to spoil all principalities and powers to make a show of them openly, triumphing over sin, Satan, sickness, and Hell itself. Somewhere in that three-day span of descending into the lower parts of the earth, there was a transition from penalty to power. It was at the time that Jesus victoriously conquered Satan and took back the keys of authority—of Hell and death!

That is why as Christians we can rejoice and shout because of the victory that Christ has given us. Oh death, where is your sting? Oh grave, where is your victory?

Scripture Reading: Deuteronomy 31, 32; Luke 1:1-23

Trivia Question: Who went into the empty tomb of Jesus first, Peter or John?

March 19

"Rise and Stand"

*Psalms 37:24 — Though he fall, he shall not be utterly cast down,
for the Lord upholdeth him with His hand.*

The Resurrection of Christ speaks of great triumph and victory. The Resurrection message is that Jesus triumphed over sin, Satan, sickness, and death. The Spirit of God, who is the power of God raised up Jesus, just as He said, from death's stronghold. Jesus truly took the sting of death, and stole the victory from the grave, and because He lives, we live!

The Resurrection means, to stand up again, a rising again. As a Christian in this life we need His Resurrection power to flow in us. At times, life situations, circumstances, or even the devil, deals us some serious and devastating blows. Some of these trials and hardships knock us down. Beloved, listen, we may at times be knocked down, but we are not out! Even if we feel like we are knocked out, it's then that we call upon God, by His Spirit, to let resurrection power rise up on the inside of us, so that we can start up again. The Lord will always be there to uphold us and keep us from staying down. Has life dealt you a serious blow? Have you been knocked down? Let His Resurrection power raise you up today, so that you will march on to victory. Romans 8:11 says, "the same spirit who raised Christ from the dead, dwells in you, and he will quicken your mortal body." Rise up in His name and power this day, to the glory of the Lord, Jesus Christ!

Scripture Reading: Deuteronomy 33, 34; Luke 1:24-56

Trivia Question: Who did Jesus appear to first after His Resurrection?

March 20

"Excellent High Priest"

*Hebrews 8:6 — But now hath he obtained a more excellent ministry,
by how much also he is the mediator of a better covenant,
which was established upon better promises.*

The Bible declares that Jesus had a more excellent ministry. Compared to what? The Word of God calls Jesus our "High Priest." (Hebrews 10:21 and Hebrews 3:1)

Compared to the old covenant. Under the Mosaic Law, Aaron was the High Priest of that day. Aaron was the High Priest over the tabernacle. Aaron had certain duties and responsibilities in the tabernacle, which had to be carried out daily. Aaron's ministry was over a building; Jesus our High Priest and His ministry are over a body. "And having a High Priest over the house of God." (Hebrews 10:21) The Body of Christ is now the

67

house of God and Jesus, our High Priest, ministers over it.

As High Priest, Jesus sprinkled His own blood upon the mercy seat in the heavenly tabernacle two thousand years ago to eternally redeem all those that come to Him in faith. As High Priest, He continues to intercede for His Body, so the church matures in every area of life. "....seeing He ever lives to make intercession for them." (Hebrews 7:25) Be encouraged today that Jesus, your High Priest, is interceding for you that your faith will not fail and that you will fulfill the destiny that God has for your life.

Scripture Reading: Joshua 1, 2, 3; Luke 1:57-80

Trivia Question: What is the goal that Paul sets before the Christians?

March 21

"Change of Heart"

Jonah 1:3 — But Jonah rose up to flee unto Tarshish from the presence of the Lord, and went down to Joppa; and he found a ship going to Tarshish: so he paid the fare thereof, and went down into it, to go with them unto Tarshish from the presence of the Lord.

The thought for today is something that we all as followers of Christ have to deal with from time to time. When God reveals to you His will for your life, and gives you clarity and direction as He did with Jonah, ("arise and go to Ninevah," Jonah 1:2), do we gladly receive His instructions and hearken to His presence, or do we respond like Jonah and run the complete other way? Do we flee from the presence of the Lord? The Hebrew word for presence in this text is (Paw-Neh), meaning "the face of God." Are we running from His face like Jonah, or allowing His face to change us like Jacob?

Jacob was also a man that had some major character flaws. Jacob was a supplanter, a deceiver and a con man. One day, Jacob had a wrestling match with a man (the Lord), and when he was overcome, looked straight into the face of God and pleaded for a blessing. (Genesis 32:24-32) Jacob finally got to the place in his life where he wanted to stop deceiving, stop running, and wanted a change. As Jacob beheld the face of God, it caused a transformation in his life. His name was changed, his character changed, and his heart changed. Do not run from the face of God, let His face and His glory change you, transform you, and preserve your life forever!

Scripture Reading: Joshua 4, 5, 6; Luke 2:1-24

Trivia Question: What did Jacob use as a pillow to sleep on in Haran?

March 22

"Remain Faithful"

Psalms 75:6-7 — For promotion cometh neither from the east, nor from the west, nor from the south. But God is the judge: he putteth down one, and setteth up another.

God is absolute promoter of our lives in all the areas, spiritual or temporal. Jesus gave us some powerful insight on how we can be promoted by God in different areas and aspects of our lives.

In Luke 16:10-13, Jesus gives us three keys to promotion. First, He said if we are faithful in that which is least, then there will be an increase to follow. In God's economy, if we prove ourselves faithful in little, then God will reward (promote) us with more. Second, we must be faithful over unrighteous mammon or money. The Bible teaches emphatically, we must be good stewards over our finances. Money is a neutral thing, and we as Christians must direct our finances in a very godly way. We must pay our bills, and give to God what belongs to Him. When we are successfully faithful over our finances, God will commit (or promote) to our trust the true riches. Third, we must be faithful to what belongs to someone else. When we faithfully support and are loyal to our employers, our spiritual leaders, our pastors, and anyone that is over us, we then qualify to be promoted. It could be a job position, a ministry position, or just a higher level of responsibility and authority in the secular world or in the Kingdom of God.

In all three examples, Jesus used the key word we see over and over, the word faithful. God does not promote talented people, but faithful people. Are you being faithful in all these areas? If the answer is yes, get ready to be promoted by God!

Scripture Reading: Joshua 7, 8; Luke 2:25-52

Trivia Question: Who said, "The silver is mine, and the gold is mine?"

March 23

"Name Change"

Genesis 35:18 — And it came to pass, as her soul was in departing, (for she died) that she called his name Benoni: but his father called him Benjamin.

This is the sad account of Rachel losing her life in child-bearing. Rachel had born one other son prior to that to Jacob, whose name was Joseph. Enroute to a place called Epthrath, Rachel went into hard labor, and had a difficult time delivering the child. Rachel knew her life was in danger, and with a last breath she named her son Benoni. Benoni means, the son of my sorrow.

Jacob, understanding the importance of a name (for he just went through a dramatic name change himself from deceiver to Prince of God), speaks up and says the boy's name shall be Benjamin. Benjamin means son of my right hand.

Beloved, maybe since you have been born again, your new birth, the world, friends, or even close relatives have been trying to label you the son of sorrow. Maybe your decision to follow Christ was not a very popular decision at home or at the office. Perhaps, people have tried to label your new birth experience as a sorrowful one. In the midst of individuals speaking negative words over your life, your Father in Heaven speaks of blessing. Your Father is saying, the old man is dead and the new man is blessed. You were born again with the blessing of God abiding on you. You are a son, or daughter of God! A son, or daughter of His right hand! The world may say, you are cursed and sorrowful, but God the Father says, you are blessed! Beloved, walk in this truth today and everyday. Never allow people (even close relatives and friends), to speak negative things over your life.

Scripture Reading: Joshua 9, 10; Luke 3

Trivia Question: How old was Jacob's father, Isaac, when he died?

March 24

"Honesty-The Best Policy"

1 Peter 3:10 — For he that will love life and see good days, let him refrain his tongue from evil, and his lips that they speak no guile.

The Bible, speaking about the Lord Jesus says, "neither was guile found in his mouth." Jesus did not sin with His mouth (or in any other way for that matter). We as Christians, need to take Jesus as our example, especially in this area. The Psalmist wrote, "I will keep my mouth with a bridle." (Psalms 39:1)

We need to watch and guard everything that comes out of our mouths. Jesus walked and talked in absolute integrity. He never was deceptive in His speech. He spoke the truth at all times.

We need to be an honest, integral people as born again believers. No guile (lying, deception), should be found in our hearts or coming out of our lips. The Word of God says, "Provide things honest in the sight of all men." (Romans 12:17)

We need to be an honest people! Yes, even during tax time! Are you my friend, providing things honest before all men?

We need to be like Nathanael in the Bible. A Christian indeed, in whom is no guile, lying, cheating, dishonesty, or deception!

Scripture Reading: Joshua 11, 12, 13; Luke 4:1-32

Trivia Question: Where did the first miracle of Jesus actually take place?

March 25

"Grace Race"

2 Corinthians 1:2 — Grace be to you, and peace from God, our Father, and from the Lord Jesus Christ.

We need to know this day that God's power twins are working mightily in our lives – His grace and His peace.

The grace of God is a gift He bestows upon us to enable us to accomplish all that He has purposed for us. Ephesians 2:8 teaches us that the grace of God is a gift, and like all gifts, it is something that is given to us freely. We didn't pay for it, and it is something we must receive thankfully. God's gift of grace is always sufficient in every circumstance and in every situation. God's grace in us; His strength for our weakness. God's grace is exchanging His ability for our inability, His sufficiency for our insufficiency! God's grace will say yes in your spirit when your flesh says no! God's grace will enable you to endure hardness as a good soldier of the Lord Jesus Christ.

Remember, we have a race to run, but we do not do this alone. God is

71

with us and when we add God to our race, He gives us the grace we need to run with patience and finish our course!

Scripture Reading: Joshua 14, 15; Luke 4:33-44

Trivia Question: What is given to every believer according to the measure of the gift of Christ?

March 26

"Perfect Peace"

2 Corinthians 1:2 — Grace be to you, and peace from our God,
our Father, and from the Lord Jesus Christ.

Jesus promised peace to us, not like the world gives, which is not genuine but a real peace that causes rest in our souls. Jesus is called the Prince of peace and offers us this perfect peace that passes all understanding. This divine peace will keep our heart and minds through Jesus Christ our Lord. (Philippians 4:7)

Losing a loved one or a relative through death is very tragic and sorrowful. Even through such a difficult time of loss and bereavement, God offers you His wonderful peace. Peace that will give you a calm in your storm, and help you to stay focused on the Prince who possesses all peace.

Do not try to figure out God's peace, or how He ministers this tranquility into your heart and soul. By faith, just receive perfect peace from the Prince of peace. Allow God to take you through even the most difficult times. Even if you lose a loved one through death, God's peace is available and will be there for you. Receive it and let it keep you calm during all the storms of life. Jesus said, "peace be still." (Mark 4:39) My friend, allow God's peace to keep you still this day!

Scripture Reading: Joshua 16, 17, 18; Luke 5:1-16

Trivia Question: Where was Jesus when His disciples were in a boat during a life-threatening storm?

March 27

"Blessed Not Cursed"

*Galatians 3:9 — So then they which be of faith are blessed
with faithful Abraham.*

God made a covenant with the Patriarch Abraham way back in the book of Genesis starting with Chapter 12. God told Abram (who later became Abraham) that He would multiply his seed as the stars of Heaven and cause him to inherit and possess a land that God would send him to.

God gave Abram a two-fold blessing in Genesis 12:2 that we as the Church of Jesus Christ can claim because we are the spiritual seed (children) of Abraham through Messiah Jesus Christ.

First, God told Abram, "I will make of thee a great nation." The Church is truly the holy nation that was prophesied about and she is great! The Church is great because we serve a great God!

Secondly, God said, "and I will bless thee." You are blessed as a new covenant child of God. You are not cursed, but blessed! Even if you have come from generations of sinful bondage and curses, when you made Jesus the Lord of your life, He reversed the curse! You are blessed!

Scripture Reading: Joshua 19, 20; Luke 5:17-39

Trivia Question: How many priests carried trumpets of rams horns while marching around the city limits of Jericho?

March 28

"Word in Action"

John 9:7 — And said unto him, Go, wash in the pool of Siloam, (which is by interpretation, Sent.) He went his way therefore, and washed, and came seeing.

When you act upon the Word of God like the blind man, you too will get results! Even though Jesus used an unorthodox method of ministering healing, the blind man responded in faith to the word of the Lord. The power was not so much in the spittle or the clay, but was manifested when the blind man decided to move out on the word of Jesus, "Go to the pool and wash." He went, and washed, and came back seeing!

Oh how we need to see as Christians the importance of acting on the

Word of God. Many times in the Bible when Jesus was ministering healing to an individual, He followed up by saying to him, "pick up your bed
and walk." (John 5:8) On other occasions, "stretch forth your hand," (Matthew 12:13) or "go show yourselves to the priest." (Luke 17:14) Jesus always
wanted to see the people's faith being expressed in His Word. That is what
faith is all about. It is acting or responding to the Word of God, and it will
bring results in your life. It worked for the blind man, and it will work for
you. What is God saying to you today from His Word? Believe His Word,
receive His Word, and then respond to His Word. It will bring results in
your life.

Scripture Reading: Joshua 21, 22; Luke 6:1-26

Trivia Question: How long was the man in John 9 blind?

March 29

"The Covering of Love"

*Genesis 9:20-27 — And Noah began to be an husbandman, and he planted a
vineyard: and he drank of the wine, and was drunken; and he was uncovered
within his tent and Ham, the father of Canaan, saw the nakedness of his father,
and told his two brethren without. And Shem and Japheth took a garment, and
laid it upon both their shoulders, and went backward, and covered the nakedness
of their father; and their faces were backward, and they saw not their father's
nakedness. And Noah awoke from his wine, and knew what his younger son had
done unto him. And he said, "cursed be Canaan; a servant of servants shall he be
unto his brethren." And he said, "blessed be the Lord God of Shem; and Canaan
shall be his servant. God shall enlarge Japheth, and he shall dwell in the tents of
Shem; and Canaan shall be his servant.*

After the flood subsided, Noah and his family only remained. God
established His covenant with Noah and blessed Him saying, "be fruitful
and multiply and fill the earth." (Genesis 9:1)

Noah became a farmer and even though God called him a just man, he
had a spiritual lapse and sinned before God. Noah drank of the wine of his
vineyard and became drunk and he was uncovered within his tent.

The text tells us that Ham, one of Noah's sons, saw the nakedness of
his father and told his two brothers. Shem and Japheth being men of love
and honor for their father, took a garment and walked backwards into their

father's tent, never looking upon his nakedness, and covered Noah with the garment they carried on their shoulders.

The Bible says in Proverbs 10:12, "love covers all sins." Love does not expose someone's faults, failures, and sin, but covers and protects so that their spiritual nakedness does not bring shame and reproach. We are not saying that we do not deal with sin, because Galatians 6:1 says, "Brethren, if a man be overtaken in a fault ye which are spiritual, restore such a one in the spirit of meekness; considering thyself, lest thou also be tempted." But godly love will correct a brother or sister in the spirit of humility and not make a public display of someone that has sinned.

Shem and Japheth did not allow Ham's contemptible attitude toward their father to influence them, but walked and operated in love and sought to cover their father's nakedness, not expose it!

Consequently, Ham's son Canaan was cursed as Noah prophesied and Noah blessed Shem and Japheth. It is true that people's actions affect their children, even their children's children.

Are you my friend exposing someone's sin bringing shame and devastation to one's life, or are you dealing with them as Christ would in the spirit of love. Remember, love always covers!

Scripture Reading: Joshua 23, 24; Luke 6:27-49

Trivia Question: How many sons did Ham have?

March 30

"Quality Time"

Genesis 12:1-8 — Now the Lord had said unto Abram, "Get thee out of thy country, and from thy kindred, and from thy father's house, unto a land that I will shew thee: and I will make of thee a great nation, and I will bless thee, and make thy name great; and thou shalt be a blessing: and I will bless them that bless thee, and curse him that curseth thee: and in thee shall all families of the earth be blessed." So Abram departed, as the Lord had spoken unto him; and Lot went with him: and Abram was seventy and five years old when he departed out of Haran. And Abram took Sarai his wife, and Lot his brother's son, and all their substance that they had gathered, and the souls that they had gotten in Haran; and they went forth to go into the land of Canaan; and into the land of Canaan they came. And Abram passed through the land unto the place of Sichem, unto the plain of Moreh. And the

Canaanite was then in the land. And the Lord appeared unto Abram, and said, "Unto thy seed will I give this land": and there builded he an altar unto the Lord, who appeared unto him. and he removed from thence unto a mountain on the east of Bethel, and pitched his tent, having Bethel on the west, and Hai on the east: and there he builded an altar unto the Lord, and called upon the name of the Lord.

After Abram was told by the Lord to leave his country, kindred, and his father's house to a land that God would show him, he obeyed, went in faith, and settled in a place called Canaan. The Lord appeared to Abram (by means of a theophany) and informed him this indeed was the Promised Land God spoke of and that this land would be Abram's and his seed's land.

Abram pitched his tent (made his home) between a place called Bethel (which means house of God) and Hai (which means a ruin), and there built an altar and called upon the name of the Lord.

Most of us live between or in the midst of Bethel, which represents the presence and power of God, and a spiritual Hai, which represents the pressures and persecutions of this life. The Bible says in Deuteronomy 11:26, "Behold, I set before you this day a blessing and a curse." Blessing and cursing, light and darkness, good and evil, the Kingdom of God and the kingdom of Satan are set before us and we live somewhere in the midst. As long as we remain at the place of blessing and continue to call on the name of the Lord at our altar of prayer, the influence of the house of God which speaks of His blessing, presence, and power will be greater in our lives than the influence of the world, which brings reproach and ruin. Jesus said we are in this world but not of this world (John 17:14-16). The truth of the matter is that righteousness and unrighteousness will always be around us. The key is establishing and maintaining a life of prayer so that godliness, righteousness, holiness, and the presence of God will prevail and overcome the present day darkness that is all around us. We must build an altar of prayer in the midst of this spiritual tug of war that we are in and allow our relationship with God to develop at our prayer altar, so we will be influenced by Bethel more than Hai!

Are you spending time with God daily at your prayer altar? It will influence and affect your life in a drastic and radical way!

Scripture Reading: Judges 1, 2; Luke 7:1-30

Trivia Question: What is a theophany?

March 31

"Altar of Blessing"

Genesis 12:9-20, 13:1-4 — And Abram journeyed, going on still toward the south. And there was a famine in the land: and Abram went down into Egypt to sojourn there; for the famine was grievous in the land. And it came to pass, when he was come near to enter into Egypt, that he said unto Sarai his wife, "Behold now, I know that thou art a fair woman to look upon: therefore it shall come to pass, when the Egyptians shall see thee, that they shall say, this is his wife: and they will kill me, but they will save thee alive. Say, I pray thee, thou art my sister: that it may be well with me for thy sake; and my soul shall live because of thee." And it came to pass, that, when Abram was come into Egypt, the Egyptians beheld the woman that she was very fair. The princes also of Pharaoh saw her, and commended her before Pharaoh: and the woman was taken into Pharaoh's house. And he entreated Abram well for her sake: and he had sheep, and oxen, and donkeys, and menservants, and maidservants, and camels. And the Lord plagued Pharaoh and his house with great plagues because of Sarai, Abram's wife. And Pharaoh called Abram, and said, "What is this that thou hast done unto me? Why didst thou not tell me that she was thy wife? Why saidst thou, she is my sister? So I might have taken her to me to wife: now therefore behold thy wife, take her, and go thy way." And Pharaoh commanded his men concerning him: and they sent him away, and his wife, and all that he had and Abram went up out of Egypt, he, and his wife, and all that he had, and Lot with him, into the south. And Abram was very rich in cattle, in silver, and in gold. And he went on his journeys from the south even to Beth-el, unto the place where his tent had been at the beginning, between Beth-el and Hai; unto the place of the altar, which he had made there at the first: and there Abram called on the name of the Lord.

Abram started to wander from the place of blessing and traveled south of Canaan. As Abram left the place where God blessed him and walked away from the altar where he communed with God, a famine hit the land. Because Abram was estranged from the prayer altar when the famine came, Abram panicked and went down into Egypt. There in Egypt, because of fear, Abram lied about his wife being his sister to Pharaoh and compromised his conviction. He put Sarai in a very vulnerable and dangerous position. Because of Abram's deceptions, the Lord plagued Pharaoh's house. Abram had to live with the guilt of putting his wife in harm's way and of Pharaoh's house being plagued because of his fear, deception, and lies. Oh what a price to pay when we forsake the place of blessing and leave our prayer altar!

When the truth was revealed to Pharaoh, he willfully gave Abram gifts, gave him his wife back, and sent them on their way. Abram came to his spiritual senses and went UP out of Egypt and returned to the place of blessing where God called him. He returned to his home and most importantly, returned to the altar that he originally built. Once again he called on the name of the Lord!

If we remain at the place God called us and linger continually at the altar of prayer, when famine, crisis, tests, trials, dry times, storms of life, sickness, or persecutions come our way, we will not panic and wander away from the things of God. "We will lift up our eyes unto the hills; from whence cometh our help? Our help comes from the Lord." (Psalm 121:1-2) We will hold onto the horns of the altar in prayer calling on the name of the Lord, and trusting in God, not man, to deliver us from all evil. "Some trust in chariots, and some in horses, but we will remember the name of the Lord our God." (Psalms 20:7)

If you have forsaken the place that God has called you and if you have left your altar of prayer, ask God to forgive and restore you, and you will be back at the place of blessing again.

Scripture Reading: Judges 3, 4, 5; Luke 7:31-50

Trivia Question: What does the word Babel mean?

April

April 1

"Wait on the Lord"

Genesis 16:1–16 — Now Sarai Abram's wife bare him no children: and she had an handmaid, an Egyptian, whose name was Hagar. And Sarai said unto Abram, "Behold now, the Lord hath restrained me from bearing: I pray thee, go in unto my maid; it may be that I may obtain children by her. "And Abram hearkened to the voice of Sarai. And Sarai Abram's wife took Hagar her maid the Egyptian, after Abram had dwelt ten years in the land of Canaan, and gave her to her husband Abram to be his wife. And he went in unto Hagar, and she conceived: and when she saw that she had conceived, her mistress was despised in her eyes. And Sarai said unto Abram, "My wrong be upon thee: I have given my maid into thy bosom; and when she saw that she had conceived, I was despised in her eyes: the Lord judge between me and thee." But Abram said unto Sarai, "Behold, thy maid is in thy hand; do to her as it pleaseth thee." And when Sarai dealt hardly with her, she fled from her face. And the angel of the Lord found her by a fountain of water in the wilderness, by the fountain in the way to Shur. And he said, "Hagar, Sarai's maid, whence camest thou? And whither wilt thou go?" And she said, "I flee from the face of my mistress Sarai." And the angel of the Lord said unto her, "Return to thy mistress, and submit thyself under her hands." And the angel of the Lord said unto her, "I will multiply thy seed exceedingly, that it shall not be numbered for multitude." And the angel of the Lord said unto her, "Behold, thou art with child, and shalt bear a son, and shalt call his name Ishmael; because the Lord hath heard thy affliction. And he will be a wild man; his hand will be against every man, and every man's hand against him; and he shall dwell in the presence of all his brethren. "And she called the name of the Lord that spake unto her, thou God seest me: for she said, "Have I also here looked after him that seeth me?" Wherefore the well was called Beerlahairoi; behold, it is between Kadesh and Bered. And Hagar bare Abram a son: and Abram called his son's name, which Hagar bare, Ishmael. And Abram was fourscore and six years old, when Hagar bare Ishmael to Abram.

Sometimes in our impatience and impetuousness, we think we have come up with a better plan than God. We live in a fast culture. We want fast food, instant coffee, quick results and immediate answers to prayer as we carry that mindset into our relationship with the Lord. We often believe He is to respond to us like one of our favorite fast food restaurants. We get tired of waiting on God and slip into despair when we do not see an answer to our prayer. Very often we come up with our own scheme.

Sarai, the wife of Abram was tired and frustrated with waiting for the promise of God to manifest. In her exasperation and impatience, she decided to suggest to Abram a better plan. God promised Abram at 75 years old that he would have a son and in him shall all families of the earth be blessed. (Genesis 12:3)

Abram was now about 85 years old and Sarai saw no baby, not even the hint of a bundle of joy. Even though God told Abram this son would come forth out of his own loins, Sarai grew tired of waiting and suggested to Abram that he "go in unto my maid; it may be that I may obtain children by her." (Genesis 16:2) Abram obliged her (what a good fellow), hearkened to her voice, went to Hagar, had physical intimacy with her and Hagar conceived.

Sarai, even though it was her own plan, became angry and jealous with Hagar and came to hate even the sight of her, especially as Hagar started to show signs of new life growing inside. Hagar gave birth to a son named Ishmael. Ishmael, the wild man, fourteen years later had a brother Isaac, who did come forth from Sarai's womb as promised. Eventually, these brothers would start an argument and a fight that has lasted over 4,000 years to the present.

Wow, we can really make a mess of things when we get impatient and try to help God out by coming up with our own ideas and plans. Friend, are you patiently waiting on God for His promise? "Though it tarry, wait for it, because it will surely come…" (Habakkuk 2:3)

Scripture Reading: Judges 6, 7; Luke 8:1-21

Trivia Question: When was Abram's name changed?

April 2

"Be a Soldier"

2 Timothy 2:3 — Thou, therefore, endure hardness,

as a good soldier of Jesus Christ.

A good warrior or soldier, before he goes into battle, makes absolutely sure that he is attired with proper clothes and weapons. Both serve to protect him and to enhance his position in gaining physical advantage over his enemy.

In his letter to the Church of Ephesus, the Apostle Paul exhorted the church and explained to them that they were engaged in spiritual warfare. He expounded on who the enemy was, how he would operate, and how the spiritual warrior should be clothed and ready to meet this adversary head on.

The born again believer needs to know that upon his/her conversion to Christ, all their sins have been washed away. Their names are written in the Lamb's Book of Life. They now can start to receive all the benefits derived from the many promises in God's Word. Most importantly, he or she has willingly enlisted in God's army. They are now soldiers for the Lord Jesus Christ. As a soldier of Jesus Christ, he needs to know precisely what war he is going into, who his enemy is, how his enemy operates, and how to combat against his enemy's attacks.

As this newly born soldier of Jesus Christ trains in boot camp, the first instruction told to him is found in Ephesians 6:10, "Finally brethren, be strong in the Lord, and in the power of His might." He is told that his own strength will not be sufficient, that he will need to receive his strength spiritually and supernaturally from the Captain of the army, who is the Lord Jesus Christ. (Hebrews 2:10)

The soldier is told that this is not a physical battle, but a spiritual one. Guns, tanks, grenades, and bombs will not give this soldier the upper hand over his enemy. 2 Corinthians 10:3,4 says, "For though we walk in the flesh, we do not war after the flesh, for the weapons of our warfare are not carnal (earthly), but mighty through God to the pulling down of strongholds."

When the Christian spiritually understands that this battle cannot be fought in the flesh (the natural or physical) and fully understands that only with the weapons that God supplies, can victory be achieved, then and only then is he or she ready to put on the Armor of God.

Remember this is spiritual armor and not physical. It needs to be viewed with deep spiritual understanding. In Ephesians 6:11, Paul exhorts us to "Put on the whole armor of God." Can you imagine going into battle and forgetting to bring with you your ammunition for your rifle? So it is as a soldier of Jesus. You need to take and put on (be clothed with) the whole armor of God.

Then Paul makes it very clear in the same verse about the Christian soldier's position during the crafty attacks of the enemy. Paul says, "Put on the whole armor of God that you may stand against the wiles of the devil." He never says sit down, layback, or even retreat. He says, stand against your adversary who is the devil.

In Ephesians 6:12, we are again reminded that we do not wrestle or fight against flesh and blood. We war against Satan and his diabolical army, which consists of principalities, powers, rulers of darkness, and spiritual wickedness in high places. The Christian solider must know who his/her enemy is - the devil and his cohorts.

Again in verse 13, Paul reiterates that the Christian soldier needs to take the whole armor of God because Satan will be going to launch out with all his sneaky deceptions and lies. The Christian will be ready as he takes and puts on the whole armor of God, "having done all to stand," the soldier will stand some more!

My friend, you are called to stand your ground this very day!

Scripture Reading: Judges 8, 9; Luke 8:22-56

Trivia Question: How does the Bible say we should enter his gates and his courts?

_____

April 3

"Circle of Strength"

Ephesians 6:13, 14 — Wherefore take unto you the whole armour of God that ye may be able to withstand in the evil day, and having done all, to stand. Stand therefore, having your loins girt about with truth, and having on the breastplate of righteousness.

In verse 14, Paul, under the inspiration of the Holy Spirit, speaks about having our loins girded about with truth. Three key words Paul uses in this verse are: *Loins, Girded,* and *Truth.* Let's look into this as we break it down.

The loins on the human body would be considered as the lower back from the ribs to the hipbone (hips and lower abdomen). This part of the body is so commonly called the belly. Proverbs 20:27 states, "The spirit of man is the candle of the Lord searching all the inward parts of the belly." The belly or the spirit of man is that place where the Holy Spirit dwells. The Bible says in Job 32:8, "But there is a spirit in man.." Man is a spirit being because he is made in the image and likeness of God (Genesis 1:26). God is a Spirit (John 4:24), hence in man's belly or spirit is where he hides the Word of God.

David said in Psalms 119:11, "Thy word have I hidden in my heart (spirit, belly)." Call it whatever you will. The heart, spirit, belly, inner man, and hidden man of the heart, are all referring to that part of a man where God's Word is rooted. Jesus said in John 7:38, "He that believes on me, as the Scripture has said, out of his belly shall flow rivers of living water." Going back to Ephesians 6:14, the verse goes on to say having our loins girded. The word girded means encircled or prepared for action. The verse continues on and declares "our loins girded about with 'truth.'" So, we see our loins or our spirit/inner man needs to be prepared or ready for action with truth, (a good soldier is always prepared for active duty).

What is truth? Jesus answers that question in John 17:17, "Sanctify them through thy truth, Thy word is truth." So, then the truth of God's Word needs to be deep rooted in our loins or hearts, ready for action and prepared to explode from us with God's given authority and power!

Scripture Reading: Judges 10, 11; Luke 9:1-36

Trivia Question: Man is a three-fold being, made up of what three components?

April 4

" No Fear in Love"

Ephesians 6:14 — Stand therefore, having your loins girt about with truth, and having on the breastplate of righteousness.

The second part of Ephesians 6:14, Paul continues "and having on the breastplate of righteousness." This part of the armor called the breastplate protects the frontal upper body of the soldier. The breastplate also protects the precious truth of God's Word that has been implanted in the loins, ready for action against the enemy's attack.

The two dynamic forces that make up the breastplate, are found in 1 Thessalonians 5:8, "Putting on the breastplate of faith and love." Paul is talking about that victorious world overcoming faith that 1 John 5:4 declares. This faith is always victorious and overcomes any attack that soldiers will ever encounter.

The other part of the breastplate is made up of love. This is the love that John wrote about in his epistle, 1 John 4:18. "There is no fear in love, but perfect (mature, fully developed) love casts out all fear." This love never fears what the enemy can do, because this love drives away any foul spirit of fear that the devil sends to intimidate the soldier of Christ. Remember what Paul said to that young soldier named Timothy, "God has not given you a spirit of fear, but love, power and a sound mind." (2 Timothy 1:7)

This is no ordinary breastplate. Paul makes it very clear and calls this part of the armor the breastplate of righteousness. The word righteousness means right standing with God, but when you look at the word in light of this spiritual battle we are in, it takes on a greater meaning. Paul said in 2 Corinthians 5:21, "For He hath made Him (Jesus) who knew no sin, to be sin for us, that we (soldiers of Christ) might be made the righteousness of God in Him."

Bless God! We are the righteousness of God in Christ Jesus. Righteousness is a God given position that no one can take away. When Jesus walked this earth, He walked with complete control and authority. He had no identity problems. Jesus knew who He was and that He was sent from the Father with a specific mission and purpose. Jesus is righteousness personified. When the soldier puts on this breastplate consisting of faith motivated by love and sealed with the righteousness of Christ, the devil should see Jesus when he looks at the soldier, (perfectly arrayed with this part of the armor).

Scripture Reading: Judges 12, 13, 14; Luke 9:37-62

Trivia Question: Who was thrown in prison for offending Pharaoh and came in contact with Joseph?

April 5

"Feet Firm"

*Ephesians 6:15 — And your feet shod
with the preparation of the Gospel of peace.*

In verse fifteen, we see the next part of the soldier's armor. This has to do with the warrior's feet, which are to be shod with the preparation of the Gospel of peace. I want you to direct your attention to the word shod. The word shod means to bind underneath. Our feet must be bound underneath with the Gospel of peace. When speaking of the anatomy, the feet of course, are very essential. The primary purpose of the feet is to keep a person stable or balanced. We also of course, use our feet to walk, run, and stand. The Christian soldier is to have his feet bound underneath with the Gospel.

When referring to the word Gospel, we mean good news, but it takes on a deeper meaning in the Scriptures. Paul states in 1 Corinthians 15:1-4, "I declare unto you the Gospel which I preach unto you…in which you stand." Then he proceeds to tell us what that Gospel actually is in verses 3 and 4. The Gospel is the message of the death, burial, and resurrection of Jesus Christ. So, we see in order to be solid, stable, or balanced, we need to be standing on the Gospel of Christ. We need to have the everlasting Gospel bound underneath us, so that it will keep us up in times of battle against the enemy.

As we stand upon God's truth and the promises contained in His Gospel, we truly experience the power of God unto salvation (deliverance) Romans 1:16. Notice that Paul refers to this Gospel as the Gospel of peace. "Peace I leave with you, my peace I give unto you." It has been said that the ultimate purpose for war is to bring about peace. In the spiritual realm, when you are in a direct confrontation with the devil, right in the midst of heated battle, you must stand on the powerful Gospel of Christ and have it's truth girding your life, then victory is inevitable and you will experience that tranquility, that calm, yes, that wonderful peace!

Scripture Reading: Judges 15, 16, 17; Luke 10:1-24

Trivia Question: How old was Joseph when he stood before Pharaoh?

April 6

"Fire Quencher"

Ephesians 6:16 — Above all, taking the shield of faith,
wherewith ye shall be able to quench all the fiery darts of the wicked.

The next part of the armor Paul describes in verse 16 is the shield of faith. We read, "Above all, taking the shield of faith, wherewith ye shall be able to quench all the fiery darts of the wicked." Paul uses the terminology above all, an interesting term that the Apostle used on other occasions to express the intensity of the message or thought that he was trying to teach. It will be a great benefit to us to pay close attention to the exhortations laid down by God through the Apostle Paul.

We read that we are to take the shield of faith. I think perhaps the best way to understand this is to simply reverse the words. Take faith as your shield. Other than love, the most powerful force God has given to His people (those who are born again believers) is faith. The Bible has much to say on this subject. The Word of God says that faith is the substance of things hoped for, the evidence of things not seen (Hebrews 11:1). In other words, our faith gives substance or reality to things we hope for, even if we do not see it with our natural eyes.

Our faith is always based on God's Holy Word that will never fail. Heaven and Earth will fail (pass away), but His Word remains forever (Mark 13:31). David said, "Thy Word, O Lord, is forever settled in Heaven." (Psalms 119:89) We need to meditate on this wonderful truth. The very foundation that Heaven sits or rests on is the Word of God. Faith in the Word enables us to raise our spiritual shield against the onslaught of the enemy. As we meditate in His Word and renew our minds in His promises, we start to walk in the light of our redemption as seen through the eyes of the Lord. Remember, God sees His army as victorious, always triumphing in Christ Jesus. (2 Corinthians 2:14)

Now, let's go back to the spiritual battle that we as soldiers of Christ are engaged in. Notice in verse 16, as we take faith as our shield, we will be able to quench all the fiery darts of Satan. Notice it does not say repel, it says, quench. Another word for quench is extinguish. This means, no matter what type of fiery darts are thrown our way, whether it be darts of depression, disease, discouragement, or any of the like, our faith shield will completely extinguish those fiery arrows at once. Yes, this is the faith that the writer of Hebrews spoke about. (Hebrews 11:33-34) "Who through faith subdued the kingdoms, wrought righteousness, obtaining promises, stopped the mouths of lions, quenched the violence of fire, escaped the edge of the sword, waxed valiant in fight, turned to flight the armies of the aliens."

Scripture Reading: Judges 18, 19; Luke 10:25-42

Trivia Question: How many times does Paul pray for the Church at Ephesus in his epistle?

April 7

"Shine Your Helmet"

Ephesians 6:17(a) — And take the helmet of salvation. . .

The next part of the armor we need to examine and understand is the helmet of salvation, found in verse 17. The helmet is the part of the armor that protects the head. When Paul wrote about the helmet of salvation, he was talking about the mind of the soldier, or the thought life. Even though this part of the armor is mentioned in the latter part of the context, it is very essential and important to us. It is in our thought life or in our mind that Satan will often attack first. Usually, the mind is the place of attack and/or surrender.

We as soldiers of Christ are called to do something with our minds. At one time we were enemies in our minds, as Colossians 1:21 says, "And you, that were sometime alienated and enemies in your mind by wicked works, yet now has he reconciled. . ." We now need to get God's Word into our minds by a process called renewing of the mind. "And be not conformed to this world, but be ye transformed by the renewing of your mind, that ye may prove what is that good, and acceptable, and perfect will of God." (Romans 12:2)

As we renew our minds with the Word of God, when Satan comes to us to attack our thought life, immediately our minds will respond with the Word of God. It is the Word of God that drives the devil far away. James 4:7 says, "Resist the devil and he will flee." How do we resist Him? We do so by having our minds renewed in the Word of God. So we see that the helmet protects those minds that have been renewed in the Word of God. Notice it says the helmet of salvation. The word salvation implies the idea of forgiveness, healing, deliverance, preservation, safety, and soundness of mind.

When our adversary comes to attack our thought life and tries to steal God's Word and to make us doubt, we remember that we have on the helmet of salvation. When he tells the Christians that they are not forgiven, immediately the renewed mind says, Romans 8:1, "There is therefore now no condemnation to them which are in Christ Jesus, who walk not after the flesh, but after the Spirit." When he gives you a thought concerning sickness, immediately the renewed mind responds with Psalm 103:3, "Who forgiveth all thine iniquities; who healeth all thy diseases." When the devil lies to you concerning still being in bondage, the mind remembers Joel

2:32, "And it shall come to pass, that whosoever shall call on the name of the Lord shall be delivered, for in Mount Zion and in Jerusalem shall be deliverance, as the Lord hath said, and in the remnant whom the Lord shall call."

When Satan says you will fail God and fall from His grace, the renewed mind expresses Psalms 32:7, "Thou art my hiding place; thou shalt preserve me from trouble; thou shalt compass me about with songs of deliverance, Selah." When Satan throws confusion, anxiety, and worry, the soldier's renewed mind rests in Isaiah 26:3, "Thou wilt keep him in perfect peace, whose mind is stayed on thee; because he trusteth in thee." No matter where the attack comes from, the helmet of salvation protects the soldier's thought life and drives the enemy back!

We never have to surrender our minds to Satan's lies. On the contrary, the Word of God that controls our thought life will bring total victory and triumph!

Scripture Reading: Judges 20, 21; Luke 11:1-28

Trivia Question: Can you name the five-fold ministry gifts that God has given to the Church?

April 8

"S - Word"

Ephesians 6:17(b) — ... And the sword of the Spirit, which is the word of God.

Without this offensive weapon, all the other parts of the armor would become ineffective. Paul says, "the sword of the Spirit, which is the Word of God." All the other defensive parts of the armor enable the soldier to stand against his enemy in a direct confrontation, without getting hurt or retreating.

The sword of the Spirit allows the soldier to achieve complete and total victory by driving his enemy into the sea. The sword of the Spirit is the spoken Word of God, flowing out of the Christian soldier's anointed mouth. Just knowledge of the Word is not enough. Just simply knowing that your sword is in the sheath is not enough; we must have the Word of God rooted in our lives. When the soldier wields the sword, he is prepared to do his enemy damage, and as the Word of God explodes from a believer's life, it will cut the enemy's head off every time.

Remember what Jesus said in Mark 11:23, "For verily I say unto you, that whosoever shall say unto this mountain, be thou removed, and be thou cast into the sea; and shall not doubt in his heart, but shall believe that those things which he saith shall come to pass, he shall have whatsoever he saith." So we see from this verse that as the spoken Word comes forth from the believer's mouth, mountains must stand to attention and obey the Word of God. If the believer commands the mountain to be removed, it must respond to the order! The writer of Hebrews 4:12 says, "God's Word is quick and powerful and sharper than a two-edged sword. . ."

That sword is so powerful and so sharp. If only the soldier can learn to use and appropriate the Word of God. In Joshua 10, Joshua, a mighty man of valor (war), defeated the cities of Libnah, Lachish, Eglon, Hebron, and Debir with the "edge of the sword." This sword was a type of the Word of God – the true sword of the Spirit.

Oh how we can utterly destroy our spiritual enemies with the edge of the sword, which is the Word of God. We need to look at Jesus in Matthew 4, when He was engaged in hand-to-hand combat against the devil. Notice the response of Jesus every time to His diabolical foe. He said, "It is written; It is written; It is written!" Satan had to flee at the anointed spoken Word of God.

So Christian solider, are you ready for battle? Do you accept the charge of Jesus in 2 Timothy 2:3, "Thou, therefore endure hardness, as a good soldier of Jesus Christ." Thank God the soldier of Jesus is thoroughly equipped with all the resources that he needs.

Jesus paid a very high price to purchase our armor. He had to give His life by being crucified. Praise God, Jesus rose from the grave and when He ascended up on high, He led captivity captive, and gave gifts unto men. Thank God for the gift of his armor! So, stand erect, put your shoulders back, and get ready for battle! If we use the armor properly, we will win every time!

Scripture Reading: Ruth 1, 2, 3, 4; Luke 11:29-54

Trivia Question: How many men in Gideon's army fought against the Midianites?

———————————————————

April 9

"Your Memorial Day"

Psalms 119:24 — Thy testimonies are also my delight and my counselors.

When Israel, under the leadership of Joshua, passed through the Jordan River on dry ground, the Lord instructed Joshua to set up twelve stones (rocks). They obtained these rocks out of the midst of the Jordan on the other side of the river at a place called Gilgal, where the Israelites camped.

These stones were to be piled up as a memorial unto the children of Israel forever. The stones were to be a witness and a testimony to all, especially the young. God did a great miracle for His people, in that they all walked through the Jordan River on dry ground. When the children would ask their parents, "what mean these stones?" (Joshua 4:6,21), the adults would testify how God made a way where there was no way.

I believe it's good to set up spiritual memorials in our lives. It is good to record and date the many times that God has made a way for us in our wilderness, the times he healed us, the many answers to our prayers, and His timely intervention in our lives. When we document and chronicle the times that God has given us miracles, and then we are faced with a crisis or go through a season of suffering, we can remember our memorial before the Lord. We remember what the Lord has done and the great testimonies we have through our past trials. That will encourage us to trust Him for the trial that we face today. Setting up memorials helps us to remember our past trials God saw us through. They also encourage us to believe that He will get us through what we face today. The past testimonies become our delight and our counselors that speak to us and tell us that we can get through our present challenges.

Friends, set up a book of memorials, when God turned your many tests into testimonies. It will counsel you and encourage you throughout your walk with the Lord!

Scripture Reading: 1 Samuel 1, 2, 3; Luke 12:1-34

Trivia Question: When the waters of Egypt were turned to blood, how long did the bloody waters remain?

———————————————

90

April 10

"God's Battle"

Exodus 14:14 — The Lord shall fight for you, and you shall hold your peace.

Sometimes the hardest thing to do when we are engaged in conflict, turmoil, or spiritual warfare is to remain silent, not speaking out in defense of ourselves but believe that God will really fight for us.

There are times when we must make our voices heard. We need to speak out on issues that are paramount to our culture and to the spiritual status of our church, community, and country. However, there are other times when the Lord speaks to our hearts, reminding us that we are His children and He is our Father. That will reassure us that He will fight the battle for us, protect us and take wonderful care of us.

We are so inclined to defend ourselves on every front that we forget at times, "it is not by might, nor by power, but by My Spirit says the Lord of hosts." (Zechariah 4:6) God told Moses to tell the people when they were so hard pressed on every side with Pharaoh and his army bearing down on them, that God would step in and fight this battle for them! All that the Israelites had to do was believe God's Word, hold their peace, and step out in faith and go forward. Sometimes, it is easier said than done!

Are you in some conflict today? Try stepping back, allow God to step in, hold your peace, trust God to fight for you, and obey His Word completely. I believe that you will see the mighty hand of God move on your behalf. Remember the battle is the Lord's and the victory will be yours! Trust Him to fight for you today!

Scripture Reading: 1 Samuel 4, 5, 6; Luke 12:35-59

Trivia Question: What plague were the magicians unable to duplicate?

April 11

"Joyful Strength"

Philippians 4:13 — I can do all things through Christ which strengtheneth me.

We as believers are faced with many challenges and circumstances that seem bigger than life and at times, insurmountable. This is when we must draw from the Lord who is El Gibbor, the God of all might and strength.

The Apostle Paul said, "Be strong in the Lord and in the power of His might." (Ephesians 6:10)

I believe it is paramount to understand a truth when standing on His promise that, "we can do all things through Christ who strengthens us." The Bible teaches in Psalms 16:11, "...In thy presence is fullness of joy. . ." And in another area, "...for the joy of the Lord is your strength." (Nehemiah 8:10) We need to grasp the truth that when we spend time in His presence through prayer, communion with Him, worship, and the study of His Word, it results in being filled with His joy because in His presence is fullness of joy. That joy that He fills us with, as we linger in His presence, becomes our strength because the joy of the Lord is your strength! Then and only then can we face every stronghold, obstacle, and challenge with God's might and boldly declare and decree, "I can do all things though Christ who strengthens me!"

His strength enables you to face any challenges head on that would try to intimidate or detour you from going forward! So, let us not forget the scriptural procedure and principles that enables us to say as Paul said, "I can do all things through Christ who strengthens me." The biblical formula is this: His presence + His joy = STRENGTH!

Scripture Reading: 1 Samuel 7, 8, 9; Luke 13:1-21

Trivia Question: How many sons did Jacob (Israel) have?

April 12

"Protect your Dream"

Proverbs 29:18a — Where there is no vision, the people perish. . .

The word for vision here is a revelation or a prophetic dream. We all need to have a prophetic dream in our lives. Dreams keep us moving forward and living with a spirit of expectation. Vision or a prophetic dream speaks of where we want to go and what we want to accomplish. Dreams keep hope alive in our hearts. God wants to give you a vision or a prophetic dream concerning your life and your future. You need to passionately pursue the Lord to find out what His purpose, plan, and prophetic dream is for your life, "For I know the thoughts that I think toward you, saith the Lord, thoughts of peace, and not of evil, to give you an expected end (a hope and a future)." (Jeremiah 29:11)

When dreams die or vision is stolen and stripped away, despair will settle in one's heart and spiritual shipwreck will result. The Bible says, "Hope deferred makes the heart sick, but when the desire (dream) cometh, it is a tree of life." (Proverbs 13:12)

Do not allow anyone or anything to steal, kill, or destroy your God given dreams, because without a vision, the people perish!

Also, be very particular whom you share your dreams with. Joseph in his immaturity shared his dreams with his brothers and they became jealous and hateful toward Joseph. Even though Joseph's dreams were authenticated from the Lord, he shared them with people that acted disdainfully toward him. Most people that have no dream or vision hate and oppose those who are full of dreams and visions.

Friend, press into the Lord this day and ask Him about His plans for your life. Receive from the Lord a vision or a prophetic dream concerning your life, ministry, and future. Allow God to breathe into your spirit His purpose, plan, and prophetic dream for your life. Others may scoff and jeer at you, but as you seek God's face and humble yourself before Him in daily study of His Word, His prophetic dream will be conceived in your heart. Eventually you will give birth to the vision of God!

Scripture Reading: 1 Samuel 10, 11, 12; Luke 13:22-35

Trivia Question: In Acts 27, the sailors were in a rough storm and realized they were approaching land. What did they plan to do?

April 13

"Don't Settle for Cattle"

Numbers 32:5-6 — Wherefore, said they, if we have found grace in thy sight, let this land be given unto thy servants for a possession, and bring us not over Jordan. And Moses said unto the children of Gad and to the children of Reuben, Shall your brethren go to war, and shall ye sit here?

The Reubenites and Gadites are perfect depictions of carnal Christians that would rather take the easy road than to face some opposition and resistance. They wanted to stay in the land most comfortable for them to raise their herds of cattle and prosper. For some Christians, hard times, suffering, opposition, and resistance will not fit or be suitable in their Christian experience and comfortable way of life. Some are spiritually spoiled and whenever anything other than smooth or velvety times is in front of them, they reject and run away. There will be no wrinkles, ruffles, or rough areas on their road!

Many Christians settle for less than God's best because they are not willing to face opposition and fight the good fight of faith.

The Reubenites and Gadites were going to settle for cattle-land instead of Canaan-Land. They were going to settle for just milk when they could have had milk and honey (cows give milk, but God promised them a land flowing with milk and honey. Exodus 3:8,17) They were going to settle for a drip and a drop when God promised a deluge and a downpour!

There are going to be times when we just do not want to go forward any longer, or we just get weary in our walk and do not receive God's best for our lives. We also settle for less than God's best. Unlike Reuben and Gad, we must be willing to fight and cross the Jordan. They settled for cattle-land and they could have had Canaan-Land. Cows are good, but Canaan is better!

Friend, what has God promised you? It is worth the fight if need be. Keep marching! He will make a way in your wilderness. He will supernaturally open up your Jordan. Don't settle for just a bit when He desires His blessing to overtake you!

Scripture Reading: 1 Samuel 13, 14; Luke 14:1-24

Trivia Question: According to the Proverbs, which emotion will cause your bones to rot?

April 14

"Blessing of Unity"

Psalms 133:1 — Behold, how good and how pleasant it is
for brethren to dwell together in unity!

There is nothing like dwelling in unity and harmony. God is able to move by His Holy Spirit and power when people are in unity. When a husband and wife love each other and dwell together, the marriage is blessed and God is able to manifest His power, presence and person through a couple like that. When children are in harmony with their parents and siblings, they love each other, and are at peace with one another. That home reflects the love of God and the blessing of God.

Paul writes in Ephesians 4:3, "Endeavoring to keep the unity of the Spirit in the bond of peace." At times we must really work at keeping unity, we must make every attempt to keep the unity of the Spirit in the bond of peace. Great results happen when we endeavor to obey God in this area.

In Acts 2, when the disciples of Jesus were gathered in the upper room, it says, "they were all with one accord in one place." These believers were in unity and harmony and in that kind of environment and spiritual climate the Lord was able to move mightily! "And suddenly there came a sound from Heaven like a rushing mighty wind, and it filled all the house where they were sitting." The Holy Spirit fell when they were fused together in God's love and unity! When people dwell together in unity it is "there the Lord commands the blessing, even life forevermore." (Psalms 133:3)

Beloved, with the help of the Lord, try to restore broken relationships if possible. Try to reach out and build bridges of reconciliation and "If it be possible, as much as lieth in you, live peaceable with all men." (Romans 12:18)

Scripture Reading: 1 Samuel 15, 16; Luke 14:25-35

Trivia Question: What is the first thing Noah did after leaving the ark?

---

cApril 15

"Oil Flow"

1 Peter 5:8 — Be sober, be vigilant; because your adversary the devil,
as a roaring lion, walketh about, seeking whom he may devour.

The amplified Bible says, "Be sober, be vigilant, because your adversary the devil, as a roaring lion, walkest about, seeking whom he may seize and devour." The word seize means to lay hold of. I maintain a belief that if Satan cannot lay hold of God's people, then he will not be able to devour them! So how can we make our lives devour-proof?

The kingdom secret is found in Psalms 133:1, 2. Once again unity is a key. The Psalmist David writes, "Behold, how good and how pleasant it is for brethren to dwell together in unity! It is like the precious ointment (oil) upon the head, that ran down upon the beard, even Aaron's beard, that went down to the skirts of his garments." David likens unity to oil being poured upon and flowing all over Aaron's body.

When we choose to flow in unity and love, it is like oil being poured all over us. Have you ever seen someone trying to get a suntan in which they oil themselves well? They put on oil in hopes of a rich dark tan. Have you ever tried to grab or lay hold of someone who has oil all over them- they are too slippery to grab hold of. The oil prevents you from laying hold of the individual. Satan cannot lay hold of us if we are oiled in unity and love.

When you take that revelation and apply it to 1 Peter 5:8, you will understand that the devil cannot "lay hold of" you and consequently, he will never be able to devour you. Staying well oiled with the Holy Spirit results from you dwelling together with your brethren in unity. Satan cannot devour your family, your finances, or your dreams because you choose to walk in love, forgiveness, and unity! The adversary cannot devour if he cannot lay hold of you! What a revelation!

Be well oiled today and every day as you walk in unity with the brethren. It will devour-proof your life.

Scripture Reading: 1 Samuel 17, 18; Luke 15:1-10

Trivia Question: Jairus' daughter was how old when Jesus raised her from the dead?

April 16

"True Freedom"

*Joshua 5:9 — And the Lord said unto Joshua,
this day have I rolled away the reproach of Egypt from off you.
Wherefore the name of the place is called Gilgal unto this day.*

After Israel crossed over the Jordan River under the leadership of Joshua, they came to a place where they abode for a season. The name of the place was called Gilgal. Gilgal means a wheel, or a rolling off. The Lord told Joshua that the reproach of Egypt was being rolled off Israel. The Israelites were slaves in Egypt for four hundred and thirty years. The oppression of the task masters, all the emotional trauma of the lack of self worth and self esteem that goes along with slavery, and the strong influence of all the false gods surrounding them caused Israel to be reproached. While they crossed over the Jordan, the Lord needed to tell them how important it was to know the reproach was rolled off of them, so that they could go forward to inherit the Promised Land. They would have to understand first that all guilt, condemnation, and reproach they incurred from living in Egypt was now being rolled off of them. That freedom would enable them to pursue the promise with passion and perseverance!

God has promised you so much in His Word. It is yours if you can believe Him with all of your heart and go after all of the promises of God passionately! You and I will never pursue God and progress in our walk with Him until we come to the realization and the revelation that the reproach of sin has been rolled off of us. The Bible says we were all slaves; meaning slaves to sin (John 8:34). Sin brings guilt, condemnation, and reproach (shame, disgrace). The Word of God teaches that the reproach on us, as a result of our sin was rolled off of us and onto Jesus. He bore the reproach of our sin, so that we could be forgiven and free.

We must understand the biblical promise, "If the son, therefore shall make you free, you shall be free indeed." (John 8:36) We have been set free by the blood of the Lamb from our sin and all the reproach that results from sinful living. We must live daily in spiritual Gilgal where we understand the reproach of our sin has been rolled off of us once and for all (because Jesus carried it on His cross). We can go forward, pursue the promises of God, and fulfill our destiny in the Lord. Our sinful lifestyle of the past and all the shame that has resulted from our sin has been rolled off of us! Praise God forever more!

Scripture Reading: 1 Samuel 19, 20, 21; Luke 15:11-32

Trivia Question: What did Israel stop eating after they crossed the Jordan River?

April 17

"Covenant God"

Joshua 5:2 — At the time the Lord said unto Joshua, make thee sharp knives, and circumcise again the children of Israel the second time.

When Israel crossed over the Jordan, the first thing God told Joshua to do was to circumcise all the males. The entire generation that came out of Egypt forty years before had died off. God told Moses because of the evil report the spies brought back into the camp of Israel, which caused doubt and fear, the entire generation would not see the Promised Land. They would die in the wilderness and their children forty years later then would inherit the promise (Numbers 14:33, 34).

That first generation failed to circumcise their children and now forty years later, God reminds Joshua, the successor to Moses, that all the males (they were adults now) had to be circumcised. These men had to be circumcised because their parents failed to do what was proper before the Lord. Even though they were adults they had to go through the pain of circumcision. When parents do not teach their children about a covenant relationship with God, it will cost their children, who eventually become adults, great pain in their lives.

Circumcision speaks of covenant. God was telling Joshua that covenant had to be reestablished. For forty years that generation wandered around in the wilderness, in doubt and fear, not understanding God's covenant promises. They forfeited the promise of God by believing ten men that reported a contrary word compared to God's Word.

Joshua reestablished the principle of the covenant with this new generation that was not taught about covenant by their parents. Circumcision speaks of covenant and we must understand that we serve a covenant God who has established His covenant with us through His Son, the Lord Jesus Christ. All of God's promises are true, because He cannot lie. He keeps all His covenant promises to us and desires us to believe and embrace them. "He hath remembered His covenant forever, the word which He commanded to a thousand generations." (Psalms 105:8)

Beloved, today look to the Lord for all that you have need of. He is Elohim (Creator/Covenant God)! Believe God and all His promises because He is your covenant God. If you have been washed in the blood of His son Jesus, then you are in covenant with God. His covenant promises are yours, if you can believe and receive by faith!

Scripture Reading: 1 Samuel 22, 23, 24; Luke 16:1-18

Trivia Question: Which chapter of the book of Psalms is the largest?

April 18

"The Work is Already Done!"

Joshua 5:8 — And it came to pass, when they had done circumcising all the people, that they abode in their places in the camp, till they were whole.

God instructed Joshua to circumcise all the males in the camp after they crossed the Jordan River and encamped in Gilgal. Before they continued their journey and progressed forward, there was a season of healing from the pain.

Believers must understand that God has given to us exceedingly great and precious promises (1 Peter 1:4), but before we can go forward, many need to be healed of pains and hurts from our past. An army cannot fight if they are hurting or handicapped. We too, as soldiers of Christ cannot do spiritual warfare, march and go forward, if there is hurt and pain in our lives. The Bible says, "He heals the broken in heart, and binds up their wounds." (Psalms 147:3)

God wants to heal all emotional hurts, wounds, and pains from our past so we can passionately pursue Him and go forward in our journey with Christ! We must get healed of our past, so we can embrace our present and thrust into our future. Jesus is a healer. Isaiah 53:4 says, "Surely He has borne our griefs, and carried our sorrows (pains) yet we did esteem Him stricken, smitten of God and afflicted." Jesus has carried our pains (spiritual, physical, and emotional). So if He has carried it, why are you still carrying it?

Imagine having someone carrying a heavy box up a flight of stairs for you only to find yourself carrying it back down so you can carry it up the stairs yourself. That would be futile because the work was already done!

When Jesus carried His cross, and went up the hill to Calvary, He carried for you all the hurt and pain in your life, so that you can be healed and never have to carry it yourself again. Jesus said, "It is finished!" (John 19:30) The work has been done! Jesus has paid the price.

Beloved, receive God's healing for you so that you become whole and you can continue your journey with Him and possess all the promises of God for your life.

Scripture Reading: 1 Samuel 25, 26; Luke 16:19-31

Trivia Question: In Proverbs 21:19 it says that it is better to live in the wilderness than to live with what?

April 19

"Passover to Crossover"

Joshua 5:10 — And the children of Israel encamped in Gilgal, and kept the Passover on the fourteenth day of the month at evening in the plains of Jericho.

Even though the Israelites under Joshua's leadership experienced a great miracle and victory at the Jordan River, they remembered that it was

God as well that delivered them so many years ago from the austere hand of Pharaoh, the oppression of Egypt, and the bondage of slavery. They were put in remembrance of the death of the first born in Egypt when the destroyer passed over their families and homes. Without a Passover there would not have been a crossover.

Keeping the Passover was a memorial and a constant reminder that God had called them, God had kept them, and the blood of the lamb delivered them from sure death!

Oh, how important it is for believers to remember that Jesus died for us 2000 years ago as our Passover Lamb. We must never forget the price Jesus paid for us and daily remember that He has redeemed us.

Whenever you are faced with a seemingly insurmountable, over-matched situation that is looking you in the face, remember because Jesus is our Passover, He will always cause you to crossover! Step into your opposition by faith and watch God do a miracle for you today!

Scripture Reading: 1 Samuel 27, 28, 29; Luke 17:1-19

Trivia Question: Who or what was Jesus talking to when He said "Peace be still?"

April 20

"Growing Fruit"

Joshua 5:12 — And the manna ceased on the morrow after they had eaten of the old corn of the land; neither had the children of Israel manna any more; but they did eat of the fruit of the land of Canaan that year.

After crossing over the Jordan, the third significant thing that happened (after they were circumcised and kept the Passover) was the manna (bread from Heaven) that God rained down on His people for 40 long years stopped in Gilgal. Six days a week for forty years God sent this bread, but as Israel settled in Gilgal for a season, suddenly there was no more bread. Gilgal was a place of maturity and growing up! The people of God had to start growing their own grain and fruit in Gilgal. If God's people were to be sustained during their campaign to possess the Promised Land, they had to learn to mature, do some things for themselves and grow their own fruit!

Christians need to develop fruit in their spiritual Gilgal and in their walk with the Lord. Jesus is not going to do everything for us forever. God expects us (especially if we have walked with Him for some time) to do some things on our own. The Lord should not have to remind us to pray and study His Word. We should mature to the place that we understand that prayer and study is our manna, our daily bread.

We should be developing the fruits of the Spirit in our lives. Love, Joy, Peace, Longsuffering, Gentleness, Goodness, Faith , Meekness and Self Control. Fruit always starts out as a seed, and a seed needs to be planted and watered, and nurtured if it is going to grow. God supplies the seed (the Word of God), but we need to do the necessary things so God can cause the seed to take root, germinate, and grow. Our prayer time with God and study of His Word will accomplish this.

Jesus said, "In this is my Father glorified, that you bear much fruit, so shall you be my disciples." (John 15:8) We are called to mature as trees of righteousness and grow fruit on our spiritual branches. Gilgal was a place where God's people had to learn to grow their own fruit. Gilgal was a place of maturity and growing up.

It is time for you to live in Gilgal where you trust God and yield to His Holy Spirit, so you can spiritually mature, grow up and bear much fruit, to glorify your Father in Heaven. Just because the manna has stopped flowing from Heaven, does not mean God is saying, "starve!" No, He is just saying start using all the tools and resources that He has provided for you to start growing your harvest!

Scripture Reading: 1 Samuel 30, 31; Luke 17:20-37

Trivia Question: Who told God that he was slow of speech and slow of tongue?

April 21

"Don't Figure it Out"

Proverbs 3:5, 6 — Trust in the Lord with all thine heart,
and lean not unto thine own understanding.
In all thy ways acknowledge Him, and He shall direct thy paths.

There are times in our lives that we go through things we really do not understand. The pain of rejection, a season of loneliness, the untimely death of a loved one or friend; it all leaves us with a sense of "what is going on in my life, I don't understand what is happening?"

At these times of uncertainty and lack of understanding we must "trust in the Lord with all our hearts!" When you feel like your life has no rhyme or reason, trust in the Lord with all your heart! When you feel like the bottom has just fallen out from underneath you, trust in the Lord with all your heart! When life or circumstance has dealt you a serious blow, trust in the Lord with all your heart!

Do not try to figure out things that are beyond you. Do not try to intellectualize or rationalize things that should be left alone and laid at the foot of the cross and on the altar of God.

In all your ways acknowledge the Lord, and He promised that He would direct your paths. God wants to direct us into the path of His peace during troubled times and storms of life. Many times when we allow God to direct us into His presence and peace we receive clarity concerning the things we do not really understand.

When we are convinced of God's love for us, we can trust in Him 100%.

The Lord will never leave you nor forsake you (Hebrews 13:5), especially when you are going through lack, and difficult and discouraging times. It is at these times, His Holy Spirit prompts you to trust in Him that much more.

When you feel like you cannot figure out what you are going through, have faith in God and He shall direct your paths!

Scripture Reading: 2 Samuel 1, 2, 3; Luke 18:1-17

Trivia Question: Who said the Word of God was in his heart like a burning fire shut up in his bones?

April 22

"Renovations"

1 Corinthians 1:26 — For ye see your calling, brethren, how that not many wise men after the flesh, not many mighty, not many noble, are called.

The Lord wants us to open up our spiritual eyes to the calling of God upon our lives. We need to SEE with the eyes of the spirit and behold what is God's purpose and plan for our lives. Too many of God's people walk through life not knowing or understanding what the will of God is for their lives. Many times we take a shot in the dark at the will of God for our lives. That kind of attempt leaves us with the sense of frustration, fruitlessness, and failure. God has a perfect will for His people, if only we would pursue Him and come the prescribed way.

The Bible says in Romans 12:1,2 "I beseech you therefore, brethren, by the mercies of God that ye present your bodies a living sacrifice, holy and acceptable unto God, which is your reasonable service. And be not conformed to this world, but be ye transformed by the renewing of your mind, that ye may prove what is that good, and acceptable, and perfect, will of God." Beloved, as we daily present our bodies a living sacrifice to God, crucify our flesh and yield uncompromisingly to His Lordship, we must resolve in our hearts that we will not conform to this world (worldly ways, philosophies and dogmas that are contrary to biblical precepts and principles).

We must be transformed by the renewing of our minds, which is done through Bible reading, study, and meditation. The process of renewing of your mind literally means to RENOVATE your thinking. As we change and make the proper renovations with our thinking to align with God's Word, a transformation takes place and we will start to understand God's perfect will for our lives. Renovation leads to transformation and that will enable you to spiritually discern God's will for your life. We can ascend from His *good will*, to His *perfect will* for our lives! As we see and understand His calling, then we passionately pursue Him with all our hearts, submitting to Him and those that He has put over our lives. Hebrews 13:17 "Obey them that have the rule over you, and submit yourselves; for they watch for your souls, as they that must give account, that they may do it with joy, and not with grief; for that is unprofitable for you."

Scripture Reading: 2 Samuel 4, 5, 6; Luke 18:18-43

Trivia Question: Who took over when Moses died?

April 23

"Surrender All"

Acts 9:6 — And he trembling and astonished said, Lord,
what wilt thou have me to do? And the Lord said unto him, Arise,
and go into the city, and it shall be told thee what thou must do.

When Saul of Tarsus was knocked off his beast and heard the voice of Jesus, it changed his life forever. Saul was an angry man who was there when Stephen was stoned and killed. He consented to Stephen's death, made havoc of the church, and finally was on a mission to travel to Damascus to find other Christians. He purposed to bring them back to Jerusalem to be tried for the same fate as the martyred Stephen. But, something happened on the way as he traveled on a dirty, dusty, Damascus Road. Saul got saved through an incredible, supernatural encounter with the Son of the living God. This encounter changed his course, direction, will, goals and objective. Saul prayed "Lord, (Kurios is the Greek which is equivalent to the Old Testament word, Adonai, interpreted as Owner, Governor, Master, and Lord) what will thou have me to do?"

Saul came to the place of surrender, which is where it all begins. Surrender is the opening gate or the starting block to our journey with the Lord. If we fail to surrender all to Jesus from our spiritual beginnings we will probably struggle throughout our walk with Him. The more junk we have in our lives like Saul of Tarsus, the more we must surrender to Jesus. We must all come to the place were we say in total surrender "not my will, but yours be done."

When Jesus went to a place called Gethsemane (which means oil press) he prayed, "Father, if thou be willing remove this cup from me, nevertheless, not MY will, but THINE will be done." (Luke 22:42) Jesus was surrendering His will to the will of the Father. He was submitting to the authority of His Father. Jesus was facing crucifixion, but the truth is, that Jesus crucified His flesh well before He was nailed to the cross! He exemplified total and complete surrender.

Beloved, if you have never come to the place of sweet surrender, let it be today! You will never come to the place of complete surrender until you come to the place of complete *smashing* of the flesh! We must all come to the place of our Gethsemane, where we allow the Holy Spirit to press out of us all that is not of God and all that hinders us from total and complete surrender to the Lord. Come to that wonderful place, and do it today!

Scripture Reading: 2 Samuel 7, 8, 9; Luke 19:1-28

Trivia Question: What did Noah put on the ark to make it waterproof?

April 24

"Epic Battle"

Galatians 5:16 — This I say then, Walk in the Spirit,

and ye shall not fulfill the lust of the flesh.

All believers need to realize that the great battle between spirit verses flesh is ongoing in a Christian's life. The struggle with disciplining your spirit man to dominate your flesh man is a struggle that Paul wrote about often in his epistles, especially in the book of Romans. "For they that are after the flesh do mind the things of the flesh, but they that are after the Spirit, the things of the Spirit. For to be carnally (fleshly) minded is death, but to be spiritually minded is life and peace…So, then, they that are in the flesh cannot please God." (Romans 8:5,6,8)

Paul described this challenge even in his own life and walk with Christ. "I know that nothing good lives in me, that is, in my sinful nature. For I have the desire to do what is good, but I cannot carry it out. For what I do is not the good I want to do, no, the evil I do not want to do-this I keep on doing." (Romans 7:18, 19 NIV)

We must learn to subdue our flesh and our fleshly nature and appetites every day. If we want to experience victory in life and God's peace daily, we must not give in to our lower nature. Paul taught us four important ways to subdue our flesh.

- MORTIFY (to kill, put to death) the deeds of the flesh. (Romans 8:12, 13) "Therefore, brethen, we are debtors, not to the flesh, to live after the flesh. For if ye live after the flesh, ye shall die; but if ye, through the Spirit, do mortify the deeds of the body, ye shall live."

- Make no PROVISION (to consider in advance, forethought) for the flesh. (Romans 13:14) "But put ye on the Lord Jesus Christ, and make not provision for the flesh, to fulfill its lusts."

- Keep my body UNDER and into SUBJECTION. (1 Corinthians 9:27) "But I keep under my body, and bring it into subjection, lest that by any means, when I have preached to others, I myself should be a castaway."

- CRUCIFY your flesh. (Galatians 2:20) "I am crucified with Christ: nevertheless I live; yet not I, but Christ liveth in me."

We must crucify, keep our body under, bring it into subjection, and make no provision for our flesh to obey its desires and demands. The war goes on between your spirit and your flesh. Which one will win the battle? "Oh wretched man that I am! Who shall deliver me from the body of this death? I thank God through Jesus Christ our Lord." (Romans 7:24)

Scripture Reading: 2 Samuel 10, 11, 12; Luke 19:29-48

Trivia Question: Who preached in a valley of dead, dry bones?

April 25

"Set Apart"

*2 Timothy 1:9 — Who hath saved us, and called us with an holy
calling, not according to our works, but according to his own purpose and grace,
which was given us in Christ Jesus before the world began.*

There are different phases to God's calling on our lives. We need to
have our spiritual eyes open to the calling of God. The first phase or level to
God's calling is the holy calling. This is the embryo phase where our spiritual eyes are not formed yet, but yet we understand that God has called us
according to His own purpose and grace before the world began. This phase
of God's calling speaks of consecration. Consecration is a theological term
that means, to set apart as holy for the service of God. Because our spiritual
eyes are not formed yet and we cannot see what God has for us, we embrace
the truth that He has called us before the world began. Think about that,
God knew us and called us before we were in our mother's womb, even
before He created the world!

Jeremiah 1:5 says, "Before I formed thee in the womb, I knew thee; and
before thou camest forth out of the womb, I sanctified thee, and I ordained
thee a prophet unto the nations." Just as God sanctified (set apart, consecrated) Jeremiah before he was conceived and formed in his mother's womb,
so it is true with you too!

We need to realize that we have been set apart for God, for His glory
and His purpose. When we grasp this wonderful truth that God has set us
apart for Himself and His service before the world began, it will dispel any
mindsets that we have about being after thoughts or accidents. No! God
saw us and called us before He spoke the world into existence. Wow! You
talk about a hope and a future. There is a destiny to be fulfilled!

If we are going to fulfill our destiny, we must understand consecration.
We must consecrate our lives before God, so He can make us vessels of
honor, fit for His service. We must say, "No" to sin and worldly lusts, and
set apart our lives as holy for His service. Paul said in 2 Corinthians 6:14-
7:1 "Be ye not unequally yoked together with unbelievers; for what fel-

lowship hath righteousness with unrighteousness? And what communion hath light with darkness? And what concord hath Christ with Belial? Or what part hath he that believeth with an infidel? And what agreement hath the temple of God with idols? For ye are the temple of the living God; as God hath said, I will dwell in them, and walk in them; and I will be their God, and they shall be my people. Wherefore, come out from among them, and be ye separate, saith the Lord, and touch not the unclean thing; and I will receive you, and will be a Father unto you, and ye shall be my sons and daughters, saith the Lord Almighty. Having, therefore, these promises, dearly beloved, let us cleanse ourselves from all filthiness of the flesh and spirit, perfecting holiness in the fear of God."

We must come out and be separate (not isolated) and touch not the unclean thing. When you understand His holy calling that speaks of consecration, and that God has great plans for you, then and *only* then are you ready to understand the next phase of God's calling for your life.

Scripture Reading: 2 Samuel 13, 14; Luke 20:1-26

Trivia Question: What big mistake did Noah make?

April 26

"Godly Character"

Ephesians 1:18 — The eyes of your understanding being enlightened;
that ye may know what is the hope of his calling,
and what the riches of his inheritance in the saints.

This second phase to understanding the call of God on your life, is termed the hope of your calling. This is when your spiritual eyes are opening so you can see where you are in character development, and see where God wants you to be. This phase speaks of character!

Our character gets developed when we find ourselves in an atmosphere that is not comfortable or easy. We find out what is inside of us when we are under great stress or pressure. How do we respond when we are backed into a corner? How do we react when we feel like the walls are closing in on us from all sides and there is no way out? How do we respond when our ministry, marriage or money is being attacked? Godly character always responds according to what the Word of God instructs. When you are being persecuted on the job, godly character will always react in a Christ

107

like manner. Godly character does not incite but will defuse situations.

You can be a great preacher, but if you lack character you will never attain God's best for your life (ministerial or otherwise). Character is how you live when all the shades are drawn in your home. Character is who you are when nobody is watching you. Developing godly character will enable you to embrace all that God has for you and His call upon your life.

Charisma is what you do (your service to the Lord, empowered by His Spirit). Character is who you are! The gifting of God empowers you for service; the character of God empowers you to do life and gives you longevity. Godly character keeps you in the race for the duration, until you cross the finish line! Our spiritual eyes need to open to this truth so that we can understand the hope of our calling!

In Isaiah's vision, he saw the Lord high and lifted up and His train filling the temple. It is interesting to note as Isaiah's eyes were opening to realization of who God was, he started to recognize his own shortcomings, sin and character flaws. "Then said I, Woe is me! For I am undone, because I am a man of unclean lips, and I dwell in the midst of a people of unclean lips; for mine eyes have seen the king, the Lord of hosts." (Isaiah 6:5) As our eyes are opening to the truth of His Word and His will for our lives, let us develop godly character so He can use us for His honor and glory!

Scripture Readings: 2 Samuel 15, 16; Luke 20:27-47

Trivia Question: Who killed James with a sword?

April 27

"Consistency"

*Philippians 3:14 — I press toward the mark for the prize
of the high calling of God in Christ Jesus.*

The third phase to the calling of God is the high calling. At this level your spiritual eyes are wide open and the prize is clearly visible. The high calling speaks of consistency. We are not called to retreat, recant, or relent, but are to always go forward with determination for the prize as we cross the finish line.

The writer of Hebrews said "Wherefore, lift up the hands which hang down, and the feeble knees." (Hebrews 12:12) We are called to run this race with endurance and perseverance. Perseverance is continuing in spite of difficulty. When we understand the high calling of God on our lives, we know that we cannot run the race with excess weight. The weight of sin will slow you down and even knock you out of this race that God has engaged you in. Consistency and endurance earmarks this phase of a Christian's life. The Christian that is pressing toward the mark for the prize, is one that will not allow sin, self, or the subtleness of Satan slow them up or disqualify them in any way.

We must all run our race with perseverance and determination. There will be obstacles, hindrances, pitfalls, detours, and better offers during your journey with Christ, but the person that understands the high calling will not be duped or deceived by the devil. They will continue in spite of difficulty, looking unto Jesus who is the author and finisher of their faith.

Remember in this race of fulfilling the call of God on our lives, it does not matter who comes in first, second, or third. All that matters is that you finish the race. Paul said in 2 Timothy 4:7 "I have fought a good fight, I have finished my course, I have kept the faith." Keeping pressing on child of God, the prize is in sight—Jesus is our Prize!

Scripture Reading: 2 Samuel 17, 18; Luke 21:1-19

Trivia Question: What man carried Jesus' cross?

April 28

"Heavenly Conviction"

Hebrews 3:1 — Wherefore, holy brethen, partakers of the heavenly calling, consider the Apostle and High Priest of our profession, Christ Jesus.

This final phase of the call of God on our lives is the heavenly calling. Not only are our spiritual eyes wide open at this level, but we are being used of the Lord to open other people's eyes! At this point we should be at the place of spiritual maturity, in which God can entrust us with His Word; bringing it to others and seeing God change lives through our witness and ministry. People who understand the heavenly calling desire to develop and mature so they can make a difference in their world, their sphere of influence, and make their lives count for God and eternity. These people "walk in the Spirit, and not fulfill the lust of their flesh." (Galatians 5:16)

When the Apostle Paul was rehearsing his extraordinary conversion to King Agrippa, and witnessing to him how Jesus came to him and revealed

Himself on that Damascus Road, Paul said, "I was not disobedient to the heavenly vision (calling)." (Acts 26:13-19) Paul purposed and resolved in his heart that he would obey what Jesus told him and fulfill the purpose and plan that God had for his life. One of the mandates that Paul had on his life was to open people's eyes to the truth that Jesus was indeed Messiah and King. (Acts 26:18)

The heavenly calling speaks of conviction. We need to have a strong conviction and be loyal and true to the call of God when we reach this level. Nothing or no one can sway us, no amount of money can seduce us and no better offer can entice us! We are sold out to Him!

Beloved, keep on walking with Jesus, continue to behold the glory of the Lord and change into the same image from glory to glory. (2 Corinthians 3:18) Continue to passionately pursue Jesus and allow His calling on your life. May the different levels of His calling be consummated and effectuated in and through you!

Scripture Reading: 2 Samuel 19, 20; Luke 21:20-38

Trivia Question: Who gave approval to Steven's death?

April 29

"True Holiness"

1 Peter 1:15-16 — But, as he who hath called you is holy,
so be ye holy in all manner of life, because it is written, Be ye holy; for I am holy.

As Christians, we are called to live holy lives, and model Christlikeness to a world who calls right wrong, and wrong right. Holiness is not someone's idea of how you should look or act, but a biblical perspective on the study of the life of Christ and establishing convictions in your own heart based on what Jesus taught and how Jesus walked. Holiness is the expression outwardly of a pure heart within. Holiness is NOT the length of one's hair, or the style or color of one's suit. It is NOT an outward enunciation of piety or the appearance of spiritual somberness. It is NOT having religious garb on outwardly, but inwardly clothed in sin and wretchedness.

Jesus challenged and rebuked those who tried to *appear* holy, but truthfully did not know anything about the holiness walk! Jesus sternly upbraided the Pharisees and scribes in Matthew 23:25-28 "Woe unto you, scribes and Pharisees, hypocrites! For ye make clean the outside of the cup and of the platter, but within they are full of extortion and excess. Thou blind Pharisee, cleanse first that which is within the cup and platter that the outside of them may be clean also. Woe unto you, scribes and Pharisees, hypocrites! For ye are like whited sepulchers, which indeed appear beautiful outward, but are within full of dead men's bones, and of all uncleanness. Even so ye also outwardly appear righteous unto men, but within ye are full of hypocrisy and iniquity."

True holiness and living a holy life is a proclamation of one's personal, passionate experience with the Holy One of Israel. One who has truly transformed his/her heart, with the washing of regeneration and renewing of the Holy Spirit! This all comes from within. The Bible teaches that we need to follow and pursue holiness and our holy walk before the Lord. "Follow peace with all men and holiness, without which no man shall see the Lord." Holiness is vital in this life and the life to come.

In the New Testament, believers in Christ are called priests. (1 Peter 2:9) In the Old Testament the Lord commanded the priests to be consecrated. Consecration means to be set apart as holy for God's service. In Leviticus 8, the priests went through a consecration ceremony with very detailed instructions from the Lord. I would like to draw from that Old Testament ceremony, and bring out some New Testament parallels for our walk with Jesus today. Let us look at these truths on New Testament holiness for the next eight days.

Scripture Reading: 2 Samuel 21, 22; Luke 22:1-30

Trivia Question: In Capernaum, whose mother-in-law was healed?

April 30

"Cleansed"

Leviticus 8:6 — And Moses brought Aaron and his sons, and washed them with water.

The first order of business for Aaron and his sons as they obeyed the Lord in the consecration ceremony, was to wash with pure water. In Scripture, water speaks of the Word of God. As Christians we must maintain a devotional life in the Word of God. The water of the Word will continually cleanse you and keep you living holy.

Jesus said that His people were not of the world, but in the world. (John

17:14) This life has a way of getting believers stained and soiled as they live out their Christian walk before the world. This is why it is expedient for Christians to maintain a daily devotional time in the Word of God. As we look into God's Word, the Lord allows His cleansing to flow over us, washing away any residue of the rudiments of the world. Jesus said, "Now you are clean through the Word which I have spoken unto you. (John 15:3) The Apostle Paul said, "That He might sanctify and cleanse it with the washing of water by the word." (Ephesians 5:26) Oh, what cleansing the Word of God gives us. We need to bathe daily in the pure water of the Word of God.

When you study about the Tabernacle of Moses in the Old Testament, after the priests sacrificed the animals at the brazen altar, they came to another piece of furniture in the courtyard, before they entered the Holy Place. This piece of furniture was called the brazen laver. The laver was made of highly polished brass, which had a top and bottom pedestal. The laver was filled with pure water and there the priests washed their face, hands and feet before entering the Holy Place. The priests would not dare enter the Holy Place unwashed or unclean.

That laver speaks to us of the Word of God and the importance of cleansing and washing in the Word of God daily, so we can go forward in God and do service for Him. Beloved, let the water of the Word cleanse you from all impediments, impurities and improprieties before you take one more step forward. It is so essential!

Scripture Reading: 2 Samuel 23, 24; Luke 22:31-53

Trivia Question: When Peter denied Christ three times, what happened?

May

May 1

"Righteous Clothes"

Leviticus 8:7-9 — And he put upon the coat, and girded him with the girdle, and clothed him with the robe, and put the ephod upon him, and he girded him with the beautifully woven girdle of the ephod, and bound it unto him therewith. And he put the breastplate upon him; also he put in the breastplate the Urim and Thummim. And he put the miter upon his head; also upon the miter even in front, did he put the golden plate, the holy crown, as the Lord commanded Moses.

After the priests were washed with pure water, they put on special garments for the consecration. Christians must be clothed always in God's righteousness knowing that we represent the Lord, the righteous King. No matter where our service to God brings us or what methodology is used to promote God's Kingdom, we must always be mindful to be arrayed in His fine linens of righteousness and true holiness. (Revelation 19:8)

Righteousness is a God-given position that He gives to His beloved upon acceptance of His dear Son, the Lord Jesus Christ. The Bible says in 2 Corinthians 5:21 "For He hath made him, who knew no sin, to be sin for us, that we might be made the righteousness of God in him." We carry the righteousness of Christ and not our own. Man's righteousness falls far short of God's standard of righteousness. Isaiah 64:6 "But we are all as an unclean thing, and all our righteousness are as filthy rags; and we all do fade as a leaf, and our iniquities, like the wind have taken us away."

Christians must be clothed in God's righteousness daily. Righteousness is right standing, right believing, and right thinking. We must stand for what Christ stands for, we must believe as Christ believes and think as Christ thinks. The fruits of righteousness are wonderful in our lives, they consist of peace, quietness, and assurance. "And the work or righteousness, shall be peace; and the effect of righteousness, quietness, and assurance forever." (Isaiah 32:17)

The garments the priests wore were to be an expression that they were God's choice servants, ministers of the altar and His representatives. The clothes spoke of the righteousness of the priests before God and man.

Because of the vicarious sacrifice of Jesus, the blood He shed and the life He has given to us, we need to understand that He has also robed us in His righteousness. Let us be His representatives and ambassadors in a sinful world that we live in and allow the world to see the righteousness of Jesus through our lives.

Scripture Reading: 1 Kings 1, 2; Luke 22:54-71

Trivia Question: Who prevented Joseph from being killed by his brothers?

May 2

"Spirit of Anointing"

*Leviticus 8:10-12 — And Moses took the anointing oil,
and anointed the tabernacle and all that was therein, and sanctified them.
And he sprinkled thereof upon the altar seven times, and anointed the altar and
all his vessels, both the laver and his foot, to sanctify them. And he poured of the
anointing oil upon Aaron's head, and anointed him, to sanctify him.*

After the priests were washed with pure water, the high priest put on his special garments. It was then time to anoint Aaron with the anointing oil. Oil is a symbol of the presence of the Holy Spirit. We know that Aaron, the high priest, was anointed from the top of his head to the soles of his feet. (Psalms 133:2)

As Christians we need to have the empowerment, the influence, and the infilling of the Holy Spirit in our lives daily. Paul said, "And be not drunk with wine, in which is excess, but be filled with the Spirit." (Ephesians 5:18) The word "filled" means to replete or fill to the brim to the point of overflowing! We must be filled with the Holy Spirit, always maintaining the highest level of the Holy Spirit's influence in our lives. We need the Holy Spirit to endow us for Christian service; in whatever capacity we serve the Lord.

Christians must always be conscious that the Holy Spirit is poured out on us, not only to manifest the power of Christ, but also to reveal the person of Christ in and through our lives as we become a holy vessel of honor, fit for the Master's service. Ask God to pour out His Spirit on your life today in a way that you will be completely immersed in His presence, His power, His person and His purity. God wants each of His beloved to have an Acts 2 experience with the person of the Holy Spirit.

The angel told Mary, "The Holy Spirit shall come upon thee, and the power of the highest shall overshadow thee." (Luke 1:35) The word "over-shadow" means to envelop in a haze of brilliancy. It comes from a root word, to superimpose. God wants His Holy Spirit, and His power and presence to *superimpose* our lives. Let the oil of His Holy Spirit be poured out on you today!

Scripture Reading: 1 Kings 3, 4, 5; Luke 23:1-26

Trivia Question: Whose armor weighed over 140 pounds?

May 3

"Sacrificial Service"

Leviticus 8:18-21 — And he brought the ram for the burnt offering; and Aaron and his sons laid their hands upon the head of the ram. And he killed it; and Moses sprinkled the blood upon the altar round about. And he cut the ram into pieces; and Moses burned the head, and the pieces, and the fat. And he washed the inwards and the legs in water; and Moses burned the whole ram upon the altar; it was a burnt sacrifice for a sweet savour, and an offering made by fire unto the Lord, as the Lord commanded Moses.

The next part of the consecration ceremony was to sacrifice a ram before the Lord. After Aaron and his sons were washed with pure water, wore special clothes, and were anointed with oil, they then had to sacrifice an animal upon the altar.

As Christians we are called to be living sacrifices before the Lord. Romans 12:1, "I beseech you therefore, brethren, by the mercies of God, that ye present your bodies a living sacrifice, holy, acceptable unto God, which is your reasonable service." Once we become Christians our lives are no longer our own but belong to God. (1 Corinthians 6:19, 20) We are called as God's servants to live sacrificial lives that will be a sweet, holy savor unto the Lord. Our sacrifice should be honorable, acceptable and pleasing to the Lord, because it is offered up to Him out of a pure, passion-ate and holy heart. We are called as Christians to be servants. As servants we are to help others and point them to the cross so they too can fulfill the destiny that God has for their lives.

When my oldest daughter was just a little girl, she walked into my study as I was preparing a sermon to preach at a church service. She looked at me with those brown eyes that seemed to say, "I want to be a part of this sermon preparation." I turned and said to her, "Pray for daddy that God will use me to help people." My little girl closed her eyes ever so tight and began to pray, "Lord, help daddy to use people!"

Sad enough there are those who use ministry opportunities as stepping-stones to bigger and better things. We are never called to use people, but to serve them, even as we live a sacrificial life in our service to God.

Scripture Reading: 1 Kings 6, 7; Luke 23:27-38

Trivia Question: What was the court in Athens called where they took Paul to question him concerning Jesus and the resurrection?

May 4

"Consecrated Christian"

Leviticus 8:22-24 — And he brought the other ram, the ram of consecration; and Aaron and his sons laid their hands upon the head of the ram. And he slew it; and Moses took of the blood of it, and put it upon the thumb of his right hand, and upon the great toe of his right foot. And he brought Aaron's sons and Moses put of the blood upon the tips of their right ears, and upon the thumbs of their right hands, and upon the great toes of their right feet: and Moses sprinkled the blood upon the altar round about.

At this point of the consecration ceremony, Aaron and his sons are instructed to take a ram, lay their hands upon the head of the ram, kill it and take the blood. Moses was to apply the blood on Aaron, his sons' right ears, thumbs of their right hands and big toes of their right feet. The right side in biblical terms always speaks of power, strength, and conviction!

As we draw some parallels from this account, we know that the blood speaks of Christ who shed His blood and paid the price for our sins on Calvary to secure our salvation and sanctification. The Bible says, "For ye are bought with a price; therefore, glorify God in your body and in your spirit, which are God's." (1 Corinthians 6:20) The child of God must walk holy and glorify God in his/her spirit and body.

The Christian's ear needs to be sanctified to the voice of the Lord. "And

116

when he putteth forth his own sheep, he goeth before them, and the sheep follow him; for they know his voice. And a stranger will they not follow, but will flee from him; for they know not the voice of strangers." (John 10:4,5) Our spiritual ears need to be discerning the voice of the Lord. There are a lot of voices speaking today. Christians are having difficulty ascertaining who is speaking. Is it God, or the devil, or even the voice of my flesh? A principle to live by is this: if it is the voice of the Lord speaking to me, it will <u>always</u> be in harmony and agreement with the Word of God. The Rhema (spoken Word of God) will always agree with the Logos (the written Word of God). This is the true test whether it is the voice of the Lord or not. Our spiritual ears must decipher who is speaking. The blood of Jesus applied by faith to our ears will enable us to discern the voice of the Lord. The Christian's hands are also very necessary to be sanctified and set apart. "Wherefore, come out from among them, and be ye separate, saith the Lord, and touch not the unclean thing, and I will receive you." (2 Corinthians 6:17) As the blood of Jesus by faith is applied to the hands of all believers, it is understood that we do not touch unclean things. Our hands speak of service to God. God's people cannot be lifting up Holy hands one moment and engage themselves in sinful practices the next. Our hands need to be sanctified.

The Christian's feet also need to be consecrated before the Lord. The feet speak of our daily walk as a child of God in front of the Lord and all people. "For the Lord God is a sun and shield; the Lord will give grace and glory. No good thing will he withhold from them that walk uprightly." (Psalm 84:11) The word uprightly means to walk with integrity, without blemish or spot. "He that saith he abideth in Him ought himself also so to walk, even as He walked." (1 John 2:6)

We must walk holy before the Lord. Jesus' walk was a walk of true love and holiness. "Be ye, therefore, followers of God, as dear children; and walk in love, as Christ also hath loved us, and hath given himself for us an offering and sacrifice to God for a sweet-smelling savor." (Ephesians 5:1,2)

Our ears, hands, and feet are to be sanctified for God's glory and honor. Are we hearing God? Are we putting our holy hands to the plow in Christian service? Are our feet and our walk before Him pleasing in His sight. Saint of God, serve Him with all your being!

Scripture Reading: 1 Kings 8, 9; Luke 23:39-56

Trivia Question: How many sons did the father of the prodigal son have?

———————————————————————

May 5

"Spirit and Truth"

Leviticus 8:27-29 — And he put all upon Aaron's hands, and upon his sons' hands, and waved them for a wave offering before the Lord. And Moses took them from off their hands, and burned them on the altar upon the burnt offering; they were consecrations for a sweet savor: it is an offering made by fire unto the Lord. And Moses took the breast, and waved it for a wave offering before the Lord; for of the ram of consecration it was Moses' part, as the Lord commanded Moses.

We come to the part of consecration when Moses put the offering in the hands of Aaron and his sons. They promptly took their hands and what was in their hands and waved them for a wave offering before the Lord. After the wave offering, Moses took the offerings and burned them on the altar for a burnt offering. It was an offering made by fire unto the Lord.

This wave offering speaks to us of pure, holy worship before God Almighty. True worship is always birthed out of the fire! Jesus said in John 4:23, "But the hour cometh, and now is when the true worshipers shall worship the Father in spirit and in truth; for the Father seeketh such to worship Him." It is easier to worship God when there is money in your pocket, your health is perfect, all your family members are Christians on their way to Heaven, and everything is wonderful. Can we worship God in the midst of a fiery trial? Peter said in 1 Peter 4:12, "Beloved, think it not strange concerning the fiery trial which is to test you, as though some strange thing happened unto you." Can we maintain a life of worship when we are going through tests, and the storms of life? As Christians and disciples of Christ we must maintain a life of worship – a continual lifting up of holy hands and worshiping the Lord in the beauty of holiness. Notice, Jesus said we must worship the Father in spirit and in truth. When carnality rules a Christian's life, they will give first place to the flesh, walk in the flesh, and be flesh ruled! Flesh is the opposite of Spirit. We cannot give true worship to God in the flesh; we must be walking in the Spirit, not fulfilling the lust of the flesh if we are going to be true worshipers. (Galatians 5:16)

Likewise, we must be walking in truth. Jesus said, "in spirit and in truth." We cannot be living a lie, or walking in deception in any way if we want to be a true worshiper of God. We cannot be living a sinful life or contrary to the Word of God and expect God to receive our sacrifice of praise or our wave offering of worship. The Bible says, "If we say that we have fellowship with Him, and walk in darkness, we lie, and do not tell the truth." (1 John 1:6)

Let us worship God in spirit and in truth. Let us offer up the sacrifice of praise to Him continually, that is, the fruit of our lips giving thanks to His name. (Hebrews 13:15)

Let us worship God with our lives! Live a life that is holy and acceptable unto God, which is our spiritual worship!

Scripture Reading: 1 Kings 10, 11; Luke 24:1-35

Trivia Question: The writer of Hebrews 12:14 said that no one will see the Lord without what?

May 6

"The Good Food"

Leviticus 8:31-32 — And Moses said unto Aaron and to his sons,
boil the flesh at the door of the tabernacle of the congregation;
and there eat it with the bread that is in the basket of consecrations,
as I commanded, saying, Aaron and his sons shall eat it.
And that which remaineth of the flesh and of the bread shall ye burn with fire.

Special food was to be eaten by the priests during the consecration ceremony. This meal was prescribed by God, and was for the priests only.

As Christians we too need to feast on spiritual food everyday. Jesus said when you pray, say to God, "Give us this day our daily bread." (Luke 11:1-4) Jesus said, "I am the bread of Life." (John 6:48) Jesus also said, "My food is to do the will of Him that sent me, and to finish His work." (John 4:34)

We must be feasting on the Word of God for self-sustenance and substance. As the Word becomes a part of us, it turns into the spiritual fuel we need to serve the Lord and fulfill the purpose of God for our lives.

Interesting when the priests ate the special consecration meal, whatever was left over they burned with fire.

The Word of God is so rich, so great and so wonderful, that as we partake of it, the Word fills us up with the truth and riches of God's Kingdom. The revelation is so great, there is an overflow and that is what we burn which becomes fuel to put our hands to the plow for the work of the Lord. So we see the Word of God enriches and blesses us. As it becomes a part of us it will spill over so we can enrich and bless others with the overflow of revelation God has given.

119

Remember, the Christian must be mindful at all times what he/she puts inside. A steady diet of things that are true, honest, just, lovely, and pure will keep his/her heart and mind holy before God. What you focus and feed on will become a part of you. Focus and feed on the Word of God!

Scripture Reading: 1 Kings 12, 13; Luke 24:36-53

Trivia Question: What Old Testament prophet spoke of Messiah riding into Jerusalem on a donkey?

May 7

"Shut In"

Leviticus 8:33 — And ye shall not go out of the door of the tabernacle of the congregation in seven days, until the days of your consecration be at an end; for seven days shall he consecrate you.

During the consecration period the priests did not go outside the tabernacle, rather were shut in with God.

There will be many times in our lives when God is calling us to get alone with Him. Nothing will seem more important than getting shut in with our heavenly Father. Jeremiah said, "And you shall seek me, and find me, when you shall search for me with all your heart." (Jeremiah 29:13) We are called to go after God with everything within us.

Jesus talked about our closet of prayer. He said when you pray, enter your closet (room) and when you have shut the door, pray to your Father. (Matthew 6:6) We need daily times in our lives where we shut out everything and everyone for a time, and shut in with the Lord for devotion and Bible meditation. This will enable us to receive the mind of the Lord for different things that we go through. He alone has the answers to all of our questions. He is the one who leads us into all truth. He will instruct and guide us as we spend time with Him. Just as the well-known saying goes, "if you are too busy to pray, then you are too busy." What joy it is to spend time with the Father, through the Son and by the Holy Spirit. What peace floods our hearts in the midst of storms when we find ourselves at His feet in Communion and prayer. A great songwriter wrote, "Oh what peace we often forfeit, Oh what needless pain we bear, all because we do not carry everything to God in prayer!"

Especially for Christians that are very active in service to the Lord, being shut in with God is paramount. There must be many seasons that ministers of the Gospel, after the multitudes are sent away, go into a place privately to pray and get alone with their heavenly Father. This is needful for refocus, refreshing, renewing, redirection, rejuvenation and refining! After Jesus had intense ministry with the people, He often went to a private place, away from the crowds to pray and get shut in with His father. How about you?

Scripture Reading: 1 Kings 14, 15; John 1:1-28

Trivia Question: After Paul healed a lame man in Lystra through the power of Christ, who did the people say Barnabus and Paul were?

May 8

"God's House"

2 Peter 1:3 — According as his divine power hath given unto us all things that pertain unto life and godliness, through the knowledge of him that hath called us to glory and virtue.

A very important aspect of our Christian lives in regards to serving the Lord, completing our call, fulfilling our destiny and finishing our course, hinges on the understanding we have of being called to glory and virtue. If we are ever going to experience higher realms of His glory, we must walk as a people of virtue. Ecclesiastes 7:8 says, "Better is the end of a thing, than the beginning thereof, and the patient in spirit is better than the proud in spirit." If we are going to finish what God has started in our lives, and fulfill the purpose and plan that He has for us, we ought to be a virtuous people.

Virtue defined is moral excellence. Why are so many believers falling short of the finish line? Many Christians may not have been diligent to develop moral excellence in their lives. For several, virtue may be void in their character, nature and the composition of their Christian experience. Where virtue is void, victory is deferred. Where virtue is void, our desire to progress in our journey with the Lord is halted.

The Bible says we must add to our faith, virtue or moral excellence. If we want to build a spiritual edifice for the Lord and allow God to take us to the place of completion in Him, we must build on our faith and moral excellence. Faith is foundational, and needs other building blocks added, to be able to express itself to the maximum potential. Without virtue or moral excellence being added to your faith, the spiritual building cannot be created and all you have is a foundation. Foundation is important, but needs blocks and floors built upon it to become something that is functional.

A building was being constructed not to far from my home. For whatever reason, the contractors only laid the foundation, and for six years I passed by only to wonder when and if there was going to be a final structure. Many Christians are just like that. They have faith, but have never added to it. 2 Peter 1:5-7 says, "And besides this, giving all diligence, add to your faith, virtue, and to virtue, knowledge and to knowledge, self control, and to self control, patience, and to patience, godliness and to godliness, brotherly kindness, and to brotherly kindness, love." God's love working through us is the greatest expression of one's faith. Paul said, "Though I have all faith, so that could remove mountains, and have not love, I am nothing." (1 Corinthians 13:2)

To develop our lives to that point and pinnacle of Christ-like expression, we must build on our faith. If faith is the foundation, then love is the Zenith. All that is in between is essential if we are to become God's building. (1 Corinthians 3:9, Ephesians 2:21, Colossians 2:7) Let us be a people that develop moral excellence or virtue in our lives so that Christ-likeness will be apparent.

Scripture Reading: 1 Kings 16, 17, 18; John 1:29-51

Trivia Question: What did Jacob buy from his brother Esau?

May 9

"Receive your Promotion"

Genesis 39:7-10 — And it came to pass after these things, that his master's wife cast her eyes upon Joseph; and she said, Lie with me. But he refused, and said unto his master's wife, Behold, my master wotteth not what is with me in the house, and he hath committed all that he hath to my hand; There is none greater in this house than I; neither hath he kept back any thing from me but thee, because thou art his wife: how then can I do this great wickedness, and sin against God? And it came to pass, as she spake to Joseph day by day, that he hearkened not unto her, to lie by her, or to be with her.

When talking about virtue, one must look to Joseph, who exemplified

122

extreme moral excellence in the face of adverse times in his life. Joseph was hated by his brothers. They conspired to kill him, threw him in a pit and eventually sold him as a slave. He was then forced to live in a foreign land with a different culture and people. Joseph was a virtuous young man and moral excellence earmarked his life. Even in the most trying of times, Joseph was promoted by God. God's divine favor was upon Joseph. Morally excellent people often get promoted and enjoy God's favor on their lives.

One day when Joseph was overseeing his master's house, Potiphar's wife tried to sexually seduce him. She attempted to have Joseph compromise his godly convictions and jeopardize his pursuit of moral excellence. Potiphar's wife was unable to succeed with her devilish wiles because Joseph's virtuous spirit prevailed. When she propositioned Joseph to sin with her, he responded with a resounding, "NO!" Joseph said, "How then can I do this great wickedness, (to Potiphar) and sin against God?"

Morally excellent people have loyalty and fidelity toward God and those they are accountable to. Even when Potiphar's wife lied and falsely accused Joseph, he stood with his convictions, remained a virtuous man and stood morally tall before God. Joseph even paid the price of going to jail on a false rape charge. Even in jail, God favored and promoted him. You just cannot keep morally excellent people down. Eventually at 30 years old, through a series of divine interventions and Joseph's interpretation of dreams, God promoted him by the hand of Pharaoh. He became prime minister or governor over the entire land of Egypt, second only to Pharaoh in the kingdom. From the pit, to the prison, to the palace.

Morally excellent people have a great future. Add to your faith, virtue and to virtue, knowledge. Knowledge is the understanding of how to live out moral excellence in your life.

Scripture Reading: 1 Kings 19, 20; John 2

Trivia Question: Jesus fed 5,000 people with five loaves of bread and how many fish?

May 10

"Compass Direction"

Deuteronomy 2:3 — Ye have compassed this mountain long enough: turn you northward.

The Israelites of long ago encircled Mount Seir for many days. After a season of surrounding the mountain, the Lord spoke to Moses and told him, it was long enough. It was time to stop going around in circles and look northward.

In our lives as Christians we too go around and around at times. There are mountains in our lives that have intimidated us, preventing us from going forward in our journey with the Lord. It is time to stop encircling our mountains and turn Godward. It is time we turn and look to the Lord for His guidance, direction, deliverance, and help. We need to look to the North – Godward! The psalmist said in Psalms 121:1,2: "I will lift up mine eyes unto the hills. From whence cometh my help? My help cometh from the Lord who made Heaven and Earth."

Mountains have prevented many of God's people from progressing and going forward in their walk with Him. There are mountains of depression, discouragement, disease, fear, rejection, past hurts, wounds, loneliness, reproach, etc. All these are mountains and could stand in our way from passionately pursing the call of God on our lives. The Bible says that our faith can move mountains, instead many of the mountains in our lives are moving our faith. We have the power in Jesus' name and by the Word of God, to see mountains be removed. Instead of compassing the mountain day after day to the point where the mountain looks insurmountable, we must blow a hole right through it, fight and continue forward with God. David wrote, "For by thee I have run through a troop, and by my God have I leaped over a wall." (Psalms 18:29)

It is time to turn Godward and get His divine plan for our lives so we can blast into our mountains and stop marching around them. Rather we need to walk through them en route to fulfilling our destiny. Child of God, you have compassed the mountain long enough, it is time to turn Godward!

Scripture Reading: 1 Kings 21, 22; John 3:1-21

Trivia Question: How old was Moses when he died?

May 11

"Early Riser"

Mark 1:35 — And in the morning, rising up a great while before day, he went out, and departed into a solitary place, and there prayed.

With our busy, quick-paced "life in the fast lane" lifestyles that many live, I wonder if prayer is the thing that gets squeezed out when we do not have the time. Many of us rush in the morning to get ready for work, school or the activities and many demands that come with the dawn of another day. Jesus knew all the many demands people were to put upon Him daily. There were sermons to preach, people that would come from all over to be healed and many lives that would need deliverance and restoration. With that understanding, Jesus would rise up a great while before the sunrise and get alone to commune with His heavenly Father. Jesus taught us a kingdom secret. If we are going to be empowered for the daily demands of each day, we need to spend time with our heavenly Father. We cannot rely on yesterday's energy supply or trust within our own abilities, strength, and expertise. It is not by our might or our power, but we must totally depend on the Holy Spirit and His anointing to endow us with all we need for everyday demands and pressures. (Zechariah 4:6)

When we forfeit our times in the presence of the Lord and fail to receive what we need, which can only come from Him, we face our world and all the challenges that will come, on our own. There is something special about getting up early, before all the action to spend some time with the Lord. David wrote "O God, thou art my God, early will I seek Thee." (Psalms 63:1) Solomon speaking on the subject of wisdom wrote, "I love those who love me, and those who seek me early shall find me." (Proverbs 8:17) As we set apart some time for God, before our busy day begins, He will meet us with His presence, guidance, love, and wisdom. Tomorrow morning the Lord will be waiting for you, don't miss out!

Scripture Reading: 2 Kings 1, 2, 3; John 3:22-36

Trivia Question: Who refused to attend his brother's welcome home party?

May 12

"Who Do You Say He Is?

James 1:1 — James, a servant of God, and of the Lord Jesus Christ, to the twelve tribes which are scattered abroad, greeting.

There are four men named James mentioned in the New Testament. James, the brother of John and the son of Zebedee. (Matthew 10:2) James,

125

the son of Alphaeus, also known as James the less. (Matthew 10:3 and Mark 15:40) James, the father of the Apostle Judas (not Iscariot). (Luke 6:16) Then we have James, the Lord's brother who got converted after the Resurrection of Jesus. (Matthew 13:55 and Acts 1:13)

James, the brother of Jesus became a strong Christian and eventually the leader over the Jerusalem church. What is very interesting about James, the Lord's brother, is that he wasn't saved or converted while Jesus ministered in His earthly ministry. As a matter of fact, James was probably in on a conspiracy to destroy his own brother. In John 7:1-5, we learn how the Jews sought to kill Jesus in the region of Judea. Jesus' brothers were encouraging Him to go down into Judea from Galilee, (his hometown region) to make Himself known to the people that were not acquainted with Him or His miracle ministry. Jesus' brothers knew right well that there were those that wanted their brother dead, but still they encouraged Him to go into the Judea danger zone! They tried to appeal to the ministry aspect of Jesus' life. "If ye do these things, show thyself to the world." (John 7:4)

Imagine the very brothers of Jesus wanted to see His life in extreme danger. The Bible says in John 7:5, "For neither did His brothers believe in Him." Was it sibling rivalry? Was it jealously over a brother who had extraordinary authority and power? Was it because Jesus got more attention than them? The answer is not clear in Scripture, but we know that Jesus' brothers did not believe He was Messiah! All Jesus was to Joseph, Judas, Simon and James was their big brother Jesus.

There are many people today that see Jesus only as a good moral man, or a dynamic teacher and communicator. Jesus asked Simon Peter and His apostles "Who do you say that I am?" Peter answered and said "Thou art the Christ, the Son of the living God." (Matthew 16:15-16) Peter's confession of Christ was powerful, ascribing all deity to Him, and recognizing that Jesus was Messiah, the anointed one! Have we come to the place that we see Him as Savior, Messiah and absolute Lord of our lives? If you have received Him as Savior, serve Him as Lord everyday of your life!

Scripture Reading: 2 Kings 4, 5; John 4:1-30

Trivia Question: Jesus healed how many men that were suffering from leprosy when only one returned to thank Him?

May 13

"True Faithfulness"

Proverbs 25:19 — Confidence in an unfaithful man in time of trouble is like a broken tooth, and a foot out of joint.

God puts a very high premium on faithfulness. Throughout the Word of God, men and women alike were applauded when there was an expression of faithfulness in their life. People need to embody faithfulness in all areas. On the job it is essential if we are going to go forward in rank and advancement within that organization. In education it is critical if we are going to excel and be head and shoulders above everyone else. Faithfulness causes individuals to stand out in the crowd.

When it comes to the spiritual realm, faithfulness is superior. The Bible says if we put our confidence in someone who is unfaithful in a time of real need or trouble, it is like a broken tooth or a foot out of joint. In other words, it will bring pain!

The Lord is looking for faithful men and women in His Kingdom. God wants to entrust His people with the riches of His Kingdom. He desires to put His confidence in us.

Christians do not realize the importance of being faithful before the Lord. God is looking for faithfulness in every aspect of our lives – faithfulness spiritually, devotionally, domestically, in good times, in bad times, in joyful times and in troublesome times. Can God count on you in times of trouble?

Most Christians think that their talents and gifts bring promotion in God's economy, but that is not how the Lord elevates His people. The Lord is looking for faithful individuals that He can trust and count on day in and day out.

In the parable of the talents in Matthew 25:14-30, Jesus rebuked the slothful servant but commended and lauded the faithful servants. At the end of our lives when we stand before the Lord, we are not going to hear, "Well done, good and *gifted* servant." We all aspire to hear those glorious words from the mouth of the Master, "Well done thou good and FAITHFUL servant, thou hast been FAITHFUL over a few things, I will make thee ruler over many things. Enter thou into the joy of thy Lord." (Matthew 25:21) Only biblical faithfulness brings true joy in one's life. Ask the Lord to help you be the faithful Christian He has called you to be. One that God can count on, even in times of trouble!

Scripture Reading: 2 Kings 6, 7, 8; John 4:31-54

Trivia Question: Whom did King David murder so he could have his wife?

May 14

"Heart Condition"

*Deuteronomy 8:2 — And thou shalt remember all the way which the Lord
thy God led thee these forty years in the wilderness, to humble thee,
and to test thee, to know what was in thine heart,
whether thou wouldest keep his commandments, or no.*

We as Christian's will go through seasons of being tested and proved by
the Lord, so He can see what is in our hearts.

When God sent the prophet Samuel to Jesse's house to choose and
anoint another king, because Saul had disobeyed the Lord and had been
rejected by God, Samuel interviewed all of Jesse's sons in hope to meet a
king. After seven of the young men (who looked like kings were supposed
to look) passed before Samuel, the question was asked, "Are all your children here?" Samuel was informed that the youngest, a shepherd boy was
in the field tending the flock. Upon summoning David to come and meet
the man of God, immediately the Lord spoke to Samuel and said, "Arise,
anoint him for this is he." David's seven brothers were head and shoulders
above him, but David was the young man that God singled out. Why?
Because "for the Lord seeth not as man seeth, for man looketh on the outward appearance, but the Lord looketh on the HEART." (1 Samuel 16:7)

It is our hearts that God is looking into. How do our hearts respond
and react during difficult times? What comes out of us when we go
through adverse seasons in our lives? Jesus said, "For out of the abundance
of the heart the mouth speaketh." (Matthew 12:34) It is interesting how
our hearts are revealed, when we go through a time of testing. Will we
keep His commandments and will our hearts stay true to God when we go
through our wilderness, humbling times, and seasons of proving?

David wrote, "Search me O God, and know my HEART, try me, and
know my thoughts, and see if there be any wicked way in me, and lead me
in the way everlasting." (Psalms 139:23-24)

We need to guard our hearts with all diligence, for out of our hearts are
the issues of life. (Proverbs 4:23)

Beloved have you filled your hearts with the Word of God? Is Christ-likeness hidden deep within your heart? Is your heart filled with the compassion of Jesus? If so, when you go through tough times of testing, Christ will be exemplified in your life as your heart is explored and revealed to all that surrounds your life.

Scripture Reading: 2 Kings 9, 10, 11; John 5:1-24

Trivia Question: Which woman had seven demons cast out of her by Jesus?

May 15

"Hidden Sin becomes Visible"

Numbers 32:23 — But if ye will not do so,
behold, ye have sinned against the Lord; and be sure your sin will find you out.

When the children of Israel took the city of Jericho, after they saw the walls fall down flat, in obedience to God's instructions, they were commanded by God not to touch the accursed things in the city. The Lord said in Joshua 6:18 "And ye in every way keep yourselves from the accursed thing, lest ye make yourselves accursed, when ye take of the accursed thing, and make the camp of Israel a curse, and trouble it." God always says what He means, and means what He says! All the gold, silver, bronze, and iron that they would recover in Jericho was to be brought into the treasury of the Lord. The instructions were very clear to all of Israel, the money is to be given to God and everything else is NOT to be touched!

There was a man by the name of Achan, whose name means "he who troubles," who thought he was an exception to the rules. There are always some who feel that the standards that are set are for everyone else but them. They do things their own way. They march to the beat of a different drum. Achan was of that persuasion!

The next city that had to be overtaken in battle, en route to the Promised Land, was a city called Ai. There were not many people in Ai and their military was small and anemic. Joshua sent only three thousand soldiers to take the city of Ai. A strange thing took place as the small army of God entered the gate of the city. The much smaller army of soldiers of Ai started to chase the Israelites and smote thirty-six soldiers in Joshua's army. God's people were devastated. Joshua was distraught. Discouragement pervaded the camp of the Lord. Joshua was so depressed that he found himself face down on the ground lamenting before the Lord, only to hear God say to him, "Get up, the reason for the defeat is because there is sin in the camp." (Joshua 7:10-12) The Israelites could not stand before their enemies, because someone disobeyed the Lord, allowed sin to enter the camp and caused God to become angry. It is true for us too that we cannot stand against our enemies (Satan and all of his demon spirits) if we have sin in our lives. When sin is evident in one's life, he or she forfeits their God-given authority!

Achan was the man who decided that he was going to take some of the accursed things from Jericho—what belonged to God (gold and silver) and keep it for himself. His selfishness, greed, and sin caused the entire camp of Israel to be affected. When God's people sin it will always affect people around them.

After Achan's sin was exposed by God, and revealed to Joshua, he made a futile attempt to confess and repent. Achan said in Joshua 7:21 "When I SAW among the spoils, a beautiful Babylonish garment, and 200 shekels of silver, and a wedge of gold of fifty shekels weight, then I COVETED them; and took them; and, behold, they are hidden in the Earth in the midst of my tent, and the silver under it."

Notice that sin is progressive. Achan saw, then he coveted, finally he TOOK of the garments and the gold and silver and hid them in his tent. Achan failed to realize that God sees everything, everywhere! The consequences for this sin in Achan's life was devastating to him and his family. Achan, his family and everything he owned were destroyed. All of Israel stoned them with stones and burned them with fire. This was all done in a valley called Achor which means trouble. So Achan, the one who brought trouble into the camp of God, is destroyed in the valley of trouble. Achan's hidden sin brought visible trouble! Achan's sin surely found him out!

God wants us to acknowledge and confess any hidden sin in our lives. His mercy is calling out to us to repent of any sin. His mercy will triumph over His judgment. (James 2:13)

The Bible says, "If we confess our sins, He is faithful and just to forgive us our sins, and to cleanse us from all unrighteousness." (1 John 1:9) Let us learn a lesson from Achan that there is a difference between true repentance and just getting caught. Hidden sin will always bring visible trouble!

Scripture Reading: 2 Kings 12, 13, 14; John 5:25-47

May 16

"The Ins and Outs"

Deuteronomy 6:23 — And he brought us OUT from thence,
that he might bring us IN, to give us the land which he sware unto our fathers.

God delivered Israel with His mighty hand out of the oppressive hold of Pharaoh, the house of bondage and set them free from all of Egypt's shackles. For over four hundred years, God's people were not living in the liberty that was promised to them. A man by the name of Moses was raised up to be the instrument and vessel God would use to deliver His people. After many encounters with Pharaoh, and ten plagues later, Pharaoh finally let the people go out into the wilderness, to sacrifice unto the Lord, and start their journey en route to the Promised Land. God was bringing Israel OUT of bondage and promised to bring them IN to a place of blessing and abundance.

It is true of us today that God has brought us OUT of the worldly system and philosophies of our culture, only to bring us IN and introduce us to His Word, way and will for our lives.

When we were slaves to sin, we were in bitter bondage. John 8:34, "Jesus answered them, 'Verily, verily, I say unto you, Whosoever committeth sin is the servant of sin." When we heard and responded to the Gospel of Jesus, we had the chains broken off our lives, through repentance and surrender to Christ. At that time God delivered us out of Satan's grip and desired to bring us in to the abundant life promised in His Word.

Maybe you feel like Israel of old when they went through a season of wilderness. You might be saying, "Where is the Promised Land God promised to bring me into?" Israel did walk around in the wilderness a long time due to a lack of faith and disobedience, but God brought their children into the Promised Land just as He said. The books of Exodus, Leviticus, Numbers, and Deuteronomy teach us about God taking them out of Egypt and their wandering in the wilderness, but the book of Joshua speaks of crossing the Jordan River and entering in the Promised Land.

Beloved, God has called you OUT, only to take you IN. It is a better place, a place of blessing and manifestations of the goodness of God.

131

There might be some wilderness between the OUT and the IN, but keep on marching, keep on pressing forward, keep on passionately pursing the Lord, and all His promises will come to pass in your life. For He is not a man that He should lie!

Scripture Reading: 2 Kings 15, 16, 17; John 6:1-21

Trivia Question: What woman drove a spike into Sisera's head?

May 17

"Learn How to Walk"

Galatians 5:16 — This I say then, WALK in the Spirit, and ye shall not fulfill the lust of the flesh.

The Bible has so much to say about our walk before the Lord. If we are walking in the Spirit, that is being led, influenced, and empowered by the Spirit of God, we will not fulfill the desires of our flesh.

Paul in Ephesians 5 writes about three ways the child of God should walk. The first is found in Ephesians 5:2. We are called to WALK in love. The preceding verse tells us to be followers or imitators of God. The Greek word *mimos* is where we get our English word mimic. Be imitators or mimics of God as His dear children. How do we imitate God? Ephesians 5:2 teaches us, "and walk in love, as Christ also hath loved us, and hath given Himself for us an offering, and a sacrifice to God for a sweet-smelling savor." To walk in love is to imitate Christ, for Jesus exemplified and modeled the love walk.

The second time Paul talks about how the Christian should walk is in Ephesians 5:8. "For ye were once in darkness, but now are ye light in the Lord, WALK as children of light."

Jesus as our light, has illuminated our lives driving out all the darkness that was resident in us. "And the light shineth in darkness, and the darkness overcame it not." (John 1:5) The child of God is called to walk as a child of light. The light of His righteousness has illuminated our path and no longer do we "have fellowship with the unfruitful works of darkness but, rather, reprove them." (Ephesians 5:11)

Third, we are called to "WALK circumspectly or cautiously, not as fools but as wise redeeming the time, because the days are evil." (Ephesians 5:15-16) We can busy ourselves with so many things in our lives, which have no eternal value. Paul teaches us to walk cautiously or smartly, not foolish, but prudent, making the most of our time. It is not time to walk in waste and unproductiveness. It is time to redeem what God has given us, understanding the days are evil in which we live and walk in the understanding of the will of God for our lives! So beloved, walk in love, walk as children of light and walk circumspectly and you will walk in the Spirit, and not fulfill the lusts of the flesh.

Scripture Reading: 2 Kings 18, 19; John 6:22-44

Trivia Question: Whose sons and husband died in Moab?

May 18

"Take the Test"

James 1:3 — Knowing this that the trying of your faith worketh patience.

There will be times very often when our faith will be tested. Whether the test is from God, the adversary or just life circumstances—tests will come. When I was in grade school, it did not matter who administered the tests, whether it was your everyday teacher, a substitute, or even a proctor. All that mattered was that you responded well, passed the test and eventually got promoted! In our walk with the Lord, it works the same way.

The Bible says that our faith (trust, reliance, and belief) in God and His Word will be tried and tested. 1 Peter 1:7 says, "That the trial of your faith, being much more precious than of gold that perisheth, though it be tried with fire, might be found unto praise and honor and glory at the appearing of Jesus Christ." Our faith will be on trial! Gold might be a precious metal, but it will perish one day. Gold and money is useless when you need a faith break through. The great possession you have is your faith; faith in God and His Holy Word. Just as gold is purified by going through extreme heat and fire to become more valuable, so it is with our faith – it will be tried with fire! When we endure the fiery trials – the fires of rejection, persecution and suffering for the cause of Christ, we will come forth from testing more valuable for the Lord and His Kingdom.

When we pass the tests of our faith, we gain priceless experience. Many Christians, at the first sign of opposition, adversity, calamity, or testing, retreat and run away. Two things happen when we shrink from the testing of our faith. First, we do not receive the victory and promotion from the

Lord. (Remember if you do not pass the test, there is no promotion.) Second, we lose out on something very valuable, the experience we receive from that faith testing. God is looking for some experienced people to entrust kingdom things to. You and I have to go through some stuff if we are to gain experience. Could you imagine having to get a root canal, sitting in the oral surgeon's chair, only to see the doctor lean over and say to you "this is a monumental occasion for me, you are my first patient that I am performing a root canal on!" I'm quite sure you would be very concerned in his dentist chair, knowing he does not have any experience in root canals.

The testing of your faith is not a rare happening in your walk with God. "Beloved, think it not strange concerning the fiery trial which is to test you, as though some strange thing happened unto you." (1 Peter 4:12) Remember the testing of your faith will work the fruit of patience in your life. Patience will come to the aid of your faith to gird you up.

Beloved, maybe your faith is on trial at this very moment and season in your life. Trust the Lord with all your heart, He will see you through and empower you by His Spirit to bring you to the place of victory and promotion in Him!

Scripture Reading: 2 Kings 20, 21,22; John 6:45-71

Trivia Question: "If you are the Son of God tell this stone to become bread," was said by whom?

May 19

"The Significant Vow"

Ecclesiastes 5:4 — When you make a vow to God, do not delay in fulfilling it, He has no pleasure in fools, fulfill your vow. (NIV)

A vow is a pledge, a promise or your word of honor that you give to someone. Since God puts a very high emphasis on words, it is easy to understand that He wants His people to keep their word to Him. He always keeps His Word to His people, "God is not a man, that He should lie, nor the son of man, that He should change His mind." (Numbers 23:19) Does He speak and then not act? Does He promise and not fulfill?" (Numbers 23:19 NIV) The Lord does not break His Word, or His promise to us. He has made a covenant with us, sealed with His Son's blood, and all His promises are yes and amen in Him! His Word is His bond.

134

The Bible teaches that born again believers are partakers of His divine nature. (2 Peter 1:4) God's nature is truth and integrity. When God speaks, you can count and rely on His Word! He will not say one thing and do another. He vows to show love to a thousand generations, to those who love Him and keep His commandments. (Exodus 20:6)

These are times that we as God's people need to vow, pledge, or make a promise to the Lord. As God keeps His Word to us, we must keep our word to Him. There are occasions in our walk, when the Lord is looking for us to make Him a promise. When we vow before the Lord we need to understand the importance of keeping our word and fulfilling our vow. It could be a vow of giving your finances, or sowing your time. Maybe it is a vow to God that you will spend more time with Him daily. (This book was written to help you spend more quality time with Jesus.) Whatever the vow is, Scripture commands us to fulfill it.

What have you promised the Lord? Most Christians are called to market place ministry (versus pulpit ministry), meaning ministry right where you are when God called you: in the market place, your place of employment, your school, right where God has placed you. Both types of ministry are essential and honorable before God. What vow have you made to God? Have you kept it? Are you endeavoring to fulfill it before the Father? It is better not to vow than to make a vow and not fulfill it. Do not let your mouth lead you into sin. (Ecclesiastes 5:5,6 NIV) God is expecting us to be people of our word and keep our promise to Him. God is seeking virtuous people — morally excellent individuals where their word is their honor. Be a virtuous man or woman that keeps his or her word to God and all that has anything to do with His business!

Scripture Reading: 2 Kings 23, 24, 25; John 7:1-31

Trivia Question: Where in the Bible do we read about 100 pound hailstones?

May 20

"Rid of I"

Philippians 2:3-5 — Let nothing be done through strife or vainglory,
but in lowliness of mind let each esteem other better than themselves.
Look not every man on his own things, but every man also on the things

of others. Let this mind be in you, which was also in Christ Jesus.

As born again believers who are mature in Christ, our attitudes should become a reflection of Him who has saved us. When we become consumed with the Lord, self will, self-centeredness, and selfishness becomes less and less. We do nothing out of selfish ambition, like the mindset, "What is in this for me?" We start however being concerned and considerate for others, more than ourselves. When we see this kind of behavior in our lives, we know we are growing in God and becoming Christ-like.

Pride is an evil enemy to our development in Christ. Pride keeps us back from forging ahead with the Lord. "Pride goes before destruction, and a haughty spirit before a fall." (Proverbs 16:18) The middle letter in the word PRIDE is I. "I" always wants to be in the center, getting all the attention. We must R-I-D ourselves from the I in P-R-I-D-E. When we crucify our flesh and R-I-D ourselves of I in PRIDE, we are left with P-R-D-E. We will be P-R-D-E (pre-dee) good Christians that are maturing and becoming like Jesus, not looking on our own interests, but on the interest of others. Our concern and consideration is no longer inward, but outward for others. Our attitudes exemplify Jesus and people see Him in us and through our lives.

Attitude is so important, because it is what people see and hear from us. The Bible says we are open epistles or letters, known and read by everyone. (2 Corinthians 3:2) Our attitudes are derived from our emotions. Christians' emotions should reflect Christlikeness. The soul of man is made up of one's will, mind, intellect, and emotions. Jesus said "In your patience, possess ye your souls (emotions)." We must have control over our emotions if we are to maintain the right attitude before God and man. Wilderness times could be hard and difficult for Christians. Maintaining the right attitude while going through a wilderness season is paramount. Think on this truth—when Israel went through their wilderness, it took them forty years to get through it because of a terrible attitude. Jesus went through His wilderness and maintained the right heart and attitude, and it took him forty days! Forty years or forty days, the choice is up to you. The right attitude will help you in your decision!

Scripture Reading: 1 Chronicles 1, 2; John 7:32-53

Trivia Question: What land was Job from?

136

May 21

"By His Strength, not Yours"

Judges 6:2 — And the hand of Midian prevailed against Israel; and because of the Midianites, the children of Israel made them the dens, which are in the mountains, and caves, and strongholds.

Israel was once again in an apostate spiritual status, serving other gods instead of the living God. As a result the Midianites oppressed them for several years. They instilled fear in Israel, discomfited the harvest fields and destroyed their livestock. The Midianites outnumbered Israel greatly and completely devastated God's people and everything they possessed. "Israel was greatly impoverished because of the Midianites, and the children of Israel cried unto the Lord." (Judges 6:6) It was truly a despondent time for God's people.

The Lord always hears the cries of His own. When Israel cried out to the Lord, God's heart was moved once again. His people were hiding out in dens, caves and strongholds for fear of Midian. (Fear should never be a place for God's elect.) God heard their cry from the caves, and sent a prophet with a word of encouragement to the people that what He did for them in Egypt, He would do again if they stopped fearing.

The Angel of the Lord appeared to a man named Gideon, who was secretly threshing wheat, and spoke over him that he was a mighty man of valor. Gideon did not feel very brave or courageous. He too was hiding out from the enemy! The Lord informed Gideon that he was the one that was going to be used by God to spearhead a campaign against the Midianites and see God turn their fear and defeat into faith and victory. Gideon, like so many of us, told the Lord that he was quite incapable of this task. Gideon looked upon the circumstances that surrounded his life and family. He said, "Who am I? I come from a poor family and I am the least in my father's house." After Gideon gave the Lord various excuses, God responded with an answer that would silence all his "spiritual loopholes" that he was suggesting. The Lord said, "Surely I will be with you!" That's what makes the difference. God does not call us to impossible tasks because of who we are, but because of who He is! Not in our own strength, but in His awesome power do we tackle the challenges that God sets before us. God told Gideon that he would smite the Midianites and Israel would prevail!

What challenge is in your life today? Does it seem bigger than life itself? What has God called you to do, you mighty man/woman of valor? Do not look within your own abilities, social status, financial condition, or your strength. Look to God and all that He is, and all that He possesses. He promises to be with you. Trust Him and He will bring it to pass. God gave the victory to Gideon and all of Israel, and He will give you victory today also. Believe His Word, step out in faith, put your eyes on God and His never-ending resources and power. Victory will be yours too!

Scripture Reading: 1 Chronicles 3, 4, 5; John 8:1-20

Trivia Question: Who was the third son born to David whose mother's name was Maacah?

May 22

"Light Shine Bright"

John 1:4-5 — In Him was LIFE, and the life was the light of men.
And the LIGHT shineth in darkness, and the darkness comprehended it not.

From the beginning of time, there was light and darkness. God always put a distinction between the two. Genesis 1:4, "And God saw the light, that it was good, and God divided the light from the darkness." Jesus said Himself, "I am the light of the world, he that followeth me shall not walk in darkness, but shall have the light of life." (John 8:12)

Those that follow Jesus need not ever walk in darkness again. His light shines bright into any dark area of life. No matter how dark it gets, the darkness cannot overcome the brightness of His light! If you ever walked into a completely dark room and light one single match, all attention goes to the light the match gives off. All the darkness in that room cannot overcome or extinguish that one light.

When Jesus' disciples were in a storm, in a boat on the Sea of Galilee, the darkness of fear gripped their heart. (Matthew 14:22-33) The Bible says in the fourth watch (between 3:00 a.m. and 6:00 a.m.), probably the darkest part of the night, Jesus came to them walking on the water.

During their darkest hour, both literally and emotionally, Jesus, the light of the world came to them! Jesus said, "Be of good cheer, it is I, be not afraid." (Matthew 14:27) In other words, Jesus was saying, "No matter how dark it is, my light will overcome and triumph over it for you!"

Jesus is also our life! He said, "I am the way, the truth, and the LIFE."

(John 14:6) Jesus said, "I come that they might have life, and that they might have it more abundantly." (John 10:10) Only Jesus can give you the full, abundant life that you desire. Only His life that He offers us is worth longing for! Light is who Jesus is. Life is what Jesus gives. His life also becomes our light. "And the life was the light of men." (John 1:4) You cannot have His life without His light!

Today, choose to walk in His light, and let it dispel all the darkness and live the abundant life that comes with walking with the true light of the world.

Scripture Reading: 1 Chronicles 6, 7; John 8:21-36

Trivia Question: Who was imprisoned with Paul at Macedonia?

May 23

"Divine Promotion"

Psalms 75:6-7 — For promotion cometh neither from the east, nor from the west, nor from the south. But God is the judge; he putteth down one, and setteth up another.

One of the greatest examples of God's promotion is portrayed in the life of Philip. The mention of Philip first appears in Acts 6. The widows were being neglected in the daily ministration. The apostles realized they could not leave the prayer altar, and the ministry of the word to serve tables. Not that serving tables was beneath them, but they understood their call to be spiritual more than temporal. After looking to the Lord, they received the direction to appoint seven men with godly character and Holy Spirit anointing to serve their widows' temporal needs. Philip was one of the godly men that were chosen.

Our next look at Philip is a couple of chapters later in Acts 8. God calls Philip to the region of Samaria, to preach Christ unto the Samaritans. The people in that area responded to Philip's preaching and many got saved, healed, delivered and set free by the power of God. Philip received promotion from God. Philip elevated from a deacon in Acts 6 to a preacher sent to a region with a miracle ministry. In Acts 8, after divine instruction from the Lord, Philip ministers to an Ethiopian man. Philip leads the man to Christ, baptizes him in water, and experiences divine transportation that few have ever encountered. "The Spirit of the Lord caught away

Philip." (Acts 8:39) From a deacon, to a preacher, to being translated, God promoted Philip because of his obedience, faithfulness, and servant's heart.

In Acts 21, Paul and his company met up with Philip in his hometown of Caesarea. Philip was now referred to as Philip the Evangelist (one of the five-fold ministry offices) as a result of his faithfulness and heart before God. (Ephesians 4:11) The Bible also says Philip had four daughters who served God with a prophetic ministry. Wow! Imagine the fantastic promotion in Philip's life. There is nothing greater than to have your family serving the Lord and being used of God in His service! It doesn't get better than that.

Philip was constantly promoted by God; from a deacon, to a Gospel preacher, to a five-fold minister (Evangelist), to a successful husband and father who joyfully watched his children serve God.

Beloved, God does not promote us because of gifting or talent. God promotes His people because they have proven faithful. Are you being faithful to the Lord and maintaining a servant's heart? If you are, you are a candidate for God's promotion in your life!

Scripture Reading: 1 Chronicles 8, 9, 10; John 8:37-59

Trivia Question: Who was David's first wife?

May 24

"Become a Vessel"

2 Timothy 2:20 — But in a great house there are not only vessels of gold and of sliver, but also of wood and of earth; and some to honour, and some to dishonour.

The great house that Paul is talking about is the house of God. The Psalmist said "I had rather be a doorkeeper in the house of my God, than to dwell in the tents of wickedness." (Psalm 84:10)

People are vessels. Vessels are to be filled and then spilled out. You and I are vessels for God. In the house of God there are vessels of gold and silver, but also of wood and earth (clay).

The Bible says some vessels bring honor and some dishonor. Paul is not talking about Christians and non-Christians. The great house is filled with different vessels, but all are saints of God.

Believers will be tried by fire, and their faith will be on trial. (1 Peter 1:7 and 1 Peter 4:12) The fire of God is intended to burn out all the dross, impurities and chaff out of our lives. Christians that are compared to the gold and silver vessels are disciples of Christ that have gladly received the baptism of fire of God's Spirit to purify them. Gold and silver, when under extreme heat, becomes more pure and valuable. Christians that are compared to the vessels of wood and clay, because they are of the earth, burn up and no longer can be filled and spilled out for God! Paul said, "If a man, therefore, purge himself from these, he shall be a vessel unto honor, sanctified, and fit for the master's use, and prepared unto every good work." (2 Timothy 2:21)

God wants His vessels sanctified—set apart as holy for His service. He wants His vessels prepared and spiritually fit–exercising faith with a steady diet on the Word of God. Vessels that are sanctified, fit, and prepared become vessels of honor, filled to overflowing with the glory of God, for the purpose of touching lives for Jesus!

Scripture Reading: 1 Chronicles 11, 12, 13; John 9:1-23

Trivia Question: Under what age did Herod order all the children to be killed?

May 25

"Spirit, Soul and Body"

1 Thessalonians 5:23 — And the very God of peace sanctify you wholly; and I pray God your whole spirit and soul and body be preserved blameless unto the coming of our Lord Jesus Christ."

We must understand that we are triune beings. God made man with three dimensions. We are spirit beings, we possess a soul, and we live in a body. We must train and discipline all three areas if we are going to be overcomers and walk in freedom and victory in Christ.

First, we are spirit beings. The Bible says in Genesis 1:26, "And God said, Let us make man in our image, after our likeness." "God is a spirit, and they that worship Him must worship Him in spirit and in truth." (John 4:24) Since God is a spirit, and we are made in His image and likeness, then we too are spirit beings. Job 32:8, "But there is a spirit in man."

The real you is a spirit. In our spirits, (not the Holy Spirit, but our human spirit) we commune with God, worship Him and hide His Word. David said in Psalm 119:11, "Thy word have I hidden in my heart, that I might not sin against thee."

The words heart and spirit can be used interchangeably in the Bible. David was saying that He meditated on the Word of God, and consequently, it went deep into his spirit! How important it is to get the Word on the inside of us; to fill our hearts with the Truth of God.

Paul called the human spirit the inward man (2 Corinthians 4:16) and Peter called the spirit of man the hidden man of the heart. Whatever you refer to, the heart, the inward man, the hidden man of the heart, they all speak of the spirit of man. Paul said, "For what man knoweth the things of a man, except the spirit of man which is in him?" (1 Corinthians 2:11)

As Christians we must meditate on God's Word. (Joshua 1:8, Psalms 1:1-3, Psalm 4:4) As we engraft God's Word into our spirits, we start training our hearts to go after Him. The spirit of man must dominate his/her walk with God. Paul said, "For God is my witness, whom I serve with my spirit in the Gospel of his Son, that without ceasing I make mention of you always in my prayers." (Romans 1:9) When we serve God with our spirits, then our souls and our bodies follow along. In 1 Thessalonians 5:23, Paul listed the spirit, soul, and body in the order of importance. We must not be fleshed ruled, but heart ruled! Hiding the Word in your heart will transition you from being flesh ruled to heart ruled, from carnality to spirituality. Imprint God's Holy Word on your spirit today and every day!

Scripture Reading: 1 Chronicles 14, 15, 16; John 9:24-41

Trivia Question: How many times did Paul beseech the Lord for his thorn in the flesh?

May 26

"Renew Your Mind"

1 Thessalonians 5:23 — And the very God of peace sanctify you wholly; and I pray God your whole spirit, soul, and body be preserved blameless unto the coming of our Lord Jesus Christ.

As a threefold dimensional being, the soul is the part of man that makes up the mind, will, intellect, and emotions. Unlike the spirit of man, which upon conversion is quickened and changed, the soul must go through a process of change and renovation. In Romans 12:2, Paul talks about being "transformed by the renewing of your mind." The soul or mind must be renewed. Meditation and study of God's Word will renew the mind so that we will have "God thoughts" instead of carnal or natural thoughts.

Paul spoke about the natural man in 1 Corinthians 2:14. Paul states, "the natural man does not receive the things of the Spirit of God, for they seem foolish to him, neither can he understand spiritual things, for they are spiritually discerned." In the original language, the natural man speaks of the soul or mind that is not renewed. Failure to renew the soul or mind will cause individuals to always think naturally, not spiritually. Natural-minded Christians cannot grasp the spiritual truths of God's Word. They will side with the sensual realm. The natural mind says, "seeing is believing," but the Word of God says, "believing is seeing." (Mark 11:24)

David said in Psalms 42:11 "Why art thou cast down, O my soul?" When we decline to renew our mind in the Word of God, and allow God to encourage us through His Word, we will experience discouragement, depression, dejection, and disheartenment. Our souls become cast down. It is mandatory that we take time in God's Word to renew our minds and restore our souls. A metamorphosis takes place when we renew our minds in the Word of God. May our prayer be, "Give us this day our daily bread."

Scripture Reading: 1 Chronicles 17, 18, 19; John 10:1-21

Trivia Question: How many characters from the Old Testament were on the Mount of Transfiguration?

May 27

"Dead and Alive"

Romans 12:1 — I beseech you therefore, brethren, by the mercies of God, that ye present your bodies a living sacrifice, holy, acceptable unto God, which is your reasonable service.

Presenting our bodies as a living sacrifice sounds paradoxical. How could something alive be dead? Well, when it comes to our walk with the Lord, we need to understand that this is not only possible, but mandatory.

We are called to be alive unto God, "And you hath He MADE ALIVE who were dead in trespasses and sins." (Ephesians 2:1) The Bible also teaches that we are crucified with Christ! (Galatians 2:20) Are we alive or dead? The answer is both. Our spirits are alive and quickened by the Holy Spirit through new birth, but our bodies need to be crucified with Christ. We are called to present our bodies a living sacrifice. The flesh, with all its affections and lusts, needs to be put under and mortified. The spirit of man needs to be alive and vibrant, ready to do God's will daily.

Sacrifices in the Old Testament were animals that were slain and then presented to God in worship and service. We are to present ourselves to God on His altar, very much dead to sin, but alive unto God and His righteousness.

As we present ourselves to God, we are saying to Him, "Here I am Lord, I am ready and available for your service, and my flesh will not stand in the way of fulfilling your will."

Our lives must be pleasing unto the Lord. The Lord never accepted an animal sacrifice that had a blemish. We must be holy, so we can be acceptable unto God! Next time you hear the words "living sacrifice," remember it speaks of you—the child of God who has learned to mortify the deeds of the flesh, and has lived a life alive unto God for His pleasure and service. Beloved, present your bodies a living sacrifice daily to the Lord and allow His Holy Spirit to work in and through you.

Scripture Reading: 1 Chronicles 20, 21, 22; John 10:22-42

Trivia Question: Joseph and his wife Asenath had how many children?

May 28

"Bad Kind of Pride"

Ezekiel 16:49 — Behold, this was the iniquity of thy sister, Sodom: pride, fullness of bread, and abundance of idleness were in her and in her daughters, neither did she strengthen the hand of the poor and needy.

When we mention the name of those twin cities of Sodom and Gomorrah, immediately what comes to mind is how God destroyed these cities and the inhabitants thereof, because of gross immorality. This is absolutely true, but this passage from Ezekiel brings out four other main sins that dominated the people of Sodom.

The first transgression that is mentioned in this portion of Scripture concerning the iniquity of Sodom is the sin of PRIDE!

Pride is an archenemy to our relationship with God. The Bible says, "Everyone who is proud in heart is an abomination to the Lord." (Proverbs 16:5) The end of the road for the prideful is disaster. "Pride goeth before destruction and a haughty spirit before a fall." (Proverbs 16:18) Pride was the sin that caused Lucifer (later known as Satan) to rebel against Almighty God, causing the Lord to kick him out of Heaven. (Isaiah 14:12-17)

Pride is akin to evil and arrogance, and opposes God, His Righteousness and the fear of the Lord. (Proverbs 8:13)

People that walk in pride are concerned about themselves. It is all about the I in PRIDE. In a day when God's grace is so desperately needed, and He desires to lavish it upon us, the sin of pride will keep God's grace from manifesting to our lives. The Lord opposes the proud in heart, but gives His grace (strength and sufficiency) to the humble in heart. "But he giveth more grace wherefore He saith, God resisteth the proud, but giveth grace unto the humble." (James 4:6) We all need God's favor and blessing in our lives. We would be foolish to remain in pride knowing that God resists the prideful.

The opposite of pride is humility. Humility is what Jesus taught and exemplified. Jesus said "Take my yoke upon you, and learn of me, for I am meek and lowly in heart, and ye shall find rest unto your souls." (Matthew 11:29) When we humble ourselves in the eyes of the Lord and array ourselves with humility, God elevates and promotes our lives. "Humble yourselves in the sight of the Lord, and He shall lift you up." (James 4:10) A good definition of pride is to trust in YOU.

There is a parable that Jesus taught contrasting two different individuals, with two very distinct attitudes. One was full of pride and the other humble. (Luke 18:9-14) Jesus addressed this teaching to certain people who trusted in themselves and were self-righteous. The first man was a Pharisee and the other a notable sinner. The Pharisee prayed to the Lord and rehearsed all his accomplishments and achievements in his life; putting down others so he would be the only one seen. Four times the Pharisee used "I."

As the other man prayed, he simply recognized his shortcomings and sins and cried out to God for mercy. He prayed, "God be merciful to me a sinner."

Jesus said, "I tell you, this man went down to his house justified rather than the other; for everyone that exalteth himself shall be abased; and he that humbleth himself shall be exalted." (Luke 18:14)

As we humble ourselves before the Lord, He will exalt us. Let us get all pride out of our lives today. Let nothing curtail or impede your relationship with your Lord!

Scripture Reading: 1 Chronicles 23, 24, 25; John 11:1-17

Trivia Question: What is the fourth commandment?

May 29

"You Gotta Give it Away"

Ezekiel 16:49 — Behold, this was the iniquity of thy sister, Sodom: pride, fullness of bread, and abundance of idleness were in her and in her daughters, neither did she strengthen the hand of the poor and needy.

The second iniquity that was found in Sodom was "fullness of bread." We can take two approaches when looking at this term. Both Isaiah 22:13 and 1 Corinthians 15:32 says, "Let us eat and drink, for tomorrow we shall die." Fullness of bread suggests that the people of Sodom, like many others, are only concerned about temporal things in life. Serving the Lord and fulfilling destiny is not priority for those who want to "live it up today, for tomorrow we die!" Paul wrote in Philippians 3:19 "Whose end is destruction, whose God is their belly (appetite), and whose glory is in their shame, who mind earthly things."

Perhaps the greater meaning of "fullness of bread" is the overwhelming abundance of revelation of the Word of God that we have obtained. Jesus said, "I am the bread of life." (John 6:48) He spoke, "Give us this day our daily bread." (Luke 11:3) Bread speaks of the Word of God. You might ask, "What is wrong, if bread speaks of the Word of God, of having 'fullness of bread?'" Nothing, unless you are full of the Word and NOT giving it out! The Bible teaches, "Freely you have received, freely give it away."(Matthew 10:8) "To much is given, much is required." (Luke 12:48)

In America and other areas of the world, there is an abundance of revelation in the Word of God. The Lord has given truth from His Holy Bible. Many of God's people just get *fat* on all of His goodness, revelation and inspirational preaching of the Gospel. Freely we have received; freely we must give it away! God never intended us to be spiritual gluttons. God's design is not for His people to get "heavy revies" (revelations), and not share those precious truths with friends, relatives, loved ones, classmates, co-workers, and the lost. We cannot be indicted like Sodom with the charge of "you have fullness of bread." We must receive our daily bread from the Lord, and then turn around and give some to others. Give and it shall be given unto you.

Let's be full of the Word of God, and also commit to the Lord that we will be faithful to give it away, and not hoard it. Many of us have been truly abundantly blessed; let's not keep it to ourselves!

Scripture Reading: 1 Chronicles 26, 27; John 11:18-46

Trivia Question: Name the first man to ever experience fear in the Bible?

May 30

"Idle Silence"

Ezekiel 16:49 — Behold, this was the iniquity of thy sister, Sodom: pride, fullness of bread, and abundance of idleness were in her and in her daughters, neither did she strengthen the hand of the poor and needy.

The third predominant sin Sodom was indicted with was the sin of "abundance of idleness." This is an interesting term, and at first glance, laziness or slothfulness comes to mind. Were the Sodomites lazy people? Was their slothfulness the cause of God's wrath being poured out? In a sense, yes! The word idleness in the original language denotes, to rest or repose. It means to be quiet, still or settled. You see, the inhabitants of Sodom kept silent and quiet in the midst of vile, repugnant and depraved sin that was going on in their city. Instead of a remnant of people rising up to speak against the wickedness and the heinousness of sin that was rampant in their city, they took a passive, quiet approach and sat idly by the wayside. Such a response is an abomination to the Lord and invokes his anger and wrath upon a people and their ungodly culture.

We too, as God's people have been silent too long! It is time for us to rise up with holy, bold, righteous indignation. We need to speak out and respond to our culture that has transgressed God's laws, rebelled against God's ways, and is ignorant to God's Word! The time for action is now. A passive or silent response is really saying to God that we are not concerned with the spiritual climate of our day. It is saying that we are content with our sub-Christian culture and plan to do nothing about it. That type of Christian has settled into the deteriorated, decadence of the immoral sin that has pervaded and permeated our communities and culture. Replace abundance of idleness with aggressive passion. We must target the issues that are bringing our family, loved ones, and friends into the oppression of our culture. The Bible says in Proverbs 14:34 "Righteousness exalts a nation, but sin is a reproach to any people." God help us, during these perilous days to "Abhor that which is evil, and cling to that which is good." (Romans 12:9) God will exalt us and this nation once again if righteousness prevails and godly men and women do not stay silent or idle. Let's be true ambassadors for the Lord Jesus Christ!

Scripture Reading: 1 Chronicles 28, 29; John 11:47-57

Trivia Question: What was the location where Paul lost his sight?

May 31

"Heart for the Poor"

Ezekiel 16:49 — Behold, this was the iniquity of thy sister, Sodom: pride, fullness of bread, and abundance of idleness were in her and in her daughters, neither did she strengthen the hand of the poor and needy.

The fourth sin that indicted Sodom was failure to minister and care for the poor and needy. There is something that will always touch the heart of God, concerning the cry of the poor. Jesus said, "For ye have the poor always with you." (Matthew 26:11)

God is for the underdog! The Lord loves the poor and needy. People will befriend others who have affluence to get something out of the relationship, but the poor and needy cannot offer that. "The poor is hated even by his own neighbor, but the rich hath many friends." (Proverbs 14:20)

In many cultures, like Sodom, the citizens looked down upon those that were less fortunate, or those that were unproductive. When there is a lack of respect for an individual because of lack of finances, and contempt toward his impoverished ways, it will lead to a condescending attitude. "Whoso mocketh the poor, reproacheth his maker." (Proverbs 17:5) To mock the poor and the needy is to attack God and His character.

There must be an outreach to the poor and needy. There must be a response to their cry. There must be a display of compassion by God's people toward those who are destitute and in despair. "Whoso stoppeth his ears at the cry of the poor, he also shall cry himself, but shall not be heard." (Proverbs 21:13)

A giver to the poor and needy, or one who sows alms will never lack. Alms, (those that minister to the poor) are to be done in secret, but are rewarded openly. (Matthew 6:2-4)

In actuality, when you and I strengthen the hand of the needy and poor, have pity on and minister to them, it is like lending to the Lord. The Lord always pays back, and will be indebted to no one! "He that hath pity on the poor lendeth unto the Lord, and that which he hath given will He (God) pay him again." (Proverbs 19:17)

Let us care for those less fortunate, and have pity upon the poor. We must put some action to our faith. Our faith must be motivated by compassion and love. James 2:14-17 says, "What doth it profit, my brethen, though a man say he hath faith, and have not works? Can faith save him? If a brother or sister be naked, and destitute of daily food, and one of you say unto them, depart in peace, be ye warmed and filled; notwithstanding, ye give them not those things which are needful to the body, what doth it profit? Even so faith, if it hath not works, is dead, being alone." A good place to start a ministry to those in need is your own family. "But if any provide not for his own, and especially for those of his own house, he hath denied the faith, and is worse than any infidel." (1 Timothy 5:8)

Let us all strengthen the hand of the poor and needy; it will be like ministering to Jesus, Himself. Jesus said, "Inasmuch as ye have done it unto one of the least of these my brethren, ye have done it unto me." (Matthew 25:40)

Scripture Reading: 2 Chronicles 1, 2, 3; John 12:1-19

Trivia Question: Why couldn't David build the temple?

June

June 1

"Return your Heart"

1 Samuel 7:2 — And it came to pass, while the ark abode in Kiriath-Jearim,
that the time was long; for it was twenty years:
and all the house of Israel lamented after the Lord.

What a sad time in Israel's history. They had been through devastation, loss of lives and humiliation caused by their enemy. Years before the Philistines defeated Israel in battle, Hophni and Phineas (the sons of Eli) were killed, the high priest and thirty thousand soldiers fell and were smitten, and most importantly, the ark of God was taken. What heartache people incur when they turn from the Lord!

During this time, God spoke to Israel through the prophet Samuel and said, "If ye do return unto the Lord with all your hearts, and put away the foreign gods, and prepare your hearts unto the Lord, and serve Him only, He will deliver you out of the hand of the Philistines (the enemy)." (1 Samuel 7:3)

What a gracious, merciful God we serve! He says, "Return to me, repent of your sin, refrain from serving the false god, refire your heart for me, refocus your affections only on me, and I will deliver you from the enemy!" What a great God!

Beloved, there are times in our lives when tragedy, misfortune, adversity, or the tough circumstances that we face have an adverse effect on our spiritual lives. We lose the joy of the Lord and gravitate to other gods. The presence of the Lord has seemingly been stolen from us, and we feel destitute and in despair. Have you ever felt far away from the Lord? Have you ever been oppressed by the enemy and lived in a constant state of lamentation?

The good news is that the Lord hears the cry of His people and will draw near to those who are of a broken heart. He saves such as be of a contrite spirit. (Psalms 34:18)

God will turn your grief into joy and replace the oppression with His overwhelming love and forgiveness. His presence will be strong in your life once again, and His joy will be your strength. Serve the Lord in gladness, and serve Him with all your heart, today, tomorrow and always!

Scripture Reading: 2 Chronicles 4, 5, 6; John 12:20-50

Trivia Question: What was the charge made by the high priest of the Sanhedrin against Jesus?

June 2

"Believer vs. Disciple"

*John 8:31 — Then said Jesus to those Jews which believed on him,
If ye continue in my word, then are ye my disciples indeed.*

We must transition from believers to disciples. A believer is what we call ourselves because we have put our trust in Christ. Being a believer is the first phase of Christianity and our walk with the Lord. Believers have faith, trust, and are sure that Jesus is savior. This is very important and the beginning of our journey with Him. The word "believers" is found only two times in the New Testament. As we continue in His Word, we transition from being only a believer to being a true disciple of Christ. The word "disciple" is found over two hundred and fifty times in the New Testament. Believers believe, but disciples follow, and therefore enter a greater relationship with Jesus.

Jesus said the key to being a true disciple, or a "disciple indeed," is to continue in His Word. John 8:31 (Wuest Translation) says, "As for you, if you remain in the word which is mine, truly my disciples you are." The word remain is a Greek word, which means to stay, abide, dwell, endure, be present, and to stand.

If we are to become true disciples of Jesus and follow Him and His ways, we need to have a constant infusion of the Word of God in our lives. We must abide and dwell in the Word of God daily! Jesus said, "If you abide (same Greek word is used here) in me, and my words abide in you, you shall ask what you will, and it shall be done unto you." (John 15:7)

Like never before, Christians need to be remaining, continuing and abiding in the Word of God. It will transition us from being just believers into being strong, unwavering disciples of Christ. Are you ready for God

152

to give you a spiritual metamorphosis? The key is continuing in His Word!

Scripture Reading: 2 Chronicles 7, 8, 9; John 13:1-17

Trivia Question: How did Solomon solve the child dispute between the two harlots?

June 3

"Know Truth"

John 8:32 — And ye shall know the truth, and the truth shall make you free.

One translation of this verse says, "And you shall know the truth in an experiential way, and the truth shall make you free." We understand that the "truth" in this passage speaks of the holy, infallible, indisputable, inerrant Word of God! Jesus said in His high-priestly intercessory prayer, "Sanctify them through thy TRUTH, thy WORD IS TRUTH." (John 17:17)

We must not only understand the truth, or study the truth, or even memorize the truth, but also experience the truth that has the power to make us free! The word "know" in this passage of Scripture means, to be aware of, to feel, to perceive, to be resolved, to be sure, to recognize. The verb is also used to convey the thought of connection or union, as between a husband and wife. Thus, the word "know" denotes intimacy and interaction between the Word of God and us. The same Greek word was used when Mary questioned the angel, "How shall this be, seeing I know not a man?" (Luke 1:34) So we conclude, it is not just the truth that will make you free, but knowing (experiencing, feeling, understanding, being sure, and intimately interacting with) the truth that makes you free!

The word "know" also suggests progress in knowledge. In other words, as Christians passionately, progressively embrace the truth of the Word of God, they grow in knowledge of His truth day by day. Just as in a marriage, as you spend quality social and intimate time with your spouse, your love and your understanding for each other grows. Paul wrote, "That I may know Him, and the power of His resurrection, and the fellowship of His sufferings, being made conformable unto His death..." (Philippians 3:10) Paul was saying, in essence, that he was growing day by day in the knowledge of the Son of God and the truth of Christ's Holy Word.

Scripture Reading: 2 Chronicles 10, 11, 12; John 13:18-38

Trivia Question: Who preached in a valley of dead men's bones?

June 4

"Your Sin Will Find You Out"

Numbers 32:23 — But if ye will not do so,
behold, ye have sinned against the Lord: and be sure your sin will find you out.

Though King David was a blessed man, had riches and honor, armies and fame, he made a terrible choice one evening and sinned greatly before the Lord. David decided to inquire about a woman who he saw bathing while he was taking a stroll on his rooftop. The lust of the eyes got the best of him and he proceeded to summon the beautiful woman to his chambers. David was informed that Bathsheba was a married woman, but still decided to pursue her. The pride of life was overwhelming in David's life. Instead of sending her back home after being told Bathsheba was another man's woman, David chose to flex his kingly muscles, have an attitude that seemed to say, "I am the king and can have anything or anyone I desire," and take the woman and commit the horrific sin of adultery. The lust of the flesh, the lust of the eyes and the pride of life enveloped David, as the sweet psalmist of Israel sinned greatly before God.

David decided to compound his sin, and after being told Bathsheba was pregnant with his child, David through deceit and deception brought Uriah, the husband of Bathsheba back home from the battlefield, hoping Uriah would spend time at home and spend intimate time with his wife. Uriah, who acted much more honorable than the king, did not go into his own house and said to David, "The ark, and Israel, and Judah abide in tents; and *my* lord, Joab, and the servants *of my* lord, are encamped in the open fields. Shall I, then, go into mine house, to eat and to drink, and to lie with *my* wife? As thou livest, and as thy soul liveth, I will not do this thing." (2 Samuel 11:11)

David, still bent on getting Uriah to be with Bathsheba, thought Uriah would weaken in his convictions by getting him drunk, but still to no avail did David convince Uriah to go into his home to be with Bathsheba. Finally, running out of schemes and diabolical plans, David ordered Uriah back to the battle to front-line duty and made sure during the heat of the

154

battle that Uriah would die from a war wound. Sure enough, it happened! Uriah died and David took Bathsheba as his own wife and thought they would live happily ever after. NOT! God sent a prophet to David several months later with a divine message, "Your sin will find you out!"

Scripture Reading: 2 Chronicles 13, 14, 15, 16; John 14

Trivia Question: What is the name of David's handsome son?

June 5

"True Repentance"

2 Samuel 12:7 — And Nathan said to David, "Thou art the man.
Thus saith the Lord God of Israel. I anointed thee king over Israel,
and I delivered thee out of the hand of Saul."

After David sinned with Bathsheba and his sin found him out, the prophet Nathan strongly rebuked David for his transgression. David must have thought that, after Uriah had died in the battle and he took Bathsheba as his wife, everything was going to be okay. Time had elapsed and he figured God was in favor of the whole situation.

The Lord sent his messenger, the prophet Nathan, to confront David with his sin. Nathan's approach was in the form of a parable about a rich man and a poor man. The rich man had much in flocks and herds. The poor man had little—just one little lamb that he treated like one of his family members. Nathan told David that a traveler came by the rich man's house, but the rich man was not willing to give the traveler a meal from his own supply of livestock. The rich man, by force, took the one little ewe lamb from the poor man, killed it, and prepared a meal for the stranger.

When David heard this story, he was filled with wrath and harshly proclaimed, "As the Lord lives, the man who has done this thing shall surely die, and he shall restore the lamb fourfold, because he did this thing, and because he had no pity." (2 Samuel 12:5-6)

How surprised David was when Nathan pointed his prophetic finger and revealed the rich man in the parable was really David, regarding the sin he committed against Uriah and Bathsheba. Sometimes, because we do not see immediate consequences to our sin or do not experience judgment right away, we conclude that everything is fine. God is always in the mercy mode and will give us time to repent! If repentance does not come from us,

155

we can be sure God will get our attention one way or the other. We will be responsible and accountable for our actions. David paid a great price for his sin. There was strife and rebellion in his own house after that with one of his sons, Absalom. The child he had with Bathsheba died, and David went through great heartache and grief.

The Bible says, "For if we would judge ourselves, we should not be judged (by God)." (1 Corinthians 11:31) We must examine our own hearts and judge ourselves and repent if need be, so that God's forgiveness can flow and mercy can be applied. There is a great difference between genuine remorse, sorrow, and repentance for the sin we commit compared to just getting caught!

Scripture Reading: 2 Chronicles 17, 18, 19; John 15

Trivia Question: Proverbs 3:6 says, if we acknowledge God in all our ways, what will He do?

June 6

"Praise God in the Storm"

1 Samuel 30:6 — And David was greatly distressed; for the people spake of stoning him, because the soul of all the people was grieved, every man for his sons and for his daughters. But David encouraged himself in the Lord, his God.

David went through a very difficult time. He had been on the run from King Saul, because Saul sought his life due to envy and jealousy. Saul knew that God had rejected him as king because of his disobedience to the Lord. (Saul had wrongly intruded into the priest's office, disobeyed God by not destroying King Agag and all the Amalekites, hunted down David like he was a wild animal, and eventually stooped so low that he consulted a witch for direction in his life). This all added up to utter contempt and defiance of God's will and way, and for his actions, he was rejected by God and the kingship was taken from him.

David was given a city called Ziklag by King Achish of Gath. David found much favor in the king's eyes and he, his family, and all the families of the men who he met and trained up at the cave of Adullam lived in Ziklag. Earlier, David, who was running from the fierce wrath of King Saul, found refuge in a cave. There at the cave of Adullam, David met four hundred men who were distressed, in debt, and discontented. There at Adullam, David became their captain and leader and turned them from men of misery to men of might. They became a part of David's new army—men of valor. Upon returning from a military campaign, David and his men witnessed a frightening sight. Ziklag had been invaded by the Amalekites, all the women and children were taken captive, the city was completely burned with fire, and everything was destroyed. The Bible says that David and his men were so distraught that they wept and wept until they had no more tears. It was a time of deep sorrow and pain for David and his small army of men. Their families were captured, their city and their homes burned, and all their dreams shattered. The Word of God says that David was greatly distressed, and to add insult to his injury, the men that he raised up from misery turned on him and wanted to stone him to death. Oh, how people quickly forget what was done for them. They were so grieved that they wanted to point the finger of blame, and David, their captain and leader, seemed to be the best candidate. The Bible says in the midst of all this sorrow, heartache, pain and false accusations that David encouraged himself in the Lord his God.

Scripture Reading: 2 Chronicles 20, 21, 22; John 16:1-15

Trivia Question: When Jesus rode into Jerusalem on a donkey, what were the people waving at Him?

June 7

"Remember the Good"

1 Samuel 30:6 — And David was greatly distressed; for the people spake of stoning him, because the soul of all the people was grieved, every man for his sons and for his daughters. But David encouraged himself in the Lord, his God.

There are times that we too, like David, will need to encourage ourselves in the Lord. There will be seasons of hardship and pain in our Christian walk, when nobody will be able to minister to us like we need. At these times, we need to encourage ourselves in the Lord. The word "encourage" in the Hebrew, pronounced (khaw-zah), means "to fasten upon, be strong, cure, help, repair, behave valiantly, restrain, to be recovered." We must keep our eyes fastened on the Lord during adverse times in our lives, and be strong in the Lord and in the power of His might!

Two ways that we need to encourage ourselves in the Lord are as follows: First, we must remember the many times that God has come through for us, the many times that He met us in our wilderness and made a way for us, the countless times He healed our hearts and our bodies from pain and hurt. We must recollect how the Lord in times past gave us a miracle in the midst of our misery, gave us His promise in the face of our problem. The Psalmist said in Psalm 119:24, "Thy testimonies also are *my* delight and *my* counselors."

David remembered all the great testimonies that the Lord had given him in times past. Though he was in distress because of what happened in Ziklag and all the loss and devastation that he experienced, David must have remembered all that God did for him in his life up to that point. He remembered when, years before, God delivered the giant Goliath into his hands, the many times he escaped from the fierce anger of Saul when the king made attempts on David's life to kill him, the *many* battles that were won under David's leadership, and the great favor the Lord gave to David in the sight of God and man. These are just a few of the testimonies of the Lord in David's life. They became his delight and counselors!

Beloved, as David encouraged himself in the Lord, his God, we too need to remember what God has done for us in times past. Yesterday's testimonies will encourage us for today's trials and give us hope for tomorrow! His testimonies will counsel us through every test and trial that we are facing today. Take time out and think, ponder, recollect and rehearse what God has done for you. It will encourage *you* right now if *you* are in the midst of a great trial!

Scripture Reading: 2 Chronicles 23, 24, 25; John 16:16-33

Trivia Question: What two chapters in the Bible are almost identical?

June 8

"Keep on Praising"

1 Samuel 30:6 — And David was greatly distressed; for the people spake of stoning him, because the soul of all the people was grieved, every man for his sons and for his daughters. But David encouraged himself in the Lord, his God.

The second way we encourage ourselves in the Lord when we go through tough, hard, and painful times is found in Paul's letter to the church of Ephesus, in Ephesians 5:19 "Speaking to yourselves in psalms and hymns and spiritual songs, singing and making melody in your heart to the Lord."

There is no doubt when David went through his time of distress and discouragement, he engaged himself in something that he did on a daily basis—PRAISING THE LORD! David was called "the sweet psalmist of Israel" (2 Samuel 23:1) and he understood the importance and benefits of praising God in psalms, hymns, and spiritual songs. David knew when he praised the Lord his spirit would be energized and strengthened. David wrote in Psalm 8:2, "Out of the mouth of babes and sucklings hast thou ordained STRENGTH, because of thine enemies, that thou mightest still the enemy and the avenger." In the New Testament, Jesus said, "Out of the mouth of babes and sucklings thou has perfected PRAISE." (Matthew 21:16)

According to these two passages, the words "praise" and "strength" are interchangeable. When we praise God in times of distress and weakness, a supernatural surge of His strength rises up within us to face the challenge at hand. Praise will also still the enemy. The Psalmist wrote, "Let the high praises of God be in their mouth, and a two-edge sword in their hand, to execute vengeance upon the nations, and punishments upon the peoples; to bind their kings with chains, and their nobles with fetters of iron; to execute upon them the judgment written. This honor have all his saints. Praise ye the Lord." (Psalm 149:6-9)

When David went through his great pain and heartache at Ziklag, he practiced what he preached –praise to God! As David praised God with psalms, hymns and spiritual songs, he encouraged himself in the Lord. How about you? Do you need encouragement today? Is your flesh weary, your soul cast down, is your spirit weak? Start to encourage yourself in the Lord by praising God. Speak to yourself in psalms, hymns and spiritual songs, singing and making melody in your heart to the Lord. You will be empowered and encouraged to keep on running the race that has been set before you!

Scripture Reading: 2 Chronicles 26, 27, 28; John 17

Trivia Question: How many years had the lame man by the pool of Bethesda been sick?

June 9

"He Carried Our Grief"

Genesis 37:35 — And all his sons and all his daughters rose up to comfort him; but he refused to be comforted; and he said, For I will go down into the grave unto my son mourning. Thus his father wept for him.

When people experience devastation and suffer great loss, perhaps the death of a loved one, a broken relationship, or even the deep pain of a tragic divorce, the emotional trauma is acute. Jacob experienced overwhelming sorrow when he was shown Joseph's coat of many colors and the testimony of Joseph's brothers that he was dead (they lied about the entire thing).

Mourning is scriptural and biblical. Loved ones mourn for a season over the death of a family member or friend. They mourned the death of the patriarchs of old (Genesis 50:3, Genesis 23:2, and Deuteronomy 34:8). Though the Bible teaches that mourning is proper and may be healthy, the time or season of mourning must come to an end. If not, mourning could turn into grief. When an individual is in grief, they refuse to be comforted. Despair has captured their souls and overwhelming sorrow has gripped their hearts. Though people around Jacob tried to comfort him, he refused. Grief is a horrible place to be. When someone is grief-stricken, they usually shut out everyone around them. Grief-laden people do not receive comfort from loved ones, friends, the Scriptures, or even God Himself. Despair controls their lives and orders their course.

Isaiah the prophet spoke concerning the coming Messiah, Jesus the Christ, about seven hundred years before the birth of Jesus. Isaiah prophesied in Isaiah 53:3-4, "He is despised and rejected of men, a man of sorrows, and acquainted with grief, and we hid as it were our faces from him; he was despised, and we esteemed him not. Surely he hath borne our griefs, and carried our sorrows; yet we did esteem him stricken, smitten of God, and afflicted."

Jesus not only was familiar and identified with grief; the Word of God says that He carried our grief for us, which means, if Jesus carried grief for us, we do not have to do it ourselves. Jesus paid the price for grief. By His stripes we are healed. Our hearts and minds and emotions can be healed from the pain and hurt of grief. When we receive that by faith, His comfort starts flowing, and the healing process begins! Hallelujah! Dear friend, if you are grieving today over a great loss, consider what Jesus has done for

160

you. Allow Him to turn your ashes into beauty, exchange the oil of joy for mourning, and the garment of praise for the spirit of heaviness, so you can be free from grief and go on for Him.

Scripture Reading: 2 Chronicles 29, 30, 31; John 18:1-23

Trivia Question: Where are we instructed to abstain from all appearance of evil?

June 10

"Our Heavenly Father"

2 Corinthians 6:17-18 — Wherefore come out from among them, and be ye separate, saith the Lord, and touch not the unclean thing; and I will receive you. And will be a Father unto you, and ye shall be my sons and daughters, saith the Lord Almighty.

Almighty God wants and even longs to be able to relate to us as our loving heavenly Father. He desires for us to live life with the confidence and assurance of who we are in Christ – manifested sons and daughters of God. However, this will only happen if we cleanse ourselves from all sin (hidden and obvious), rid our life from any fleshly and carnal desires, free ourselves from every habit that will hold us back, and cast off heaviness that tries to weigh us down. You see, our Father knows best! He knows that these things will contaminate our spirits, souls, and bodies. They will hinder us from walking in the authority God has granted to us and inhibit the establishment of His Kingdom on the Earth.

Let us mature in holiness, so that we declare like Jesus did, "I only do those things that please the Father." This will cause His Kingdom to come and His will to be done on Earth as it is in Heaven. True satisfaction, contentment and fulfillment in life only come as we do the will of the Father.

Scripture Reading: 2 Chronicles 32, 33; John 18:24-40

Trivia Question: How many men conspired to kill Paul at Jerusalem, taking a vow not to eat or drink until Paul was killed?

June 11

"Love in Action"

John 3:16 — For God so loved the world that He gave His only begotten Son, that whosoever believes in Him should not perish but have everlasting life.

This is probably the most well-known verse in the New Testament. This verse declares to all humanity the magnitude of God's love. The foundation of the entire plan of God for man, as revealed in the Scriptures, is encapsulated in this passage. God loves us so much that he actually took upon Himself flesh and blood and became a man to live the perfect life we never could. Then, after he fulfilled the righteous requirements of the law, He died for our sins so we could have eternal life. What love! He became sin so that we could become righteous in Him. Love for the world motivates Jesus to reach out to us and save us!

We will only be effective in soul-winning if we allow this same love that Christ has to compel us to reach out and touch someone. The Holy Spirit has impregnated our spirits with love for humanity. However, we must allow the seed of the love of God to germinate into fruit, as we pray for our enemies, do good to those who hate us, and bless those who curse us. As we are moved with compassion (which is God's love in action), we will be able to do the works of Christ and see many saved, healed and delivered by this manifested love of God.

Scripture Reading: 2 Chronicles 34, 35, 36; John 19:1-22

Trivia Question: Who found himself eating with the pigs after detaching from his father and his house?

June 12

"Go"

Matthew 28:18-20 — And Jesus came and spake unto them, saying, "All power is given unto me in Heaven and in earth. Go ye therefore, and teach all nations, baptizing them in the name of the Father, and of the Son, and of the Holy Spirit: Teaching them to observe all things whatsoever I have commanded you: and, lo, I am with you always, even unto the end of the world. Amen."

"GO, GO, GO" should not only be a rally cry at sporting events, but it should be the battle cry of the church as we obey "The Great Commission." We are called to go and make disciples of all nations, and as we do, God will validate His Word with healings, miracles, and wonders. (Mark 16:15-20) Luke 14:23 commands us to go into the highways (public places) and hedges (private places) and compel people to come to Christ.

It is God's heart for your loved ones, friends, neighbors, co-workers, and the people you see every day to come to Christ.

Scripture Reading: Ezra 1, 2; John 19:23-42

Trivia Question: How many yokes of oxen was Elisha plowing the field with when Elijah cast his mantle on him?

June 13

"He is Alive"

Matthew 28:1-7 — After the Sabbath, as the first light of the new week dawned, Mary Magdalene and the other Mary came to keep vigil at the tomb. Suddenly the earth reeled and rocked under their feet as God's angel came down from Heaven, came right up to where they were standing. He rolled back the stone and then sat on it. Shafts of lightning blazed from him. His garments shimmered snow-white. The guards at the tomb were scared to death. They were so frightened, they couldn't move. The angel spoke to the women: "There is nothing to fear here. I know you're looking for Jesus, the One they nailed to the cross. He is not here. He was raised, just as he said. Come and look at the place where he was placed. "Now, get on your way quickly and tell his disciples, 'He is risen from the dead. He is going on ahead of you to Galilee. You will see him there.' That's the message." (MSG)

As Mary sat and watched over the tomb that had Jesus' body lay within, she was forever filled with such longing to see Him again. Would He come back like He said? She could rehearse over and over the scenes in her mind of how they crucified her Christ, and she yearned for His gentle words of life again. Then, all of a sudden, the earth began to quake and the walls around the opening once concealing her Savior were being shaken. The hope and anticipation that was welling up inside her was almost unbearable. Suddenly, a voice beckoned to her the message that was to be told to all the world – Jesus is ALIVE!

Being a Christian means that we have been commissioned to take the message of hope and forgiveness found only in Jesus Christ and bring it to those who are spiritually dead. It is a message that turns people from darkness to light and turns their mourning into dancing. Mary Magdalene could proclaim that message of hope easily because it was so real to her. We too need to allow Jesus Christ to become so real in our life that proclaiming the good news to every living creature and giving him or her hope is a result of a vibrant intimate relationship with our Savior! Jesus is alive. Let us live like we know it and proclaim it like we believe it!

Scripture Reading: Ezra 3, 4, 5; John 20

Trivia Question: What was the result when certain young people acted irreverent and mocked the prophet Elisha?

June 14

"Faithful God"

Deuteronomy 11:13-14 — And it shall come to pass, if ye shall hearken diligently unto my commandments which I command you this day, to love the Lord your God, and to serve him with all your heart and with all your soul, That I will give you the rain of your land in his due season, the first rain and the latter rain, that thou mayest gather in thy corn, and thy wine, and thine oil.

God puts such an importance on faithfulness in the Kingdom of Heaven because it is part of His own very nature. This faithfulness that God has denotes being able to be trusted, relied upon, and able to carry out a command. 1 Corinthians 1:9 says that "God is faithful," and we can rest in knowing that He will watch over His Word to perform every single thing that we believe Him for and make it come to pass, because He is faithful to His promises. He also knows exactly the perfect timing of when you will receive the greatest blessing, making everything beautiful in its time. (Ecclesiastes 3:11)

We also have the perfect example of faithfulness in Jesus. He was faithful to the call of God on His life, at all cost. It was only by the power of the Holy Spirit that Jesus could have completed this enormous mission, and today, because of His obedience, we now have salvation as a result.

As the children of God, we have been given the Holy Spirit to carry out the things we have been asked to do by our heavenly Father. Through prayer, we put a demand on God's faithfulness for Him to carry out His oaths. We also, through our actions, are expected to earnestly obey in order to reap the harvest in our own lives. Let us be more concerned about being faithful to the things that God has entrusted to us, than adhering to our own agendas. 2 Peter 1:4 says that we have been given exceedingly great and precious promises. He will be faithful to bring them to pass. Let us be faithful to Him by aligning ourselves to receive them.

Scripture Reading: Ezra 6, 7, 8; John 21

Trivia Question: How long did the Ark of the Covenant remain in Obed-Edom's house?

June 15

"Revealed"

Luke 10:22 — All things are delivered to me of my Father:
and no man knoweth who the Son is, but the Father;
and who the Father is, but the Son, and he to whom the Son will reveal him.

Prophets, kings, priests and judges of old could only hope for the Messiah to come, rule and reign. People and leaders of Old Testament times never saw the things that you and I are privileged to witness.

Jesus came to Earth to die for our sins and give His life a ransom for all. He came to manifest the Kingdom of God, through preaching the Gospel, healing the sick, raising the dead, casting out devils and cleansing the lepers. He also came to bring a revelation of His Father. Jesus said that His Father delivered all things to Him. He had the mandate to keep those things from the wise and proud and reveal them to the simple and innocent. (Luke 10:21)

The greatest revelation Jesus gives us is an understanding of the Father, His love, character, holiness and plan. The Son has come to reveal the Father to us. May you ask the Son to give you a revelation of our heavenly Father in a greater way today. The Father waits to lavish His love on you right now. Receive the revelation of His greatest attribute –perfect, endless, love. See the Father as Jesus reveals Him to you. "Blessed are the eyes which see the things that ye see." (Luke 10:23)

Scripture Reading: Ezra 9, 10; Acts 1

Trivia Question: Who was the father-in-law of Caiaphas the High Priest?

June 16

"Worthy of Our Worship"

*Matthew 28:17 — When they saw Him,
they worshiped Him; but some doubted.*

This short verse of Scripture is packed with valuable revelation! First, it teaches us that Jesus Christ is Jehovah God, because only Jehovah God is worthy of all our worship, praise, and adoration. The Ten Commandments state that we are to have no other gods before Jehovah and bow down to none other but Him. Jesus would only accept worship if He was God.

Secondly, as the disciples saw Him risen from the dead (just as He said He would), they were overwhelmed knowing that He cannot lie and had fulfilled His promise to them. He then spoke to them and gave them the directive for their future and His plan to advance His Kingdom through them. When you realize that He watches over His Word to perform it in your life, and that all the promises of God (in the Bible) are yes and amen in Christ Jesus, then you will begin to thank Him for His goodness. As you get a greater glimpse of who He is and what He has done for you, awe will fill your heart, causing you to bow prostrate in pure, spontaneous, unadulterated worship! Through your worship, He will flood your heart with His purposes for your life and empower you to fulfill His destiny through you.

Thirdly, notice that there were doubters even in the midst of this historic resurrection scene. If some could dare to doubt His presence when he had walked among them, understand that there will always be those who doubt in and around your life. No matter if you are at church, at home, or on the job, skeptics will be there! You must make a conscientious decision to believe that He is with you, wherever you are, whatever you are going through, because He is the omnipresent, omniscient One. As you praise Him, it will keep you in faith, in fellowship with the Almighty and prevent your feet from slipping into areas you should not go!

Scripture Reading: Nehemiah 1, 2, 3; Acts 2:1-13

Trivia Question: According to Proverbs, where is the king's heart?

June 17

"Faith, Hope, Love"

1 Corinthians 13:13 — And now abideth faith, hope, charity, these three; but the greatest of these is charity.

Let us get back to the basics of our Christian faith. As long as we remain on this Earth, we must always walk by faith, live a life of love, and have hope as an anchor for our souls.

Our walk of faith will enable us to look not at the things of this world, which can make us discouraged, but on the things of God, which will encourage us to serve Him. As we come to the realization of how much God loves us, then we will be able to love Him with all of our heart, soul, mind, and strength. His love will so captivate us that we will be capable of truly loving ourselves. Then His love, which has been poured into our hearts, will emanate out love for others. Our hope in the future return of our Lord and Savior Jesus Christ and His promise to us of our eternal home in Heaven will help to keep our lives in proper perspective. As we continually remind ourselves that our reward is in Heaven, we will daily look for His return, living each day as if Christ's return is imminent.

Scripture Reading: Nehemiah 4, 5, 6; Acts 2:14-47

Trivia Question: How many princes did Darius the King set over his kingdom?

June 18

"Righteousness and Rebirth"

Psalms 85:10 — Mercy and truth are met together; righteousness and peace have kissed each other.

The psalmist gives us insight into the intimacy between righteousness and peace. The Scripture says that they (righteousness and peace) have kissed each other. The word "kissed" means to touch, to be attached, or to be fastened together. The word also implies a military connotation, which means to be equipped with weaponry as an armed soldier.

When we understand the righteousness of God from a biblical teaching, we receive by faith the impartation of God's righteousness through

Christ into our lives. Paul wrote in 2 Corinthians 5:21, "For He has made Him (Christ) to be sin for us, who knew no sin, that we might be made the righteousness of God in Him." What this means simply stated: Though our righteousness is as filthy rags (Isaiah 64:6), the blood of Jesus, through the blood covenant that is understood and appropriated, has washed away our sin, removed our transgression, and placed the born again child of God in right standing with the sovereign of the Universe. This righteousness resulting from the new birth not only gives us right thinking, right believing, and right standing with God, but like an armed soldier, it gives us a weapon that will overcome and defeat Satan at all times.

When Satan comes at you and attempts to attack using condemnation tactics, trying to convince you that you are not loved by God, that you are not saved or forgiven by God, or that you are wretched and undeserving of God's blessings, you must retaliate by using the weapon of God's righteousness. You must tell Satan that he is a liar, and decree and declare that the precious, powerful, efficacious blood of Jesus has made you the righteousness of God in Christ Jesus. You WILL extinguish all those fiery darts of condemnation, guilt and unworthiness. Thank God for the weapon of God's righteousness! Use it and defeat the devil every time.

Scripture Reading: Nehemiah 7, 8; Acts 3

Trivia Question: What two "power twins" give favor and good understanding in the sight of God and men when tied around our necks and written on the tables of our hearts?

June 19

"Fight with Peace"

Psalm 85:10 — Mercy and truth are met together; righteousness and peace have kissed each other.

We talked about God's imparted righteousness to us as a weapon that we use to defeat condemnation, guilt, and unworthiness, but the Psalmist said that righteousness and PEACE have kissed each other. The peace of God can and should also be used as a weapon against the devil.

When Satan uses anxiety, inferiority, terror, and fright against you, the armed soldier of God can attack back with the peace of God. We must decide what will rule our hearts. Will it be anxiety (Philippians 4:6) or the peace of God? (Colossians 3:15)

God desires His absolute peace to rule in and reign over our hearts. Jesus said in John 14:27, "My peace I leave with you, my peace I give unto you: not as the world giveth, give I unto you. Let not your heart be troubled, neither let it be afraid." Isaiah 26:3 says, "Thou wilt keep him in perfect peace, whose mind is stayed on thee, because he trusteth in thee." Jesus who is the prince of peace (Isaiah 9:6) will give you perfect peace in the face of fear as you decree and declare that God's peace rules your heart, even in the midst of peril. The peace of God that passes all understanding keeps your heart and mind (Philippians 4:7) and becomes a weapon against Satan and his fear and terror tactics.

Execute God's righteousness and God's peace as mighty weapons to thwart the enemy's attack and attempt on your life. Righteousness and peace have kissed each other!

Scripture Reading: Nehemiah 9, 10, 11; Acts 4:1-22

Trivia Question: In what month did the angel Gabriel visit Mary in Nazareth?

June 20

"Pray for Leaders"

1 Timothy 2:1-4 — I exhort therefore, that, first of all, supplications, prayers, intercessions, and giving of thanks, be made for all men; For kings, and for all that are in authority; that we may lead a quiet and peaceable life in all godliness and honesty. For this is good and acceptable in the sight of God our Saviour; Who will have all men to be saved, and to come unto the knowledge of the truth.

God is not a respecter of people or nations. His Word is true, and He is the same today, just as He was in biblical times.

2 Chronicles 7:14 gives us the key to repentance and the continual blessing of God for every nation that embraces it. God is waiting for His people, those who love the name of Christ, to humble themselves and pray. He is looking for the church to seek Him for the salvation of our nation. Once we do this, He will then forgive our sins and heal our land. According to the Scripture, it is the Church's prayers that determine the course of our nation. That is why it is imperative for us to pray for every person in a governmental office. Pray that those who do not know God would have a Damascus Road experience like the great Apostle Paul did and humbly

turn to Him. (Acts 9:1-19) Pray that godliness and holiness would govern all the affairs of the country now and forevermore. (Proverbs 14:34)

Scripture Reading: Nehemiah 12, 13; Acts 4:23-37

Trivia Question: How many warnings should be given to a heretic (a person who holds a belief that is different from the truth) before rebuke and rejection?

June 21

"Wait and Expect"

Psalm 27:14 — Wait on the Lord: be of good courage,
and he shall strengthen thine heart: wait, I say, on the Lord.

When we hear the word *wait*, perhaps many things come to mind. *Wait* for some might mean a testing of their patience, others might envision time elapsing from one event to another, still others might see themselves on a street corner anticipating the arrival of a taxi or bus. Though these are all valid and true descriptions of the word wait, in Scripture and particularly this verse, the word we understand as *wait* brings a greater understanding of the Lord and our relationship to Him, especially during the greatest trials of life.

In Psalm 27:14, the word *wait* (pronounced Kaw-Vaw in the Hebrew) means to expect. Our expectation in God must be beyond someone waiting for a taxi or bus. There are circumstances that could cause the taxi driver or bus driver to be tardy or never even arrive. Weather, a detour, accidents, road blocks, and even unfaithfulness on the part of the driver could cause our waiting to be in vain. In these examples, our expectation would end with disappointment, but not when it comes to waiting on God.

Nothing prevents our heavenly Father from making good on His Word! "He watches over His Word to perform it." (Jeremiah 1:12) "My covenant will I not break, nor will I alter the thing that is gone out of my lips." (Psalm 89:34)

"The grass withers, the flower fades, but the word of our God shall stand forever." (Isaiah 40:8)

We can wait on the Lord, expecting Him to be who He says He is and to do what He says He will do. Waiting on the Lord is expectation in the Lord. Nothing holds Him back or prevents Him from making good on His Holy Word.

Trivia Question: When a father walks in integrity, how does that affect his children?

June 22

"One with His Word"

Psalm 27:14 — Wait on the Lord: be of good courage,
and he shall strengthen thine heart: wait, I say, on the Lord.

There is another Hebrew definition for the word *wait* that we need to understand, especially if we are going to be of good courage and allow God to strengthen our hearts during times of great testing and trials. The thought is to be intertwined or bound together with God. Picture in your mind's eye, two wires being twisted together tightly; each one is wrapped around the other, touching each other and becoming like one. It is almost impossible to disconnect them. That is what the word *wait* in Bible language means - me in God and God in me.

God's Word in me and me in His Word. Jesus said in John 15:7, "If ye abide in me, and my words abide in you, ye shall ask what ye will, and it shall be done unto you." Abide means to live in or to be vitally united with Him. When you are waiting on God, you are not idle, passive, complacent or indifferent. You are actively, aggressively going after Jesus and His Word. You are *getting* into His promises, and in turn, His promises are *getting* into you – giving you the faith you need to wait in anticipation of the promise of your Father to come to pass. This understanding on the biblical definition of wait will also renew your strength and cause you to "mount up with wings like eagles." (Isaiah 40:31)

Scripture Reading: Esther 4, 5, 6; Acts 5:17-42

Trivia Question: Before Christ's ascension, in what region did he say disciples would be witnesses for Him by the Spirit's Power?

June 23

"Rock of Ages"

Exodus 33:20-23 — And he said, Thou canst not see my face: for there shall no man see me, and live. And the Lord said, Behold, there is a place by me, and thou shalt stand upon a rock: And it shall come to pass, while my glory passeth by, that I will put thee in a clift of the rock, and will cover thee with my hand while I pass by: And I will take away mine hand, and thou shalt see my back parts: but my face shall not be seen.

Moses had an unusual request, "show me your glory." The Lord responds that He would reveal His goodness, graciousness and mercy. The Lord forbids Moses to see His face, which is reserved for most of us in the splendor of Heaven. God told Moses to stand in the opening of a rock as He passed by and the Lord's hand covered him. God only allowed Moses to see His back.

I believe it is noteworthy that the great Pastor Moses was only allowed to view God's back. On another occasion, we are told that God spoke to Moses face to face. (Exodus 33:11) In this portion of Scripture, Moses had just received the order for the building of the tabernacle, which would be a portable temple for God's presence to meet His people. Moses got everything he needed to construct the tabernacle and resume their journey in pursuit of the Promised Land.

It is imperative as we travel life's journey and continue our walk with God, that we see His back. When we behold God's hinder parts, we are assured He is leading and we are following. The danger of getting ahead of God, which many people do, is much less if we continue to see His back.

Do not get ahead of God. Do not allow impetuousness or your own agenda to take the leading of the Lord out of your life's equation. It is dangerous to lead yourself or get in front of God and His will. Allow God, by His Spirit to lead you. "For as many as are led by the Spirit of God, they are the sons of God." (Romans 8:14)

May you always see the back of God and be assured as He leads you, that you are in a safe, secure and stable place.

Scripture Reading: Esther 7, 8, 9, 10; Acts 6

Trivia Question: What man cast stones at Kind David, cursed at him and called him a bloody man and was allowed to live?

172

June 24

"Grander Thoughts"

Exodus 13:17-18 — And it came to pass, when Pharaoh had let the people go, that God led them not through the way of the land of the Philistines, although that was near; for God said, Lest peradventure the people repent when they see war, and they return to Egypt: But God led the people about, through the way of the wilderness of the Red Sea: and the children of Israel went up harnessed out of the land of Egypt.

When God delivered Israel from the slavery of Egypt after four hundred and thirty years of bondage, one might think that He would take them the quickest and most direct route to the Promised Land of Canaan.

The Bible says God's ways are higher than man's ways, and God's thoughts are not as man's thoughts. (Isaiah 55:8-9)

Consider this: In one minute, light travels 11 million miles. In one day, light travels 160 billion miles. In one year, light travels 5 trillion, 865 billion, 696 million miles! That is just one light-year! The outer edge of the universe, according to astrophysicists, is 15.5 billion light-years away. That is incomprehensible and unfathomable, yet it is true. This is the distance between God's thoughts and our thoughts. We fall short of trying to figure out why God is doing something we do not comprehend or taking us a direction we have not chartered out or calculated. Actually, we fall short 15.5 billion light-years away! God truly is 15.5 billion light-years smarter than us and ahead of us.

The way of the land of the Philistines, geographically speaking, is the closest and most direct route from Goshen in Egypt to the Promised Land, but God took the people of Israel the long and hard journey down the Sinai Peninsula. The Lord knew that His people would not be prepared for the battles that were awaiting them, militarily speaking. Don't forget, they were not trained soldiers, but trained slaves. It takes time for God to teach and train His soldiers. There would be much *boot camp* to come for His people, preparing them to conquer and possess the Promised Land.

Perhaps you cannot figure out or understand the journey God has you on, or the direction He is taking you, but He who knows the end from the beginning, He whose thoughts are 15.5 billion light-years greater than our thoughts, is ordering your steps and taking you out to bring you in—from a slave to a soldier of Christ.

The way may not always be comfortable or pleasant, but it will be the right way as long as the Holy Spirit is leading you. (Romans 8:14)

There is much for you to learn in this wilderness journey so that your life can be used to bring glory to God and much blessing to others. Refuse the temptation of trying to figure everything out that God is leading you to do, rather trust Him with your life.

Scripture Reading: Job 1, 2, 3; Acts 7:1-19

Trivia Question: Who was the bald prophet that 42 young people mocked?

June 25

"Guiding Light"

Psalm 36:9 — For with thee is the fountain of life: in thy light shall we see light.

One of the first things God did after He created the light and saw that it was good, was to divide or separate the light from the darkness. (Genesis 1:3-4)

Light is good. Light leads, darkness limits. Jesus is the light of the world. (John 8:12)

Life has a way of obscuring us from the true light. As we journey in life, there is much we need to know and understand. Who do I marry? What vocation is right for me? Is God calling me into ministry or the mission field? What home should I purchase? Where and what do I invest in? What school should I attend?

Question after question demands an answer because we all want to do what is right, in the perfect will of God, and pleasing to our heavenly Father. God has promised us a "fountain of life." Jesus described it as "abundant life." (John 10:10) The way we receive answers to our questions, direction in life, and leading of the Lord, is to seek Him (Jesus), who is the true light. In Him is life, and the life (abundant life) was the light of men. His is the true light, which lighteth every man that cometh into the world. (John 1:4-9)

In other words, if we purpose in our hearts to seek Him, the true light, in His light, shall we see light. He will illuminate our hearts to His perfect will and direct us by His Holy Spirit. We receive light as we seek and pursue light. His light dispels any obscurity and darkness that keeps us from enjoying His fountain of life, from experiencing abundant life, or from the peace that comes from knowing you are living in His perfect will.

Seek Jesus, for as you seek Him through His Word, He will illuminate you and you shall see light in His light.

Scripture Reading: Job 4, 5, 6; Acts 7:20-43

Trivia Question: How long did David reign as king?

June 26

"Sow Your Seed"

Genesis 8:22 — While the earth remaineth, seedtime and harvest, and cold and heat, and summer and winter, and day and night shall not cease.

There are laws that govern nature, laws that govern physics and laws that govern science. These laws are immutable. They are forever established by God and sealed into the fiber of our existence. Take the law of gravity for example. Even if one would will to defy this law, one jump off a high cliff would convince the gainsayer that the law of gravity is irreversible.

So it is with the law of harvest. This law, also known as the law of increase, has four components to it. If one is to receive a harvest in the area of horticulture or farming, there must be: seed, a sower, soil, and the proper season.

God's law of harvest or increase in all areas works the same. Increase or harvest comes many ways—in the form of relationship blessing, financial blessing, healing or health blessing, even raising godly children blessing.

Here is how the law of harvest works. There first must be the sowing of seed. In a relationship, the seed of love and time must be sown. If one is believing God for a healing harvest, there must be the sowing of the seed of the Word of God. Nothing grows without first starting with a seed. How ridiculous is the thought of a farmer going out to his field, expecting a crop, if he never sowed seed in the field? For every need, one must sow a seed. We could never expect a financial harvest without sowing a seed. God has placed seeds within the fruit, so that there can be a continued harvest in life. As long as we do not eat the seed to be sowed for future harvest, we can have a perpetual harvest. He gives seed to the sower and bread to the eater. (Isaiah 55:10) If the seed that is to be sown is consumed, there will be no bread for the eater.

This is true in every potential harvest. If you have a need for increase in your life, God has placed within you a seed to sow, so you can see the law of harvest work in your life.

"And God said, let the Earth bring forth grass, the herb yielding seed, and the fruit tree yielding fruit after his kind, whose seed is in itself upon the Earth; and it was so." (Genesis 1:11) The seed you need to sow is not far off; it is within you. So start your harvest and sow your seed today. Tomorrow we will look at the second step: time!

Scripture Reading: Job 7, 8, 9; Acts 7:44-60

Trivia Question: What king, at the end of his life, charged his son to be a man?

June 27

"Waiting Time"

Genesis 8:22 — While the earth remaineth, seedtime and harvest, and cold and heat, and summer and winter, and day and night shall not cease.

Planting seed is not difficult. Waiting for a harvest is! Planting seed takes diligence. Waiting for a harvest requires patience and even at times longsuffering. The waiting process of time that elapses between planting the SEED and reaping the HARVEST is a hard place to be. The farmer that plants seed expecting a crop has to be patient before he sees any sign of the fruit of his labor. Patience is vital to reap a harvest in our lives. Many times adversities and challenges rise up in the waiting phase of your harvest. Your faith will be tested if you are to receive any type of blessing, harvest or increase from God!

James 1:3-4 says, "Knowing this, that the trying of your faith worketh patience. But let patience have her perfect work that ye may be perfect (complete) and entire, wanting nothing." (When you receive your increase or harvest, you do not want anymore.)

Just as the farmer has to wait for his harvest after planting seed, so does the child of God need to wait for his/her harvest. "Be patient therefore, brethren, unto the coming of the Lord. Behold, the husbandman waiteth for the precious fruit of the earth, and hath long patience for it, until he receive the early and latter rain. Be ye also patient; establish your hearts: for the coming of the Lord draweth nigh." (James 5:7-8)

You might be thinking, "What do I do, what do I say during this waiting process." The Bible gives us tremendous insight to the answers of both questions. "What do I do while I am waiting?" When Abraham received the promise that God had planted in him, that he was to have a son, he did not realize then that this seed that God planted in him would take twenty-five years to materialize. So what did Abraham do between the planting of the seed (the promise of God) and the harvest (his son being born to him and Sarah)? Abraham worshipped God! "And being not weak in faith, he considered not his own body now dead (he was 75 years old when he received the promise), when he was about one hundred years old, neither yet the deadness of Sarah's womb: He staggered not at the promise of God through unbelief, but was strong in faith, giving glory (worship) to God." (Romans 4:19-20) Abraham worshipped while he waited.

"What do I say while I am waiting?" The answer to that question is found in Hebrews 10:23. "Let us hold fast the profession (confession) of our faith without wavering, for He is faithful that promised." Speak the promise of God over and over again while you're waiting. As we worship God and give Him glory and continually speak and rehearse the promise given to us by God, the waiting or time phase will become more faith-filled as we anticipate the harvest of God. Tomorrow we will look at the third step: Harvest!

Scripture Reading: Job 10, 11, 12; Acts 8:1-25

Trivia Question: Where did the Lord first appear to Solomon?

June 28

"Share the Harvest"

Genesis 8:22 — While the earth remaineth, seedtime and harvest, and cold and heat, and summer and winter, and day and night shall not cease.

Well, it is harvest time! After a farmer breaks up the fallow ground with his plow, the field is ready to plant seed. After the seed has been sown, time takes center stage and the waiting process begins. After proper continual watering, sunlight and care, time continues to elapse.

After the prescribed time according to the laws of agriculture, there are the first signs of true HARVEST! When harvest is manifested, embraced and enjoyed, you almost forget the pain of plowing, the sweat of sowing, and the work of waiting, because harvest has a way of causing all of that to be a dim memory.

The Kingdom of God is like a farmer's harvest. The seed of the Word of God is sown, time elapses as we continue to speak and rehearse the promises of God, always giving God glory in the wait, and then in His impeccable season, His harvest (increase and blessing) come in. Oh, the joy of the goodness and blessings of God when they are manifested in our lives.

This is a kingdom law: seed-time-harvest. Just like the law of gravity cannot be reversed, so also is the law of the harvest—first seed, second time, and third harvest.

What are you believing God for in your life? What harvest are you looking forward to enjoying? Operate in the principles of the Kingdom of God and the law of harvest will happen for you. There must be a sowing of seed, then time and waiting on God, and then seeing and enjoying His harvest that He will bring you.

Remember this: when your harvest appears and you are blessed, it is to be shared with others. Never *eat* all your harvest (blessing), or you will *eat* all your seed. Sow your seed from your harvest to guarantee future harvests in your life! Share the blessing!

Scripture Reading: Job 13, 14, 15; Acts 8:26-40

Trivia Question: Who was the king of Israel that fell down through a lattice in his upper chamber in Samaria?

June 29

"The Good Neighbor"

Luke 10:30-37 — And Jesus answering said, A certain man went down from Jerusalem to Jericho, and fell among thieves, which stripped him of his raiment, and wounded him, and departed, leaving him half dead. And by chance there came down a certain priest that way: and when he saw him, he passed by on the other side. And likewise a Levite, when he was at the place, came and looked on him, and passed by on the other side. But a certain Samaritan, as he journeyed, came where he was: and when he saw him, he had compassion on him, And went to him, and bound up his wounds, pouring in oil and wine, and set him on his own beast, and brought him to an inn, and took care of him. And on the morrow when he departed, he took out two pence, and gave them to the host, and said unto him, Take care of him; and whatsoever thou spendest more, when I come again, I will repay thee. Which now of these three, thinkest thou, was neighbour unto him that fell among the thieves? And he said, He that shewed mercy on him. Then said Jesus unto him, Go, and do thou likewise.

What a wonderful story of compassion and mercy. Sometimes the people that we expect to rise up and respond to a need, do not. There are many people that feel stripped, beat up and left for dead without a hope in the world. Like the man in the parable who lost his money and momentum in life, as he was interrupted by men who robbed him, beat him and left him to fend for himself. There are many people like that today, traveling along life's journey with a dream and a plan only to be hindered by the enemy of lack, poverty, sickness, divorce, emotional pain and crisis of all types. They too feel stripped, beat up and emotionally dead.

The priest and the Levite in the parable offered no help and no hope. God however will always raise up a *good neighbor* with compassion to step out and offer a helping hand. Because God is watching out for you, He will always touch someone's heart to bring mercy to you. From sending someone to pick you up off the ground to minister to your wounds, to giving you an encouraging word during a low point in your life. Let us all strive to be a good neighbor to someone, showing compassion and mercy when needed. Jesus does that for us! May we do that for others and become a good neighbor.

Scripture Reading: Job 16, 17, 18; Acts 9:1-22

Trivia Question: Who was Absalom's counselor?

June 30

"His Spirit, Our Blessing"

Acts 19:1-2 — And it happened, while Apollos was at Corinth, that Paul, having passed through the upper regions, came to Ephesus. And finding some disciples he said to them, "Did you receive the Holy Spirit when you believed?" So they said to him, "We have not so much as heard whether there is a Holy Spirit. (NKJV)

Have you received the Holy Spirit since you believed? God has blessed His children with so many wonderful gifts, but on the top of the list must be the gift of His Holy Spirit. Just the thought that the third person of the Holy Trinity would make His abode in us is unthinkable. Yet He does, when we acknowledge God's gift and desire it.

179

Jesus put it like this, "If a son shall ask bread of any of you that is a father, will he (the earthly father) give him a stone? Or if he asks for a fish, will he for a fish give him a serpent? Or if he (a son) shall ask for an egg will he offer him a scorpion? If you then being evil know how to give good gifts unto your children how much more shall your heavenly Father give the Holy Spirit to them that ask Him?" (Luke 11:11-13)

The gift of the Holy Spirit is for all born again believers, just for the asking! God's Spirit will help us to be the ambassadors and witnesses for Christ that we desire to be. It is not by our power or might, but by His Spirit. (Zechariah 4:6)

We need to be empowered by the Spirit of God for any kind of Christian service. Not relying totally on God's Spirit would result in trusting in self. Self will fail and fall short. The Spirit will always empower believers so that they can glorify God.

Acts 1:8 says, "But ye shall receive power, after that the Holy Spirit is come upon you: and ye shall be witnesses unto me both in Jerusalem, and in all Judaea, and in Samaria, and unto the uttermost parts of the earth."

We could never be the witnesses that God desires us to be, and that we desire to be, without the indwelling presence of God's Spirit.

Are you filled with the Holy Spirit? If not, God is waiting for you to ask Him. Why not ask Him right now! He will give you this precious powerful gift—the Holy Spirit!

Scripture Reading: Job 19, 20; Acts 9:23-43

Trivia Question: What was the initial evident sign that the 120 believers were filled with the Holy Spirit on the day of Pentecost?

July

July 1

"The Lord's Covering"

2 Kings 14:15-19 — Now the rest of the acts of Jehoash which he did, and his might, and how he fought with Amaziah king of Judah, are they not written in the book of the chronicles of the kings of Israel? And Jehoash slept with his fathers, and was buried in Samaria with the kings of Israel; and Jeroboam his son reigned in his stead. And Amaziah the son of Joash king of Judah lived after the death of Jehoash son of Jehoahaz king of Israel fifteen years. And the rest of the acts of Amaziah, are they not written in the book of the chronicles of the kings of Judah? Now they made a conspiracy against him in Jerusalem: and he fled to Lachish; but they sent after him to Lachish, and slew him there.

If you were asked, "What was the greatest sin Israel committed before God?" Would you say adultery, complaining, idolatry, or lust? The Psalmist, as he rehearses and recounts the wilderness journey of God's people, says this amazing statement: "How often did they provoke Him (God) in the wilderness, and grieve Him in the desert? Yea, they turned back and tempted God, and *limited* the Holy One of Israel." (Psalms 78:40-41)

Elisha the prophet is ready to go be with the Lord. The Syrians have been oppressing Israel and threatening to attack again. Joash king of Israel weeps over the dying prophet and Elisha shares his last words directly with the king. Elisha instructs the king to shoot an arrow out of a window, symbolizing a victory over Syria and deliverance from the enemy. Elisha covered the king's hand with his own hand while Joash shot the arrow. The meaning of all this simply is letting the king know that the Lord, the God of Israel is covering His people, leading them by His Spirit, and all it will take to defeat the enemy will be an arrow.

Then Elisha gives a strange command, "Take the arrows (left in the quiver) and strike the ground with those arrows!" Joash takes the remain-

181

ing arrow and smites the ground three times and then stops suddenly. Elisha gets angry with the king and tells him that he should have struck the ground five or six times with the arrows. He tells the king there would be only three triumphs militarily. That is just what happens in 2 Kings 14:25. Syria would continue to be an enemy of Israel in the future.

The king's expectations were too low. Joash needed a bigger revelation of God! Joash was *limiting* the Holy One of Israel. Can you imagine if he struck the arrow ten times? Twenty times? How do you see your God? Do you see Him as Lord over all or limited? Is His promise greater than your problem? How many times will you strike your arrows? Elisha told the king that God would have destroyed and annihilated the enemy completely if he had that type of expectation. How far can our faith take us? What can we believe God for today?

Our God is greater, our God is stronger, our God is high over all! Get your expectation and your faith out there and watch God give you total victory in every area of your life today!

Scripture Reading: Job 21, 22; Acts 10:1-23

Trivia Question: When children are well taught of the Lord, what will they possess?

July 2

"Falling vs. Failing"

*Matthew 11:29 — Take my yoke upon you, and learn of me;
for I am meek and lowly in heart: and ye shall find rest unto your souls.*

What man calls failure, God calls learning. As Christians and followers of Jesus, we may stumble and fall during our journey with Christ. The voice of condemnation will tell us that, in our fallings we are failures, we have displeased God to the point that he is disgusted with us and gives up on us. That is a LIE!

When a toddler is learning how to walk for the first time, (and even beyond that) that child has many encounters with the floor or ground with his/her bottom. The point is, when the child falls down, he or she is not failing, but learning how to walk. As long as that child keeps trying and trusting, they will learn how to walk, then skip, then run, then sprint, and then gain the potential to be a champion.

What we call failing, God calls learning, as long as we keep on getting up again when we fall (trying) and holding on to the hand of Jesus, just like a child would hold on to his/her father's hand (trusting).

Failure is not recognized in Heaven. God sees only a people who FALL from time to time, only to keep *trying* and *trusting*, so we can learn who He is and what He wants us to give back to Him. Keep learning as you keep trying and trusting Him.

Scripture Reading: Job 23, 24, 25; Acts 10:24-48

Trivia Question: How many wives did Solomon's son Rehoboham have?

July 3

"Word Over World"

Mark 4:19 — And the cares of this world, and the deceitfulness of riches, and the lusts of other things entering in, choke the word, and it becometh unfruitful.

Jesus taught in the parable of the sower the concepts of seed, soil, and season (the key to the law of increase). In the parable, the seed is the Word of God and the soil is the condition of your heart.

There are so many distractions that try to entice us away from God and His Word. The world with all its flamboyancy, glitter, glamor, and glory seeks to seduce us into things that displease God while distracting us away from godly things that cause us to please God. The Word of God attracts us to Jesus. The world distracts us away from Jesus.

The Word of God brings us into relationship with the Father, Son, and Holy Spirit, and brings love, peace, joy, and righteousness.

The world brings tribulation (John 16:33), hatred (John 17:14), enmity with God (James 4:4), and the possibility of losing your own soul. (Mark 8:36)

Are there things in your life that are distracting and pulling you away from Jesus and His Kingdom? If yes, then that is the world trying to draw you away from God.

Jesus and His Word are attractive. Choose the Word over the world and live in the peace, promises, and purposes of God today!

Scripture Reading: Job 26, 27, 28; Acts 11

Trivia Question: Who said, "We ought to obey God rather than men"?

July 4

"True Freedom"

John 8:36 — If the Son therefore shall make you free,
ye shall be free indeed.

True freedom is only obtained when we learn to abide in the Word of God. In this passage of Scripture (John 8:31-36), Jesus is talking to believers. He makes a distinction between being a believer and becoming His disciple. The path from believer to disciple (learner under discipline) is walked by those who abide and remain in the Word of God. As you continue to read, meditate, and study the Scriptures, you will gain a more comprehensive and clearer understanding of who God is and what He has done for you. Then, as the eyes of your understanding are enlightened, you will be able to grasp who you are in Christ and what God has for you! This knowledge of God's plan and purpose for your life will liberate you to fulfill your destiny.

Citizens of the United States of America celebrate Independence Day to remember freedoms and liberties. Moreover, as citizens of the Kingdom of Heaven, we should celebrate freedom every day – Christ has set us free! You have been set free from Satan's dominion, sin's punishment and the control of the flesh. So rejoice and walk in the light of your redemption.

Scripture Reading: Job 29, 30; Acts 12

Trivia Question: What does God make our feet like so that He can set us upon the High Places?

July 5

"Patience through Suffering"

Psalm 121:1, 2 — I will lift up mine eyes unto the hills, from whence cometh my help. My help cometh from the LORD, which made Heaven and earth.

The Psalmist David found himself being treated unfairly and unjustly. David was reaping for something that he did not sow. Have you ever been there? Treated like a criminal, when all you tried to do is serve. David was Saul's armor-bearer, anointed musician, and faithful servant, and in return for all that, Saul tried to kill him as he hunted him down like an animal.

(Jealousy was the root cause for Saul's misconduct.)

David wrote, "God is our refuge and strength, a very present help in trouble."

If you find yourself today or in this season of your life being treated unfairly or being paid evil for good, remember the Lord is your refuge and strength. He who is called faithful and true will help you in your time of testing, tears, and trouble. Peter said, "For what glory is it if, when you are buffeted for your faults, you shall take it patiently? But if, when you do well and suffer for it, you take it patiently, this is acceptable with God." (1 Peter 2:20)

Scripture Reading: Job 31, 32; Acts 13:1-23

Trivia Question: According to Paul's letter to Titus, what has appeared to all men?

July 6

"Knowledge from On High"

Proverbs 4:7 — Wisdom is the principal thing; therefore get wisdom: and with all thy getting get understanding.

The Bible calls Jesus "the wisdom of God." (1 Corinthians 1:24b) There is a saying that our culture has coined, "knowledge is power." Natural knowledge or wisdom has its limitations. If you complete the eighth grade, then you have an eighth grade education. If you have completed and graduated high school, then you have a high school education. The wisdom and knowledge the Bible talks about is from above, not from a certain level of education. It is not a part of the academic process of education to higher levels of intellectual learning. It is divine wisdom. The wisdom and knowledge of God cannot be learned in a classroom. The wisdom of God and of Jesus flows from Him to us as we engraft His Word into our spirits through study and meditation, and spending much time with Him in prayer.

James writes, "If any of you lack wisdom, let him ask of God, who gives to all men liberally and upbraideth not, and it shall be given him." (James 1:5)

James was not saying that God would increase your intellect or give you a greater capacity to store more data in your brain. Education is good. God's divine wisdom and counsel is better! Wisdom is the principal thing, therefore get God's wisdom.

Scripture Reading: Job 33, 34; Acts 13:24-52

Trivia Question: How many pillars are in the house that wisdom has built?

July 7

"Stand Under to Understand"

Proverbs 4:7 — Wisdom is the principal thing; therefore get wisdom: and with all thy getting get understanding.

What is godly understanding? The best way we can define God's understanding is: the ability to execute and appropriate the wisdom of God. Understanding is the manifestation of the genius of God. Wisdom and understanding go together. Receiving the wisdom of God is not enough; we need to know how to bring His wisdom into the earthly realm. How does God's divine wisdom and will translate into life and someone's personal walk with God? Through understanding. That is why Solomon said, "Get God's wisdom and with all your getting, get understanding."

I like to put it this way: wisdom comes from God above. If we "stand under" the wisdom of God, the mind and will of God drops down into our spirits, our spirits grasp what God is revealing to us, and then we respond and act accordingly.

To "stand under" (understand), will take submission to His Lordship, waiting on Him prayerfully, and constantly bathing in the water of the Word of God. You will then start to receive understanding by revelation of God's divine wisdom and carry out what God is saying. This is understanding. Understanding is the fleshing out of execution of the wisdom of God. "How much better is it to get wisdom than gold. And to get understanding is rather to be chosen than silver." (Proverbs 16:16)

Scripture Reading: Job 35, 36, 37; Acts 14

Trivia Question: What happens to a wise man when given instruction?

July 8

"True Service"

1 Corinthians 3:5-17 — Who then is Paul, and who is Apollos, but ministers by whom ye believed, even as the Lord gave to every man? I have planted, Apollos watered; but God gave the increase. So then neither is he that planteth anything, neither he that watereth; but God that giveth the increase. Now he that planteth and he that watereth are one: and every man shall receive his own reward according to his own labour. For we are labourers together with God: ye are God's husbandry, ye are God's building. According to the grace of God which is given unto me, as a wise master builder, I have laid the foundation, and another buildeth thereon. But let every man take heed how he buildeth thereupon. For other foundation can no man lay than that is laid, which is Jesus Christ. Now if any man build upon this foundation gold, silver, precious stones, wood, hay, stubble; Every man's work shall be made manifest: for the day shall declare it, because it shall be revealed by fire; and the fire shall try every man's work of what sort it is. If any man's work abide which he hath built thereupon, he shall receive a reward. If any man's work shall be burned, he shall suffer loss: but he himself shall be saved; yet so as by fire. Know ye not that ye are the temple of God, and that the Spirit of God dwelleth in you? If any man defile the temple of God, him shall God destroy; for the temple of God is holy, which temple ye are.

This powerful portion of Scripture is part of Paul's letter to the people of Corinth. They were growing in their walk with Jesus, although expressions of carnality were still present within them. They were being challenged by the apostle concerning their Christian service to Christ and His Kingdom.

In regard to our Christian service to the Lord, Paul states five facts that he wanted the church to know and understand.

Fact #1, according to 1 Corinthians 3:7—God is the focus.

Ministry to others and Christian service has been reduced in some Christian circles as a "side show" and has taken on the look of "self." Christian service has never been about *our* gift or how well *I* sing or communicate. The word minister means to serve. When you are engaged in genuine service to others, it is never about you. Paul stated that it does not matter who does the planting or the watering, it is God who gives the increase.

Let us always remember the commission is from God, for the glory of God and to advance God's Kingdom. God is the focus.

July 9

"Let God Work"

1 Corinthians 3:5-17 — Who then is Paul, and who is Apollos, but ministers by whom ye believed, even as the Lord gave to every man? I have planted, Apollos watered; but God gave the increase. So then neither is he that planteth anything, neither he that watereth; but God that giveth the increase. Now he that planteth and he that watereth are one: and every man shall receive his own reward according to his own labour. For we are labourers together with God: ye are God's husbandry, ye are God's building. According to the grace of God which is given unto me, as a wise masterbuilder, I have laid the foundation, and another buildeth thereon. But let every man take heed how he buildeth thereupon. For other foundation can no man lay than that is laid, which is Jesus Christ. Now if any man build upon this foundation gold, silver, precious stones, wood, hay, stubble; Every man's work shall be made manifest: for the day shall declare it, because it shall be revealed by fire; and the fire shall try every man's work of what sort it is. If any man's work abide which he hath built thereupon, he shall receive a reward. If any man's work shall be burned, he shall suffer loss: but he himself shall be saved; yet so as by fire. Know ye not that ye are the temple of God, and that the Spirit of God dwelleth in you? If any man defile the temple of God, him shall God destroy; for the temple of God is holy, which temple ye are.

Fact #2 stated by Paul concerning our Christian service and its reward is: God works with us!

It is not by our might, or our power, but it is by God's Spirit, says the Lord of Hosts. (Zechariah 4:6)

In 1 Corinthians 3:9, Paul exhorts the church that we are workers together with God. We are not on our own, flying solo or on a one-man quest. God works with us, enabling and empowering us to do and accomplish the assignment He has ordained.

When we believe we are out there in Christian ministry or service by ourselves, then we look to ourselves for strength, ability, opportunity, and results. This type of approach will be tedious, laborious, and frustrating.

Disappointment will surely be evident and one will become "burned out," delusional, and dissatisfied.

Jesus taught us that after His death, burial and resurrection, and ascension, He and His Father would send us the Holy Spirit. The Holy Spirit would engage and empower us for the task at hand. As we submit to God and receive the aid of the Holy Spirit, we are able to accomplish the assignment given to us by God. God works with us in the person of the Holy Spirit.

How refreshing and rewarding it is when we yield to the Holy Spirit in our Christian service. He will work with us and help us to be impacting, influential, and effective in our service to God. When we try to work on our own, it is for our glory. When we covet the help of God, by His Spirit, the Lord receives all the glory.

According to Mark's Gospel, after the ascension of Christ and him giving the disciples the Holy Commission, they went forth and preached everywhere, the Lord WORKING WITH THEM (by His Spirit), and confirming the word with signs following (Mark 16:19,20). God works with us.

Scripture Reading: Job 40, 41, 42; Acts 15:22-41

Trivia Question: What does Solomon to compare a woman void of discretion?

July 10

"His Grace, Our Race"

1 Corinthians 3:5-17 — Who then is Paul, and who is Apollos, but ministers by whom ye believed, even as the Lord gave to every man? I have planted, Apollos watered; but God gave the increase. So then neither is he that planteth anything, neither he that watereth; but God that giveth the increase. Now he that planteth and he that watereth are one: and every man shall receive his own reward according to his own labour. For we are labourers together with God: ye are God's husbandry, ye are God's building. According to the grace of God which is given unto me, as a wise masterbuilder, I have laid the foundation, and another buildeth thereon. But let every man take heed how he buildeth thereupon. For other foundation can no man lay than that is laid, which is Jesus Christ. Now if any man build upon this foundation gold, silver, precious stones, wood, hay, stubble; Every man's work shall be made manifest: for the day shall declare it, because it shall be revealed by fire; and the fire shall try every man's work of what sort it is. If any man's work abide which he hath built thereupon, he shall receive a reward. If any man's work shall be burned, he shall suffer loss: but he himself shall be saved; yet so as by fire. Know ye not that ye are the temple of God, and that the Spirit of God dwelleth in you? If any man defile the temple of God, him shall God destroy; for the temple of God is holy, which temple ye are.

Fact #3 concerning our Christian service to God and His reward is found in 1 Corinthians 3:10: According to the grace which is given to me. It is God who provides the grace for the race He has chosen for us. It is an overwhelming feeling to be called to something that is beyond yourself, beyond your own ability or skillfulness, and to think you must accomplish the assignment with your own emotional, physical, and financial resources. Not true, for this is where you must understand that, if God has called you to do something for His Kingdom, He will supply the measure of grace needed to perform the task. Grace is more than God's unmerited favor. It is a divine exchange between God and us—His strength for our weakness, His ability for our inability, His sufficiency for our insufficiency, His limitless supply for our limited resources, His courage for our cowardice. He gives grace for the race He has chosen for us. We do not run it alone. We have a friend who is closer than a brother.

The recipient of God's grace recognizes he or she cannot do it in their own strength or efforts. They simply receive through divine exchange the measure of grace they need from the outset of their God-given assignment. Friend, receive His grace right from the starting line. It will take you through the journey (your race) to the finish line.

Scripture Reading: Psalm 1, 2, 3; Acts 16:1-15

Trivia Question: Counsel is in the heart of man like deep waters. Who will draw it out?

July 11

"Strong Foundation"

1 Corinthians 3:5-17 — Who then is Paul, and who is Apollos, but ministers by whom ye believed, even as the Lord gave to every man? I have planted, Apollos watered; but God gave the increase. So then neither is he that planteth anything, neither he that watereth; but God that giveth the increase. Now he that planteth and he that watereth are one: and every man shall receive his own reward ac-cording to his own labour. For we are labourers together with God: ye are God's husbandry, ye are God's building. According to the grace of God which is given unto me, as a wise masterbuilder, I have laid the foundation, and another buil-deth thereon. But let every man take heed how he buildeth thereupon. For other foundation can no man lay than that is laid, which is Jesus Christ. Now if any man build upon this foundation gold, silver, precious stones, wood, hay, stubble; Every man's work shall be made manifest: for the day shall declare it, because it shall be revealed by fire; and the fire shall try every man's work of what sort it is. If any man's work abide which he hath built thereupon, he shall receive a re-ward. If any man's work shall be burned, he shall suffer loss: but he himself shall be saved; yet so as by fire. Know ye not that ye are the temple of God, and that the Spirit of God dwelleth in you? If any man defile the temple of God, him shall God destroy; for the temple of God is holy, which temple ye are.

Fact #4 regarding our Christian service to God and His reward is in 1 Corinthians 3:11: God is our foundation!

Jesus taught us that there are two different foundations. One is the Word and the other, the world. He defined the two foundations as the rock verses the sand. Both are very different. Jesus taught about the wise man who built his house (ministry, service to God, God given assignment) upon a rock. When the rain came down, the floods started to rise and the winds blew, but the house did not fall, for it was founded upon a rock. Paul said, "For other foundation can no man lay than that which is laid, which is Jesus Christ." Jesus is the rock, "and did all drink the same spiritual drink, for they drank of that spiritual rock that followed them, and that rock was Christ." (1 Corinthians 10:4)

Conversely, Jesus taught about the foolish man who built his house upon the sand. And the rain came down, the floods started to rise, and the winds blew, and the house fell, and great was the fall of it. (Matthew 7:24–27) What are we building our ministries on? What foundation is the base for our Christian service to God? Have we built our ministries on our own platforms of self-confidence, self-pontification, and self-glorification? Have we trusted in the arm of the flesh or put our faith in the wisdom of man? These are all "sand" foundations. We can be sure when the tests and trials come, (the rain, floods and wind) what we built in the flesh for our own pleasure and promotion will surely fall.

When the foundation for what we are going to do for God is God him-self, then we can be assured that whatever may come against us and our

God given assignment will not triumph over us. Jesus, the rock, is our only platform, and he protects and preserves what has been built for His honor and glory.

Is what you are doing for God giving Him all honor and glory? Are you promoting His Kingdom? Are you lifting up His name? Are you decreasing, so He is increasing? (John 3:30) Jesus must be the foundation for anything and everything we build for God. All other platforms are sinking sand.

Scripture Reading: Psalm 4, 5, 6; Acts 16:16-40

Trivia Question: According to Jesus, if someone looks on someone with lustful eyes and motives, what sin do they commit?

July 12

"What's the Motive?"

1 Corinthians 3:5-17 — Who then is Paul, and who is Apollos, but ministers by whom ye believed, even as the Lord gave to every man? I have planted, Apollos watered; but God gave the increase. So then neither is he that planteth anything, neither he that watereth; but God that giveth the increase. Now he that planteth and he that watereth are one: and every man shall receive his own reward according to his own labour. For we are labourers together with God: ye are God's husbandry, ye are God's building. According to the grace of God which is given unto me, as a wise masterbuilder, I have laid the foundation, and another buildeth thereon. But let every man take heed how he buildeth thereupon. For other foundation can no man lay than that is laid, which is Jesus Christ. Now if any man build upon this foundation gold, silver, precious stones, wood, hay, stubble; Every man's work shall be made manifest: for the day shall declare it, because it shall be revealed by fire; and the fire shall try every man's work of what sort it is. If any man's work abide which he hath built thereupon, he shall receive a reward. If any man's work shall be burned, he shall suffer loss: but he himself shall be saved; yet so as by fire. Know ye not that ye are the temple of God, and that the Spirit of God dwelleth in you? If any man defile the temple of God, him shall God destroy; for the temple of God is holy, which temple ye are.

Fact #5 concerning our Christian service to Christ and His reward is: God will test or prove all of our works. This truth is most interesting, along with being very sobering. Think about it, all of our works of service to God will be tested by God to see if they are properly mandated and motivated by Him. Have we done our own thing for our own reasons? Or, have we carried out His God-given mandate, being motivated by His love, and for His glory? The Bible says (1 Corinthians 3:13), everyone's works shall be made manifest for the day (Judgment Seat of Christ) shall declare it, because it shall be received by fire, and the fire shall test everyone's work of what sort it is.

Wow, the purifying fire of God will be applied to the work we have done for Him. Fire not only consumes, it also cleanses. God's fire testing will reveal if our Christian service to God and the works we have done in His name were carnally-directed or Christ-directed. The fire test by God will reveal quite different results.

The wrongly-motivated works are likened to wood, hay, and stubble. The Christ-directed, and love-motivated works are like gold, silver, and precious stones. Obviously, when fire is applied, the former is burned up, consumed to worthless ashes. The latter will purify and cause these "gem works" to become more valuable and long lasting. Paul said if someone's work abides and remains, they shall receive God's reward. (1 Corinthians 3:14)

Conversely, if someone's work be burned up and consumed, they shall suffer the loss of no reward. (1 Corinthians 3:15)

It all comes down to this: Did God direct me to do what I am doing? And what is my motivation for doing it?

A very sobering portion of Scripture is found in Matthew 7:21-23: "Not everyone that saith unto me, Lord, Lord, shall enter into the Kingdom of Heaven; but he that doeth the will of my Father which is in Heaven. Many will say to me in that day, Lord, Lord, have we not prophesied in thy name? And in thy name have cast out devils? And in thy name done many wonderful works? And then will I profess unto them, I never knew you: depart from me, ye that work iniquity."

If these people were lying about their accomplishments for Christ, Jesus would have called them liars. He did not, he said, "I never knew you, depart from me, you that work iniquity."

Apparently, their motives did not line up with the Word of God and biblical ministry as taught by Jesus himself.

Is what I do for the Kingdom motivated with the love of Jesus and for His glory? Everything else is ashes!

Scripture Reading: Psalm 7, 8, 9; Acts 17:1-15

July 13

"Tower of Safety"

Proverbs 18:10 — The name of the Lord is a strong tower;
the righteous runneth into it, and is safe.

In a world that is full of debauchery, darkness and danger, it is comforting and reassuring knowing that our Lord is our strong tower.

Towers in biblical settings and even in some places today are designed and intended to keep residents safe and enemies out.

The name of Jesus is our strong and high tower. Just the mention of His name in faith brings instant safety and protection. The name of the Lord Jesus is higher than any other name (everything has a name).

"Wherefore God has highly exalted Him and given Him a name which is above every name: that at the name of Jesus, every knee should bow, of things in Heaven and things in Earth, and things under the earth; and that every tongue should confess that Jesus Christ is Lord, to the glory of God the Father." (Philippians 2:9-11)

The name of Jesus is greater, stronger, and above every other name. His name is above fret, worry, anxiety, depression, lust, sickness, disease, loneliness, rejection, sin, Satan, Hell, and death!

King David, who was being hunted down by Saul like a wild animal, walked in the light of the revelation that the Lord was His strong tower, who kept him safe and secure from all danger and alarm. Psalm 18:2-3 says, "The Lord is my rock and my fortress, and my deliverer; my God, my strength, in whom I will trust; my buckler, and the horn of my salvation, and my high tower. I will call upon the Lord, who is worthy to be praised: so shall I be saved from mine enemies."

Psalm 61:1-3 says, "Hear my cry, O God; attend unto my prayer. From the end of the earth will I cry unto thee, when my heart is overwhelmed: lead me to the rock that is higher than I. For thou hast been a shelter for me, and a strong tower from the enemy."

Beloved, whatever you are facing today, whatever giant is staring you down, whatever danger is lurking in your midst, know that the name of the Lord is your strong and high tower. He will keep you safe and protect you from the fiery darts of the wicked. The righteous run to Him and are safe.

He promises us that the wicked one will not touch us (1 John 5:18), and He does not lie (Titus 1:2).

Be safe and secure from all alarm. He is our strong tower!

Scripture Reading: Psalm 10, 11, 12; Acts 17:16-34

Trivia Question: Who remains in the congregation of the dead?

July 14

"God is Good"

John 5:2-8 — Now there is at Jerusalem by the sheep market a pool which is called in the Hebrew tongue Bethseda, having five porches. In these lay a great multitude of impotent folk, of blind, halt, withered, waiting for the moving of the water. For an angel went down at a certain season into the pool, and troubled the water: whosoever then first after the troubling of the water stepped in was made whole of whatsoever disease he had. And a certain man was there, which had an infirmity thirty and eight years. When Jesus saw him lie, and knew that he had been now a long time in that case, he saith unto him, "Wilt though be made whole?" The impotent man answered him, "Sir, I have no man, when the water is troubled, to put me into the pool: but while I am coming, another steppeth down before me." Jesus saith unto him, "Rise, take up thy bed and walk."

What a great demonstration of God's love and kindness toward this man, who had been handicapped for thirtyeight years. The word "Bethsada" means house of kindness. What a kind Jesus we have! Our thoughts toward God probably bring a diversity of words. God is love, good, merciful, gracious, etc. God manifested through His Son Jesus is also kind.

When you dwell on the love and kindness of the Lord, you become aware of how utterly good He is and the sensitive side of God that truly understands exactly who we are and what we face in life. God is the author of life (Acts 3:15) and has breathed into us the breath of life. (Genesis 2:8) God who is the author of life and the breath of life has given each one of us in this life to enjoy His goodness, mercy, and grace that has been made available through His Son, Jesus Christ. Forgiveness in this life is available to whoever is in need of it.

King David, who needed forgiveness from God, makes reference to God's kindness in Psalm 63:3-4. "Because your loving-kindness is better than life, my lips shall praise thee."

195

David understood that the kindness of God that results in God's love and forgiveness is even better than life itself.

There are people that have life, but are not living life the way God intended. The author of life, who gives the breath of life, desires to extend to you His life-changing kindness. Will you receive God's kindness right now to change your circumstance, forgive your sin, heal your body, restore your soul and bring you into a new place of oneness with Him?

David received that revelation. His lips were constantly praising his God, and his outstretched arms giving continued thanksgiving to the one whose kindness is better than life itself.

Receive God's kindness today and start to walk in thankfulness, praise to God, and victory!

Scripture Reading: Psalms 13, 14, 15, 16; Acts 18

Trivia Question: There is no wisdom, nor understanding, nor counsel against whom?

July 15

"What Are You Reflecting?"

Proverbs 27:19 — As in water face answereth to face, so the heart of man to man.

The NIV reads like this, "As water reflects a face, so a man's heart reflects the man." With all that we have to "marinate" ourselves with, i.e. creams, lotions, anti-aging gels, etc., we can camouflage much and put forth an image of self that is tainted and less than forthright.

Have you ever gone to the side of a lake and bent over to see your reflection in a sun-drenched watery mirror? When the sun's rays are hitting the water just right, you can see a detailed image and reflection of your face. Water can reflect the face of a man, but only what is inside can really reflect who you are!

One's heart when expressed openly and honestly reflects who a person really is. If your heart was exposed and expressed today, what would it say about you?

One can only hope that integrity, honesty, love, loyalty etc, dwells within. If a heart is home to Christlikeness and the fruits of the Spirit, that expression will work its way out and reveal to all just who you really are. A man's heart really does reflect the man.

May our greatest objective in this life be to have a heart like Jesus. As Jesus was recognizable by all through His heart's actions, may we too let all know that we are disciples of Christ, through our heart's actions reflecting who we really are as Christians. Water can reflect our face, but our hearts reflect who and what we really are...followers of Jesus!

Reading: Psalms 17, 18; Acts 19:1-20

Trivia Question: According to Proverbs 30, how many daughters does the horseleach have?

July 16

"The Greatest Love"

Jude 21 — Keep yourselves in the love of God,
looking for the mercy of our Lord Jesus Christ unto eternal life.

The best way to keep ourselves in the love of God is for the love of God to be in us. When someone gives their life to Jesus, His love comes to make residence inside that new creation in Christ. Like all other seeds, in order to grow and mature into what God created that seed to be, it must be planted, watered, cared for, and take root.

Paul says we must be rooted and grounded in love. (Ephesians 3:17) As we continue to study His Word and meditate in it, the love of God starts to be perfected (mature, grow). (1 John 4:17)

The way to keep ourselves in the love of God is to let the love of God remain in us. God's love is the greatest force on planet earth. His love will keep you during unstable times. His love will protect you during danger and uphold you when you think you are falling into oblivion. His love covers us, cleanses us, corrects us, connects us, commands us, collects us and cares for us.

Stay in the love of God by protecting the love of God that is in you. Grow and develop in God's love. Let His love overshadow you right now. Whatever trial you are facing, His love will bring you through! It really will!

Scripture Reading: Psalm 19, 20, 21; Acts 19:21-41

Trivia Question: God is not the author of confusion, but the author of what?

July 17

"Found"

Psalms 23:6 — Surely goodness and mercy shall follow me
all the days of my life: and I will dwell in the house of the Lord forever.

Have you ever heard someone say, "I found the Lord?"

Truth of the matter, the Lord did not need to be found, he was not ever lost. Indeed, the Lord found us. "All we like sheep have gone astray, we have turned everyone to his own way..." (Isaiah 53:6) We are the ones that were lost!

Jesus who is the personification of goodness and mercy pursued us even when we were rebellious, on the run, anti-God, and doing our own thing. He was tracking us as the hound of Heaven nipping at our heels.

Sometimes it is hard to imagine that God incarnate, Jesus the Son of God, would love us so much as to chase after us trying to apprehend us, so that He can reveal Himself to us and give us the revelation that He is God, the answer to all our questions, the sum total of everything we could imagine, and the truth that will set us eternally free.

God knows that within you is a gift that He Himself engrafted inside of you, that needs to be developed and then released to touch someone else to change them for time and eternity.

This is why His goodness and mercy will continue to follow you—to let you know how much He loves you and wants you to be in His great family and to mature and grow the wonderful gift He put inside of you, so that you can fulfill His divine calling on your life and be a blessing to someone. There is somebody out there that needs what only you have from God!

Just as that spiritual rock followed Israel in the desert, Jesus who is that rock follows you. (1 Corinthians 10:4)

Let Him apprehend you today. It will be the greatest catch you will ever experience.

Scripture Reading: Psalms 22, 23, 24; Acts 20:1-16

Trivia Question: What were the four major sins of Israel as they traveled in the wilderness?

July 18

"Listening Ears"

Proverbs 1:5 — A wise man will hear, and will increase learning; and a man of understanding shall attain unto wise counsels.

A wise individual today is defined many ways. If a person has been educated, displays intellect, and is skilled in a certain discipline or vocation, that person may be considered wise.

The truth of the matter is, from God's dictionary, a wise man and the subject of wisdom take on a different definition and meaning.

Intellect is man-given. Wisdom is God-given. Intellect can be eventually diminished and lost. Wisdom stays with you even through eternity. Intellect best expresses itself in a favorable environment. God's wisdom thrives in any environment, condition, or surrounding.

A wise man will hear. Notice a hearing ear is essential to possess God's wisdom. A "know-it-all" mentality will short-circuit God's divine wisdom to an individual. "Faith comes by hearing, and hearing by the Word of God." (Romans 10:17) It is impossible to attain God's wisdom apart from His Word. His Word goes beyond man's intellect or making one smarter. His wisdom put inside man is the very genius of God. "Christ the power of God, and the wisdom of God." (1 Corinthians 1:24) When Christ and His Word is in you, God's wisdom resides and manifests the very character and expression of God Himself.

When a Christian will purpose in his/her heart to hear God through His Word, and continue to hear and hear and hear, the Bible says they will increase in learning. When we learn, we become more equipped. When we become more equipped, we become more apt. When we become more apt, we become more available. When we become more available, we become more useful—to God and His service. Truth becomes real to us, changes us and empowers us to bring change to others.

Conversely, there will be those who ever are learning (intellectually) and never able to come to the knowledge of the truth (fruit of God's wisdom). (2 Timothy 3:7)

Desire more than natural intellect that comes from education. Desire God's wisdom that derives from hearing, and hearing and hearing the Word of God. Intellect is good, wisdom is great!

July 19

"Sweet Sleep"

Psalms 3:5 — I laid me down and slept; I awaked;
for the Lord sustained me.

When someone gives their life over to the Lord Jesus, they eventually stop taking things for granted. Even the little things that were overlooked in the course of life are now appreciated.

If an individual suffered from a sleep disorder, that person values a good night sleep in a tremendous way. The average person that is tired goes to sleep and wakes up, rarely acknowledging God for that good night of sleep or His sustaining grace during the restful period.

Scripture does not reveal to us that David had a sleep disorder, but it does give light concerning David's sleep. This Psalm was probably written when Absalom, David's son, was rebelling and causing impending harm to his father. If you have sleep deprivation, have to sleep with one eye open, or sleep knowing you could be in harm's way, then a restful, peaceful, uninterrupted night of sleep is enjoyed and causes a thankful acknowledgment to the one who is the author of peace, rest, and sleep – Almighty God.

David said that He who neither slumbers or sleeps sustained and watched over him while he slept. (Psalm 121:4)

Even if you have been blessed with the ability to go to sleep and get a good night's rest, wake up and be mindful that God who never sleeps was the one making sure that your sleep was sweet and restorative. God was protecting you and sustaining the one He calls His special treasure – you!

Be thankful for the little things that we take for granted at times. Acknowledge God and His sustaining power and grace that He extends to you each time you lay your head down and sleep. Sleep is not only needful for the body to replenish, restore, and heal itself. Sleep is a gift from God. Enjoy it and be thankful to God for it. (Psalms 4:8, Psalms 91:5, Psalms 127:2, Proverbs 3:24)

Scripture Reading: Psalms 28, 29, 30; Acts 21:1-14

July 20

"That Still Small Voice"

1 Samuel 3:1-10 — And the child Samuel ministered unto the Lord before Eli. And the word of the Lord was precious in those days; there was no open vision. And it came to pass at that time, when Eli was laid down in his place, and his eyes began to wax dim, that he could not see; And ere the lamp of God went out in the temple of the Lord, where the ark of God was, and Samuel was laid down to sleep; That the Lord called Samuel: and he answered, "Here am I." And he ran unto Eli, and said, "Here am I; for thou calledst me." And he said, "I called not; lie down again." And he went and lay down. And the Lord called yet again, "Samuel." And Samuel arose and went to Eli, and said, "Here am I; for thou didst call me." And he answered, "I called not, my son; lie down again." Now Samuel did not yet know the Lord, neither was the word of the Lord yet revealed unto him. And the Lord called Samuel again the third time. And he arose and went to Eli, and said, "Here am I; for thou didst call me." And Eli perceived that the Lord had called the child. Therefore Eli said unto Samuel, "Go, lie down: and it shall be, if he call thee, that thou shalt say, 'Speak, Lord; for thy servant heareth.'" So Samuel went and lay down in his place. And the Lord came, and stood, and called as at other times, "Samuel, Samuel." Then Samuel answered, "Speak; for thy servant heareth."

The people of God were going after worldly pleasures and other gods. They were worshipping Ashtoreth (the sex goddess) and pledging their allegiance to Baal. The priesthood was producing sons that did not know or serve the Lord. The leaders were causing God's people to look on the holy sacrifices with disdain and contempt. Sexual sin was occurring within the tabernacle! The congregation and the culture were in apostasy.

In the midst of all the evil, God was raising and rearing up a young boy by the name of Samuel. Samuel was his mother's answer to her desperate prayer a few years before. Hannah promised God, if He would give her a son, she would give him to the Lord all the days of his life, sanctified for God and His service. (1 Samuel 1:11)

God indeed granted her the petition and Samuel was born. Samuel was brought up in the temple, trained and taught by Eli, the priest. As Samuel ministered before the Lord (1 Samuel 2:18), and grew before the Lord (1 Samuel 2:21), he started having favor with God and man. (1 Samuel 2:26) It was then time for God Himself to speak to Samuel and personally call Him into His service. Man can teach and train, but God must do the clear calling on one's life.

Samuel, hearing a voice, was too young and immature to discern that it was the voice of God. Eli was too old and out of touch to discern it was God calling Samuel. Finally Eli deduced it might be God's voice and instructed Samuel to answer the voice from Heaven. The fourth time God called Samuel, he answered and reassured God that he was hearing and obeying.

Jesus taught us in the New Testament that his sheep hear His voice, know His voice, and follow Him. (John 10:27)

In the midst of immorality and immaturity, chaos and confusion, spiritual decay and debauchery, lewdness and loneliness, God wants to speak to you!

Will you hear Him today? Will you rightfully discern the voice of God? Will you set apart yourself and give the God of time and eternity your time?

The Lord wants His people to hear Him. Do not allow what is going on around you to influence you. Do not allow the culture to cause you to be cold.

Hear God today! Know His voice. Follow His ways. Be a servant that will speak His Word to your generation. Be a part of "the Samuel Generation." Because Samuel chose to hear God and obey Him, revival eventually came to the nation.

Scripture Reading: Psalms 31, 32, 33; Acts 21:15-40

Trivia Question: Where did Samuel live?

July 21

"Weight the Change"

Proverbs 24:21 — My son, fear thou the Lord and the king: and meddle not with them that are given to change.

Change is good. Change is bad. Change is good when it results in behavior adjustments and conforms more to Christlikeness. Change is good when speaking about metamorphosis or transformation concerning the glory of God and "changing" into the same image of Christ. (2 Corinthians 3:18) Change is good when transitioning from our terrestrial bodies to our celestial bodies at the "catching away" of the church. (1 Corinthians 15:51, 1 Thessalonians 4:14-17)

Change is NOT good when someone divorces, disconnects, detaches, or discerns wrongfully the great tenets of the faith, which are the great beliefs and principles that are derived from the Holy Scriptures. "For I am the Lord, I change not." (Malachi 3:6)

When it comes to the character of God, the integrity of His Word, the orthodoxy of all inspired Scripture, and the heart of our heavenly Father, there is no change! God means what He says, and says what He means. God is not a man that He should lie, neither the Son of man (Jesus), that he should repent or change. (Numbers 23:19)

In a very fast-moving, volatile, ever-changing world in which we live, we must be very circumspect concerning the stability and the immutability of God.

It should be comforting to know that God's love is unchangeable. His grace, mercy, forgiveness, favor, pardon, and loving-kindness do not change with the season or society.

My friend, always fear (reverence) the Lord and do not meddle with them that are given to change. (Proverbs 24:21) That means, those that are seeking to redefine who God is, what God says, and how God responds.

Change is healthy in many areas of life and our journey with Jesus, but not when it comes to biblical principles, promises, practices, and protocol. Obey the Lord in your life by honoring Him and His unchanging word. You will be glad you did!

Scripture Reading: Psalms 34, 35; Acts 22

Trivia Question: How many children did God give Hannah?

July 22

"His Will to Heal"

Jeremiah 17:14 — Heal me, O Lord, and I shall be healed, save me and I shall be saved, for thou art my praise.

God says what He means, and means what He says. Are you in need of healing today? Are you in need of His salvation today? Are you in need of His deliverance today? Call on the name of the Lord and He will answer.

He is a present help in our time of need. (Psalms 46:1, Psalms 145:18)

We have a Father in Heaven who hears us when we call on Him! If it is a healing cry from our hearts of faith to God, then it is a healing response from God to us we will have.

He is our healing and health. He is our salvation. He is all we need. Call on Him right now. Cry out to Him in faith. Receive from Him at this moment in Jesus name. He is your well that will never run dry. Hope thou in God, for I shall yet praise Him, who is the health of my countenance and my God. (Psalms 42:11) Be healed in Jesus' name! Be made whole in Jesus' name! Enjoy your healing and health today.

Scripture Reading: Psalms 36, 37; Acts 23:1-11

Trivia Question: What was the second miracle recorded in Cana?

July 23

"The Leading Shepherd"

John 10:11 — I am the good shepherd.
The good shepherd giveth his life for the sheep.

Jesus is the good shepherd. What a wonderful Jesus we serve. As our good shepherd, He leads us, feeds us, protects us, and preserves us.

What a contrast between a good, true shepherd and someone who is hired just to do a job of watching the sheep. Jesus said that someone who is just in it for a paycheck (hireling), when he senses pressure or danger imminent, runs and saves his own skin. A hireling does not really care for the sheep because he is just in it for the monetary gain. (John 10:12-13)

Jesus is the good shepherd, who knows his sheep by name, personality traits, behavior patterns, and innermost thoughts. (John 10:14) Even though Jesus knows everything about us (the good and the bad), He was willing to go to the cross, shed His blood, be crucified, and give His life for us. Wow, what a good shepherd. What a great shepherd. Jesus' part in salvation as the good shepherd was to give His life for us.

What is your part as a sheep? It is to hear His voice and follow Him! (John 10:27) Are you listening to the voice of the good shepherd today? Are you following Him and His ways? He is the good shepherd. Are we the good sheep that hear, obey, and follow Him? Purpose in your heart to be a good sheep that follows the good shepherd.

July 24

"Don't Prevent your Blessing"

Proverbs 3:9–10 — Honour the Lord with thy substance,
and with the firstfruits of all thine increase: So shall thy barns be filled with
plenty, and thy presses shall burst out with new wine.

Every Christian should honor the Lord with first fruits, or the tithe. The tithe is holy before God. We give God 10% of our income, He blesses 100%, and the 90% is left for us to live on.

In the school of biblical finance and kingdom giving, learning to give God our tithe should be the learning level of pre-school or kindergarten. Every Christian should understand that God is so good and He gives grace, empowerment, ability, and strength to us so that we can earn income through a skill, vocation, trade, or some form of employment. Saying thank you to God is our tithe, 10% or first-fruits to your local church or storehouse, so that there will be a continual supply of "meat," or the Word of God, to feed the congregation on an ongoing basis. (Malachi 3:10)

Simply put, the people tithe, the local church continues, and the ministry is able to serve the needs of the congregation, spiritually and otherwise.

We should tithe or give first fruits not only with the expectation of getting back, but first and foremost out of love and adoration, thanksgiving and appreciation for all that God has done for us. Loving and thankful people have no issue on giving tithes or first-fruits...none!

Scripture Reading: Psalms 41, 42, 43; Acts 24

Trivia Question: After Jesus raised Lazarus from the dead, many of the chief rulers of the synagogue believed on Jesus. Why then did they not confess their faith in Christ publicly?

July 25

"A Holy Temple"

*1 Corinthians 6:20 — For ye are bought with a price:
therefore glorify God in your body, and in your spirit, which are God's.*

Someone said that the gift of salvation is free. This statement is true for the ones who are the recipients of the wonderful gift. Jesus was brutally scourged, beaten, mocked, ridiculed, and spit upon. His facial hair was ripped out, He was hung on a cross, His blood was shed, and He was crucified. Jesus paid a very high price for our salvation. It was a free gift to us, but costly for Him! Our salvation was bought and paid for by Jesus Himself. That was His part in the divine transaction.

Our part is living our lives well-pleasing to Him. We are to bring Him glory in our lives daily. Two ways we glorify God are with our spirits and our bodies.

When our spirits are born again, filled with His Word, tender before the Father, willing to serve, obedient to His will, and yielded and surrendered to His Lordship, we bring Him glory.

Giving God glory in our bodies at times is more challenging. Our spirits desire to serve God. (Romans 1:9) Our bodies, however tend to want to serve self. Our bodies must be denied the demands that they dictate to us. We must bring our bodies into subjection and submission to the Word of God, the will of God, and the ways of God. (1 Corinthians 9:27)

When we starve the extreme appetites of our flesh and walk in the spirit so we do not fulfill the lust of our flesh, then we can glorify God in our bodies.

They might be our bodies, but they are God's temples. We must be ever mindful that as Christians, God makes His abode in us, in the person of the Holy Spirit. God dwells in us! We must not defile that temple of God in any way.

Sin, self-hatred, sexual misconduct, even any kind of abuse to our bodies (His temples) can bring defilement. (1 Corinthians 3:17)

May we bring glory to God in our spirits and our bodies, which belong to God. Remember we have been bought and redeemed with a price – the blood and sacrifice of Jesus.

Scripture Reading: Psalms 44, 45, 46; Acts 25

Trivia Question: How many Philistines did Samson kill with a jawbone of a donkey?

July 26

"Faith Challenge"

Mark 5:36 — As soon as Jesus heard the word that was spoken,
he saith unto the ruler of the synagogue, Be not afraid, only believe.

People have great needs. The maladies of life put individuals in desperation. The ruler of the synagogue, Jairus by name, had a 12-year-old daughter who was dying. Plain and clear, she was on her deathbed, her life being ripped away from her, death being the apparent victor.

In desperation, Jairus made an appeal to the Healer of Galilee. He asked Jesus to come to his home, lay hands on his daughter and heal her. Jairus was desperate but did not lack in his determination. He strongly persuaded Jesus and received a positive response from the Master. Jesus would indeed go to his home!

On the way, Jesus was interrupted and delayed however, with another urgent request. A woman who was hemorrhaging for twelve years sought healing for her body. She had an unforgettable encounter with Jesus, receiving healing and wholeness to her body. The plague was gone, her life was changed, and peace was her result. In the process of her miracle, some time had elapsed. (Sometimes miracles take time to manifest.)

Jesus was delayed, and a bad report was brought to Jairus on the road to his home with his heavenly companion and Healer. The messengers reported, "Your daughter is dead. Do not have Jesus come one more step!"

Jesus, knowing that despair, discouragement, and fear would grip Jairus' heart with those kinds of tidings, said immediately, "Be not afraid, only believe." Jesus spoke the words of faith. Nothing changed from the Lord's perspective. He promised that he would go to Jairus' home and heal his daughter. Just because Jesus was delayed with another need did not negate His promise. Delay is not denial. Your miracle is on the way! Wait on God, continue to believe, and you will see God's promise come to pass.

When fear knocks on your door, answer the door with the words of faith. Faith will dispel, disband, demobilize and drive off fear. Be quick to answer fear's attempt to bring you into doubt and unbelief with faith words, which are His Word. Faith will dismiss fear every time.

Scripture Reading: Psalms 47, 48, 49; Acts 26

Trivia Question: After Noah left the ark, what was his first recorded action?

July 27

"Your Help Is Coming"

*Psalms 20:2 — Send thee help from the sanctuary
and strengthen thee out of Zion.*

Help is on the way for you! Help is on the way for you!

Very few people can do life alone. I am sure there are those who have tried, but unsuccessfully. The truth is that we need others to help us in this life. The assignment that God has for you requires others to hold up your hands. The mission that you seek to fulfill may require others to fuel and finance it. The dreams that God has put in your heart will need others to "buy into" those dreams in one or more ways. Clearly, we need the help of people in our lives to fulfill our destinies.

The good news is that God has promised to send help from the sanctuary. Every Christian should be connected to a local New Testament church, a place where you go regularly to worship, learn His Word, fellowship with those of like precious faith, and be strengthened and empowered overall. Within that body of believers, God has prepared someone to help you with your walk with God, your stewardship questions and concerns, your challenges vocationally, etc. God has ordained someone to help you. Since help comes from the sanctuary, you must be in the sanctuary so God's helpers can connect with you. Do not believe people who try to convince others that the local church and the assembly of the saints are outdated and unimportant. (Hebrew 11:25)

Zion speaks of the presence of God, the church of God, or the people of God that His presence is within. Help is being sent to you from the sanctuary and you will be strengthened out of Zion. Help is on the way!

Scripture Reading: Psalms 50, 51, 52; Acts 27:1-25

Trivia Question: Jacob is regarded as the father of the Israelites and Esau is considered the Father of the _____ .

July 28

"Turn Back"

Zechariah 1:3 — Therefore say thou unto them, Thus saith the Lord of hosts;
Turn ye unto me, saith the Lord of hosts, and I will turn unto you,
saith the Lord of hosts.

The backdrop of this admonition from the Lord comes from a 70-year captivity in Babylon. Because of the apostasy of the southern kingdom of Judah, the nation was besieged by Nebuchadnezzar and brought into exile.

Under King Darius the Mede, more of the Jewish captives after this 70-year period were allowed to start going home to Jerusalem. The temple was destroyed, the walls torn down, but God was bringing His people home.

Zechariah gives a stern warning from the Lord. He states that the Lord had been displeased with their forefathers, their compromise, contempt and lack of conviction for the holy things of God. So the decree goes forth, "Turn to me, and I will turn to you." A better way to say it was simply, "Return back to me with all your hearts, and my presence, power, purity, and person shall return back to you."

The Lord is still lovingly calling individuals to turn back to Him. God is saying to His creation, "Turn to me." Man has tried and strived desperately to do life on his own, only to find himself captive to the insurmountable issues of life. It is time for this generation to turn back to their creator, to turn back to the true lover of their souls, to turn back to God!

Will you help others today to turn to the Lord? No God...no peace. Know God...know peace.

The choice is up to people. God made His choice. He is waiting on His creation to make their choice. Turn to God, and He will turn to you.

Scripture Reading: Psalms 53, 54, 55; Acts 27:26-44

Trivia Question: After what occasion did Miriam, the sister of Moses, lead a procession of praise to God?

July 29

"Pursue your Dream"

Genesis 50:22-23 — And Joseph dwelt in Egypt, he, and his father's house:

and Joseph lived a hundred and ten years.
And Joseph saw Ephraim's children of the third generation: the children also
of Machir the son Manasseh were brought up upon Joseph's knees.

At seventeen years of age, Jacob's son Joseph was a dreamer. Joseph had ten brothers older than him and one younger. Joseph was highly favored by his dad. The ten older brothers were jealous. They hated him because of his dreams which indicated that they all would bow and serve their young brother. They conspired to kill him and put an end to the dreamer and his dreams.

Joseph was thrown into a pit, sold as a slave, accused falsely of rape, thrown in jail, forgotten in prison, and left to die. Joseph, however, refused to let go of the dream that God put in his heart. After a series of sovereign, supernatural events, God brought Joseph out of the prison and into the palace. Joseph became prince of Egypt, had stewardship over all of the grain to sustain Egypt, his family, and the surrounding nations. Joseph saw his dreams come to pass as his brothers eventually bowed to him after a period of not communicating or seeing him for over twenty years.

The devil tried to squash his dream, snuff him out, destroy any possibility of prosperity and posterity, but God who was the one who put these dreams inside of Joseph, and He saw to it that these dreams would come to pass and to fruition. The dream was determined!

At the end of Joseph's life at 110 years old, we have a visual. The children of Machir, the son of Manasseh, who is the son of Joseph, are on his lap.

Joseph and his dream at seventeen was supposed to die, but now we see Joseph with his great grandchildren imparting to them at the end of his days. The teenager that was supposed to die is touching four generations with his life and dream that God preserved. The dreamer is still depositing at the point of death. Joseph refused to abort what God put in his heart. It took some years for the dream to come to pass, but it eventually indeed became a reality.

Do not give up on your dream. Do not abort the promise of God. Do not relinquish His prophetic word to you. It will indeed become a reality. May you too impart and touch up to four generations with your life and what God put into your heart.

Scripture Reading: Psalms 56, 57, 58; Acts 28:1-15

Trivia Question: What was the second of ten plagues visited upon Egypt for keeping the Hebrew people in bondage?

July 30

"Troubled Waters"

*John 5:4 — For an angel went down at a certain season into the pool,
and troubled the water: whosoever then first after the troubling of the water
stepped in was made whole of whatsoever disease he had.*

An expression of God's grace and mercy was manifested at the pool of Bethesda (house of kindness or favor) from time to time. People who were sick, diseased, and infirmed would gather, waiting for the "troubling" (the stirring or agitation) of the water in the pool. Whoever would step into the pool first would be healed and made whole of their plagues.

From time to time, God is troubling or stirring up the waters of our heart. What is your passion today? What desires are stirring up within you? What dreams do you have that are unfulfilled?

God is stirring you up at this very season in your life. He wants to get your attention, so you can recognize that He is stirring up your waters. Respond to His stirring, step out and step into what God has for your life!

We do not receive from God by being passive, complacent, lazy, or indifferent.

We must be proactive, aggressive, diligent, and have "feet" to our faith!

Go ahead and step out in the waters that you believe God is stirring in your life. Your future may depend on it.

Respond to God, and you will be glad you did! Go for it!

Scripture Reading: Psalms 59, 60, 61; Acts 28:16-31

Trivia Question: When David was old and at the end of his life, what did his servants suggest that he should have for warmth and comfort?

July 31

"Godly Leaders"

*Proverbs 29:2 — When the righteous are in authority,
the people rejoice: but when the wicked beareth rule, the people mourn.*

As Christians, we need to understand the importance of having godly leaders in government.

A brief tour through the book of 1 Kings and 2 Kings and 1 Chronicles and 2 Chronicles will underscore the tremendous benefit of having righteous rulers. Simply put, when a king of Israel (northern kingdom) or a king of Judah (southern kingdom) served, honored, and obeyed the Lord, their enemies did not penetrate. The culture was charged with the blessings of God and the people prospered.

Conversely, when a king chose to dishonor, disobey, and discredit God and His Holy Word, the nation of Israel fell into complacency, indifference, and apostasy.

Israel needed righteous kings and rulers just as America needs godly men and women that sit in seats of authority.

When we pray for politicians and vote our biblical values, we have a better chance to see the righteous in authority. When ungodly, wicked, anti-Bible people rule, we will go through a season of mourning. You can make a difference by understanding the current issues of our day and praying daily for your nation and its leaders.

Scripture Reading: Psalms 62, 63, 64; Romans 1

Trivia Question: Name the prophet that declared the Savior was to be born in Bethlehem.

August

August 1

"Harvest Isn't Tidy"

Proverbs 14:4 — Where no oxen are, the crib is clean:
but much increase is by the strength of the ox.

The oxen are beasts of burden. They plow the fields, pull the loads and endure the heavy weights that are put on them. Oxen are workaholics!

A farmer in biblical times without oxen is likened to a carpenter without a hammer and his saw.

Along with the work that only the oxen can produce, also comes the unclean, dirty stalls. That is just the way it goes! There is a trade-off when it comes to the performance and productivity of these beasts of burden. The oxen work hard, but the farmer has to work hard as well cleaning out the crib (stall). Oh my!

No oxen leads to clean stalls, but also no plowed field for harvest or increase.

People that have to have their lives "neat and tidy" all the time, usually do not produce much. It takes a team to fulfill a dream. You will need people around you, working with and for you. Where there are people, there is often mess –it just comes along with the package. However if you want increase in your life, you will probably need some hard working people to help you fulfill your desires, dreams and destiny. You will have to take the good with the bad. Dedicated, devoted, hard working people will help you get the job done, but sometimes we will have to clean up the messes that come along with prosperity and productivity. Increase is by the strength of the ox.

Decide if you want increase. If you do, you will need some oxen. The stalls will need cleaning, but your harvest will be fruitful!

Scripture Reading: Psalms 65, 66, 67; Romans 2

August 2

"God is Truth"

Titus 1:2 — In hope of eternal life, which God, that cannot lie, promised before the world began.

God cannot lie! The text does not say "God will not lie," it states, "God cannot lie." God is absolute truth, there is nothing false in Him. Jesus is truth incarnate. Jesus said Himself that He came into the world to bear witness to the truth. (John 18:37)

Since God the Father is totally truth and Jesus who came to reveal to us the Father's character and heart, is the truth, we can take God at His Word—every time!

Every word Jesus spoke was inspired by His Father. Every teaching, every exhortation, every admonition, and every sermon given by the Lord Jesus is truth. Truth spoke truth. Jesus is the truth. (John 14:6) God cannot lie. Jesus cannot lie. The Holy Spirit cannot lie.

Today you can trust God, and take Him at His Word. All His promises are true. Every promise in His Word is yours, and you can believe in them. Whatever you are going through at this moment, at this time and season of your life, may you trust in a God who speaks truth, who is truth, who cannot lie!

Scripture Reading: Psalms 68, 69; Romans 3

Trivia Question: According to the book of James, what has the Lord promised to them who endure trials and temptations?

August 3

"Of Sound Mind"

Jeremiah 17:7 — Blessed is the man that trusteth in the Lord, and whose hope the Lord is.

There is a great blessing for the ones who put their trust in God. In order for someone to trust another, that person would have to be trust-worthy. Scripture teaches us that God is truly trustworthy. He does not alter His Word or change His character. God is not a man that He should lie, neither the Son of man that he should repent. He has said, and shall He not do it? Or has He spoken, and shall He not make it good? (Numbers 23:19)

Man changes his mind, his motives and his message, but God does not. You can take God at His Word. Search out all of His promises; they are all true. You will be blessed as you put your trust in the Lord. God will do what He has promised. He will make good on His Word. Believe in, cling to, rely on, and trust in God and all His promises. He will not fail you. Today, be blessed as you put your trust in the Lord.

Scripture Reading: Psalms 70, 71, 72; Romans 4

Trivia Question: In the Beatitudes, what group of people will be called, "the children of God?"

August 4

"Love is the Life Saver"

Song of Solomon 8:7a — Many waters cannot quench love, neither can the floods drown it.

One thing remains through all the tests, trials, troubles and tears of life. That is the love of Jesus. Through all of the storms of life, God's love will keep you. The love of God remains faithful and never leaves you, even when others run off on you in the midst of challenges and crises.

The prophet Isaiah said, "when you pass through the waters, I will be with you, and through the rivers, they shall not overflow you." (Isaiah 43:2)

The love of Jesus will keep you from being overwhelmed, overcome and overwrought. His love will keep you from falling.

If you are facing a storm of some sort, or going through deep waters, the love of God will keep you afloat. His love is a life-saver in the midst of the storm. Many waters cannot overcome love, neither can the floods drown it. Rest in God's love. This love is shed abroad in our heart by the Holy Spirit. His love will prevent you from drowning. Trust in His love today and may His love take you to higher heights, deeper depths and cause you to fly higher than you ever have before.

215

Scripture Reading: Psalms 73, 74; Romans 5

Trivia Question: Who said, "Follow my example as I follow the example of Christ."

August 5

"The Anointing"

Acts 10:38 — How God anointed Jesus of Nazareth with the Holy Spirit and with power, who went about doing good and healing all who were oppressed by the devil, for God was with Him. (NKJV)

What does the theological word, anointing mean? How is it defined in biblical language? More importantly, what does anointing do for me today?

The prophet Isaiah teaches that this "anointing" will take burdens off of shoulders and take yokes (or anything that causes pain) off of necks, and completely destroy or annihilate the yoke. (Isaiah 10:27)

In the Old Testament when Samuel, to appoint the next king of Israel, sought the young shepherd boy out, David had to be anointed first. "Then Samuel took the horn of oil and anointed him (David) in the midst of his brothers and the Spirit of the Lord came upon David from that day forward." (1 Samuel 16:13)

We see that the anointing of God and the Spirit of God are coupled together. The anointing and the Spirit of God are also linked to the power of God. The text says, "God anointed Jesus of Nazareth with the Holy Spirit and power who went about doing good and healing all those that were oppressed of the devil, for God was with Him." Anointing, the Holy Spirit and power work together.

So the anointing defined is the manifestation of the presence and the fullness of the Holy Spirit who is the power of God demonstrated to others.

Let His anointing lift your burden right now. Let His anointing take, remove and destroy any yoke that has you bound and in pain. The Holy Spirit and His power with the anointing will do it for you. Just believe and receive.

Scripture Reading: Psalms 75, 76, 77; Romans 6

Trivia Question: What did the apostle Paul teach is the fulfilling of the law?

August 6

"Your Best Friend"

John 15:13 — Greater love hath no man than this,
that a man lay down his life for his friends.

From time to time we all experience seasons of loneliness. Times that we *feel* like we do not have a friend in the whole world. Have you ever felt that way?

Truth is, at one time or another we all go through that emotion. Jesus is a friend who sticks closer than a brother. (Proverbs 18:24) Jesus is a friend who loves you at all times. (Proverbs 17:17) Even when we are unlovable, Jesus' love never fails or gives up on us. (1 Corinthians 13:8a)

Jesus loves you so much, that He was willing to go to the cross and die for you. He proved His love to us. There is no greater love than someone who gives his life. Jesus gave his life for us. You are His friend. Jesus is your best friend. Jesus who is Savior/friend took away your sin. He has redeemed us and ransomed us. He paid the price of ransom with His own life. What a friend!

Next time you feel all alone without a friend in the whole world, remember your friend Jesus and the ultimate gift He has purchased for you—the gift of salvation, forgiveness and His friendship. "Henceforth I call you not servants, for the servant knows not what his lord does, but I have called you friends." (John 15:15)

Love Jesus today with all your heart. He loves you and proved His love. He died on the cross for you and He calls you His friend.

Scripture Reading: Psalms 78; Romans 7

Trivia Question: The psalmist said "If I regard iniquity in my heart the Lord _____."

August 7

"Entrusted Overseers"

1 Corinthians 4:2 — Moreover, it is required in stewards
that a man be found faithful.

A steward is someone who has been entrusted by an authority to oversee someone (people), something (places) or some event (things). A steward is one who assumes the responsibility to oversee what has been entrusted to him. A steward takes ownership.

It is required that a steward be found faithful. An overseer is who a steward is, and faithful is how he gets the job done.

God wants to entrust His people with people, places and things. Abraham had stewardship over his nephew Lot. (people) (Genesis 12:5) Adam had stewardship over the garden that God put him in and was told to care for it. (place) (Genesis 2:15) The servants were entrusted and had stewardship over the talents that their employer put in their care. (things) (Matthew 25:15)

What has God entrusted to you? What does God want you to be a faithful steward over? What do you need to take ownership of?

As you become more faithful before God in areas like your time, talents and treasure, God will call you to stewardship. You too can be an entrusted overseer for God and His Kingdom.

Scripture Reading: Psalms 79, 80, 81; Romans 8:1-18

Trivia Question: Why did Jesus say earthly treasures are uncertain?

August 8

"Safe Counsel"

Proverbs 11:14 — Where no counsel is, the people fall:
but in the multitude of counsellors there is safety.

There will be times in your life that you will need help, godly help! No one can do everything that life demands by themselves; good godly instruction and counsel is needed. More than a voice of reason is needed, but a godly voice in season. It could make the difference in one's life between victory or defeat, winning or losing, slipping and sliding or soaring and gliding.

We must seek out godly counsel when needed—someone who has studied God's Word and has it in his/her heart. When godly counsel is needed, but not sought after, the results can be dangerous. "Where no counsel is, the people fall."

God has raised up individuals in our sphere of influence that have a gift of counseling –people that are gifted and anointed by the Spirit of God to impart truth. Jesus was the greatest counselor and has given that gift to others. "And the Spirit of the Lord shall rest upon him, the spirit of wisdom and understanding, the spirit of counsel and might, the spirit of knowledge and the fear of the Lord." (Isaiah 9:6, Isaiah 11:2)

"Counsel in the heart of man is like deep water; but a man of understanding will draw it out." (Proverbs 20:5)

May we all seek to hide God's Word in our hearts so that we too can refresh the weary soul with sound, wise counsel from the Word of God.

There is safety in much counsel. More of godly counsel, more of the Word and more of the truth will take us out of the *danger zone* and put us in a safe place.

May God bring you good, godly counsel when you need it.

Scripture Reading: Psalms 82, 83, 84; Romans 8:19-39

Trivia Question: What were the names of the two midwives in Egypt who were instructed by Pharaoh to have all the male babies killed?

August 9

"Divine Purpose"

Exodus 2:1-4 — And there went a man of the house of Levi, and took to wife a daughter of Levi. And the woman conceived, and bare a son: and when she saw him that he was a goodly child, she hid him three months. And when she could not longer hide him, she took for him an ark of bulrushes, and daubed it with slime and with pitch, and put the child therein; and she laid it in the flags by the river's brink. And his sister stood afar off, to wit what would be done to him.

The Pharaoh made the decree, "all the baby boys born shall be cast into the Nile River and drowned." Egypt and Pharaoh were paranoid because the Hebrews were growing and multiplying. Pharaoh set task masters over God's people, and made them slaves in hopes that their will would break and they would become anemic physically, spiritually and emotionally. "But the more they (Egyptians) afflicted them, the more they multiplied and grew." (Exodus 1:12)

Amram and Jochabed gave birth to a baby boy. Jochabed, his mother, was able to hide him from the authorities for just three months. The mother refused to give into fear. She defied the decree of the king. Jochabed believed if God gave her a baby boy, there must have been a divine purpose for his life. She made a little "baby boat" and brought him to the place where many babies met their watery grave; a place of death. Jochabed believed God, even in the face of death threats and the place where death had been experienced, her boy would live. God's purpose was stronger than Pharoah's decree. God's purpose causes fear to back down. When purpose is saturated in faith, it causes you to step out and persevere. "By faith, Moses when he was born was hidden three months by his parents, because they saw he was a beautiful child, and they were not afraid of the king's commandments." (Hebrews 11:23)

Wow! Parents that believed in a purpose for their child!

Friend, your heavenly Father believes in a purpose for you, His child. Believe today!

No matter what negative words have been spoken over you, in spite of your background, your race, your portfolio, your social status, or no status at all. God has a divine purpose for you. To find it out will be your greatest goal in life. Seek God for a divine revelation concerning His divine purpose.

Remember, people that pursue purpose, do not fear what man says or the threats of the culture. God has a divine purpose for you!

Scripture Reading: Psalms 85, 86, 87; Romans 9

Trivia Question: In the parable, the pearl of great price, what did the merchant do when he found a pearl of tremendous value?

August 10

"Hide and Seek"

Isaiah 55:6 — Seek ye the Lord while He may be found,
call ye upon Him while He is near.

Is God hiding on you? Is God trying to make Himself obscure, making it difficult to recognize Him?

The Lord is not hiding, nor is He trying to make Himself obscure. He is not afar off.

Jeremiah 29:13 says, "And you shall seek me and find me, when you search for me with all your heart."

God is looking to reveal Himself to those who are passionately pursuing Him, hungry and thirsty for Him, and are seeking Him above and beyond anyone or anything else.

God wants to make Himself known to anyone who is diligently seeking Him. He will answer when you call upon Him. He is not only near, He is here!

David said in Psalms 27:8, "When you said, seek my face, my heart said to you, thy face, Lord will I seek."

"O God, you are my God, early will I seek thee, my soul thirsts for you, my flesh longs for you in a dry and thirsty land, where no water is." (Psalms 63:1)

Scripture Reading: Psalms 88, 89; Romans 10

Trivia Question: According to the Apostle Paul what cannot the eye say to the hand?

August 11

"How Big is God?"

Psalms 34:3 — Oh, magnify the Lord with me,
and let us exalt His name together.

When observing some people's attempt to read the small print on a label or jar, it is very common for them to use a magnifying glass. Obviously, the magnification causes the words to be enlarged, making it easier to read.

When a Christian goes through tough times, the storms of life or the darkest season they ever encountered, it could seem that the problem is bigger and greater than the promise of God.

It is during those times that we need to do what David did—magnify the Lord! Magnify in this context means, to make large or promote. When we magnify the Lord, we are making Him larger than what we are going through. When we magnify the Lord, He becomes bigger than what we are facing.

One way you can magnify the Lord is by meditating on His Word and promises. When the Word is deep down on the inside of you, you get a biblical image of who God is—the Great I Am! Another way to magnify the Lord is by lifting Him up in your praise. When you exalt the Lord in praise, you are placing Him higher than anyone or anything else. He is higher than your problem! He is higher, greater, bigger and stronger than any test that you face! How big is God? As big as you see Him in the Word, as big as you praise Him in your life. May God's greatness be revealed to you today. Oh, magnify the Lord with me, and let us exalt His name together.

Scripture Reading: Psalms 90, 91, 92; Romans 11:1-21

Trivia Question: Who are the three that bear record in Heaven?

August 12

"Buried Treasure"

2 Corinthians 4:7 — But we have this treasure in earthen vessels, that the excellency of the power may be of God, and not of us.

On the inside of every believer is a wonderful treasure. God chose to make His abode in us in the person of the Holy Spirit.

Jesus said, "and I will pray to the Father, and He shall give you another comforter (the Holy Spirit) that He may abide with you (or in you) forever."

Wow! God is in us! Christ is in us the hope of glory. The Spirit of God dwells on the inside. The Holy Spirit of God who demonstrates the power of God, lives on the inside of the believer. Paul said, "And my speech and my preaching was not with enticing words of man's wisdom, but in demonstration of the Spirit and of power…" (1 Corinthians 2:4) The Spirit of God and the power of God cannot be separate, both live on the inside of the born again believer. The power is not man-made, manufactured or manipulated. This power is of God, and not of us.

Stop saying that you are weak. God's treasure is on the inside of you. His power resides in your re-created spirit. The power of God lives in you. You are an overcomer—saved, healed and delivered by the power of God. This power remains in you by the Holy Spirit. His power is excellent and available today. Draw from His excellent powerful treasure. Change is on the way for you!

Scripture Reading: Psalms 93, 94, 95; Romans 11:22-36

Trivia Question: Who betrayed Jesus for 30 pieces of silver?

August 13

"Team Work"

Romans 15:7 — Wherefore receive ye one another,

as Christ also received us to the glory of God.

The word "team" defined, is a cooperative unit, two or more to pull something, or individuals that harmoniously work/minister together to achieve a common goal. To make the dream work, you have to make the team work. You can have a great dream, but without a team, it will only remain in the womb of anticipation and expectation.

On any team there will be diversities, differences and dichotomies. There will be cultural, racial and background distinctions. The Word of God exhorts us to receive one another. It is so important if we are serving on the same team, whether it is a vocational, athletic or ministry team, that there is a respect for one another. If one person on a team thinks he/she is superior to the rest, then schisms will be evident. When a team works together to achieve a common goal, with mutual respect for each other, the chances of attaining the prize or goal is much better.

Paul said to receive one another as Christ received us! Wow, the thought that Jesus received us with all our quirks, personality flaws, shortcomings and challenges helps us to remember when someone is very *different* from us, we must receive him/her just as Jesus received us.

May we all see our dream work with great teamwork, as we receive and respect one another for Jesus' sake.

Scripture Reading: Psalms 96, 97, 98; Romans 12

Trivia Question: Who did the Apostle Paul team up with on his first missionary journey?

August 14

"God's Love"

John 3:16 — For God so loved the world that He gave His only begotten Son, that whosoever believeth in Him would not perish but have everlasting life.

Love is an action word. God is love. God proved His love for all humankind by sending His Son to this world to suffer and die for all of man's sin. Jesus took our place on the cross—the sinless one bearing the sin of all. "But God commendeth his love toward us, in that, while we were yet sinners, Christ died for us." (Romans 5:8)

There is no excuse for anyone to go to Hell. Jesus paid the price for all.

Even while we were sinners, Jesus died for us. That is unconditional love. If you feel unloved today, just get a glimpse of the cross. Behold the blood stained tree of Calvary. God is love. Jesus is love. The Holy Spirit is love!

God has made a way for all to be saved. No one has to perish, but believe in Jesus for eternal life. Receive God's love today and share God's love with someone. Tell somebody God has made provision for them to make Heaven their home. He sent His Son Jesus to pay the price. May the whole world know that God is love. Love sent Jesus to the world. Love motivated Jesus to die for all mankind's sin. Love is going to cause Jesus to come back again.

Scripture Reading: Psalm 99, 100, 101, 102; Romans 13

Trivia Question: What kind of sleep does God promise us in His Word?

August 15

"Turn to Me"

Zechariah 1:3 — Therefore say thou unto them, Thus saith the Lord of hosts; Turn ye unto me, saith the Lord of hosts, and I will turn unto you, saith the Lord of hosts.

In a day of complacency, indifference and apostasy, the Lord is calling His people once again to turn to Him. He says if we would turn to Him, then He will turn to us.

The prophet Zechariah encouraged God's people after seventy years in Babylonian captivity to turn back to God with all their hearts. God's people, because of their ungodly ways and unrighteous behavior, went into exile in Babylon. Through God's mercy, the heart of the king of Babylon was touched and softened by God and the people of the Lord were released to return to their homeland. The Lord warned and admonished them, if they did not, "turn to the Lord" another captivity would be inevitable. The Lord never wants to be distanced from His people. This is why in the new covenant Jesus came to bridge the gap between sinful man and a Holy God. Jesus died on the cross, shed His blood to cleanse our sin, and made a way for us to approach and turn Godward. As we turn to God, through the righteousness of Christ and His holy blood, God turns to us. May sin never detach us from our God. If you know someone who is away from God, simply tell him/her to turn back to Him. He will turn His favor and forgiveness toward the penitent heart. What a loving Father we have. Turn to Him!

Scripture Reading: Psalms 103, 104; Romans 14

Trivia Question: Who stood up on the day of Pentecost and preached with great influence and power?

August 16

"Believe and Speak"

*2 Corinthians 4:13 — We having the same spirit of faith,
according as it is written, I believed, and therefore have I spoken;
we also believe, and therefore speak.*

There are different ways we release faith that is in our hearts. One way is by confession or speaking through your mouth what is in your heart. Jesus taught, "For out of the abundance of the heart, the mouth speaks." (Matthew 12:34b)

It is expedient to meditate on God's Word and promises. Hide His Word in your heart. (Psalms 119:111) Let your heart become a reservoir filled with abundant words of God. "Faith comes by hearing, and hearing by the word of God." (Romans 10:17) When we fill our hearts with God's Word, faith will come and come in abundance—the same spirit of faith that Paul possessed and talked about in 2 Corinthians 4:13. Paul went through trials and troubles, heartache and heartbreak, dark times and desperate times. Through it all, he believed in a God through His Son Jesus to deliver him from all affliction and attacks. Paul quoted David, who also went through difficult seasons, from Psalms 116:10. Both Paul and David believed and spoke His Word. We release the faith that is in our hearts through our mouths.

Do you believe Jesus is your deliverer? Then speak His promise of deliverance out of your mouth. (Psalm 32:7) Do you believe Jesus is your healer? Then speak His healing promises out of your mouth. (Isaiah 53:5, Matthew 8:17, 1 Peter 2:24, 3 John 2, Acts 10:38) Do you believe Jesus redeemed you from the curse of the law, then speak it out of your mouth. (Galatians 3:13)

Believe God and His Word, and speak it out our your mouth. The spoken Word releases your faith!

Scripture Reading: Psalms 105, 106; Romans 15:1-20

Trivia Question: How many souls were saved after Peter preached his sermon at Pentecost?

August 17

"Heart to Heart"

Colossians 3:23 — And whatsoever ye do, do it heartily,
as to the Lord, and not unto men.

The expression "do it with all your heart" is biblically based. Some peoples' hearts are not in the things they do, or in their job performance, or even their relationships. You can only do something with all your heart from a thankful heart. People that are appreciative in life usually respond with heartfelt actions.

When we really understand Calvary, the cross and the price Jesus paid for our salvation, we become a thankful people—a people full of thanksgiving. Out of that thankful heart we respond whole-heartedly to the requests and demands of life. If we understand, doing all things heartily as unto the Lord and not unto men, even the things we do for men will be done with our whole heart. This is because we are thankful to God for all the blessings He has bestowed on us. If our whole heartedness stems out of a thankful heart to God, our response to men becomes easier, not burdensome.

Be thankful today to God. It will cause you to be a better friend, employee, brother or sister, citizen, etc. Thankful people respond to the demands of life, remembering that they do all things heartily, as unto the Lord.

Scripture Reading: Psalms 107, 108; Romans 15:21-33

Trivia Question: How many pillars does wisdom hewn out?

August 18

"The Redeemer Rewards"

Colossians 3:24 — Knowing that of the Lord ye shall receive
the reward of the inheritance: for ye serve the Lord Christ.

The Bible talks about crowns or rewards the Savior bestows upon his faithful, hard working servants. It teaches on five specific crowns. The first is the Incorruptible Crown. (1 Corinthians 9:24-27) This crown awaits all those that have completed the call, fulfilled their God-given destiny, accomplished their assignment, finished their course and have run their race. This is "the finishing the course crown."

Many have started out well, but have not finished well. There are many examples in the Bible of people who started to run their race, but sin, character flaws, the pleasures of this world, the lust of other things and deceitfulness of riches derailed them, and so they never completed their race or journey. "Better is the end of a thing than the beginning thereof..." (Ecclesiastes 7:8)

God has set each and every one of us in our race, and is cheering us on to complete the call on our lives. (Hebrews 12:1)

Purpose and resolve in your heart to run your race well, and determine to finish your course. The incorruptible crown awaits you in the day when you see Jesus face to face. May you hear the words of the Master, "well done, thou good and faithful servant thou hast been faithful over a few things, I will make thee ruler over many things: enter thou into the joy of thy lord." (Matthew 25:21)

Scripture Reading: Psalms 109, 110, 111; Romans 16

Trivia Question: What did the Master do to the servant who hid the talent that was given to him in the parable of the talents?

August 19

"The Crown of Rejoicing"

I Thessalonians 2:19 — For what is our hope, or joy, or crown of rejoicing? Are not even ye in the presence of our Lord Jesus Christ at his coming.

The second crown mentioned in the Bible is the Crown of Rejoicing. This crown is the soul winner's crown.

We are to give away our faith. Jesus said, "freely you have received, freely give." (Matthew 10:8) We are called His witnesses in Acts 1:8, and as witnesses we are to share with people the wonderful Gospel or goodness of the Kingdom of God. Our family, friends, co-workers, classmates and associates need to hear how much God loves them—in sending His Son to die for them on a cross, shed His blood and gave His life. Jesus loved people to death.

Today, will you purpose in your heart to be salt and light and tell someone the great love story that Jesus shed His blood to forgive all his/her sin? They can become a child of God. People need to know we are all God's creation at our natural birth, but we do not become God's child until we experience our spiritual birth by being born again.

When we determine to be soul-winners, share the Gospel to many, lead individuals to Christ, and joyfully see people born into the Kingdom of God, we become candidates for the Crown of Rejoicing or the soul winner's crown. Let us spread the seeds of God's Word, and see them grow into salvation in our friends, family, coworkers, classmates, neighbors and associates. "He that goeth forth and weepeth, bearing precious seed, shall doubtless come again with rejoicing, bringing his sheaves with him." (Psalm 126:6)

Scripture Reading: Psalms 112, 113, 114, 115; 1 Corinthians 1

Trivia Question: How many people did Jesus feed with only five loves of bread and two small fish?

August 20

"Overcomers"

James 1:12 — Blessed is the man that endureth temptation:
for when he is tried, he shall receive the crown of life,
which the Lord hath promised to them that love him.

Another crown or reward that will be offered by Jesus to those faithful followers is the Crown of Life.

This reward is for those who have persevered, have overcome temptation, and have remained faithful to Jesus even in the face of adverse situations and circumstances.

When Jesus addressed one of the seven churches in Revelation (Smyrna), he said, "be faithful unto death, and I will give thee a crown of life."

So this crown is for those who do not succumb to temptation and stay faithful to God and His Word.

In a day where there is so much coming at you, a culture where it is easier to quit than to continue, Jesus is empowering His own to overcome temptation by the devil. Purpose in your heart to remain faithful to God, His Word, His ways and His will.

Learn to endure and overcome temptation like Jesus did, by speaking God's Word to every temptation you face. (Matthew 4, Luke 4)

The Crown of Life awaits all those that endure temptation and remain faithful to God until the end.

Scripture Reading: Psalms 116, 117, 118; 1 Corinthians 2

Trivia Question: What was the animal that spoke to Balaam?

August 21

"The Crown of Righteousness"

2 Timothy 4:8 — Henceforth there is laid up for me a crown of righteousness, which the Lord, the righteous judge, shall give me at that day: and not to me only, but unto all them also that love his appearing.

Are you looking for Jesus? Do you believe He is coming back? The Bible says, "this same Jesus who is taken up from you into Heaven, shall so come in the like manner as ye have seen Him go into Heaven." (Acts 1:11b)

I do not believe God wants us to be gazing up into Heaven waiting for Jesus to come back, while our dreams are not pursued, our destiny unfulfilled, and the downcast unattended. The Gospel must be preached, the sick must be prayed for, the lost must be found.

While we are impacting our world for Christ, there must be anticipation for the *catching away of the church*, and the appearing of our Lord. The Bible does not teach a passive Christianity, but a proactive faith. Simultaneously we are looking for His appearing, but living for Him actively.

Those that "love His appearing" are a people that are living holy and are ready for the announcement of Gabriel and the trumpet of God, all indicating that Jesus is appearing to take all believers with Him to their heavenly home. (1 Thessalonians 4:13-18)

Are you ready? Are you looking? Are you living for Him? A Crown of Righteousness awaits you.

Scripture Reading: Psalm 119:1-48; 1 Corinthians 3

Trivia Question: Who was the priest that discovered the book of the Law in the temple during King Josiah's reign?

August 22

"The Crown of Glory"

*1 Peter 5:4 — And when the chief Shepherd shall appear,
ye shall receive a crown of glory that fadeth not away.*

What an honor it is for those who have been mandated by Christ to teach, preach and care for God's people. The call to shepherd God's flock is truly a privilege. This Crown of Glory has been promised to all those who take feeding, leading and protecting the sheep of God's pasture very seriously. Those that understand their assignment from the Chief Shepherd, as under-shepherds, to passionately care for the sheep, await this wonderful reward.

Jesus, who is called the Good Shepherd, Great Shepherd and Chief Shepherd in Scripture, shall appear one day soon with a Crown of Glory to the faithful stewards. The Crown of Glory will never fade away.

Have you been called by God to care for someone? If you have been, do it with all your heart. Not because you have to, but because you want to. Not because of money, but because it is God's mandate on your life. Overseeing God's people is an awesome task. A Crown of Glory will be yours!

Scripture Reading: Psalm 119:49-104; 1 Corinthians 4

Trivia Question: How many wise men came to visit the baby Jesus?

August 23

"Soar like an Eagle"

*Psalm 103:5 — Who satisfieth thy mouth with good things;
so that thy youth is renewed like the eagle's.*

While some ornithologists (people who study birds), believe it to be legend; others believe for the eagle to have the longest lifespan of the species, it must go through a difficult, renewing process. For an eagle to reach the age of about 70 years, it must make a hard decision. In its 40's, its long and flexible talons become stiff and brittle and can no longer grab prey, which serves as food. Its long and sharp beak that catches larger prey becomes bent. Its aged and heavy wings, due to its thick feathers, become stuck to its chest and make it difficult to fly. Then the eagle is left with only two options: die or go through a painful process of change, which lasts around five months.

The process requires that the eagle fly to a mountaintop and sit on its nest. There the eagle knocks its beak against a rock until it falls out. After having the beak plucked out, the eagle will wait for a new beak to grow back and then it will pluck out its talons. Eventually when the new talons grow back, the eagle starts plucking its age-old feathers. After five months, the eagle takes its famous flight of rebirth and can live another thirty years.

Is there anything in your life that is making it difficult for you to fly high? God wants each of us to soar to greater heights. He wants to renew our youth like the eagle. In order to do that, we too must be willing to go through a painful process of change. We must be willing to pluck out the age-old feathers and shed off anything and everything that is making it difficult to soar in God. We too were made to fly high, over our problems, crises and circumstances. We must be willing to shed off sin that keeps us grounded—lust, unforgiveness, jealousy, gossip, over-eating, under-eating, etc. May God give grace to pluck out the old, aged, weighty feathers in our lives so we can soar to new heights. Fly high!

Scripture Reading: Psalm 119:105-176; 1 Corinthians 5

Trivia Question: How many things work together for good to those who are called according to His purpose?

August 24

"Contender not Pretender"

Jude 3 — Beloved, when I gave all diligence to write unto you of the common salvation, it was needful for me to write unto you, and exhort you that ye should earnestly contend for the faith which was once delivered unto the saints.

We live in perilous times with false doctrines, false prophets and false apostles. We face complacency, indifference and apostasy in our culture. The devil works hard and furious to take people off course, to detour and derail them. Terrorism puts fear in many. False religions seem to pop up overnight regularly. We must contend for the faith. The Lord is exhorting us through Jude to defend that, which has been entrusted to us through the Scriptures. Scripture is holy, unadulterated, immutable and inerrant. We must defend the Holy Writ.

One of the definitions for "contend" is, to compete for something or to be engaged in a fight. We are competing for the souls of men. All of the falsehood attempts to deceive men and draw them away from Jesus the truth. We are in a spiritual fight to believe, communicate and uphold truth. We must not pretend to know truth, we must believe, receive and embrace truth. "And you shall know the truth, and the truth will make you free." (John 8:32) The battle is on—truth verses error, light verses darkness, good verses evil and Jesus verses Satan. Be on the side of truth and defend it, on your job, in the schoolhouse, in the church house and in the state house. May truth and freedom ring! Be contenders of the faith. The Bible is truth. Truth brings faith. Fight to defend faith –faith in God and His Holy Word.

Scripture Reading: Psalm 120, 121, 122, 123; 1 Corinthians 6

Trivia Question: What other name did Jesus give to Peter?

August 25

"STRONG"

Ephesians 6:10 — Finally, my brethren, be strong in the Lord, and in the power of his might.

There are times during testing, challenge, sorrow and loss, well meaning people have given advice, "Be strong." This sounds good and correct, but what if we have exhausted all of our strength. What if the strength tank is running on fumes at best.

God does not expect us, especially during times of peril and distress to muster enough strength within ourselves to try to get through the difficult and hard season that is confronting us. Rather, the Lord encourages us to draw strength from Him, who is the God of all strength and might. His well never runs dry! (Psalm 46:1, Psalm 81:1)

Be strong in God and draw from His power and might. Maybe you are facing things today that seem insurmountable, bigger than life, mountains that will not seemingly move. The God of Israel is He who gives strength and power unto His people. (Psalm 68:35)

Draw from "El Gibbor," the God of all might and power and He will strengthen your heart, and you will be able to endure your battle and come out victoriously!

Scripture Reading: Psalms 124, 125, 126, 127; 1 Corinthians 7:1-24

Trivia Question: What is a key to being delivered from confusion?

August 26

"Why Worship?"

Psalm 81:10 — I am the Lord thy God, which brought thee out of the land of Egypt: open thy mouth wide, and I will fill it.

Never forget what God has done for you. Never take for granted the amazing things God has brought you through. God delivers us out of bondage to bring us into blessing.

Israel constantly committed the sin of forgetfulness. They forgot that God delivered them from Egyptian bondage. During their wilderness journey, when faced with trials and tribulations, instead of worshipping for the wonderful deliverance, they murmured because of the circumstance. They forgot that the Lord gave them a mighty deliverance.

In our journey with Jesus, we too will face tests, trials, troubles and tears. May we never forget that the Lord has delivered us from sin, Satan, sickness and spiritual slavery.

Remember always what God has done for you and you will be a constant, perpetual worshipper. Our mouths will be filled with thanks and wonderful worship to the Lord. Why worship? Because He has brought us out of bondage!

Scripture Reading: Psalm 128, 129, 130, 131; 1 Corinthians 7:25-40

Trivia Question: What were the four empires that Daniel spoke about in his vision?

August 27

"Correct Connections"

Amos 3:3 — Can two walk together, except they be agreed?

There is great danger in connecting with those that are not walking in the same direction that you are. Those who are not in covenant with the Jesus you love and serve.

Ephesians 5:11 says, "And have no fellowship with the unfruitful works of darkness, but rather reprove them." In these last days of perilous times and a culture of compromise, we have to make correct choices about who we connect with, fellowship with, are yoked with in business, partner with, do ministry with and marry!

This is important to understand, because Satan will try to get you watered down for Christ, get you off your focus, detour, discredit, defame, depress and derail you any way he can.

You have a destiny to fulfill, allow nothing or no one to short circuit you. Three things to help you be successful in life and to accomplish your God-given assignment are: know who you are in Christ, know where you want to go in life, and choose correct connections that will help you get there. Enjoy the journey!

Scripture Reading: Psalms 132, 133, 134, 135; 1 Corinthians 8

Trivia Question: How many admonitions (warnings) do you give a heretic before you reject them?

August 28

"The Passionate Pardone"

*Micah 7:18 — Who is a God like unto thee, that pardoneth iniquity,
and passeth by the transgression of the remnant of his heritage?
he retaineth not his anger for ever, because he delighteth in mercy.*

What a merciful God we serve. What a wonderful Savior. What an amazing giver of grace. A Master of mercy!

God will have a remnant in these last days that understands the mercy and forgiveness of God. A people who have been pardoned from their iniquity and transgression and have truly repented and turned from their sins.

A God who delights in mercy is a God that desires fellowship with His people. Sin has and always will separate people from God and His Holiness. Jesus came to bridge the breach that sin has caused between the Father and us. Jesus connects us with the Father through His death, burial, resurrection and ascension.

When someone is pardoned, they are forgiven, their debt has been paid, their slate wiped clean and they have been given another chance to start over. When someone is pardoned they are excused of an offense, they are formally liberated!

The Passionate Pardoner has liberated us from the offense, the shame and the slavery of sin!

Jesus is not angry with you, He delights in mercy and is ready to pardon. Just ask Him if you need forgiveness. He delights in manifesting His pardon to you. He is truly the Master of Mercy.

Scripture Reading: Psalms 136, 137, 138; 1 Corinthians 9

Trivia Question: In the book of Romans what was Paul's earnest desire and prayer for Israel?

August 29

"Ministering to the Lord"

Acts 13:1-2 — Now there were in the church that was at Antioch certain prophets and teachers; as Barnabas, and Simeon that was called Niger, and Lucius of Cyrene, and Manaen, which had been brought up with Herod the tetrarch, and Saul. As they ministered to the Lord, and fasted, the Holy Spirit said, Separate me Barnabas and Saul for the work whereunto I have called them.

The Christians that were in Jerusalem scattered because of major persecutions that came to the church. The Jerusalem church was made up of Jewish believers. The Antioch church was multicultural and filled with diversity. (Heaven will be multi-ethnic and multi-racial.)

At a gathering of Christian leaders made up of prophets and teachers in Antioch, the people were seeking the Lord. The text says, "As they ministered to the Lord and fasted..."

What does it mean to minister to the Lord? How do we minister to a great God? Does He even need ministering? The true essence of the word minister means to serve. There are different ways Christians serve the Lord. One way we minister to the Lord is through prayer. When Christians pray, they serve the Lord in a major way. Many times in the Bible fasting is coupled with prayer. It is most likely these Christian leaders were having an old fashioned prayer meeting as they were fasting. They needed answers, direction and guidance. Notice in the Scripture, as they ministered to the Lord (prayer and praise), the Holy Spirit spoke. God gave direction for Saul and Barnabas in the assignment that God ordained for them. The Lord spoke clearly in the midst of prayer and fasting and gave to His choice servants the clarion call. Hence, Paul's first missionary journey was birthed.

Do you need direction and guidance in your life? Do you need a clear understanding of what God has for you in the next chapter of your life?

Try ministering to the Lord. Prayer, coupled with fasting, will cause God to speak to you by the Holy Spirit. Prayer and fasting is vital in our serving the Lord. The same Holy Spirit that spoke to Barnabas, Simeon, Lucius and Manaen, while ministering to the Lord, will speak to you. You can count on it!

Scripture Reading: Psalms 139, 140, 141; 1 Corinthians 10:1-13

Trivia Question: What was made flesh and dwelt among us?

August 30
"The Road Less Traveled"

Matthew 7:13-14 — Enter ye in at the strait gate: for wide is the gate, and broad is the way, that leadeth to destruction, and many there be which go in thereat: Because strait is the gate, and narrow is the way, which leadeth unto life, and few there be that find it.

The crowd is not always right. Jesus gives us truth in this portion of Scripture that we need to direct our attention to. Jesus said there are two roads in life. One road has a wide gate or entranceway that leads to a broader way. Many travel that road, but it leads to destruction. It is a road of deception. It looks inviting, it looks popular, it looks well-traveled, and it looks like many have chosen that way; but it leads to devastation and destruction.

Do not travel down that road. All that glitters is not gold!

Few travel the road with the narrow gate or entranceway that leads to a hard way. It is not inviting, it is not popular, there are only a few journeyers, but this less traveled road leads to life. It is the road of truth. Jesus is the truth. Jesus is the right way. Jesus leads us into life.

Choose the right road. Travel the way of truth. Do not be hoodwinked by the crowds or the glitter. Choose Jesus and His Word. He will lead you into life, abundant and eternal. Bigger is not necessarily better. More is not necessarily right. Jesus is the right way. Choose Jesus and His way.

Scripture Reading: Psalms 142, 143, 144; 1 Corinthians 10:14-33

Trivia Question: What married couple deceived Peter and lied to the Holy Spirit with fatal consequences?

August 31

"Missing the Target"

Romans 3:23 — For all have sinned and come short of the glory of God.

Not one person in the whole human race, past, present and future is flawless. No one has arrived. Not one person is without sin. We all have broken God's laws. (James 2:10)

When Paul used the term, "come short," the inference is an archer who draws back his bow and arrow, aims at his target and misses it. The archer tries to hit the bull's eye, but misses the target completely.

We have all missed the mark. We have all tried but failed to hit the goal. We all fall short of God's standard and God's holiness. We have sinned. Sinners need a savior. God sent Jesus to die and offered grace for us, even though we missed His target.

His grace is available for all. Jesus paid the price for each one to receive forgiveness for their sins. "Being justified freely by His grace through the redemption that is in Christ Jesus." (Romans 3:24)

Do not fret about missing the mark, coming short or not hitting the target, everyone fails. Jesus has washed us clean through His blood. Rejoice and receive His redemption today!

Scripture Reading: Psalms 145, 146, 147; 1 Corinthians 11:1-15

Trivia Question: Who is the faithful witness, first begotten of the dead, and the prince of the kings of the Earth?

September

September 1

"Attitude of Gratitude"

Psalm 107:1 — O give thanks unto the Lord, for he is good:
for his mercy endureth for ever.

When we get a revelation that the Lord is so good, we will always maintain a thankful heart. God's goodness is beyond fathoming at times. His goodness is boundless and endless. He is good. God cannot tempt us. There is no evil in God. God is good. "Let no man say when he is tempted, I am tempted of God, for God cannot be tempted with evil, neither tempts he any man (or woman)." (James 1:13) Satan is evil. God is good. The Lord lavishes us with His goodness every day. This is why we can give thanks to God. Focus on His goodness instead of the negative and the evil that is in the world. To focus on evil is to focus on the devil. To focus on good is to focus on God.

Be thankful today because your Father in Heaven is going to bless you, be kind to you and abundantly bestow His divine goodness on you. Have an attitude of gratitude and watch how your day will be more pleasant, more peaceful and more powerful. Oh, give thanks to the Lord!

Scripture Reading: Psalms 148, 149, 150; 1 Corinthians 11:16-34

Trivia Question: Who beheld Satan as lightning fell from Heaven?

September 2

"The Compassionate Christ"

Mark 6:34 — And Jesus, when He came out, saw much people
and was moved with compassion toward them, because they were like sheep

239

not having a shepherd: and He began to teach them many things.

God is love. (1 John 4:8) Jesus is God. (Hebrews 1:2,3) Jesus is love personified.

One of Jesus' ministries is being a pastor or shepherd. Shepherds are unique individuals with a special concern and love for their flock. Shepherds understand their responsibilities to lead, feed and protect their flocks.

In our text, the people are pressing and running to have an audience with Jesus. There are so many people, they are running here and there, scattered abroad with no direction, like lost sheep.

Jesus the shepherd is moved with compassion. Through His shepherd's eyes, he sees them as sheep that are lost, hungry and unsafe. He begins to feed them the Word of God. Sheep need to eat. We need to eat. The compassionate Christ who is our shepherd wants to feed us the Word of God. The Word is good food. The shepherd wants to teach us many things. Before Jesus fed these people (sheep) with fish and bread, he fed them the Word of God. "Man shall not live by bread alone, but by every word that proceeds out of the mouth of God." (Deuteronomy 8:3, Matthew 4:4)

Will you give time and place for the shepherd to feed you? He will feed you spiritually and naturally. He is the compassionate Christ and He is moved today to teach you many things.

Scripture Reading: Proverbs 1, 2; 1 Corinthians 12

Trivia Question: What is impossible for God to do?

September 3

"Blind Faith"

Matthew 9:27-31 — And when Jesus departed thence, two blind men followed him, crying, and saying, Thou son of David, have mercy on us. And when he was come into the house, the blind men came to him: and Jesus saith unto them, Believe ye that I am able to do this? They said unto him, Yea, Lord. Then touched he their eyes, saying, According to your faith be it unto you. And their eyes were opened; and Jesus straitly charged them, saying, See that no man know it. But they, when they were departed, spread abroad his fame in all that country.

"Two blind men FOLLOWED him…" This is amazing! Jesus did not follow the blind men, but the blind men followed Him! That was not an easy endeavor. We are not told how they followed Him, but we know they followed Him all the way into the house. We know Jesus was ministering in His home region of Galilee, so it is possible that it was the home of Jesus in Nazareth that they followed Him to.

There is a persistent pursuit of true faith. True faith perseveres in the face of opposition. True faith hurdles obstacles. True faith never quits or forfeits. The pursuit of faith causes individuals to progress even while handicapped.

These two blind men pursued Jesus. They knew Jesus had their miracle. Sometimes you have to "chase down" your miracle. Sometimes Jesus touches you, other times you must passionately pursue to touch Him.

May your faith not waiver today. Jesus is the miracle worker. He has your answer. In the face of opposition, hindrances and handicaps, may you keep on keeping on. Pursue Him! Faith says, "I will not give up!" The pursuit of faith will result in blessing. The two blind men received their miracle. You will too!

Scripture Reading: Proverbs 3, 4; 1 Corinthians 13

Trivia Question: Who was the apostle Peter's brother?

September 4

"God Thoughts"

Psalm 139:17-18 — How precious also are thy thoughts unto me, O God! how great is the sum of them! If I should count them, they are more in number than the sand: when I awake, I am still with thee.

What an amazing, encouraging truth. God is thinking about me today, every day and many, many times during the day. Jeremiah 29:11 says, "For I know the thoughts that I think toward you, saith the Lord, thoughts of peace, and not of evil, to give you an expected end." God's thoughts toward us are peaceable and precious! He is thinking of His people constantly and continually. His precious and peaceable thoughts toward me are more numerable than I can count. Can you tally the grains of sand on the shoreline? Can anyone count that high?

He is thinking good thoughts toward you today, not evil or negative thoughts, or thoughts of your failure. He is thinking thoughts about your future. He gives you hope in your heart today for tomorrow, a hope and a future, an expected end, and a determined destiny to fulfill.

With God on your side and His constant thinking of good thoughts toward you, you cannot fail, falter or fizzle out. The Creator of the universe, the Sovereign of all earth, He who sits upon the circle of the earth, the One who inhabits eternity, the high and lofty One is thinking about you, and His thoughts are precious and peaceable. May you think on that today, that He is thinking about you!

Scripture Reading: Proverbs 5, 6; 1 Corinthians 14:1-20

Trivia Question: What are we to cast upon the Lord?

September 5

"The Searchlight of God"

Psalm 139:23, 24 — Search me, O God, and know my heart: try me, and know my thoughts: and see if there be any wicked way in me, and lead me in the way everlasting.

David the sweet Psalmist of Israel is writing about all the enemies of the Lord. Those that try to come against God and His righteousness, David said, "your enemies Lord will be my enemies." This is a statement of devotion and loyalty. David was a man of war. Well acquainted with blood, the blood of his own soldiers and enemy soldiers who would rise up against him and the kingdom of Israel.

David understands the fine line between anger and righteous indignation. David understands the thin veil between flesh and spirit. David understands the difference between human warfare and holy warfare.

David prays and asks the Lord to search his heart and test his thoughts. Is his heart upright before God? Are his thoughts in line with God and His Word? Is this just a fleshly attempt to vent on David's part or blow off some spiritual steam? David continues, "Lord, see if there is any wicked or offensive way in me, and lead me in your everlasting way."

We must always examine our motives. Do we use our liberty to give place to our flesh? Are we just blowing off steam, or are we speaking against things that God Himself speaks against? Are we promoting ourselves or are we promoting God? Are we His masterpiece, or are we just giving people a piece of our mind?

A sure test is to ask God to search our hearts and test us, and our thinking process. If we pass the test then we will know we are being moved to react, speak or stand up to the things that God reacts, speaks or stands up to. We become His ambassadors.

Some people feel the Lord has nothing to say about injustice, poverty, sickness or enemies of righteousness. He has much to say about these and other subjects. He is not a passive God. Find out how God feels about things and speak up for Him, always with the correct motives, pure heart and right thoughts. God needs you, your voice and your convictions. Speak up for Him today!

Scripture Reading: Proverbs 7, 8; 1 Corinthians 14:21-40

Trivia Question: How many original apostles were there?

September 6

"Walking in the Truth"

3 John 3 — For I rejoiced greatly, when the brethren came and testified of the truth that is in thee, even as thou walkest in the truth.

John the beloved, the great revelator, is addressing his friend Gaius. He writes him in his third epistle and gives him quite a compliment by saying in his salutation that he rejoices because Gaius is "walking in the truth."

What does it mean to walk in truth? By the truth John means not only the revealed truth of the Scriptures (the written Word), but also Jesus Christ who is Himself the Truth incarnate (the Living Word). When one has a revelation of the written Word (logos) and an experience with the Living Word (Jesus), an expression of the spoken Word (Rhema) will flow from their lives. The Word of God is the Truth (John 17:17). To "walk in truth" is to walk in the Word of God.

When one walks, the inference is to get somewhere - to progress from one place to another. If we walk backward we digress. If we walk sideways, we remain in the same place and do not advance, but to walk forward is to progress.

Gaius was progressing in truth. He was progressing in the Word of God. Gaius was advancing with the written Word. He was progressing in his experience with the Living Word (Jesus) and progressing in his execution of the spoken Word.

Are you walking in truth? Are you walking in the logos (written Truth)? 2 Timothy 3:16 says, "All Scripture is given by inspiration of God, and is profitable for doctrine, for reproof, for correction, for instruction in righteousness…" Are you walking with Jesus (the Living Truth)? John 14:6 says, "Jesus saith unto him, I am the Way, the Truth, and the Life: no man cometh unto the Father, but by me." John 1:14 states, "And the Word was made flesh, and dwelt among us, (and we beheld his glory, the glory as of the only begotten of the Father,) full of grace and truth." Are you walking in Rhema (the spoken Truth)? Ephesians 4:15 says, "But speaking the truth in love, may grow up into him in all things, which is the head, even Christ…"

May we learn from John's friend today and receive the challenge to walk in the Truth and progress in the Word of God – the written Word, the Living Word and the spoken Word. John 8:32, "…you shall know the truth, and the truth shall make you free."

Scripture Reading: Proverbs 9, 10; 1 Corinthians 15:1-32

Trivia Question: Who was the apostle that leaned on Jesus' bosom?

September 7

"Choices"

Deuteronomy 30:19 — I call Heaven and earth to record this day against you, that I have set before you life and death, blessing and cursing: therefore choose life, that both thou and thy seed may live…

Life is full of choices – decisions, decisions, decisions! Our choices and decisions that we make today determine our tomorrow. Decisions that we make today will determine our destiny.

God sets before us life and death, blessing and cursing, right and wrong, good and evil. God is not the author of death or evil, but He allows these things to be set before His people daily. God has clearly laid out in His master plan (the Bible) what He wants for our lives. God's thoughts toward us are peaceable, precious and prosperous. The Lord has given us all free will to choose right or wrong, good or evil, blessing or cursing. God's choice for us is good, blessings, life and happiness. He will not, however, force us to make the right choice or override our will in any way. He puts these choices before us and then, through our knowledge of His Word, desires us to choose the right things and make good spiritual decisions.

God is not looking for a robotic creation to be pressured or strong-armed by the Creator. He is looking for a people who, out of there own volition, love Him and desire to honor Him with proper godly choices.

Yes, your choices and decisions that you make today could very likely affect you for time and eternity. Make good, godly choices. Make Bible-based decisions that God will back you up on. Jeremiah 1:12 says, "...thou hast well seen, for I will hasten (watch over) my word to perform it." May the Spirit of God and the Word of God help you make the right choices – your destiny depends on it!

Scripture Reading: Proverbs 11, 12; 1 Corinthians 15:33-58

Trivia Question: How many years did the southern kingdom of Judah spend in captivity in Babylon?

September 8

"Aim to Please"

Revelation 4:11 — Thou art worthy, O Lord,
to receive glory and honour and power: for thou hast created all things,
and for thy pleasure they are and were created.

We were created to give God glory. We were created to give God honor. We were created to give God praise. We were created to give pleasure to God. Our daily goal is to live our lives to please God.

In the selfish, self-centered, self-absorbed, self-gratifying world that we live in, the thought of living your life to please someone else is balked at and rejected. We are living in a culture of "selfies."

Jesus teaches us truth. He is the truth embodied and personified. When He walked the Earth, every chance He received from His Father, He taught truth. He is still teaching us truth from His Word and by His Spirit. Jesus said some profound words of selflessness in John 8:29, "And he that sent me is with me: the Father hath not left me alone; for I do always those things that please him."

On the top of the Son of God's priority list was to always please the Father. Jesus lived a life of self-sacrifice, unselfishness and altruism. His concern was not for Himself, but for others.

That kind of life pleases our heavenly Father. When you know your assignment like Jesus did and you know the Father is always with you to help, comfort and strengthen you to fulfill what He is requiring of you, you also will be motivated to please Him and be empowered to bring Him pleasure.

May we too live unselfish lives, be concerned for the well-being of others, be determined to accomplish our assignments given to us by God, and be convinced that He is with us and will not leave us alone, so that we also can "do always those things that please Him."

Aim to please Him and you will be blessed in return.

Scripture Reading: Proverbs 13, 14; 1 Corinthians 16

Trivia Question: Who probably founded the church at Colossae?

September 9

"Where are the Fathers?"

1 Corinthians 4:15 — For though ye have ten thousand instructors in Christ, yet have ye not many fathers: for in Christ Jesus I have begotten you through the Gospel.

Paul founded the church of Corinth during his second missionary journey. Apostolically he taught the Corinthians foundational truths, the dynamics of the Kingdom of God, how to live holy lives, great doctrines concerning the death, burial, and resurrection of Jesus Christ, marriage, ministry gifts, and other great fundamental truths that Christians live by today. Paul remained at Corinth for one year and six months. (Acts 18:11)

Paul was more than a Bible teacher to the flock at Corinth. He was a spiritual father. Paul, in his letter, probably written to them at the close of his three year residence in Ephesus (1 Corinthians 16:8), was letting them know they can have thousands of Bible teachers, but not many fathers. He indeed was a father to them. Why was this important for the Corinthians to understand that Paul was a spiritual father to them?

The main four-fold purpose of a father who is likened to a spiritual shepherd is to lead, feed, correct and protect.

Teachers teach. Fathers lead, feed, correct and protect. Paul was not only affirming his apostolic authority, but endearing the flock at Corinth that he loved and cared for them as a father. Just as a biological dad would care for his children, Paul led the people to Christ and wanted to see them grow, mature and develop as true saints of God. The heart of a father is to see their children blossom in every area of life - spiritually, physically, emotionally, socially and even financially.

God is our heavenly Father and in His love for us, He has given us fathers in the faith to speak into our lives (feed), direct and guide us (lead), discipline us if need be (correct), and be willing to lay down their lives for us in the face of imminent danger (protect).

May we thank God for true spiritual fathers and pastors that love God and love us. Pray for these special gifts from God daily.

Scripture Reading: Proverbs 15, 16; 2 Corinthians 1

Trivia Question: What great sin did Paul have to address with the church at Corinth?

September 10

"Anointed for Action"

1 Samuel 11:6 — And the Spirit of God came upon Saul when he heard those tidings, and his anger was kindled greatly.

Nahash, the king of the Ammonites, enemies of Israel, were pressing hard against God's people. Invasion was imminent and God's people, who lived in Jabesh-Gilead, were troubled, concerned and afraid. The people of God attempted to "cut a deal" with their enemies that if they didn't wipe Israel out in war, they would serve them.

Nahash agreed on one condition and that was that he would spare them, BUT the Ammonite army would gouge out all the right eyes of the Israelite army. The men of Jabesh-Gilead said, "give us seven days to think on your condition," and sent messengers to all of God's people throughout the region. When the gruesome message was heard throughout the land, all of the Israelites started to weep. What could they do? They were outnumbered, outmanned and outmatched by such a foe!

When King Saul heard of the diabolical plot against His people, he was stirred up. The Bible says that the Spirit of God came upon King Saul and holy indignation was greatly kindled in him.

Previously (1 Samuel 10:10), when the Spirit of God came upon Saul, it resulted in King Saul having a "prophesying party" with some of God's other prophets as they enjoyed the anointing and the presence of the Lord.

This time when the Spirit of God came upon him, the results were quite different. Saul's heart was moved in such a manner that this anointing caused him to be proactive, aggressive and engaging. He sent word to all of the soldiers that it was time to help their comrades in Jabesh-Gilead. The people rallied (330,000 men) and came against Nahash and the entire Ammonite army. God was with His people and gave them a swift and complete victory over the enemy!

What effect does the anointing of God have on you? The anointing of God has not been given to His people exclusively to make us feel good. The anointing calls us to action. The anointing makes us proactive. The anointing causes us to be passionate for the things that God is passionate about. Thank God for His Spirit, thank Him for His anointing on you, and then ask Him where He wants you to be directed to be proactive and passionate. You might be surprised where He guides you and what He wants you to become involved with. The anointing does not only make us feel good, the anointing makes us do good! (Acts 10:38)

Scripture Reading: Proverbs 17, 18; 2 Corinthians 2

Trivia Question: We should not be drunk with wine, but instead filled with what?

September 11

"Rejoice"

Philippians 4:4 — Rejoice in the Lord always
and I will say it again, Rejoice. (NKJV)

Happiness depends on happenings! If I feel well, I am happy. If I get a promotion on my job, I am happy. If my friends applaud me, I am happy. If my children are well behaved, I am happy. Happiness is contingent on happenings.

Joy is totally a different expression. Joy does not depend on what is going on with your life, but rather what is going on in your life. Jesus is the joy-giver. John 15:11, "These things have I spoken unto you, that my joy might remain in you, and that your joy might be full."

When an individual becomes born again, the joy of Jesus enters your life. It is a fruit of the spirit that comes into your recreated spirit in seed form and needs to be developed. As you develop the joy seed in your life by watering it with the word, joy will start to mature and grow. There will be a plethora of joy. So you can rejoice again and again. May the joy of Jesus be yours today as you are very aware that Jesus, the joy-giver, lives in you.

Scripture Reading: Proverbs 19, 20; 2 Corinthians 3

Trivia Question: What should we not let the sun go down upon?

September 12

"Overpower Evil"

Romans 12:21 — Be not overcome by evil, but overcome evil with good.

The Phillips translation says, "Overpower evil and offensively overpower evil with good."

Many people have walls up around their lives. Past pain and emotional scars have caused them to be "defensive" as it were. It is extremely difficult to overpower the evil that is coming against you when you are in a defensive posture. Even the best defense on a football team will give you, at best, a tie score. Many individuals live a status-quo life because of the defensive walls they built around themselves to protect them from any future emotional pain. It is time to break down the walls of defense around our lives and be on the offensive, so we can overcome and overpower evil en-route to a win! God has given us plenty of weaponry to offensively overcome evil. His Word, His name, His authority, His blood, His angels, and His Spirit. We cannot let evil win any longer because of our lack of counterattack. Let us be aggressive, overpowering evil. God's love overpowers Satan's hatred. Healing overpowers sickness. Hope overpowers despair. Respect overpowers disdain. Passion overpowers indifference.

Overpower evil with good. God is good. Overpower evil with God! Overpower evil with God and His Word. Victory is yours.

Scripture Reading: Proverbs 21, 22; 2 Corinthians 4

Trivia Question: Who did Paul and Barnabas take with them on their first missionary journey?

September 13

"No God, No Peace...Know God, Know Peace"

Romans 3:17 — And the way of peace they have not known.

People are in perpetual pursuit of finding peace. Some believe temporary and artificial peace comes as a result of doing a drug, alcohol, or even an illicit relationship. Peace is not some THING you chase down, wrestle to the ground and claim as your own. Peace is a person - the person of Jesus. Isaiah 9:6, "for unto us a child is born, unto us a son is given: and the government shall be upon his shoulder: and his name shall be called Wonderful, Counselor, the mighty God, the everlasting Father, the Prince of Peace."

The great messianic prophecy, written about 700 years prior to the birth of Jesus, reveals not only who Jesus is, but what He brings to humanity. The Prince of peace (Jesus) brings perfect peace to you. (Isaiah 26:3)

Having a relationship with Christ is paramount, for He truly is the author of peace. There is not and will not be peace in the world, but there certainly can be peace in your heart. (Matthew 10:34)

Know Him today and you will know peace! No Christ, no peace!

May Jesus, the Prince of peace, give you perfect peace, especially in the midst of your turmoil, trouble and tears. His peace is greater than the trial you are facing. Maintain a relationship with Him during the trial and you will maintain His peace. Know God, know peace.

"And the peace of God, which passes all understanding, shall keep your hearts and minds through Christ Jesus." (Philippians 4:7) Peace be with you, peace be in you.

Scripture Reading: Proverbs 23, 24; 2 Corinthians 5

Trivia Question: During Paul's second missionary journey, where did the Holy Spirit forbid him to preach?

September 14

"Delivered and Translated"

Colossians 1:13 — Who hath delivered us from the power of darkness, and hath translated us into the kingdom of his dear Son.

There are no real grey areas in the Bible, or in our service to God. There is truth and there is error. (1 John 4:6) There is life and there is death. (1 John 3:14) There is righteousness and unrighteousness. (2 Corinthians 6:14) There is good and there is evil.

We have been delivered from the power of darkness. As God is ruler over light and is light, Satan conversely rules over darkness and is darkness. Darkness includes all that Satan is and the power thereof. (Ephesians 6:12) Sin is darkness. Disobedience is darkness. Rebellion against God and His Holy Word is darkness. The dark world is all about hating God and living for the lust of the flesh and the demands of the darkness.

If you are born again and walking in Christ's light, you have been delivered from darkness and all its power or hold that once chained you. Jesus' finished work on Calvary, the blood that He shed and the cleansing of our sin that He offers, breaks the hold that the power of darkness has over our lives.

Reformation, resolution or even religion cannot break the stronghold of Satan on our lives. Only Jesus can deliver us. Only Jesus can break the bondage of sin and darkness. Only Jesus and His light can illuminate the darkness.

Here is good news! We do not have to grope around in darkness or be enslaved in sin because the light of Jesus, through His work on the cross, has delivered us from the power of darkness.

Scripture Reading: Proverbs 25, 26, 27; 2 Corinthians 6

Trivia Question: What is the only substance that can wash away sin?

September 15

"God Never Forgets"

Hebrews 6:10 — For God is not unrighteous to forget your work and labour of love, which you have shewed toward his name, in that you have ministered to the saints and do minister.

Nothing goes unnoticed from Heaven's vantage point. All service to God and His work will be rewarded. Many times in this life, but absolutely in eternal life.

We are called as Christians to be actively engaged in the affairs of Heaven, the work of the Kingdom, and be about our Father's business.

Once you are born again (we are saved by grace alone), it is required to do good works. "We are His workmanship created in Christ Jesus unto good works, which God has before ordained that we should walk in them." (Ephesians 2:10) God sees everything that we do to help people, to bring them to an understanding of the salvation that Christ provides, to advance

His Kingdom, and to promote and steward the Gospel in every way. God sees it all and is well pleased with His children that are engaged in godly affairs. God does not forget or dismiss your work, labor of love, which you have shown toward His excellent name, and the ministry to His wonderful people that you have extended your helping hand to. Great is your reward. Nothing is unnoticed by God. (Colossians 3:23-24) "Whatever you do, do it heartily as to the Lord, and not unto men; knowing that of the Lord you shall receive the reward of the inheritance: for you serve the Lord Christ."

Scripture Reading: Proverbs 28, 29; 2 Corinthians 7

Trivia Question: What does Barnabas's name mean?

September 16

"Balancing Yourself"

Proverbs 11:1 — A false balance is abomination to the Lord: but a just weight is his delight.

God wants our house to be well balanced. When we overemphasize certain areas of our lives, it could result in malfunction. When we are out of balance and the scale tips in favor of one area over another, it could lead down a road of hurt and disappointment.

For example, if our emotions demand all of our attention, then other parts of our lives will be neglected and could lead to "false balance."

The Scripture gives us insight into a well-balanced life. All we have to do is take a look at the life of Jesus. Luke 2:51-52 is very insightful and practical. With the emphasis on verse 52, let's first look at verse 51.

"And he went down with them, and came to Nazareth, and was subject unto them: but his mother kept all these sayings in her heart. And Jesus increased in wisdom and stature, and in favour with God and man." (Luke 2:51-52)

The backdrop of the text teaches us that Mary, Joseph and Jesus, were on their way home with other family and friends to Nazareth in Galilee from Jerusalem upon completing the celebration of the Passover feast. When the mother and foster father of Jesus checked on their twelve-year-old son, Jesus, much to their horror, they discovered the child was not with the caravan going home to Nazareth.

They scurried back to Jerusalem and, after three days of anxiety, found

Jesus in the temple with the adults, conversing about the Kingdom of God. The emotions of these parents were of both relief and rebuke (Luke 2:46-48).

As Joseph, Mary and the child Jesus returned to their homeland, the Bible states that Jesus grew in wisdom, stature, favor with God and favor with man. Verse 51 reveals to us the truth that we should never overlook. Jesus was SUBJECT to His parents. The word simply means that Jesus submitted to His parents and was under obedience. The outcome was Him growing in wisdom, stature, and favor with God and man (verse 52). What a truth, the Son of God obeying Mary and Joseph.

Jesus taught us accountability and submission by the way He lived His life.

One of the keys to living a balanced life is understanding submission to authority and accountability. Accountability unlocks the door to a healthy, balanced life. If you desire to advance and grow in wisdom (intellectually), stature (physically and healthy), favor with God (spiritually and relationally) and favor with man (socially) choose to live your life with accountability, submission and obedience to God and to those that God has put over your life.

Scripture Reading: Proverbs 30, 31; 2 Corinthians 8

Trivia Question: Who was John the Baptist's mother?

September 17

"Grow in Wisdom"

Luke 2:52 — And Jesus increased in wisdom and stature, and in favor with God and man.

Jesus lived a well-balanced life. The word "increased" in the original Bible language means to advance, to grow, to go forward. Jesus grew in wisdom. Jesus grew educationally and intellectually. We know that Jesus was a carpenter by trade. He had to go through natural or secular training to develop and perfect His skill. That took place educationally, as He studied, learned and was mentored by Joseph and others. He grew in natural wisdom. The word wisdom not only embraces the natural or secular areas of our lives, but also the growth or advancement in spiritual wisdom. The Bible says in James 1:5, "If any of you lack wisdom, let him ask of God, that giveth to all men liberally and upbraideth not; and it shall be given him."

Spiritual wisdom is needed for guidance, direction, decision-making and destiny success. Proverbs 4:7, "Wisdom is the principal thing; therefore get wisdom: and with all thy getting get understanding." Proverbs 3:13, "Happy is the man that findeth wisdom, and the man that getteth understanding."

Wisdom comes from God. All wisdom comes from Him, even if it is in the natural areas of our lives. Divine wisdom is needed to make practical decisions. If you are born again, God's wisdom is on the inside of you. Jesus lives in you by His Spirit. Christ the power of God, and the WISDOM of God. (1 Corinthians 1:24)

Jesus grew, advanced and went forward in wisdom - both naturally and supernaturally. Because His Spirit lives in you, His wisdom is in you. Tap into that divine intellect today. Stop making guesses and start drawing from God's wisdom. We must all grow in wisdom to live a well-balanced life.

Scripture Reading: Ecclesiastes 1, 2, 3; 2 Corinthians 9

Trivia Question: What two sons of Aaron offered "strange fire" before the Lord?

September 18

"Grow in Stature"

*Luke 2:52 — And Jesus increased in wisdom and stature,
and in favor with God and man.*

The word stature in the Greek means simply to mature. How important it is for Christians to mature. To grow in their faith (heart), to grow in their soul (emotions) and to grow in their bodies (health). If we are not growing and maturing in spirit, soul and body then we have become stagnant.

The Scripture gives us the key to the maturation process. The key to grow and develop is not obscure in the Bible. Paul addresses the subject in the book of Ephesians. "But speaking the TRUTH in love, may GROW UP into Him in ALL things, who is the head, even Christ." (Ephesians 4:15)

The truth will mature us in every way. What is truth? Jesus answered that question in John 17:17, "sanctify them through thy truth, thy word is truth." Yes, the Word of God will mature you. Hearing the Word, reading the Word, and speaking the Word will cause growth in all aspects of our lives. We must grow in stature if we want to live a well-balanced Christian life. May you increase in stature today and be used mightily for Jesus in the Kingdom of God.

Scripture Reading: Ecclesiastes 4, 5, 6; 2 Corinthians 10

Trivia Question: Where was the man from who appeared to Paul in a vision asking for him to "come and help us?".

September 19

"Grow in Favor with God"

Luke 2:52 — And Jesus increased in wisdom and stature, and in favor with God and man.

Growing in favor with God speaks of spiritual growth. Growth spiritually is probably the most important of the fourfold growth process that we learn from Jesus' young life. Jesus grew in wisdom (intellectually), grew in stature (physically), grew in favor with God (spiritually) and grew in favor with man (socially).

We too need to grow spiritually. Growing up spiritually will allow you to grow in your relationship with God. The parallels between the natural life and the spiritual life are similar. Just as newborns need their mother's milk, so babies in Christ need the pure or sincere milk of the Word. (1 Peter 2:2) Babies need milk and nourishment to grow physically and young Christians need the Word to grow spiritually. However to see an adult drinking from a bottle would be very concerning to say the least, so it is with older Christians who should graduate from milk to meat. The writer of Hebrews says, "for everyone that drinks milk is unskillful (spiritually immature) in the word of righteousness, for he is a babe." (Hebrews 5:13)

Our desire for God's righteousness and more of His Word matures us spiritually and will cause us to grow in favor with God. Have you transitioned from milk to meat? Do you carve out time each day for Bible study and prayer? Are you growing spiritually in favor with God? You are God's favorite. Is He your favorite?

Purpose today to grow spiritually and grow your relationship with Jesus through His Word!

Scripture Reading: Ecclesiastes 7, 8, 9; 2 Corinthians 11:1-15

Trivia Question: Who warned us to test the spirits whether they are of God, because many false prophets are gone out into the world?

September 20

"Grow in Favor with Man"

Luke 2:52 — And Jesus increased in wisdom and stature,
and in favor with God and man.

Growing in favor with man speaks of social or relational growth. Jesus grew in wisdom (intellectually), grew in stature (physically), grew in favor with God (spiritually) and grew in favor with man (socially).

How needful it is for us to grow in our relationships with others –especially good, godly relationships. In this day of depersonalization with the use of the internet, Twitter, Instagram, etc., face to face social interaction is becoming less emphasized. Growing socially in our relationships is extremely beneficial to us. It truly does matter whom you socialize with! Ungodly social relationships will pull you down and defer your destiny. The Apostle Paul said, "be not deceived: evil company corrupts good morals." (1 Corinthians 15:33) In another place, "and have no fellowship with the unfruitful work of darkness but rather reprove them. For it is a shame even to speak of those things which are done of them in secret." (Ephesians 5:11, 12)

Godly relationships are great and will build you up and should draw you closer to God. A good friend will always tell you the truth. "Faithful are the wounds of a friend, but the kisses of an enemy are deceitful." (Proverbs 27:6)

Cultivate and develop good, godly relationships. Jesus did just that. He had twelve friends that he interacted with, interceded for, imparted to, and invested in. John 15:15, "Henceforth I call you not servants; for the servant knoweth not what his lord doeth: but I have called you friends; for all things that I have heard of my Father I have made known unto you."

Grow in favor with man (relationships) and ask God to connect you to the right and righteous people. Your future could depend on it!

Scripture Reading: Ecclesiastes 10, 11, 12; 2 Corinthians 11:16-33

Trivia Question: What two women were having a disagreement in the church at Philippi?

_____

September 21

"For by Faith You Stand"

2 Corinthians 1:24 — Not for that we have dominion over your faith,
but are helpers of your joy: for by faith ye stand.

What really matters at the end of the day through all the trials, troubles and tears is our stance of faith. Are we still standing in faith as we confront problems, pressures and persecution?

Rocky Balboa just wanted to be standing after his first fight with Apollo Creed in that blockbuster movie in the 70s *Rocky*. Imagine after fifteen rounds of confrontation and fight, his only desire was that he would be able to stand after it was all said and done.

Our faith will be tried, tested, zapped, taxed and attacked. 1 Peter 1:7, "That the trial of your faith, being much more precious than of gold that perisheth, though it be tried with fire, might be found unto praise and honor and glory at the appearing of Jesus Christ." Will you still be standing after your faith is tested and tried?

What is faith? The biblical answer is found in Hebrews 11:1, "Now faith is the substance of things hoped for, the evidence of things not seen." In practical terms, faith is simply trusting God! Faith is believing and receiving what God says to you through His Word. Faith is holding on to His promises regardless of what you see or feel. Faith is soaring to new heights even though the circumstances are trying to ground you. Faith is taking God at His Word. Faith is getting up in the morning even when your body says no. Faith is showing up knowing that there will be a showdown. Faith is stepping out even when you do not see a step. Faith is being bold enough to say the same thing that God says. Faith still believes though you feel beat up! Beloved, through it all continue to trust in Jesus, continue to lean on Him and depend on His Word. Continue to stand by faith. For by faith you stand!

Scripture Reading: Song of Solomon 1, 2, 3; 2 Corinthians 12

Trivia Question: Which animals entered Noah's ark in groups of seven?

September 22

"Happy Birthday from God"

Romans 12:3, — For I say, through the grace given unto me, to every man that is among you, not to think of himself more highly than he ought to think; but to think soberly, according as God hath dealt to every man the measure of faith.

There are two distinct births the Bible teaches. The first one of course is when you are born into the world, your birthday. The second is when you are reborn to come out of the world, meaning the worldly system. This is called new birth or being born again. (John 3:1-8)

When you are born into this world, God gives you the gift of life. When you become born again, there is another gift God gives you – the gift of *seed* faith. Seed faith is a Happy Birthday gift from God our Father at the time of our spiritual new birth. Romans 12:3, " For I say, through the grace given unto me, to every man that is among you, not to think of himself more highly than he ought to think; but to think soberly, according as God hath dealt to every man the measure of faith."

The measure of faith or, seed faith, like any other seed must be watered, nurtured and helped to grow to its maximum potential. God puts inside of us upon the new birth experience a seed called faith. God gives the gift, what we do with the gift is up to us. Just like in our natural birth, God gives us the gift of life; what we do with that gift is also up to us.

A doctor asked me once, "Is faith volumized?" In other words, if faith needs to grow just as a seed has a journey for maturation, are there different levels of faith?" The answer is yes. There are different levels or dimensions of faith. Our faith can indeed grow. Let us go on a little tour of what the Bible teaches on different levels of faith.

Faith (Colossians 1:23)
Tiny Faith (Luke 17:6)
Little Faith (Luke 12:28)
Weak Faith (Romans 14:1)
Failing Faith (Luke 22:32)
Vain Faith (1 Corinthians 15:14)
Increasing Faith (Luke 17:5)
Full Faith (Acts 6:5)
Overcoming Faith (1 John 5:4)
Precious Faith (2 Peter 1:1)

Great Faith (Luke 7:9)

Most Holy Faith (Jude 20)

Perfect Faith (James 2:22)

Faith of Jesus (Galatians 2:20)

Faith of God (Mark 11:22)

Wow! Faith must grow, faith must develop, faith must progress. Are you growing in your birthday gift from God? Your faith can and will grow. Faith comes (and grows) by hearing, and hearing by the Word of God. Water your gift of seed faith with God's Word and watch it grow. You will be glad and blessed you did!

Scripture Reading: Song of Solomon 4, 5; 2 Corinthians 13

Trivia Question: When Adam and Eve realized that they had sinned, what did they do?

September 23

"Faith Agreement"

Matthew 18:19 — Again I say unto you,
that if two of you shall agree on earth as touching any thing that they shall ask,
it shall be done for them of my Father which is in Heaven.

When we hear about the subject of agreement we often think of two individuals that share the same convictions, creed and character. Amos 3:3 says, "how can two walk together except they be agreed?" Have you ever considered being in agreement with the Lord in your faith stand? Can you think of a better agreement partner? God says, "my covenant will I not break, nor will I alter the thing that is gone out of my lips." (Psalm 89:34) The Lord will not waver, wobble or wash out. He is a solid rock.

I believe God is looking for someone to agree with Him. Who will believe His work with Him? There must be an agreement of faith to receive from God. Agreeing by faith in God's Word is one of the fundamental principles of faith. James 1:6-7, "But let him ask in faith, nothing wavering. For he that wavereth is like a wave of the sea driven with the wind and tossed. For let not that man think that he shall receive anything of the Lord." There must be an agreement with God and His Word if we are going to receive from God.

There is a story in the Word about two blind men who were follow-

259

ing Jesus (It was always interesting to me that blind men were following Jesus – that takes faith.) When Jesus arrived to the house (very possibly his house) the blind men followed him in. Jesus asked them a question, "Do you believe that I am able to do this?" Of course Jesus knew that He was able and willing to cure them. Jesus was trying to get them to agree with Him for this miracle. (Matthew 9:27-29) They agreed in faith and received their miracle!

Agree with God today. What are you believing for? What break-through is desired in your life? Your faith agreement will bring a miracle manifestation in your life.

Scripture Reading: Song of Solomon 6, 7, 8; Galatians 1

Trivia Question: Who walked with God and was eventually taken straight to Heaven?

September 24

"Faith Announcement"

Hebrews 10:23 — Let us hold fast the profession of our faith without wavering; (for he is faithful that promised).

The writer of Hebrews says to hold fast to the profession or confession of our faith. A better way to say it is "hold tight". A person who wears a hat in a driving wind and rainstorm will often hold tight to their hat because the wind will attempt to knock it off. That is the idea behind our faith announcement or our confession of faith. The devil, evil powers, even the storms of life attempt to get us off our faith stand and the principle of our faith confession. Hold on to your profession of faith! Continue to believe and speak the promises of God over your life, your body, your circum-stances, your finances, your family, etc. Holdfast to your faith confession, and do not let go!

1 Peter 2:24 says, "Who his own self bare our sins in his own body on the tree, that we, being dead to sins, should live unto righteousness: by whose stripes ye were healed." The Bible teaches us that Jesus has provided healing for us. Isaiah 33:24 says, "And the inhabitant shall not say, I am sick: the people that dwell therein shall be forgiven their iniquity." We therefore shall not say I am sick. Our faith confession should be if we really believe that Jesus carried our sicknesses in his own body, I am healed!

(Matthew 8:16-17) Is it easier to say, "I am healed or I am ill?"

Let the poor say I am rich. Let the weak say I am strong. Let the bound say I am free and let the blind say I can see! Consider these verses for additional Bible study on the subject of faith announcement or faith confession.

Proverbs 18:21
Matthew 12:37
Ephesians 4:29
Proverbs 16:24
James 3:6-10

Announce boldly what you believe; faith has a voice and it uses your mouth!

Scripture Reading: Isaiah 1, 2, 3; Galatians 2

Trivia Question: Who adopted baby Moses?

September 25

"Faith Action"

James 2:14-26 — What doth it profit, my brethren, though a man say he hath faith, and have not works? can faith save him? If a brother or sister be naked, and destitute of daily food, And one of you say unto them, Depart in peace, be ye warmed and filled; notwithstanding ye give them not those things which are needful to the body; what doth it profit? Even so faith, if it hath not works, is dead, being alone. Yea, a man may say, Thou hast faith, and I have works: shew me thy faith without thy works, and I will shew thee my faith by my works. Thou believest that there is one God; thou doest well: the devils also believe, and tremble. But wilt thou know, O vain man, that faith without works is dead? Was not Abraham our father justified by works, when he had offered Isaac his son upon the altar? Seest thou how faith wrought with his works, and by works was faith made perfect? And the scripture was fulfilled which saith, Abraham believed God, and it was imputed unto him for righteousness: and he was called the Friend of God. Ye see then how that by works a man is justified, and not by faith only. Likewise also was not Rahab the harlot justified by works, when she had received the messengers, and had sent them out another way? For as the body without the spirit is dead, so faith without works is dead also.

The Apostle James teaches us that our faith is an action and it must do something in our lives. Faith agreement, faith announcement and faith

261

action are three major principles of biblical faith and how we receive from God. We must act upon the Word of God! We must put feet to our faith! When Jesus healed the man with the withered hand in the Temple, he told him to stretch forth his hand. The man acted upon the words of Jesus, putting action to his faith and received full restoration of that limb. (Mark 3:1-5) Jesus spoke to the paralytic and told him, "arise take up your bed and go to your house." The man acted upon Jesus' words, puts feet to his faith and received his miracle! (Matthew 9:1-7)

When Jesus was recruiting his team of men he would work with, teach and impart to, he went to a man named Matthew at a tax booth. He said, "Follow me." Matthew arose, put feet to his faith and followed Jesus. Matthew acted upon the word of Christ. Acting upon just two words changed the tax collector's life and gave us a rich discourse called the Gospel according to St. Matthew. (Matthew 9:9)

Peter the Apostle acted on just one word of Jesus, "Come" and he walked on water. (Matthew 14:29)

So put feet to your faith, act upon the words of Jesus, step out on the Word of God and see what the Lord will do for you. Do it today!

Scripture Reading: Isaiah 4, 5, 6; Galatians 3

Trivia Question: How many soldiers actually went with Gideon into battle?

September 26

"Breakthrough"

1 Corinthians 15:57 — But thanks be to God,
which giveth us the victory through our Lord Jesus Christ.

Breakthrough is victory. You are not breaking down, you are not breaking up, you are not breakdancing or even going to break-fast – you are going to have a breakthrough!

Breakthrough defined is a sudden, dramatic and important discovery or development. When we discover new and fresh encounters with God and are determined to develop a relationship with Him, you can count on eventual breakthrough.

Where do you need a breakthrough in your life? Have you been pounding on the pavement too long? Is there more month than money in your finances? Do you feel like you're hitting your head against the proverbial wall? You need a breakthrough!

Encounter and experience Jesus in a fresh way today. Say goodbye to the old, dried up, religious routines of meeting God and ask Him for a fresh anointing, a new encounter, a better experience with Him. It starts through daily prayer, Bible study and an infusion of God's Word and His love.

May breakthrough earmark your life today and going forward. May you discover Jesus in a way you never have before.

Scripture Reading: Isaiah 7, 8, 9; Galatians 4

Trivia Question: How many chapters are in the book of Isaiah?

September 27

"Truth"

3 John 12 — Demetrius hath good report of all men, and of the truth itself: yea, and we also bear record; and ye know that our record is true.

The epistle of 3 John has a wonderful theme – walking and living in truth.

Gaius was a man who walked in truth. (3 John 1-3, "The elder unto the wellbeloved Gaius, whom I love in the truth. Beloved, I wish above all things that thou mayest prosper and be in health, even as thy soul prospereth. For I rejoiced greatly, when the brethren came and testified of the truth that is in thee, even as thou walkest in the truth.")

Diotrephes was a man who misapplied and abused truth, wanting to be number one because of pride. (3 John 9-11, "I wrote unto the church: but Diotrephes, who loveth to have the preeminence among them, receiveth us not. Wherefore, if I come, I will remember his deeds which he doeth, prating against us with malicious words: and not content therewith, neither doth he himself receive the brethren, and forbiddeth them that would, and casteth them out of the church. Beloved, follow not that which is evil, but that which is good. He that doeth good is of God: but he that doeth evil hath not seen God.")

Demetrius was a man who lived the truth. Jesus is the truth. (John 14:6, "Jesus saith unto him, I am the way, the truth and the life: no man cometh unto the Father, but by me.") Jesus came to bear record of the truth. (John 18:37, "Pilate therefore said unto him, Art thou a king then? Jesus answered,

'Thou sayest that I am a king. To this end was I born, and for this cause came I into the world, that I should bear witness unto the truth. Every one that is of the truth, heareth my voice.") Jesus came to bring freedom resulting from the truth. (John 8:31-32, "Then said Jesus to those Jews which believed on him, If ye continue in my word, then are ye my disciples indeed. And ye shall know the truth and the truth shall make you free.") Jesus came to reveal himself as the living Word of God, which is truth. (John 17:17, "Sanctify them through thy truth: thy word is truth.")

Demetrius lived in the truth, that is, he allowed the living one, Jesus, to be revealed in him and through his life. Jesus is called the express image of the Father. (Hebrews 1:3, "Who being the brightness of his glory, and the express image of his person, and upholding all things by the word of his power, when he had by himself purged our sins, sat down on the right hand of the Majesty on high.") Jesus came to reveal the Father to us. John 14:9, "Jesus saith unto him, Have I been so long time with you, and yet hast thou not known me, Philip? He that hath seen me hath seen the Father; and how sayest thou then, shew us the Father." As the body of Christ, Christians are to reveal Jesus the Truth to a lost world. (2 Corinthians 3:2-3)

As Christians we are called to live in truth and have the truth live in us, and reveal the Truth (Jesus) to our friends, family, and even our foes. It is said of Demetrius that he had a good witness of all men (inside and outside Christian circles) of the Truth itself (Himself). Are you like Demetrius living in truth?

Scripture Reading: Isaiah 10, 11, 12; Galatians 5

Trivia Question: What archangel contended with the devil over the body of Moses?

September 28

"Truth, Part 2"

3 John 12 — Demetrius has received a good testimony from everyone, and from the truth itself. We also add our testimony, and you know that our testimony is true. (ESV)

What does it really mean to live the truth? The answer is simply allowing the living Truth who is Jesus Christ to live his life through you. Someone said to me once, "Pastor, I cannot live my life for the Lord anymore, it's too hard." I replied, "Good don't do it!" To their shock I continued with my answer, "Stop trying to live for the Lord based on your merits, strivings, and hard work. Let the living Lord who is Truth, live his life through you." (It takes a lot of pressure off of you.)

It is great to walk in truth like Gaius (3 John 1-3), but to get to the place that truth lives in you for all to see and witness is much greater. Consider these verses.

"And now come I to thee; and these things I speak in the world, that they might have my joy fulfilled in themselves. I have given them thy word; and the world hath hated them, because they are not of the world, even as I am not of the world. I pray not that thou shouldest take them out of the world, but that thou shouldest keep them from the evil. They are not of the world, even as I am not of the world. Sanctify them through thy truth: thy word is truth. As thou hast sent me into the world, even so have I also sent them into the world. And for their sakes I sanctify myself, that they also might be sanctified through the truth. Neither pray I for these alone, but for them also which shall believe on me through their word; That they all may be one; as thou, Father, art in me, and I in thee, that they also may be one in us: that the world may believe that thou hast sent me. And the glory which thou gavest me I have given them; that they may be one, even as we are one: I in them, and thou in me, that they may be made perfect in one; and that the world may know that thou hast sent me, and hast loved them, as thou hast loved me." John 17:13-23

"But ye shall receive power, after that the Holy Spirit is come upon you: and ye shall be witnesses unto me both in Jerusalem, and in all Judaea, and in Samaria, and unto the uttermost part of the earth." Acts 1:8

"Now then we are ambassadors for Christ, as though God did beseech you by us: we pray you in Christ's stead, be ye reconciled to God." 2 Corinthians 5:20

"Who now rejoice in my sufferings for you, and fill up that which is behind of the afflictions of Christ in my flesh for his body's sake, which is the church: Whereof I am made a minister, according to the dispensation of God which is given to me for you, to fulfill the Word of God; Even the mystery which hath been hid from ages and from generations, but now is made manifest to his saints: To whom God would make known what is the riches of the glory of this mystery among the Gentiles; which is Christ in you, the hope of glory." Colossians 1:24-27

"For it is God which worketh in you both to will and to do his good pleasure." Philippians 2:13

May we earnestly desire and strive to be Jesus with flesh on. May all people see Jesus (the Truth) within us. May we be a manifestation of His love, power, holiness, mercy, grace, comfort, conviction, biblical standards, forgiveness, kindness and goodness to a searching culture, so that it can be said of us, "we have a good report of all men, of the truth itself (or Himself)."

Is the truth living big in me? Is the Word living big in me? Am I receiving what I am asking God for?

John 15:7, "If you abide (live) in me and my word (truth) abide (live), in you, you shall ask what you will, and it shall be done unto you."

That my friend is the truth!

Scripture Reading: Isaiah 13, 14, 15; Galatians 6

Trivia Question: What is the fifth commandment?

September 29

"Help God"

Psalms 46:1-5 — God is our refuge and strength, a very present help in trouble. Therefore will not we fear, though the earth be removed, and though the mountains be carried into the midst of the sea; Though the waters thereof roar and be troubled, though the mountains shake with the swelling thereof. Selah. There is a river, the streams whereof shall make glad the city of God, the holy place of the tabernacles of the most High. God is in the midst of her; she shall not be moved: God shall help her, and that right early.

The Bible teaches that God hears our cries and His ears are open to our prayers. (1 Peter 3:12) Even a simple cry for help gets the attention of our loving heavenly Father.

Help defined: to make things better or easier, to aid, to assist, to remedy, to serve or wait on. God wants to bring us aid, He wants to assist us in life, He truly wants to make things better for us. He wants to help!

His name brings help. Psalm 124:8, "Our help is in the name of the Lord, who made Heaven and earth." Call on His name today.

Worship involves help. Matthew 15:25, "Then came she and worshiped him, saying Lord, help me." The Syrophoenician mother received a miracle for her daughter as she worshiped and cried for help from Jesus. Worship the Lord today!

Grace brings help. Hebrews 4:16, "Let us therefore come boldly unto

266

the throne of grace, that we may obtain mercy and find grace to help in time of need." His throne is full of grace and goodness. Go boldly to that place and discover His grace. His grace will help you get through anything, anytime. Find His grace to help you today!

His name brings help. Worship invokes His help. His grace brings help. He is our help. When you discover Jesus as your help, "You may boldly say, the Lord is my helper and I will not fear what man shall do to me." (Hebrews 13:6)

Scripture Reading: Isaiah 16, 17, 18; Ephesians 1

Trivia Question: Who was Solomon's mother?

September 30

"Pull Out the Root"

Hebrews 12:15 — Looking diligently lest any man fail of the grace of God; lest any root of bitterness springing up trouble you, and thereby any be defiled.

Bitterness will leave you always at a dead end. If allowed to control you, the grace of God will be of no effect. We cannot live without God's grace, His goodness, mercy, kindness, favor and strength. Bitterness short circuits the force of grace that is available to us. The longer bitterness grows in us, and the longer it is left unattended, it will become deeply rooted within our emotions. Bitterness will trouble you and those around you. Do not prune or play with bitterness. Pluck up that root. You do not prune, water or tolerate ugly weeds in a beautiful garden because the weeds will compromise it.

Do not water bitterness, or only prune it (it will come back). Pull it out from the root and remove it from your life forever. You are beautiful. Do not allow bitterness weeds that have deep roots to enter your life. Pull out the root today!

Scripture Reading: Isaiah 19, 20, 21; Ephesians 2

Trivia Question: After being crowned king in Hebron, David defeated the Jebusites and made what city his capital?

October

October 1

"The Kingdom Within"

Luke 17:20-21 — And when he was demanded of the Pharisees,
when the kingdom of God should come, he answered them and said,
The kingdom of God cometh not with observation: Neither shall they say,
Lo here! or, lo there! for, behold, the kingdom of God is within you.

We must realize, as children of God, we already possess the Kingdom of God within us. God's presence is already resident in all who are born again by the Holy Spirit. The Kingdom of God is not some outward phenomena, nor does it come to us with a lot of pomp and circumstance. The Kingdom of God is really God's rule and reign in our lives. We allow the Lord to rule our lives as we yield every area of our life to Him by obeying His commandments and submitting to His Word. Jesus said that if we love Him, we will obey Him and keep His commandments. (John 14:15; 1 John 5:3)

The Scriptures declare that those who receive the gift of righteousness shall rule and reign in life through Jesus Christ. (Romans 5:17) It has always been God's divine intention to exhibit His kingdom authority through the church of Jesus. We are His body and His presence on the Earth. If He is to establish His Kingdom on the Earth, it must be through our lives, as we yield to His Lordship and obey His Word. Throughout history God has chosen to manifest Himself to, and then through, human vessels. Will you allow Him to use you to express His love, mercy, forgiveness and grace to bring others into a relationship with Him? His influence in, and then through, our lives is what will turn others from darkness to light, from the kingdom of Satan to the Kingdom of God and from an eternity in Hell to the glorious riches of Heaven.

Scripture Reading: Isaiah 22, 23; Ephesians 3

Trivia Question: How did Samson die?

October 2

"In His Image"

Genesis 1:26-27 — And God said, "Let us make man in our image, according to our likeness; let them have dominion over the fish of the sea, the birds of the air and over the cattle, over all the earth and over every creeping thing that creeps on the Earth." So God created man in His own image; in the image of God He created him; male and female He created them.

How amazing that Almighty God created us in His image. His perfect plan is for us to walk in and exercise the authority He has given us over all things. We are called to go boldly into this world for His purpose to touch the hearts of those who are hurting and in need of His saving grace. We have the right given to us by God Himself, as believers, to defeat the enemy and his tactics and to be overcomers in Christ. We are called each day to "put on the whole armor of God, that you may be able to stand against the wiles of the devil" (Ephesians 6:11), so we can reach this lost and dying world.

Our heavenly Father desires for us to live life and walk this earth with the confidence and assurance of who we are in Christ. Be salt and light to all those you meet in the marketplace, on your jobs, or in school. As Paul said in 1 Corinthians 9:22, "I have become all things to all men, that I might by all means save some." Let us live in faithfulness and obey God's Word so we can walk more like Jesus did and continue to complete the work He has prepared for us.

Scripture Reading: Isaiah 24, 25, 26; Ephesians 4

Trivia Question: What did God promise to give King Solomon that he had not requested?

October 3

"Authority"

Matthew 28:18-19 — And Jesus came and spoke to them, saying, "All authority has been given to Me in heaven and on earth. Go therefore and make disciples of all the nations, baptizing them in the name of the Father and of the Son and of the Holy Spirit. (NKJV)

Jesus has commissioned us as the church and His body, with His authority, to advance the Kingdom of God here on Earth. He promised to be with us wherever we go, as we bring this grand and glorious Gospel to our lost and dying world.

Just as Christ epitomized a servant, we too must realize that a servant-spirit is essential to fulfilling this Great Commission. As we humble ourselves before the Lord, He will work through us, confirming His Word with manifestations of His power and glory. However, the enemy will try to take us off course, burdening us down through strife, bitterness, jealousy, complaining, etc. That is why it is vital for us to keep our eyes on Him who loves us. He is the only one who can heal us from our emotional pains and spiritual sorrows.

We must remember that Jesus has bruised (snapped) the head of Satan so that we can stand boldly in our position within the body of Christ. However, if we allow the devil to keep us focused on our hurts and pains, we will stay spiritually lame and become a heel in the body of Christ. When we do not receive our healing from the Lord, we give Satan the right to control and manipulate us. Remember, we are the head and not the tail; above and not beneath. (Deuteronomy 28:13) Let the love of God compel us to love our neighbors as ourselves and allow us to be the light of the world, the salt of the earth and God's ambassadors to all mankind. I encourage you to be edified daily with His transforming, empowering, authoritative Word.

Scripture Reading: Isaiah 27, 28; Ephesians 5

Trivia Question: God changed Abraham's name to Abraham from what other name?

October 4

"Thanksgiving"

Psalm 136:1-4 — Oh, give thanks to the Lord, for He is good! For His mercy endures forever. Oh, give thanks to the God of gods! For His mercy endures forever. Oh, give thanks to the Lord of lords! For His mercy endures forever. To Him alone who does great wonders, For His mercy endures forever.

Psalm 136 is a psalm of thanksgiving to the Creator of Heaven and earth! This psalm is also reminiscent of God's awesome deliverance to the children of Israel. As you understand that our heavenly Father is the God of all gods and Jesus Christ is the Lord of all lords, then you can grasp the reality that He will deliver you from any oppression, bondage, trial or tribulation that you may be facing. Each verse of this psalm ends with the statement that, "His mercy endures forever!" He is the Father of mercy and the God of all comfort (2 Corinthians 1:3); therefore, you can come confidently to His throne of grace to obtain mercy and to find grace to help you in your time of need! (Hebrews 4:16) Thanksgiving is an attitude of the heart, which keeps us in a state of expectation, because we are continually reminding ourselves of God's goodness to us. Four times in Psalm 107 the psalmist reminds us to thank God for His goodness, which is manifest in the wonderful works and marvelous miracles He does for us.

Scripture Reading: Isaiah 29, 30; Ephesians 6

Trivia Question: When Abraham was visited by 3 men, they left to go where?

October 5

"He is Alive"

Mark 16:6-7 — And he saith unto them, Be not affrighted: Ye seek Jesus of Nazareth, which was crucified: he is risen; he is not here: behold the place where they laid him. But go your way, tell his disciples and Peter that he goeth before you into Galilee: there shall ye see him, as he said unto you.

As the women went to the tomb early that Sunday morning to anoint Jesus' body, their hearts must have been so heavy from seeing their Lord crucified just three days earlier. What a great loss this was to them and all His disciples. They must have been wondering what He had meant by saying, "You shall see me again!" (John 16:16) Arriving at the tomb, they saw that a great earthquake had rolled back the stone at the entrance. As they looked up, there appeared an angel of the Lord bringing them the good news that "Jesus is alive!" With great joy and excitement, they ran to bring His disciples word of this great miracle.

As we always celebrate the resurrection of Jesus Christ and His victory over sin, Satan, sickness and death, we must first remember the cross and the crucifixion that Jesus endured for us. In Christ's suffering and death, He who knew no sin became sin and became the atonement for our greatest need, the forgiveness of our sin. (2 Corinthians 5:21) By paying the ultimate price, laying down His life, He became the perfect sacrifice, and paid the ransom for the judgment we should have received.

The prophet Isaiah prophesied 700 years earlier about this perfect sacrifice, the final Lamb that was led to the slaughter. How amazing to see the prophecy come to pass through the Gospel of Christ. As Christians, we have been called to share the message with others that He carried our sorrows, was wounded for our transgressions, bruised for our iniquities and by His stripes we are healed. (Isaiah 53:3-7)

Scripture Reading: Isaiah 31, 32, 33; Philippians 1

Trivia Question: What is the first commandment that was given to Moses at Mt. Sinai?

October 6

"Our Past Deleted"

2 Corinthians 5:17 — Therefore if any man be in Christ, he is a new creature: old things are passed away; behold, all things are become new.

In Paul's letter to the Corinthians, he speaks of the new man who is created in us when we accept Jesus Christ as our Lord and Savior. Webster's dictionary defines the word "new" as fresh or unused, clean, spotless, unmarked or untouched. How awesome that we receive a fresh start, a clean slate, as our lives become spotless, white as snow as we are washed in Jesus' cleansing blood. As we draw near to Him and we enter into His presence, He draws near to us and His Spirit dwells within us. (James 4:8) God desires us to fellowship with His Son, Jesus Christ, and as we do, we become one in Christ and identify with His death and resurrection.

In John 3:3, Nicodemus questioned how one could be "born when he is old?" Does God forget our sins, our past? Yes, our sins are forgotten and we become children of the most-high living God! We can rest in the truth that with new birth we become justified (as if we never sinned), and we enter into a new realm of God's Kingdom.

Scripture Reading: Isaiah 34, 35, 36; Philippians 2

Trivia Question: A virtuous woman's price is compared to what?

October 7

"Faithfulness"

Proverbs 31:10, 30 — A capable, intelligent and virtuous woman
—who is he who can find her? She is far more precious than jewels
and her value is far above rubies or pearls. Charm and grace are deceptive
and beauty is vain (because it is not lasting), but a woman who reverently
and worshipfully fears the Lord, she shall be praised! (AMPC)

God chose Mary to be the mother of our Lord Jesus Christ because she was highly favored and "blessed among all women." (Luke 1:28) Mary led a faithful, pure life and the Lord found her to be a willing vessel to bear God's Son. She exemplified a life that God desires each of us to lead. God puts such an importance on faithfulness because it is part of His very own nature. This faithfulness that God has denotes being able to be trusted, relied upon and one who has a servant's heart.

As we live our lives under the awesome covering of God, we are able to draw closer to Him who is loving and merciful from generation to generation. When we are open to Him, God can perfect His Word within us so He can manifest His promises in our lives. God has prepared wonderful things for those who love Him. Let your life be a holy sacrifice so that you may receive all that God has in store for you and your family. 2 Peter 1:4 says that we have been given exceedingly great and precious promises by which we can be partakers of His divine nature. As we are faithful to get to know Him more, more of His nature, life and godliness will be evident in us.

The fruit of the Holy Spirit develops in our spirit as we abide in Christ and His Word abides in us. (Galatians 5:22-23) As Jesus says in John 15, a branch cannot bear fruit of itself unless it abides in the vine. Abide in Jesus Christ so that He may abide in you. As you do, knowledge, perseverance, godliness, kindness, love and virtue will be added unto you so that Christ's likeness will be seen in you.

Scripture Reading: Isaiah 37, 38; Philippians 3

Trivia Question: How did Joseph gain his freedom from prison in Egypt?

October 8

"Peace and Rest"

Matthew 11:28-30 — Come unto me, all ye that labour and are heavy laden, and I will give you rest. Take my yoke upon you, and learn of me; for I am meek and lowly in heart: and ye shall find rest unto your souls. For my yoke is easy, and my burden is light.

Jesus makes an amazing and heart warming declaration in this passage of Scripture! He invites everyone to come and find rest for the soul through Him. As we can see all around us, our entire world is in a state of extreme anxiety and turmoil. Natural disasters are increasing, wars and conflicts are expanding, and financial crisis is escalating. The collapse of governments, the economy and the biosphere has caused the world to be filled with anxiety, fear and despair. People's hearts are failing them.

Beloved, what the human race is looking for can only be found in Christ. This intrinsic peace will not be found in any human endeavor or accomplishment. It cannot be produced by the latest technology. The beauty of nature itself cannot give us lasting peace. Yet Christ offers this contentment freely to all who are willing to develop a personal and intimate relationship with Him. Maybe God is allowing this entire world system to fail, so that His crown creation, mankind, will stop and hear Him say, "These things I have spoken to you, that in Me you may have peace. In the world you will have tribulation; but be of good cheer, I have overcome the world." (John 16:33) Peace (or rest of soul) cannot be found in a bottle, or a pill, not even in another human relationship, but only comes from the Prince of peace, the Lord Jesus Christ.

Scripture Reading: Isaiah 39, 40; Philippians 4

Trivia Question: What is pure and undefiled religion according to the Apostle James?

October 9

"True Rest"

Acts 3:19, 20 — Repent ye therefore, and be converted, that your sins may be blotted out, when the times of refreshing shall come from the presence of the Lord.

And he shall send Jesus Christ, which before was preached unto you.

True rest and refreshing does not come from a week or two of vacation, although we all need some time away from our normal pace of life. True refreshing can only come from the Lord.

If we only rest our bodies and do not learn how to enter into these times of refreshing in the presence of the Lord, as soon as we leave that vacation and return to our normal routine, we will realize that we are as tired and weary as we were before. As important as it is to get away, this alone cannot truly refresh us. Jesus spoke about a rest for our souls, that is available to us as we stay hooked up to Him. (Matthew 11:28-30) As a matter of fact, the presence of the Lord is with us and available to us twenty-four hours a day, seven days a week if we do what the Apostle Peter commands us to do. We must first repent, change our thinking and then be converted, change our behavior, then Jesus Christ Himself, the very presence of God will revive and renew us.

Scripture Reading: Isaiah 41, 42; Colossians 1

Trivia Question: Hearing of his wisdom, who visited Solomon?

October 10

"Restoration and Renewal"

Acts 3:19-21 — Repent ye therefore, and be converted, that your sins may be blotted out, when the times of refreshing shall come from the presence of the Lord. And he shall send Jesus Christ, which before was preached unto you: Whom the heaven must receive until the times of restitution of all things, which God hath spoken by the mouth of all his holy prophets since the world began.

The word restoration in this passage of Scripture means to bring back to a former state. His desire is to restore us back to the position that the church, which is His body, had in the beginning, as the manifested sons and daughters of God. The church was birthed in power. As we become the habitation of God by His Spirit (Ephesians 2:19-22), we will once again move out in the power of Christ and the miraculous proofs of His ministry will be evident in us. We must be a praising church and a praying church if we desire to experience His presence and fulfill His plans for our lives. As we preach the Gospel in the power of the Holy Spirit, we will populate the Kingdom of God. However, with any great move of God, Satan will try to stop us with persecution from those who oppose God's Kingdom. We must permit these persecutions to unite us and not divide us. Jesus said that a house divided against itself will not stand. Let us be prepared so that when persecution does arise, we will know from whom it is coming and not allow the persecution to turn us against each other, but unite us in the love of God and continue to support and serve one another.

Scripture Reading: Isaiah 43, 44; Colossians 2

Trivia Question: What Old Testament prophet speaks of Messiah's agony and suffering on the cross?

October 11

"Humble Leaders"

3 John 9-10 — I wrote to the church, but Diotrephes, who loves to have the preeminence among them, does not receive us. Therefore, if I come, I will call to mind his deeds which he does, prating against us with malicious words. And not content with that, he himself does not receive the brethren, and forbids those who wish to, putting them out of the church.

One of the first requirements to being a leader in the church is a humble spirit. The Bible speaks of a man in 3 John, named Diotrephes who displayed contrary characteristics. He was a man who not only disliked correction, but forbid any leaders or mentors from speaking into his life or his church. He had a spirit that wanted the preeminence and superiority, and refused any help or counsel. John speaks of Diotrephes not welcoming him as the apostle over him in the church. He had a domineering manner and was out of divine order.

The Bible says, "Pride goes before destruction and a haughty spirit before a fall." (Proverbs 16:18) To think that we have it altogether and do not need any spiritual direction or counsel will lead us on a destructive path. When we look at the character of Jesus, His greatest attribute was humbleness. His ministry was enveloped by this main characteristic, which allowed His Father to exalt Him. We must do the same – humble ourselves and pray and turn from our wicked ways! (2 Chronicles 7:14)

One of the main purposes of coming together as a church is to connect to pastors, leaders and others that God puts into our lives to shape us. Correction or counsel may sometimes feel as "spiritual sandpaper," but God uses those people and opportunities to shape us into His likeness and help make us whole. As a leader we need those over us to speak into our lives, to stretch us, correct us, encourage us and often lead us in the way of truth.

We do not want domineering leadership, but strong leadership. Strong leaders are often put into our lives to lead us in a way that we could not do on our own. Strong leaders that walk in righteousness can lead and make a difference in the church house, State House and White House. We cannot have a spirit of Diotrephes on any level of church leadership! We cannot feed our pride, but must serve and minister.

Humble yourself today before God and allow him to make you strong. Whether you are a leader in the church, or a new congregant, let God use the people he puts into your life to shape you into Christ-likeness. Remain in humbleness and He will ultimately lift you up!

Scripture Reading: Isaiah 45, 46, 47; Colossians 3

Trivia Question: According to the Gospel of John, who participated in creation along with the Father?

October 12

"Cleansing"

2 Corinthians 6:16-7:1 — And what agreement hath the temple of God with idols? for ye are the temple of the living God; as God hath said, I will dwell in them, and walk in them; and I will be their God, and they shall be my people. Wherefore come out from among them, and be ye separate, saith the Lord, and touch not the unclean thing; and I will receive you. And will be a Father unto you, and ye shall be my sons and daughters, saith the Lord Almighty. Having therefore these promises, dearly beloved, let us cleanse ourselves from all filthiness of the flesh and spirit, perfecting holiness in the fear of God.

For us to have an increased and persistent habitation (not just a visitation) of the Shekinah Glory of the Lord, we must do what the Apostle Paul challenges the church in Corinth to do. We should cleanse ourselves from anything that has even the slightest potential to corrupt or defile us. As we put away from our lives the sins of the flesh and the worldly enticements that work to ensnare us, we will complete and then execute the process of holiness in our lives. God is holy and He commands us to be holy as He

Himself is holy. (1 Peter 1:15-16)

Scripture Reading: Isaiah 48, 49; Colossians 4

Trivia Question: Who moved upon the face of a dark and formless world in the beginning?

October 13

"Magnifying Glass"

Psalm 69:30-31 — I will praise the Name of God with a song,
and will magnify Him with thanksgiving. This also will please the Lord better
than an ox or bull, which has horns and hoofs. (NKJV)

In this passage of Scripture, the Psalmist King David teaches us one of the secrets to having God's continual saving, delivering and healing power available. As you magnify God with thanksgiving, your trials, troubles and tribulations will not be able to overwhelm you. Whatever you magnify in your life will become more prevalent to you and more powerful over you. The Hebrew word for "magnify" means to twist rope together, which exponentially magnifies each strand of strength. As you praise the Lord with a song and magnify Him with thanksgiving you will be entwining your life with His. As life's circumstances, situations and issues pull at you from all directions, you will not snap or break because His strength becomes yours.

Many times when we go through trouble, we look for things that we can sacrifice or give up as a bargaining chip to manipulate God to move on our behalf. However, what truly pleases Him is not our sacrifices at the altar, but the sacrifice of thanksgiving which is the fruit of our lips. (Hebrews 13:15) As you daily endeavor to magnify the Lord, He will deliver you from all of your fears and troubles. (Psalm 34:3-6)

Scripture Reading: Isaiah 50, 51, 52; 1 Thessalonians 1

Trivia Question: What did God call the two "great lights" that separated day from night?

October 14

"Reflect on the Word"

John 1:14 — And the Word was made flesh, and dwelt among us,
(and we beheld his glory, the glory as of the only begotten of the Father,)
full of grace and truth.

The incarnation of God in flesh occurred so that He could dwell in the midst of the human race as Jesus Christ, the Word. (John 1:1-4) As the Holy Spirit overshadowed the Virgin Mary, the Word of God was birthed as the Babe in the manger. (Luke 1:31-38) The Word was manifest in the flesh so that He could accomplish the perfect will of God for us. As a man, Jesus Christ fulfilled every aspect of God's righteousness. As the unblemished Lamb of God, He became our sin sacrifice, so that we could become God's righteousness and sons and daughters of Almighty God.

As you daily reflect on the birth of Christ, remember that the Word of God became flesh in the person of Jesus Christ. We too are born again, through the Word of God, as babes in Christ. It is through a hunger and a thirst for the Word of God that we grow into disciples of the Lord. (1 Peter 1:22-23) As we meditate on the written Word of God, it will govern every thought we have and every decision we make. We will then walk in grace and truth, manifesting to the world the Glory of God.

Scripture Reading: Isaiah 53, 54, 55; 1 Thessalonians 2

Trivia Question: What reason did God give for creating a companion for Adam?

October 15

"Lasting Joy"

Psalm 16:11 — Thou wilt shew me the path of life: in thy presence
is fulness of joy; at thy right hand there are pleasures for evermore.

Take heed to the words of the sweet psalmist of Israel and spend quality time in the presence of the Lord. His presence will fill you with divine joy and give you divine pleasure. True and lasting joy (not just happiness), permanent contentment and enduring satisfaction in life can only come from a more intimate relationship with your Creator and the Lover of your soul. No other person, relationship, object, hobby, or occupation can give purpose, meaning or direction for your life, only Jesus can!

As you walk with Jesus, by obeying His Word and the leading of the Holy Spirit, God promises: divine protection from the wicked, divine purification from sin, divine provision from Heaven, divine power over the mountains you face and divine purpose for your life.

Scripture Reading: Isaiah 56, 57, 58; 1 Thessalonians 3

Trivia Question: What was man's first occupation in the Bible?

October 16

"Spiritual Maturity"

Ephesians 4:12-16 — For the perfecting of the saints, for the work of the ministry, for the edifying of the body of Christ: Till we all come in the unity of the faith, and of the knowledge of the Son of God, unto a perfect man, unto the measure of the stature of the fulness of Christ: That we henceforth be no more children, tossed to and fro, and carried about with every wind of doctrine, by the sleight of men, and cunning craftiness, whereby they lie in wait to deceive; But speaking the truth in love, may grow up into him in all things, which is the head, even Christ: From whom the whole body fitly joined together and compacted by that which every joint supplieth, according to the effectual working in the measure of every part, maketh increase of the body unto the edifying of itself in love.

In this portion of Scripture, the Apostle Paul declares that we can grow from a babe in Christ, through spiritual childhood to a mature son or daughter of God. Jesus is truth personified and the Word manifest in the flesh. (John 1:14) Divine perfection (maturity) is a result of us embracing the truth (John 8:32) and allowing His Word to set us apart for His service and glory. (John 17:17) As we grow into spiritual maturity as Christians, Christ becomes evident in our lives. This will cause the fulfillment of Jesus' words in Matthew 5:48, "therefore you shall be perfect, just as your Father in Heaven is perfect."

Scripture Reading: Isaiah 59, 60, 61; 1 Thessalonians 4

Trivia Question: What was Noah's occupation after the flood?

October 17

"Great Love"

1 John 3:1a — Behold what manner of love the Father has bestowed on us, that we should be called children of God.

The Apostle John challenges us to contemplate and understand the unfathomable quality and quantity of love our Father God has lavished on us! It is almost incomprehensible that a holy, righteous God, the Creator of the universe would become our Father and adopt us as His children. (Romans 8:15-16)

How great is this love for us? He loved us even when we were sinners and living an ungodly lifestyle. While we were still enemies of the Cross, the Father's love was manifested in Christ reconciling us to Himself. (Romans 5:6-11)

How much love does the Father have in His heart for us? Our heavenly Father's immeasurably profound and boundless love is made evident because He gave His Son, to die in our place. Jesus prayed that we would comprehend that the Father loves us with the same love and to the same extent that He loves Jesus, the Son of God. (John 12:20-26) We can only truly love Him as we begin to know and believe in the unchanging love of our heavenly Father. As we realize and appreciate the nature of God's love, the love of God that is already in our hearts will grow. (Romans 5:5) This mature (perfect) love will enable us to fulfill the commandment that Jesus left us, to love each other to the same dimension and degree that He loves us. (1 John 4:16-21)

Scripture Reading: Isaiah 62, 63, 64; 1 Thessalonians 5

Trivia Question: Abraham and Sarah migrated from Ur to what place?

October 18

"Unshaking Faith"

1 Corinthians 15:3-8 — For I delivered unto you first of all that which I also received, how that Christ died for our sins according to the scriptures; And that he was buried, and that he rose again the third day according to the scriptures: And that he was seen of Cephas, then of the twelve: After that, he was seen of above five hundred brethren at once; of whom the greater part remain unto this present, but some are fallen asleep. After that, he was seen of James; then of all the apostles. And last of all he was seen of me also, as of one born out of due time.

The Gospel, the good news of man's salvation, is succinctly stated by the Apostle Paul in his first letter to the Church at Corinth. The death, burial and resurrection of our Lord and Savior Jesus Christ are not only foretold in the Scriptures, but are historical facts, witnessed by well over 500 people. Many of these eyewitnesses of Christ's resurrection were still alive at the writing of Paul's letter. Their lives were transformed and changed after their personal encounter with the risen Christ that they went everywhere testifying of this experience. God blessed their witness and validated their preaching with signs, wonders, healings and miracles.

Thomas would not believe that Christ had risen until he saw him personally. He had to touch the Lord's wounds before he would believe. Our gracious Lord and Savior shocked Thomas by answering his request and appearing to him so that he would not be unbelieving but believe. Christ then makes a startling statement declaring, "Blessed are those who have not seen and yet believe." (John 20:24-29) How could this be? Why would a person be more blessed to believe without seeing the risen Christ, than those who were alive at the time of His resurrection?

Hebrews 11:6 explains why, "Without faith it is impossible to please God, for he who comes to God must believe that He is and that He is a rewarder of those who diligently seek him." In Matthew 8, Jesus stated that the centurion had great faith when he believed that Jesus' spoken Word was enough to heal his daughter. God is well pleased and delights in those who believe His Word. He rewards and blesses a person according to their faith. It is still true today that whoever chooses to believe in the resurrection of Christ will see the glory of God manifested in their lives. (John 11:40)

As the world is in a panic due to the economic, moral and political crisis that confronts us, be bold witnesses of the resurrected Christ. Do not be afraid to preach Christ crucified! This profound message of His death, burial and resurrection may confuse some, but it is the power of God that sets mankind free. (1 Corinthians 1:18) An individual does not have to see to believe (as Thomas thought). As you share your testimony and the message of His love with others, faith will rise up in the hearer's heart. He/she will then receive the forgiveness, mercy, love and peace that our heavenly Father has for all.

Scripture Reading: Isaiah 65, 66; 2 Thessalonians 1

Trivia Question: Why did Abraham and his family change course and go south into Egypt?

October 19

"Protection Promise"

Hebrews 13:5-6 — Let your conversation be without covetousness;
and be content with such things as ye have: for he hath said, I will never leave
thee, nor forsake thee. So that we may boldly say, The Lord is my helper,
and I will not fear what man shall do unto me.

What an awesome faith stirring promise that God has made to His people, throughout Scripture. Regardless of what we are going through or the challenges that confront us, He is always with us. God told Jacob that He would be with him and never leave him until His promises had come to pass. (Genesis 28:15-16) Moses, upon his death, declared to the nation of Israel as they entered the Promised Land, that God would defeat all of their enemies. Moses encouraged them not to have any fear and to be strong and have great courage because the Lord their God would go with them. To emphasize this awesome truth, Moses called Joshua forward in front of the entire nation and reiterated the fact that God, the One who promises His Presence, will always be with them. (Deuteronomy 31:1-8) After Moses died, in case Joshua had any doubt of God's continual protection, the Lord Himself spoke personally to him and commanded Joshua to be strong and have great courage. The Lord his God promised to be with him wherever he went. (Joshua 1:9)

The foundation for Hebrews 13:5 is the promise of God's continual presence, protection, provision and providence that was shown to the saints in the Old Testament. As New Testament believers, the Lord is our helper and we DO NOT have to fear, despite the hard times we may face. Jesus emphasized this truth again when he declared, "I am with you always even unto the end of the age." (Matthew 28:20) During tests, trials and tribulations, our faith in Christ will cause us to overcome as we cleave to Him. (John 16:33 and 1 John 5:4, 5)

Scripture Reading: Jeremiah 1, 2; 2 Thessalonians 2

October 20

"Remain Faithful"

Psalm 63:1-3 — O God, thou art my God; early will I seek thee: my soul thirsteth for thee, my flesh longeth for thee in a dry and thirsty land, where no water is; To see thy power and thy glory, so as I have seen thee in the sanctuary. Because thy lovingkindness is better than life, my lips shall praise thee.

In the above Scripture, King David gives us instruction on how to walk through wilderness times and seasons when life's circumstances try to overwhelm us. Our first response in the midst of calamity or uncertainty should be to seek God. Even if the economy dries up, you lose your job or your house goes into foreclosure, God is still in control and is watching over you! These adverse situations can cause us to either run to God or from Him. Running away from God will only lead you further into your wilderness and keep you from blessings. During troublesome times we must maintain our focus on God and hold onto the promises found in Psalm 34:8-10. He will bless us as we trust in Him, He will meet all of our needs as we reverence Him, and He will provide us all the good things of life as we continually seek Him.

It is in the presence of God that we see His power and glory manifested to us. DO NOT stop going to the house of the Lord during periods of deficiency or death in your life. Hebrews 10:25 declares that we must not forsake the assembling of ourselves together as the day of Christ's return approaches. The tendency of the carnal Christian is to stop going to the house of God as the times become more and more evil. However, notice that the Psalmist David declares that it is in the Sanctuary where we experience God's power and glory. The Sanctuary of God is the place where the saints (the Church) gather together for cooperation in worship and prayer and where the Word is preached under the anointing of God. This is the place where the Spirit of God moves confirming His Word in the lives of all who seek Him. As you seek God in the midst of His people you will be inspired and encouraged to continue on your walk of faith. You will be assured once again that nothing in this life can separate you from the love of God, which is found in and through Jesus Christ. (Romans 8:35-39)

Scripture Reading: Jeremiah 3, 4; 2 Thessalonians 3

Trivia Question: Where was Joseph taken by traders who removed him from the pit?

October 21

"Faith Ingredients"

*2 Peter 1:5-8 — And beside this, giving all diligence,
add to your faith virtue; and to virtue knowledge;
And to knowledge temperance; and to temperance patience;
and to patience godliness; And to godliness brotherly kindness;
and to brotherly kindness charity. For if these things be in you,
and abound, they make you that ye shall neither be barren nor unfruitful
in the knowledge of our Lord Jesus Christ.*

Faith additives are spiritual qualities that you must add to your faith so that you stay prepared for the harvest that the Lord wants you to enjoy. When baking a cake, the main ingredient is usually flour, however the recipe will always require many other ingredients to complete the process, such as sugar, shortening and flavoring. In the same way, the Apostle Peter gives us the formulas for a productive Christian walk.

Apostle Peter first declared that we have the same quality and value of faith (like precious faith) as he had received from the Lord. What an amazing truth, that our faith is the same as this apostle who walked on water, raised the dead and healed the sick. However, to be able to live the same faith life as this great man of God, we must be sure to follow these instructions for success and make every effort to mix our faith with all the components listed above. This will establish us in the Lord and make us fruitful in our knowledge of Christ. As we mature, a multiplying effect of His grace and peace will operate in our lives. As we grow in grace and in the knowledge of Christ, His divine power will enable us to live godly in the midst of this crooked and corrupt generation. We will then fulfill Jesus' declaration in John 15 that as we abide in Him, we will bear much fruit, showing the world that we are His disciples as we walk in love, doing the works of Christ.

Scripture Reading: Jeremiah 5, 6; 1 Timothy 1

October 22

"Mature in Love"

2 Peter 1:5-8 — And beside this, giving all diligence,
add to your faith virtue; and to virtue knowledge;
And to knowledge temperance; and to temperance patience;
and to patience godliness; And to godliness brotherly kindness;
and to brotherly kindness charity. For if these things be in you,
and abound, they make you that ye shall neither be barren nor unfruitful
in the knowledge of our Lord Jesus Christ.

The love of God operating in and through our lives is the culmination of all our worship, prayer time, study of the Word of God and acquisition of the knowledge of Christ. The love of God has already been placed in our hearts by the Holy Spirit. (Romans 5:5) Our maturity as Christians is measured by the increase of this most essential fruit of the Spirit in our lives!

The Apostle John states, "...God is love and he who abides in love, abides in God and God in Him." (1 John 4:16) In essence, God's very nature is love! The Lord's very desire is for you to be a partaker, an active participant and partner of His divine nature. (1 Peter 1:2-4) We have the privilege, right and responsibility to develop the love of God in our lives. Paul declared that if we do not have the love of God as our focal point, all that we say, all that we do and all that we give has no meaning or benefit to us, nor to God. (1 Corinthians 13) As your family, friends, coworkers and associates are able to eat the fruit of God's love from your "tree" they will recognize and know that you are a child of God and disciple of Christ.

Scripture Reading: Jeremiah 7, 8; 1 Timothy 2

Trivia Question: What did Jacob say upon being reunited with Joseph in Egypt?

October 23

"Being God-Like"

*2 Peter 1:5-8 — And beside this, giving all diligence,
add to your faith virtue; and to virtue knowledge;
And to knowledge temperance; and to temperance patience;
and to patience godliness; And to godliness brotherly kindness;
and to brotherly kindness charity. For if these things be in you,
and abound, they make you that ye shall neither be barren nor unfruitful
in the knowledge of our Lord Jesus Christ.*

Godliness is defined as holiness, reverence, piety and respect toward God. Simply put, godliness is God-like-ness, or being conscious of how Jesus would handle every situation He faces. The Apostle Peter declares that we possess God's nature and can be partakers of His moral excellence to help us escape the worldly lusts and social depravity that confronts us every day. (2 Peter 1:3, 4)

Truth will always lead you to God-like-ness. (Titus 1:1) Therefore, know the Word and know Jesus Christ more intimately, because as you do, God's divine nature will manifest in you, causing you to walk circumspectly in the midst of the hedonism, humanism and materialism that tries to distort our thinking and pervert our behavior.

In 1 Timothy 4:7,8, the Apostle Paul states that godliness is a spiritual exercise that we must participate in and practice every day. Living holy and reverent before God on a daily basis will not only benefit us in the life to come, but will bring blessings to us today. If you truly want to see God's presence, protection and promised blessings in your life, you must live holy as Jesus, Himself is holy. You can do it! You have the Holy Spirit within you! As you understand the grace of God toward you, His love, mercy and kindness for you will teach you how to live a life of holiness and piety.

Scripture Reading: Jeremiah 9, 10; 1 Timothy 3

Trivia Question: Why was Moses given that name by the daughter of Pharaoh?

October 24

"Waiting for Him"

2 Peter 1:5-8 — And beside this, giving all diligence,
add to your faith virtue; and to virtue knowledge;
And to knowledge temperance; and to temperance patience;
and to patience godliness; And to godliness brotherly kindness;
and to brotherly kindness charity. For if these things be in you,
and abound, they make you that ye shall neither be barren nor unfruitful
in the knowledge of our Lord Jesus Christ.

We are looking at the importance of living godly in the midst of this evil generation. As our culture becomes more corrupt and each day dawns darker and darker, the second coming of Christ looms larger. We can discern from the signs of the times that the season of His return is imminent. (Matthew 16:3)

The Apostle Paul states, "For the grace of God that bringeth salvation hath appeared to all men, Teaching us that, denying ungodliness and worldly lusts, we should live soberly, righteously, and godly, in this present world; Looking for that blessed hope, and the glorious appearing of the great God and our Saviour Jesus Christ; Who gave himself for us, that he might redeem us from all iniquity, and purify unto himself a peculiar people, zealous of good works." (Titus 2:11-14) The Apostle John declares that if we are hoping for His return we will persistently purify ourselves in anticipation of seeing Him. (1 John 3:2-3) As a bride readies herself for her bridegroom, so must we, the Bride of Christ, continually prepare ourselves for His return. (Ephesians 5:27) Our expectation of seeing the Lord will be the catalyst for our purification. Let God's grace, which is His ability within you, become the driving force, enabling you to live soberly, righteously and godly in this present age of hedonism, materialism and humanism.

Scripture Reading: Jeremiah 11, 12, 13; 1 Timothy 4

Trivia Question: Why did Moses slay an Egyptian?

_____

October 25

"Confidence in Christ"

1 Thessalonians 1:1-3 — Paul, and Silvanus, and Timotheus, unto the church of the Thessalonians which is in God the Father and in the Lord Jesus Christ: Grace be unto you, and peace, from God our Father, and the Lord Jesus Christ. We give thanks to God always for you all, making mention of you in our prayers; Remembering without ceasing your work of faith, and labour of love, and patience of hope in our Lord Jesus Christ, in the sight of God and our Father...

God, the Father, notices when the things we do for Him and for His body are done out of a heart of love and not out of religious obligation. It is only the things we do in love and inspired by love that count for eternity. The love of God, which has been poured into your heart by the Holy Spirit will manifest in all that you do and say. It is the love of God and the love for His church that will establish us blameless in holiness, so that we are ready to meet Jesus when He returns to take us home. (1 Thessalonians 3:12-13)

Hope is the confident expectation that what has been promised shall be accomplished. Our hope must be based on the promises of God. God's Word is clear, Jesus has promised that He is coming back to receive us in the Father's house (Heaven). It is this confident expectation of seeing Jesus Christ that anchors our soul, that is, our mind, will and emotions. (Hebrews 6:19) As we focus on the hope of Heaven, we will be inspired to mature in higher dimensions of holiness. Looking up toward Heaven causes us to become more rooted and grounded in the faith. (Colossians 1:5, 22, 23)

Scripture Reading: Jeremiah 14, 15, 16; 1 Timothy 5

Trivia Question: Why did God appoint Aaron as spokesman for Moses?

October 26

"Kingdom Within"

Luke 1:30-33 — And the angel said unto her,
Fear not, Mary: for thou hast found favour with God. And, behold, thou shalt
conceive in thy womb, and bring forth a son, and shalt call his name Jesus.
He shall be great, and shall be called the Son of the Highest: and the Lord God

shall give unto him the throne of his father David: And he shall reign over the house of Jacob for ever; and of his kingdom there shall be no end.

Let us always remember the main reason that Jesus came to Earth. He was born to die and, through His death, destroy the power that Satan had over our lives. (Hebrews 2:14-15, 1 John 3:8) Once we are redeemed from Satan's control, we make Jesus Christ our new Lord and allow Him to establish His eternal kingdom in and through us, His body, the Church.

God had to become a man so that He could redeem back what the first man, Adam, lost; that is the rule and reign of mankind on the Earth. The first Adam lost this privilege and responsibility; however, the Last Adam, the Son of God, has once again for all eternity set the Kingdom of God in and through believers. Since Christ is God in the flesh, the kingdom promised to Adam and then given to David now becomes Christ's kingdom, since He was born the Son of David. As you honor the Lord, the Babe born in that manger, reflect on the truth that His life has now been birthed into all who have been born again. His life initiates the Kingdom of God within us. He lives through us so that we can rule and reign in this life, causing His Kingdom, of which there will be no end, to advance throughout the world.

Scripture Reading: Jeremiah 17, 18, 19; 1 Timothy 6

Trivia Question: Why was Miriam stricken with leprosy in the wilderness?

October 27

"Made New"

Isaiah 43:18-19 — Remember ye not the former things, neither consider the things of old. Behold, I will do a new thing; now it shall spring forth; shall ye not know it? I will even make a way in the wilderness, and rivers in the desert.

God will do something new, fresh and different for you. Trust Him to make a way out of your wilderness experience. Look to Him to give you refreshing and rest in your desert time. See Christ in your crisis and watch Him make a testimony out of your test.

The Scripture tells us not to remember the past, but look to the future and expect God's blessing, benefits and bountiful harvest to overtake us.

The Apostle Paul declares that a mature believer is able to forget what is behind and look forward to what is ahead, pressing on towards the perfect will of God. (Philippians 3:12-15)

Scripture Reading: Jeremiah 20, 21, 22; 2 Timothy 1

Trivia Question: Why did God tell Moses to remove his shoes?

October 28

"Why Fast?"

Matthew 6:1-18 — Take heed that ye do not your alms before men, to be seen of them: otherwise ye have no reward of your Father which is in Heaven. Therefore when thou doest thine alms, do not sound a trumpet before thee, as the hypocrites do in the synagogues and in the streets, that they may have glory of men. Verily I say unto you, They have their reward. But when thou doest alms, let not thy left hand know what thy right hand doeth: That thine alms may be in secret: and thy Father which seeth in secret himself shall reward thee openly. And when thou prayest, thou shalt not be as the hypocrites are: for they love to pray standing in the synagogues and in the corners of the streets, that they may be seen of men. Verily I say unto you, They have their reward. But thou, when thou prayest, enter into thy closet, and when thou hast shut thy door, pray to thy Father which is in secret; and thy Father which seeth in secret shall reward thee openly. But when ye pray, use not vain repetitions, as the heathen do: for they think that they shall be heard for their much speaking. Be not ye therefore like unto them: for your Father knoweth what things ye have need of, before ye ask him. After this manner therefore pray ye: Our Father which art in Heaven, Hallowed be thy name. Thy kingdom come, Thy will be done in earth, as it is in Heaven. Give us this day our daily bread. And forgive us our debts, as we forgive our debtors. And lead us not into temptation, but deliver us from evil: For thine is the kingdom, and the power, and the glory, for ever. Amen. For if ye forgive men their trespasses, your heavenly Father will also forgive you: But if ye forgive not men their trespasses, neither will your Father forgive your trespasses. Moreover when ye fast, be not, as the hypocrites, of a sad countenance: for they disfigure their faces, that they may appear unto men to fast. Verily I say unto you, They have their reward. But thou, when thou fastest, anoint thine head, and wash thy face; That thou appear not unto men to fast, but unto thy Father which is in secret: and thy Father, which seeth in secret, shall reward thee openly.

Jesus commanded us to give, pray and fast. He says, *when* you give, *when* you pray and *when* you fast, not if you do these things. Giving, praying and fasting should be the three staples of a Christian's life and ministry. Many of us have done well in our prayer life and our giving, but have not heeded the biblical mandate to include fasting as a spiritual discipline. Maybe this is a reason that some of our prayers have not been answered like the Word says they should be. Could this be one of the explanations as to why God's blessings have not overtaken us?

Jesus, who is God in the flesh, had to fast and pray to defeat Satan's tactics against Him. (Luke 4:1-15) How much more must we engage in this necessary spiritual combat to break demonic strongholds and controls in our lives and the lives of others. Remember, even though Jesus had given His disciples power over demons to cast them out and to heal all kinds of diseases, (Matthew 10:1) He also declared that some demonic oppositions will not come down until we fast and pray. (Matthew 17:19-21)

Fasting does not change God, nor do we fast to twist God's arm and force Him to do something for us. However, as we fast and pray, it will make us more sensitive to hear His voice and believe His Word. Fasting helps us to be in alignment with His will and position us for His promises to be fulfilled in our lives.

Scripture Reading: Jeremiah 23, 24; 2 Timothy 2

Trivia Question: Who was Joshua's father?

October 29

"Life Light"

John 1:4 — In Him was life; and the life was the light of men.

In Christ is the LIFE of God, and this life is available to us through His resurrection. It is because He still lives that we can live as well. Faith in Christ causes us to pass from spiritual death into spiritual life. (John 5:24) Before we believed in Christ, we were dead in our trespasses and sin. We were walking dead men. (Ephesians 2:1-3) However, Christ gives the life of God freely to everyone who receives Him as their Lord and Savior. (1 John 5:11-13) It is this life of God in us that gives us light, inspiration, illumination and understanding into the true purpose and meaning of our lives. It is His life that shines in us and then through us. (John 8:12; John

12:36) As the life of Christ radiates through us, we become the light of the world. We must let our life (light) shine so bright, that all around us will see our good works and give glory to God. (Matthew 5:13-16) It is the light of God's love shining through us that will enlighten others to the good news of salvation through the resurrection of the Savior of the world. (Acts 4:32-35; Philippians 2:14-15)

Scripture Reading: Jeremiah 25, 26; 2 Timothy 3

Trivia Question: What was God's exhortation to Joshua as he succeeded Moses?

October 30

"The Lamb"

1 Corinthians 5:7 — Purge out therefore the old leaven, that ye may be a new lump, as ye are unleavened. For even Christ our passover is sacrificed for us.

There are three major principles found in the Passover story from Exodus 12 and 13. These principles will keep the destroyer from our lives and allow the blessings, benefits and promises of God to rest upon us. Since Jesus Christ has become our Passover, we are not under religious obligation to fulfill the Passover rituals. However, as we apply these three principles in our lives, we can reap all that our Passover Lamb has provided for us in this New Testament dispensation.

The first major principle is that we must remove all leaven from our houses (lives). In the New Testament, leaven represents two main things: wrong doctrine (teaching) and sin. The false teachings that we must avoid are two-fold, that of the teaching of the Sadducees who denied the resurrection and the supernatural, and the false teaching of the Pharisees who followed a doctrine of good works and self-righteousness to gain eternal life. (Matthew 16:5-12) The second thing that leaven represents in the New Testament is sin. If we are to enjoy the benefits of our covenant with God, we must rid ourselves from all sin. (1 Corinthians 5:6-8, Galatians 5:7-9)

The second major principle is that God has established a Sabbath rest for His people. (Hebrews 4:1-11) This rest is much more than a one-day a week rest. It is a repose we find in Christ as we understand that God has everything under control. As we mix our faith with the Word of God, we can trust and rely on Christ's finished work; that is, from eternity past and before He created the world, He has met every one of our needs. This will give us great peace and assurance of heart causing us to rest in the promises God has for us.

The third principle is that we must understand and appropriate the blood covenant. It was the blood of the lamb that protected the Jewish homes from the destroyer. Today, it is the blood of Jesus Christ that we apply to our lives that enables us to overcome Satan's tactics, schemes and diabolical plans against us. (Revelation 12:11)

We are redeemed from the entire curse put upon the human race. (Galatians 3:13-14) Not only that, God has promised that His blessings would come upon us and overtake us. (Deuteronomy 28) As we put into practice these three spiritual principles taken from the Passover account, we will enjoy the total and complete redemption purchased for us by the blood of Jesus Christ.

Scripture Reading: Jeremiah 27, 28; 2 Timothy 4

Trivia Question: Who was the fourth judge of Israel?

October 31

"Satan the Deceiver"

2 Corinthians 11:14-15 — And no marvel;
for Satan himself is transformed into an angel of light.
Therefore it is no great thing if his ministers also be transformed as the ministers
of righteousness; whose end shall be according to their works.

We are living in a day that was predicted many years ago by God's prophets. A day of great deceit, deception and danger. People who are demonically inspired, being used as tools of Satan, are seeking to destroy the innocent's faith. Whatever measures it takes, Satan and his demonic army are attempting to misguide, mislead and mess up people's lives spiritually and otherwise.

Jesus said, "Beware of false prophets, which come to you in sheep's clothing but inwardly they are ravening wolves."(Matthew 7:15) Satan is a master of disguise and deception. Satan will appear to be a harmless friend but inwardly has another agenda. Satan is a wolf, and the objective of the wolf is to prey on the sheep. Satan's representatives may come to you looking like sheep, smelling like sheep and acting like sheep, but inwardly a ravening wolf! Ouch! Watch out!

"Test the spirits whether they are of God, do not believe every one and everything you hear, because many false prophets are gone out into the world." (1 John 4:1)

The Litmus test for Christians to discern truth vs. error is the Word of God. If someone is peddling and promoting a Bible teaching, size it up to the inerrant Word of God. You will be surprised who does not make the cut. Romans 16:17, "Now I beseech you, brethren, mark them which cause divisions and offences contrary to the doctrine which ye have learned; and avoid them." Not everyone that knocks on your door is sent from God! Promote truth and renounce error.

Scripture Reading: Jeremiah 29, 30; Titus 1

Trivia Question: What were Stephen's last words before he died as a Christian martyr?

November

November 1

"Progressing in God, Part 1"

*Ephesians 4:13 — Till we all come in the unity of the faith
and of the knowledge of the Son of God, unto a perfect man,
unto the measure of the stature of the fullness of Christ.*

Paul's discourse to the church at Ephesus was both corrective and challenging. Ephesus was a city of idolatry, immorality and a culture filled with anti-God practices. Paul loved the church that was established there and held the people dear to his heart. Paul spent at least three years there on his third missionary journey. Paul's letter to them is powerful, with a strong emphasis on the theme of "The Church, Christ's body." As any founder of a company, organization or sports franchise, the growth, maturity and progression of the *team* is paramount. Paul was no different with his concern of the progression of the people in the Ephesian church.

Paul uses words in our text in Ephesians 4:13 like, *perfect (or mature) man, measure* and *fullness.* All these words bring the idea of progression. With this in mind, let us look at what I call "Five Levels of Relationship with Christ." Our relationship with the Lord could and should progress. If I only know my wife in the same way today as when we were first married, there probably was not much growth. My relationship with my wife has increased, developed and progressed considerably after almost 40 years of marriage.

Desire, devotion and determination are really the backdrop of any relationship that is going to develop and progress. This is also the truth about our relationship with Jesus.

The beginning level or phase of our relationship is called being a believer. Acts 16:31 says, "and they said, believe on the Lord Jesus Christ, and thou shalt be saved, and thy house." Paul and Silas speaking to the guard in the jail they were incarcerated in after a mighty deliverance, answered the

297

question, "What must I do to be saved?" The answer then is the same answer now. It is not what I can do; our good works are not good enough (Ephesians 2:8, 9) and our righteousness is dirty. (Isaiah 64:6) Jesus did all the work by sacrificing His righteous life for us. We must do the believing!

When the Ethiopian eunuch met Phillip and heard the Gospel of Jesus Christ, he responded and told Philip he wanted to be identified with this Jesus. (Acts 8:26-40) The man said, "I believe that Jesus Christ is the Son of God." The first level in our relationship with God through Christ and by the Holy Spirit is being a believer.

Believing in the Lord Jesus Christ is glorious, life-changing, and wonderful, but that is not the end-all. Believing starts you on your way to a strong, intimate relationship with the Lord, but you must progress. Believing is good, but the demons also believe in God and tremble. (James 2:19)

If a Christian only remained in the believing phase of relationship with Christ, they too will tremble, that is, only see one facet of God – a judge for their rebellion and sin.

We must progress in our relationship with the Lord to know Him in all of His many facets. We need a terrific relationship with Him, not a trembling one!

We must move on to a new level of relationship with Christ, called disciples.

Scripture Reading: Jeremiah 31, 32; Titus 2

Trivia Question: Who wrote, "A double minded man is unstable in all his ways?"

November 2

"Progressing in God, Part 2"

*Ephesians 4:13 — Till we all come in the unity of the faith
and of the knowledge of the Son of God, unto a perfect man,
unto the measure of the stature of the fullness of Christ.*

As we desire to progress from believer to the next phase of relationship with Christ as a disciple, there must be a strong desire to get to know Him through His Word. Jesus is the Word of God.

The way I have grown closer to my wife in my marriage relationship is spending time with her over the years and communicating. It takes words to communicate, and there have been many words that we have shared with each other over almost 40 years of marriage.

In any relationship, words are important. If you desire to grow any relationship it will take more than a few words spoken once in a while. There must be a constant flow of communication for that relationship to have the potential to blossom.

Jesus said in John 8:31, "If you continue in my word, then are you my disciples indeed." There must be a continual, constant interaction with the Word of God to become true disciples of Christ. A disciple is one that is disciplined; one that takes the time to get into God's Word and lets God's Word get into them.

Failure to discipline your life in the Word of God will stagnate you and slow down the progression of your relationship with Jesus. Of course you are still a believer, but God wants you to progress to a disciple. A disciple is continually, "in my word." (John 8:31)

Decide today to discipline yourself to get into the Word daily. Bible reading, devotions and study of the Scriptures will bring you to a place in your relationship with Christ called discipleship.

Scripture Reading: Jeremiah 33, 34, 35; Titus 3

Trivia Question: Abraham's son Isaac was a father of two boys. What are their names?

November 3

"Progressing in God, Part 3"

Ephesians 4:13 — Till we all come in the unity of the faith and of the knowledge of the Son of God, unto a perfect man, unto the measure of the stature of the fullness of Christ.

As we develop and grow from believers, to disciples, the next phase of a deeper relationship with Christ is called a convert. This might surprise you, but allow me to prove it by the Scriptures.

There is a beautiful story of an intimate dialogue between Jesus and His friend Peter. Luke 22:31-32 reads, "And the Lord said, Simon, Simon, behold, Satan hath desired to have you, that he may sift you as wheat. But I have prayed for thee, that thy faith fail not: and when thou art converted, strengthen thy brethren."

Notice Peter already was a believer, he was already called a disciple of Christ. Jesus was challenging Peter to a new level of relationship with Him. "When you are converted, strengthen your brothers." According to Jesus, His friend Peter who was walking with Him for almost three years was not converted yet. Believers and disciples have their focus for the most part on themselves. But when you rise to the level of convert, your focus and concern turns towards others. True converts of Christ want to help others become strong in their relationship with Christ. When your attention gets off of self and on to others that is an indication that you are progressing in your relationship with Jesus. Jesus is all about serving and strengthening others. (Mark 10:45) Let us progress to biblical conversion and begin to strengthen others. "Look not every man on his own interests, but every man also on the interests of others. (Philippians 2:4)

Scripture Reading: Jeremiah 36, 37; Philemon 1

Trivia Question: What three items were placed in the hands of Gideon's soldiers for the battle with the Midianites?

November 4

"Progressing in God, Part 4"

Ephesians 4:13 — Till we all come in the unity of the faith and of the knowledge of the Son of God, unto a perfect man, unto the measure of the stature of the fullness of Christ.

As we progress in relationship with Christ, developing from a believer, to a disciple, to a convert, we are now ready to step into stewardship. A steward is one who has been entrusted by God to oversee and lead people, places or things. A steward is responsible and accountable to God and those that God sets over them. Stewards that oversee and lead God's entrusted people, places and things treat them as their very own, although always remain aware they have been entrusted by God with them. Stewards are faithful overseers. 1 Corinthians 4:2 says, "Moreover it is required in stewards, that a man be found faithful." Believers believe, disciples follow, converts strengthen others and stewards are faithful overseers to who and what they have been charged with. Stewards are individuals that are selfless, sacrificial people who are deep in their relationship with the Lord. God feels comfortable entrusting and empowering them with His precious commodities: people, places (lands and properties) and kingdom things (money, etc.)

Can God trust you with such precious cargo? Are you at the place that you are entering stewardship? Are you faithful in the small so that God can trust you with more? Be a steward for God and be entrusted by the Creator with His creation.

Scripture Reading: Jeremiah 38, 39; Hebrews 1

Trivia Question: How many years did the Israelites spend wandering in the desert before settling in Canaan?

November 5

"Progressing in God, Part 5"

Ephesians 4:13 — Till we all come in the unity of the faith and of the knowledge of the Son of God, unto a perfect man, unto the measure of the stature of the fullness of Christ.

I believe God wants to bring us to a revelation of relationship with Him, to the point of the understanding becoming co-heirs. Romans 8:17 says, "And if children, then heirs of God, and joint-heirs with Christ; if so be that we suffer with him, that we may also be glorified together." Wow, what a relationship position – children of God, heirs of God and joint or co-heirs with His Son Jesus Christ. When we walk in that kind of relationship, knowing we are co-heirs with Jesus, we become more Kingdom minded, more Holy Spirit directed, more soul-saving conscious, and more God pleasing. Jesus came to do the will of His Father and to please Him. (John 8:29) If we are co-heirs, we also are co-laborers with Christ. (1 Corinthians 3:9, 2 Corinthians 6:1)

Our relationship with the Father should be such that when we wake up in the morning, we are very aware of the fact that we are sons (and daughters) of God, and even greater, that we are co-heirs with Jesus Christ. As Jesus was determined to say what the Father wanted Him to say, go where the Father wanted him to go and do what the Father wanted him to do, we too would have that kind of desire, determination and dedication to do the will of the Father and all of Heaven's requests.

May we all progress to that level of revelation of relationship that we are about our Father's business (Luke 2:49) and seek through our obedience to please Him by doing His will daily. (John 4:34)

Scripture Reading: Jeremiah 40, 41, 42; Hebrews 2

Trivia Question: Who advised Moses to select capable leaders to help him counsel the people and settle disputes?

November 6

"How Great Thou Art"

Psalm 92:5 — O Lord, how great are thy works!
And thy thoughts are very deep.

God is great! Because He is great, He does great things. How great are His works! There is nothing average, or common about God. God loves you greatly and wants to do great things in your life. "Now unto Him that is able to do exceeding abundantly above all that we ask or think, according to the power that worketh in us." (Ephesians 3:20)

Exceedingly, abundantly, above all that we can ask, think of or even imagine, that is what our great God wants to do for you today!

What is your need in your life at this very moment? God is thinking of you, (Jeremiah 29:11) and loves you with a never ending, never failing love, (1 John 4:16) and desires to do great works on your behalf. (Matthew 7:7-8)

Just ask Him in faith, believe and trust Him, wait on Him and see what your great God will do for you!

Scripture Reading: Jeremiah 43, 44, 45; Hebrews 3

Trivia Question: Why did Naomi and her husband Elimelech leave Bethlehem to settle in Moab?

November 7

"Healing Hands"

Matthew 8:14-15 — And when Jesus was come into Peter's house,
he saw his wife's mother laid, and sick of a fever. And he touched her hand,
and the fever left her: and she arose, and ministered unto them.

Jesus was invited to Simon Peter's house one day. Upon entering His friend's home, He discovered that Peter's mother-in-law was ill with a high fever. (Perhaps Peter's mother-in-law was visiting, took ill and remained there unable to leave, or maybe Peter's mother-in-law lived with them.)

Jesus immediately saw the need, was moved with compassion and did what He does best—touched her. His healing hand touched her hurting head, and the results – the fever left her, she got up and fixed Him a meal. (Maybe some good mother-in-law matzo ball soup.)

Are you in need of His healing hand? Invite Him to your home today. He will have compassion on you and He will touch you, heal you and raise you up. He is your shield, your burden bearer and the lifter up of your head. (Psalm 3:3) Let His healing hand touch your hurt right now!

Scripture Reading: Jeremiah 46, 47, 48; Hebrews 4

Trivia Question: Why did God order Gideon to reduce his army?

November 8

"The Early Bird Get's the Worm"

Psalm 63:1 — O God, thou art my God; early will I seek thee: my soul thirsteth for thee, my flesh longeth for thee in a dry and thirsty land, where no water is.

There is something about starting your day God conscious, God communicating and God connecting. The Psalmist that said, "early will I seek thee," probably was referring to early in his day. Life is filled with problems, pressures and pulling from all directions. I have personally experienced starting out my day in prayer and devotion helps my day go better. I encourage you to seek Him early in your day. If early is not for you, seek Him during *some* time of your day. David said, "my soul is thirsty for you, my flesh longs after you." David's soul (emotions) were dry, his flesh needed the touch of God, he knew his remedy would not be found in the world. The world has nothing to offer. The land is dry and thirsty. No natural water will suffice. David needed living water to quench his thirsty soul and satisfy the hunger in his heart. Only God and His Word can fill and satisfy. (John 4:14-15)

Purpose in your heart and life to seek God and put Him first. Give Him the first part of your day. The early bird may get the worm, but if you seek Him early you will get wisdom, blessings and direction.

Scripture Reading: Jeremiah 49, 50; Hebrews 5

November 9

"Peace"

John 16:33 — These things I have spoken unto you, that in me ye might have peace. In the world ye shall have tribulation: but be of good cheer; I have overcome the world.

I have learned in my Bible studies that the subject of faith is deep and has different dimensions to it. People can possess *no faith* (2 Thessalonians 3:2) to *perfect faith.* (James 2:22) Faith can grow, expand and increase. So it is with peace. Peace also is a fruit of the Spirit that we receive in seed form upon believing on the Lord Jesus Christ. As we water *seed faith* with the Word of God, so also *seed peace* needs to be watered by the Word and developed in our lives. Jesus said, "that in me you might have peace." (John 16:33) Peace is initiated by Jesus, is developed by Him in our lives and concludes with Him. Hebrews 12:14 says to "follow peace." Peace is on the move, aggressively going forward, developing and growing and therefore we must go after peace.

Sadly, there are individuals all around us that have no peace. "There is no peace, saith my God, to the wicked." (Isaiah 57:21) Unfortunately there is wickedness in the world, done by wicked people; people who have rejected God and His Christ, and those that are contemptible toward God and His holiness. The ungodly may experience temporary peace in their life, but not perfect peace that only comes from the Lord. May we introduce the Prince of peace to those who are engaged and engulfed in wickedness, so they too can know peace of God.

Scripture Reading: Jeremiah 51, 52; Hebrews 6

Trivia Question: What did Nathan the prophet tell David the consequences would be for taking and having Uriah killed?

November 10

"Living in Peace"

2 Corinthians 13:11 — Finally, brethren, farewell. Be perfect, be of good comfort, be of one mind, live in peace; and the God of love and peace shall be with you.

What does it mean to live in peace. I believe it starts with you making a conscious effort to bring in Jesus, the Prince of peace, who gives perfect peace into every situation no matter how tumultuous it is. In every storm of life, He is our peace. In every battle we go through, He is our peace. In every confusion that clutters our minds, He is our peace. In every sorrow, He is our peace. In every problem we face, He is our peace.

We have to invite Jesus, our peace, into our storms, battles, confusions, sorrows and problems, so that the manifestation of His presence and peace can flood our lives. If we are living our lives in Him, then we are living in peace. Trying to fix everything ourselves, and attempting to push all the right buttons, especially during adverse seasons in our lives, will only lead to frustration, fear and failure. We need God all the time. It is not a sign of weakness not to invite Jesus into every situation that we face, it is a sign of pride. "I can figure this out myself, I will get through this on my own," – famous (or should I say infamous) last words. Live in Christ, live in His presence, live in His Word and live in His peace. His peace will calm the troubled sea. Live in peace today!

Scripture Reading: Lamentations 1, 2; Hebrews 7

Trivia Question: In what town of Galilee was Jesus when He healed a nobleman's son who was at the point of death in Capernaum?

November 11

"The Place of Peace"

Haggai 2:9 — The glory of this latter house shall be greater than of the former, saith the Lord of hosts: and in this place will I give peace, saith the Lord of hosts.

Did you ever notice that God created places before He created people? God created the Garden of Eden before He created Adam. God put the man in the place called Eden. I believe it is important for us to be in the right place that God has planted us. When we are in the place God puts us, His peace will be there.

Are you in the right place? Have you allowed God to place you where He desires? Are you in the will of your heavenly Father? His peace will be in that place!

We have a tendency to wander from the place that God has created for us. The farther we go from the place that God has led us, the less peace we experience. Ask God today if you have wandered. Ask Him to reveal to you His perfect will. Walk in obedience wherever God leads you, no matter what it looks or feels like. God will provide peace at that place.

Scripture Reading: Lamentations 3, 4, 5; Hebrews 8

Trivia Question: What were Nicodemus's credentials as a Jewish leader?

November 12

"Prevailing Peace"

Colossians 3:15 — And let the peace of God rule in your hearts, to the which also ye are called in one body; and be ye thankful.

"Rule in your hearts!" That is the kind of peace that governs and prevails in your heart, even in the presence of problems, pains, pressures and persecution! The verb "rule" means to govern or manage. Some synonyms for "rule" are: to be in authority, control, dictate, dominate, predominate, prevail, reign, and take over. This kind of peace supersedes everything that would try to bring you into an arena of darkness and despair, confusion and chaos, or stress and overwhelming circumstances. The peace of God dominates all situations. Every emotion contrary to God must bow to God's peace when it is ruling in your hearts.

So let His peace dictate and control your life, even if you feel like your life is speeding down the highway out of control. Develop peace, water the seed of peace and watch it rise up out of obscurity to take charge of the situation and bring balance and stability in your life. His peace will win every time!

Scripture Reading: Ezekiel 1, 2, 3; Hebrews 9

Trivia Question: Who did Paul exhort to fulfill the ministry that God entrusted to him?

November 13

"Abundant Peace"

Psalm 72:7 — In his days shall the righteous flourish;
and abundance of peace so long as the moon endureth.

Abundance means a very large quantity of something. God wants you, the righteous, to flourish. He desires increase in our lives.

As we feast on His Word and continue to fill up the storehouse of our spirits, peace will flourish, increase and grow. All the fruits of the Spirit (Galatians 5:22, 23) start out in their seed state. As we water the seed with the Word of God, the seed will grow and flourish. God desires for us to have a plethora of peace even during the most difficult and dark times.

Joseph stored up grain during the years of harvest so that he and Egypt (and eventually his own family) would have plenty in the season of famine. You never know when you will be going through a dry, disturbing season. Let God's peace grow and develop in you so that abundant peace overcomes the stress in your life. God says His peace will be in abundance for you, as long as the moon endures. The moon is not going anywhere soon. Let His abundant peace "keep your hearts and minds through Christ Jesus." (Philippians 4:7)

Scripture Reading: Ezekiel 4, 5, 6; Hebrews 10:1-23

Trivia Question: Who brought Simon Peter to Jesus?

November 14

"Great Peace"

Psalm 119:165 — Great peace have they which love thy law:
and nothing shall offend them.

People that walk in the peace of God do not allow offense in their lives. Offended individuals usually are bitter people and lose sleep at night. Offense will emotionally cripple you and cause you to digress. God's great peace can squash offense under your feet. When you have the Word of God, you start to infuse God's ways, God's will and God's Word into your spirit. God's Word will start to build immunity to offense and cause His great peace to bring victory.

Are you offended easily? Do people around you have to tiptoe and watch everything they say? If so, offense could be a giant that you have to conquer. God's Word brings great peace. His peace will act like a weapon to defeat offense. Offense is good if you are playing football, but not in the Kingdom of God.

Love God's Word, have great peace and let NOTHING offend you.

Scripture Reading: Ezekiel 7, 8, 9; Hebrews 10:24-39

Trivia Question: According to the Psalmist David, what is forever settled in Heaven?

November 15

"Perfect Peace"

Isaiah 26:3 — Thou wilt keep him in perfect peace,
whose mind is stayed on thee: because he trusteth in thee.

How challenging it is to focus on Jesus and His truth when thoughts are bombarding our minds. It is an exercise that will take practice, practice, and more practice. Nevertheless, it all comes back to trusting in God. Isaiah teaches us if we are trusting God through every trial and circumstance, and focusing our mind and thought life on God and His promises, then peace will follow – perfect peace! His perfect, complete peace will overshadow you. Having our minds stayed on Him, allows God to manifest Himself to you.

Jesus is the embodiment and personification of peace. He is the Prince of peace. (Isaiah 9:6) Jesus is the Head of peace, the Chief Captain of peace, the General of peace, the Governor of peace, the Lord of peace, the Keeper of peace and the Master and Ruler of peace.

Keep on meditating in God's Word especially when facing tests and trials. Trust Him and His perfect peace will cause you to triumph.

Scripture Reading: Ezekiel 10, 11, 12; Hebrews 11:1-19

Trivia Question: Who was the devout Roman officer who was instructed in a vision to contact Simon Peter?

November 16

"Different Types of Prayer"

Matthew 7:7-8 — Ask, and it shall be given you; seek, and ye shall find; knock, and it shall be opened unto you: For every one that asketh receiveth; and he that seeketh findeth; and to him that knocketh it shall be opened.

There are times and circumstances the Holy Spirit will direct you to ask God one time as you petition him prayerfully and never again. But there will be other times that you ask and keep on asking, seek and keep on seeking, knock and keep on knocking. All prayer is not thrown into the same pot. When I was a boy my mom would cook a stew and put many different vegetables and ingredients in one pot, the result was a delectable meal. On the other hand when she made her famous signature dish, eggplant parmesan, she was careful to make it with just a few ingredients.

There are different types of prayer for different types of needs. For example, if you are praying for the sick or even for your own physical healing; the prayer of faith should be prayed, God's gift of healing received and then thanksgiving should continually follow. However, there are prayer requests you can pray for daily, such as for your church, ministries that God has entrusted to you and even for revival in your land. I encourage you to make a Bible study on different types of prayer. There are various situations, conditions and needs, so when it comes to prayer, one size does not fit all.

Scripture Reading: Ezekiel 13, 14, 15; Hebrews 11:20-40

Trivia Question: When Jesus fed the people with five loaves of bread and two fish, how many men ate?

November 17

"Not Taking No for an Answer"

Matthew 15:21-28 — Then Jesus went thence, and departed into the coasts of Tyre and Sidon. And, behold, a woman of Canaan came out of the same coasts, and cried unto him, saying, Have mercy on me, O Lord, thou son of David; my daughter is grievously vexed with a devil. But he answered her not a word. And his disciples came and besought him, saying, Send her away; for she crieth after us. But he answered and said, I am not sent but unto the lost sheep of the house

of Israel. Then came she and worshipped him, saying, Lord, help me. But he an-
swered and said, It is not meet to take the children's bread, and to cast it to dogs.
And she said, Truth, Lord: yet the dogs eat of the crumbs which fall from their
masters' table. Then Jesus answered and said unto her, O woman, great is thy
faith: be it unto thee even as thou wilt. And her daughter was made whole from
that very hour.

Persistence many times will result in breakthrough. There is a story in the Bible about a mother whose daughter was demonically attacked. The mother came to Jesus imploring His help. To her dismay, Jesus did not respond to her urgent request and to add to her consternation, Jesus did not even say a word to her. His disciples also urged Him to rid of her. The mother would not take no for an answer. She had a dire, emergent need that demanded Jesus' attention and response. Her importunity and persistence compelled Jesus to grant her request and give a command for her daughter's healing and freedom.

There are times you will have to be a *pit-bull* in the spirit. I believe Jesus always intended to heal this young lady, but still provoked this mother to continue to exercise her faith. Faith has always and will always move the hand of God. Do not accept no, when Jesus says yes; at times you may have to press in more aggressively. "The kingdom of heaven allows for violence, and the violent take it by force." (Matthew 11:12)

Scripture Reading: Ezekiel 16; Hebrews 12

Trivia Question: What shall the person that endures temptation receive as a reward?

November 18

"Broken Tooth, Broken Foot"

*Proverbs 25:19 — Confidence in an unfaithful man in time of trouble
is like a broken tooth, and a foot out of joint.*

These are troublesome times. God needs faithful men and women that He can trust and rely on. He is looking for those that He can have confidence in, and will carry His everlasting Gospel to the world.

It is painful enough in good times to trust and put confidence in unfaithful, unreliable and undependable people, but in tough times it is much more painful. Solomon likens this type of experience of putting confidence and trust in unfaithful people, like a broken tooth, and a broken foot. Double pain!

A broken tooth will affect your talk and a broken foot will affect your walk. There are people that you think are in covenant with you, only to prove themselves unfaithful in tough times, especially when you're counting on them the most.

Are you in covenant with people that will stick by you in troublesome times, through stormy seasons and through the financial challenges of life? It is easy to stay engaged and connected when everything is going well, but what about in times of trouble?

Covenant with those that *God* shows you to covenant with—in marriage, in business, in relationships and in ministry. Psalms 118:8, 9 says, "It is better to trust in the Lord than to put confidence in man. It is better to trust in the Lord than to put confidence in princes."

Scripture Reading: Ezekiel 17, 18, 19; Hebrews 13

Trivia Question: According to Solomon in Proverbs, which is the strongest of beasts?

November 19

"Press On"

Proverbs 24:10 — If thou faint in the day of adversity, thy strength is small.

The word faith in this text means to forsake or to leave. We have to purpose in our hearts that we will not give up or quit even when adversity comes, and adversity will come. People that quit during times of testing indicate that they are not drawing strength from God. The Lord can see you through any trial or storm, the key is to have a reservoir of His strength inside of you. That is accomplished by having a steady diet of prayer and Bible meditation. If we fail to replete the reservoir of God's strength, when adversity comes we will only possess *small strength.*

We must press on in the Kingdom of God and persevere on our journey with Jesus. We have to endure hard times if we are truly soldiers of Christ. (2 Timothy 2:3) We must continue in the strength of Christ to speak to the mountains if need be. (Mark 11:23) We must continue in spite of difficulty, opposition, pressure, persecution and pain. Hebrews 12:1-2, "Wherefore seeing we also are compassed about with so great a cloud of witnesses, let us lay aside every weight, and the sin which doth so easily beset us, and let us run with patience the race that is set before us, Looking unto Jesus the author and finisher of our faith; who for the joy that was set before him endured the cross, despising the shame, and is set down at the right hand of the throne of God."

Nehemiah faced great opposition in his quest to rebuild Jerusalem's walls. He said, "I am doing a great work so that I cannot come down. Why should the work stop while I leave it, and come down to you?" (Nehemiah 6:3)

Stay on the wall, stay the course, stay in the fight. Most of all stay in the Word and God's presence to give you the strength you need to press on and persevere. Remember beloved, you are a soldier!

Scripture Reading: Ezekiel 20, 21; James 1

Trivia Question: What king allowed the remnant of the Jews in captivity to return to Jerusalem?

November 20

"This is Your Season"

Galatians 6:9 — And let us not be weary in well doing: for in due season we shall reap, if we faint not.

Satan cannot prevent your harvest from coming to you because he is not the author of seasons, God is.

God stated, "While the earth remaineth, seedtime and harvest, and cold and heat, and summer and winter, and day and night shall not cease." (Genesis 8:22) This is a law of God —a law that governs the Earth. "The Earth belongs to God and the fullness thereof." (Psalm 24:1)

Solomon said, "To everything there is a season, and a time to every purpose under the heaven." (Eccelsiastes 3:1) Seasons belong to God and are His gift to us. The promise is, "in due season we shall reap, if we faint not." (Galatians 6:9) As we continue to persevere in our walk with Christ, and our marriages, parenting, relationships, ministries and studies, continue to be tenacious; God will bring the season to receive your harvest that He promised. Do not get weary, do not become fainthearted, do not get worn down or worn out. Your harvest is on the horizon. This is your season! Remember, our diligence – His reward.

Scripture Reading: Ezekiel 22, 23; James 2

Trivia Question: What three apostles are regarded as members of Christ's inner circle?

November 21

"My Brother's Keeper"

James 5:19-20 — Brethren, if any of you do err from the truth, and one convert him; Let him know, that he which converteth the sinner from the error of his way shall save a soul from death, and shall hide a multitude of sins.

In this self-centered, self-absorbed, self-indulgent culture that we live, we as Christians have to be aware of the need to be concerned about others (especially their walk with God).

Though we are not called to judge people's heart, we need to judge behavior patterns. If we see someone stray from the truth, it is our Christian responsibility to reach out and try to bring correction by compassion. James tells us in this text, someone who errs from truth can end up in death –spiritually and sometimes worse.

We have to be concerned for others, especially fallen comrades. Paul said in Galatians 6:1, "Brethren, if a man be overtaken in a fault, ye which are spiritual, restore such an one in the spirit of meekness; considering thyself, lest thou also be tempted." The strong helping the weak is God's way. In another area of Scripture, "We then that are strong ought to bear the infirmities of the weak, and not to please ourselves." (Romans 15:1)

Reaching out to the Christian who is downtrodden, discouraged or even deceived has to be on our agenda. Look around you, is there one that once walked the way, but now is wandering away, ask God to give you compassion and an understanding heart and rescue them from spiritual and possibly eternal disaster. I am my brother's keeper!

Scripture Reading: Ezekiel 24, 25, 26; James 3

Trivia Question: What Jewish Queen risked her life to intercede for her people before the Persian king?

313

November 22

"Love Me More than These"

John 21:15 — So when they had dined, Jesus saith to Simon Peter, Simon, son of Jonas, lovest thou me more than these? He saith unto him, Yea, Lord; thou knowest that I love thee. He saith unto him, Feed my lambs.

After Christ's resurrection, He appears once again (the third time) to His disciples. Jesus walks to the seaside and meets Peter, Thomas, Nathaniel, James, John and the others. The disciples do not recognize Jesus at first (some could still not process what they witnessed at Calvary and the empty tomb), but Jesus engages His friends. The disciples were fishing all night but caught nothing. Did you ever feel that all your efforts to do something only resulted in emptiness and frustration?

Jesus asked them if they had any food. This only added to their frustration. Asking this of a fisherman, who spent all night fishing with no results, is like asking a boxer who has been through 15 rounds of getting his body beaten up and finally knocked out, "Did you win?"

Jesus instructs them to try again but His way this time. He said, "Cast the net on the right side." They did and caught a multitude of fish –153 in all. As they eventually came to shore, they smelled the aroma of grilled fish prepared for them exclusively by Jesus. (Jesus has his own source of getting fish.) Jesus is cooking the meal for them with His heavenly catch and now invites them to come and dine. Jesus then breaks some bread and starts to serve the fish dinner to His friends on a beautifully decorated dinner table. Imagine Jesus provides the fish (His own and the miracle of their catch), prepares the meal and then serves them. (John 21:1-14) Jesus is our Savior, our friend, our caregiver, our provider and our servant!

After they have dined and finished the delicious meal, Jesus asked Simon Peter a very interesting question. "Simon, son of Jonah, do you love me *more than these*?"

This question to Peter attracts my attention. I too would want to respond with the right answer if that question was proposed to me from Jesus. We have to really understand the question before we give a hasty answer.

"More than these." What are *these*? Some scholars suggest *these* are friends of Peter. I see a slightly different meaning with a fresh appreciation for what it REALLY means to love Jesus! Do you want to know "*what are these*"? Good! I will tell you in tomorrow's devotional.

Scripture Reading: Ezekiel 27, 28; James 4

Trivia Question: Who defied her husband to provide food for David's men in the wilderness?

November 23

"Love Me More than These, Part 2"

John 21:15 — So when they had dined, Jesus saith to Simon Peter, Simon, son of Jonas, lovest thou me more than these? He saith unto him, Yea, Lord; thou knowest that I love thee. He saith unto him, Feed my lambs.

We have learned in yesterday's devotional that the third time Jesus appeared to His friends after the Resurrection, He gives them the ability to catch fish that they previously could not. Jesus also supernaturally provides, prepares, cooks and serves them a meal. Wow, what a savior, what a friend, what a caregiver, provider and servant!

After they dine, their bellies are full and are probably feeling quite good about the day. They are possibly excited about their extraordinary catch of 153 fish in their net. Jesus then turns to Peter and asks, "Do you love me more than these?"

What are *these?* "Peter, do you love me more than the ability to catch fish, earn a living and an income? Peter, do you love me more than my miraculous provision and blessings I bestow upon you? Peter, do you love me more than the things I do for you – providing, preparing, cooking and serving you? Peter, do you love me more than the 153 fish?"

What are *these* in your life? Do you love Him more than what He does for you? Do you love Him more than the stuff He gives you? Do you love Him more than His provision? Do you love Him more than anyone or anything else? Do you love the healing more than the Healer? Blessings, harvest, provision, possessions and meals are great, but do you love him more than these?

If you love the person of Jesus more than the provisions of Jesus, then you must live your life accordingly. If you really love Him more than anyone or anything, you will feed His lambs, (young Christians) so that before a young believer learns to fall in love with stuff, they will first fall in love with Him! Live life loving the Lord and share the message with other believers, to love Him more than *these.* May all the *these* that He provides for you take a backseat to Him.

315

Scripture Reading: Ezekiel 29, 30, 31; James 5

Trivia Question: Where did the widow live who fed the prophet Elijah from her last handful of meal?

November 24

"Give Thanks"

Ephesians 5:20 — Giving thanks always for all things unto God and the Father in the name of our Lord Jesus Christ.

If you sit down and really think about how much you have to be thankful for, it would probably take some time. We truly have so much to be thankful for.

As our nation commemorates one special day called Thanksgiving, it seems that our culture has lost the true meaning of the day. Somewhere between turkey, football, special desserts and an afternoon nap, the real purpose of the day has been eclipsed.

As Christians, we should be very aware that God is good, and every good gift is from Him. "Every good gift and every perfect gift is from above, and cometh down from the Father of lights, with whom is no variableness, neither shadow of turning." (James 1:17) May we be thankful for every good gift – all of them! I encourage you to write down ALL that you are thankful for. Your list will most likely be long. Take one thing you are thankful for and make it a theme for one day. For example, if you are thankful for your family, then in your devotions focus on family through prayer and intercession and speak the Word over them. If on your list is your job, then make that the focus on day two. Being thankful will enhance and enrich your focus and your prayer life too.

Scripture Reading: Ezekiel 32, 33; 1 Peter 1

Trivia Question: Who was the Moabite widow who left her homeland to follow her mother-in-law to Bethlehem?

November 25

"Stir it up"

2 Timothy 1:6 — Wherefore I put thee in remembrance that thou stir up the gift of God, which is in thee by the putting on of my hands.

As a young boy, I often went to my grandmother's home. Those were great days – rich in love and family values. I remember watching my grandfather, a man of few words, drinking his coffee at the kitchen table. It was strange to me to watch grandpa put four to five heaping teaspoons of cane sugar into that black cup of coffee. That was unique enough, but what would really get my attention, even as a youngster, is grandpa would never stir the sugar in the cup. I would watch and observe, (it happened every time) as he made his way to the bottom of the cup. The expression he made with his face would entertain me as he sipped the sugary syrup at the bottom. I would laugh, not letting him see me of course. Grandpa never stirred it up!

Paul says, "Stir up the gift of God which is in you." I would think when I was at grandpa's house, "what a waste of sugar." Grandpa couldn't finish the cup, because of the bottom was filled with only sugar. He could have used one or two teaspoons, stirred it up and enjoyed the cup from top to bottom.

God has put gifts and anointing into His people, but like my grandfather they refuse to stir it up! Consequently these gifts settle to the bottom of our spirits, not being exercised or used for God's glory. One way you stir up a gift is by stepping out and acting on what you believe God has put into you. Stir it up, and let all of God's sweetness touch every area of your life from top to bottom. Do not let your gift be buried deep inside you; stir it up! Ask God what gifts He has put into you, and then stir it up, step out, and be a blessing to someone. Friend, stir it up!

Scripture Reading: Ezekiel 34, 35; 1 Peter 2

Trivia Question: What woman of Jericho gave lodging and protection to Joshua's spies?

November 26

"Lessons Learned in the Fire"

Daniel 3:23-25 — And these three men, Shadrach, Meshach, and Abednego, fell down bound into the midst of the burning fiery furnace. Then Nebuchadnezzar the king was astonished, and rose up in haste, and spake, and said unto his counsellors, Did not we cast three men bound into the midst of the fire? They answered and said unto the king, True, O king. He answered and said, Lo, I see four men loose, walking in the midst of the fire, and they have no hurt; and the form of the fourth is like the Son of God.

The Israelites were taken away captive into Babylon (as predicted by the prophets), because of their apostasy. Daniel and his three friends are in a strange land and culture, but stay loyal to the Lord and His ways. They find themselves in a very difficult position. They are told in a decree from the King of Babylon, to bow to a graven image or burn in a fiery furnace.

Shadrach, Meshach and Abednego know the consequences but determine not to bow to the statue, and doing so they defy the king. The result is a furnace of fire for them. The furnace is heated seven times hotter than normal – an order from the king for the youth's insolence. They are tied up, thrown in the fire and left to become cremated. To the king's surprise, when he takes a peek into the furnace expecting to see nothing, he sees four men untied and walking around in the middle of the blazing incinerator.

The God that these young people revered and honored came through for them!

God could have prevented them from going into the fire. He could have extinguished the fire with one breath of His nostril. He even could have sent a fireproof angel to cover them in the furnace. God chose however, to allow them to go into the fire, loose them from their shackles and protect them, all while the fire was still roaring. It is one thing for God to take you from a dangerous situation, it is another to go through the danger, unharmed and unscathed. Yes, God gets more glory when He delivers you in the midst of the fire. Those around you see it, and must recognize that your God is God! May He deliver you today in the midst of your fiery trial.

Scripture Reading: Ezekiel 36, 37; 1 Peter 3

Trivia Question: What was Nebuchadnezzar's new decree after he witnessed the delivering power of the Hebrews' God?

318

November 27

"Perspective that Brings Change"

Psalm 118:23 — This is the Lord's doing; it is marvellous in our eyes.

God is always revealing Himself to us. He is good and shows His goodness to us. He is always doing good, in hope that we see and recognize that He has initiated His goodness to us.

Sometimes our view and impression of things are skewed. We can often see things obscured and our perspective is not valid or accurate.

God wants our perspective to bring positive change in our lives. The Lord wants to show us what truth is and what it is not. Only then we will have the right perspective.

A number of years ago I went to Ghana, West Africa on a mission's trip. I was there for seventeen days (including travel) and saw God do great things. I was even privileged to pray over a 9-year-old boy that was born blind, and see God give him back his sight. I will never forget that experience.

Like many of us, I had become used to living well in the United States – a nice car, good meals, a fine home, etc. In my home state of New Jersey, however, traffic was terrible and as a result complaining and murmuring often flowed easily from my lips.

While in Africa, I observed much. I lived with the people, ate with them and endured the same challenges that the precious people of Ghana have to endure, not just seventeen days, but every day. The conditions were difficult – no plumbing, no hot water, bugs in the beds, electricity that turned off each day and long hot journeys in the mission van to various places of ministry. I lost sixteen pounds (which I probably needed to), but I witnessed many things that moved my heart. I saw the great love, devotion and faithfulness of the people in Ghana.

When I got back to the States, I had found that I changed. The traffic jams didn't bother me; the pollution didn't move me and the complaining and murmuring stopped. Why? I saw things differently. My perspective had changed. God did something in me and, "it was marvelous in my eyes." That new perspective led to new priorities and changes in my life.

May we see life as God shows it to us. May we receive God's impressions on people, places and things, so we can have new priorities in our lives.

Scripture Reading: Ezekiel 38, 39; 1 Peter 4

Trivia Question: Who killed the Canaanite commander, Sisera, by nailing a tent peg through his head while he slept?

November 28

"The Purpose for God's Anointing"

*Isaiah 10:27 — And it shall come to pass in that day,
that his burden shall be taken away from off thy shoulder, and his yoke
from off thy neck, and the yoke shall be destroyed because of the anointing.*

Burdens shall be lifted off of shoulders, yokes from off of necks and yokes (bondages) shall be destroyed, because of the anointing!

God's anointing is awesome and sobering at the same time. It is humbling to think that the God of the universe would come down and manifest His presence in a special way that brings transformation for time and eternity. God's anointing is not intended for us to misuse, abuse, to just give spiritual goose bumps, or to be marketed or merchandised in any way. God's anointing is to help heal and set people free. The anointing is to do the service of ministry, not have ministry serve you.

Isaiah 61:1-3 says, "The Spirit of the Lord God is upon me; because the Lord hath anointed me to preach good tidings unto the meek; he hath sent me to bind up the brokenhearted, to proclaim liberty to the captives, and the opening of the prison to them that are bound; To proclaim the acceptable year of the Lord, and the day of vengeance of our God; to comfort all that mourn; To appoint unto them that mourn in Zion, to give unto them beauty for ashes, the oil of joy for mourning, the garment of praise for the spirit of heaviness; that they might be called trees of righteousness, the planting of the Lord, that he might be glorified."

So with God's anointing go preach, heal, liberate, deliver, proclaim, comfort and give people Jesus! The world needs Him and His wonderful anointing now.

Scripture Reading: Ezekiel 40; 1 Peter 5

Trivia Question: Where and when did Jesus say Isaiah 61:1-3 was fulfilled?

November 29

"Teacher's Silence"

Psalm 28:1 — Unto thee will I cry, O Lord my rock; be not silent to me: lest, if thou be silent to me, I become like them that go down into the pit.

Tests and trials are part of a Christian's life. 1 Peter 4:12, "Beloved, think it not strange concerning the fiery trial which is to try you, as though some strange thing happened unto you." Just as you would prepare for a scholastic test with study and meditation, so it is with preparation for a spiritual test. Not too many people enjoy tests, but they are indicators to us of what we have digested and absorbed. Tests are also a way of knowing if we are to be promoted to the next level or grade.

Psalm 83:1, "Keep not thou silence, O God: hold not thy peace, and be not still, O God."

Have you ever noticed in school that the teacher is usually not communicating with students during the test? Study and questions asked should be done prior to the test. Sometimes as Christians, going through tests are challenging, but even more difficult when the Lord is not speaking to us. David went through times like this. Psalm 13:1, "How long wilt thou forget me, O Lord? How long wilt thou hide thy face from me?" Many times we have to embrace, believe and stand upon the truths and promises God taught us prior to the test. Draw from those truths. Even if God does not say anything to us during the test, you can be assured His promises will get you through to pass the test and be promoted. Draw from your relationship with the Lord. What He has taught you and what He has brought you through previously will be a great source of strength and comfort. "Thy testimonies also are my delight and my counselors." (Psalm 119:24) You will pass this test!

Scripture Reading: Ezekiel 41, 42; 2 Peter 1

Trivia Question: Why did Naomi ask the people of Bethlehem to call her Mara?

_____

November 30

"Parents"

2 Corinthians 12:14 — Behold, the third time I am ready to come to you; and I will not be burdensome to you: for I seek not yours but you: for the children ought not to lay up for the parents, but the parents for the children.

What an awesome responsibility. What an amazing ministry God has entrusted to some, the ministry of parenting. Parents are called to *lay up* for their children. That does not mean play a game of basketball with them (though I've done that many times with my son). To *lay up* as the King James version states, is to put a deposit or treasure into the children that God has blessed you with. What does it mean to deposit or store treasure in children?

Many parents only believe it is buying them designer jeans and sneakers, driving them to endless soccer and basketball games, allowing sleepovers with unruly classmates and basically going into debt to keep up with the other kids. Is laying up more than sending our children to a college or university, knowing they will have to pay the financial debt for a good part of their lives? Is storing treasure all about our children landing great jobs to produce high income, so that when they get married and have children of their own they continue the cycle of a godless heritage?

I think God has a different objective. Jesus said, "For what is a man profited, if he shall gain the whole world, and lose his own soul?" (Matthew 16:26)

Imagine providing everything you can for a child, but that child who grows up to adulthood is impoverished spiritually. What does it cost a parent "in exchange for his/her soul?" We must deposit or store up treasures spiritually first and foremost to our children. Providing for them a rich godly heritage that will stay inside of them like rich treasure all the days of their lives. We must store the Word of God into our children, and in turn they will deposit the Word into their children, so on and so forth. "As for me, this is my covenant with them, saith the Lord; My spirit that is upon thee, and my words which I have put in thy mouth, shall not depart out of thy mouth, nor out of the mouth of thy seed, nor out of the mouth of thy seed's seed, saith the Lord, from henceforth and for ever." (Isaiah 59:21) "Only take heed to thyself, and keep thy soul diligently, lest thou forget the things which thine eyes have seen, and lest they depart from thy heart all the days of thy life: but teach them thy sons, and thy sons' sons." (Deuteronomy 4:9)

Parents are instructed to impart, deposit and store up the treasure of God's Word into their children. May our children growing up in the present culture, "be strong in the Lord and in the power of His might." (Ephesians 6:10)

I always thank God for the parents He gave me. They were examples of God's love, support and provision. Dad worked tirelessly to provide, and mom labored at home making our lives as children so blessed, and lacking nothing. You do not get to choose your parents, however, I thank God that He chose the perfect two for me. Mom is in Heaven now, enjoying her great reward. What a soldier for Jesus she was and is! Love you Mom and Dad; you did well!

In Memory of Mom.

Scripture Reading: Ezekiel 43, 44; 2 Peter 2

Trivia Question: What did Solomon say you should not forsake of your mother?

December

December 1

"Remember"

1 Corinthians 11:23-25 — For I received from the Lord that which I also delivered to you, that the Lord Jesus in the night in which He was betrayed took bread; and when He had given thanks, He broke it and said, "This is My body, which is for you; do this in remembrance of Me." In the same way He took the cup also after supper, saying, "This cup is the new covenant in My blood; do this, as often as you drink it, in remembrance of Me.

Holy Communion is a sacrament (sacred thing) the Christian church observes, reveres and celebrates. It is remembering the ultimate price that Jesus paid to provide and secure our salvation. The communion table is not a wake or funeral service, or some sorrowful event. On the contrary, it is a celebratory remembrance of our wonderful Savior and His proven love for us.

At that famed Passover meal that Jesus shared with His friends, He took bread and broke it, signifying that His own body would be broken for them. Isaiah 53:5 foretold the coming event, "But he was wounded for our transgressions, he was bruised for our iniquities: the chastisement of our peace was upon him; and with his stripes we are healed." The word bruise means to crush, crumble, break and beat to pieces. Certainly the prophet was referring to the brutal scourging, beating, abuse and ultimately the crucifixion of Jesus. (Matthew 27:26-50)

Jesus then lifted the chalice at the same meal. He told His friends that the fruit of the vine represented His blood that would be shed and spilled for man's sins to be remitted and removed.

The Christian Church should not partake of communion from a ritualistic or religious posture, but from their personal relationship with Christ. It should be done with the understanding that His body was beat and broken; His blood was shed and spilled personally for each individual. We

325

remember what Jesus, through His amazing love, did for us.

May your experience with Christ be fresh and new each day, never mundane. May your experience with God at each communion time, be fresh, inspiring and exhilarating as you once again, remember!

Scripture Reading: Ezekiel 45, 46; 2 Peter 3

Trivia Question: What sign of betrayal did Judas do to inform the chief priests that Jesus was the one they were looking for?

December 2

"My Meditation"

Psalms 119:97 — O how love I thy law! It is my meditation all the day.

How important it is to take time to meditate in the Word of God. Feeding on the Word of God continually will build up your spirit man, especially during challenging and troublesome times. Jesus said that His Words are spirit and life (John 6:63), and if one would abide (live in, be vitally united) in the Word, they would receive what they ask God for. (John 15:7)

There is much information today to dwell on. Some of it will not build you up, but rather bring you down. Joshua 1:8 says, "This book of the law shall not depart out of thy mouth; but thou shalt meditate therein day and night, that thou mayest observe to do according to all that is written therein: for then thou shalt make thy way prosperous, and then thou shalt have good success." Psalms 1:1-3 states, "How blessed is the man who does not walk in the counsel of the wicked, nor stand in the path of sinners, nor sit in the seat of scoffers! But his delight is in the law of the LORD, and in His law he meditates day and night. He will be like a tree *firmly* planted by streams of water, which yields its fruit in its season and its leaf does not wither; and in whatever he does, he prospers."

Take time each day to meditate on His Word. Like David fell in love with His Word, it will be your meditation all day long.

Scripture Reading: Ezekiel 47, 48; 1 John 1

Trivia Question: When did the Lord turn Job's maladies and situation around?

December 3

"Faith Spark"

Galatians 5:6 — For in Jesus Christ neither circumcision availeth any thing, nor uncircumcision; but faith which worketh by love.

I have learned when your faith is just about on empty and running on fumes, the love of God is like a spark that will ignite it again. You will be able to continue to believe God for the manifestation of His answer to your prayer.

Have you ever felt that you have used up all the faith you possessed? When I was going through an extended health battle in my life, I felt that way often. It was always then that I drew from the love of God deep inside of me to give my faith the spark it needed. (Ephesians 3:17) Paul says, "faith works by love." In the original language it means faith is energized or ignited by love. You can have a 100-gallon hot water heater in your home that runs on natural gas, but if the pilot light goes out, you will take cold showers and freeze in the winter. You must give that heater a spark, ignite the pilot and enjoy all the hot water you want.

Love is the spark that energizes and ignites your faith. Give your faith a spark today by being rooted and grounded in God's love. Draw from His unfailing love during times you feel like you are running on "faith fumes". His love will energize your faith again.

Scripture Reading: Daniel 1, 2; 1 John 2

Trivia Question: What is everyone given according to the measure of the gift of Christ?

December 4

"Water those Seeds"

1 Corinthians 3:6 — I have planted, Apollos watered; but God gave the increase.

I had some bare patches of grass on the front lawn of my home. Bugs and deer traffic left it quite a sight. The ground was sinking a bit, so I spread topsoil over the sinkholes. I raked it all even and then planted grass seed on the newly spread soil. There were about seven large patches in all. I knew with proper watering, the seed would grow into lush grass and blend in to complement the entire front lawn.

Knowing the principles of the law of harvest, most days I was diligent to water the seed. One sows, others water and God gives the increase. This was particularly true with my lawn. The landscaper planted the seed, I watered it and then trusted God and His laws of increase to see a new front lawn. It worked just like the Bible teaches, except for two patches on the left side. The landscaper prepared the troubled area and planted the seed, but because I did not water that area, it did not grow grass. (The garden hose did not stretch that far and I got lazy.) The rest of the yard looked very good, but those two patches on the left side were as bare and grassless as I started with.

You must water seed if you want to see it grow. We desire all kinds of harvest in our lives. Every harvest demands a certain kind of seed to be planted. It is not enough to just plant the seed, it must be watered to see increase. Plants, vegetables and fruit can only be enjoyed if they are watered as seeds.

God's Word is like water and needs to be applied to every seed you sow. If you plant a financial seed, water that seed by speaking the Word over it. Speak the Word over every seed you plant, and you will receive a harvest. Do not get lazy like me with my front lawn; be diligent to water your seed and enjoy the increase of God.

Scripture Reading: Daniel 3, 4; 1 John 3

Trivia Question: How does Jesus want to present His body (the Church) to Himself?

December 5

"The Dream Legacy"

Proverbs 29:18 — Where there is no vision, the people perish: but he that keepeth the law, happy is he.

I have learned that making Heaven will be fairly easy. Jesus did all the work through His vicarious sacrifice, scourging, crucifixion, descending into the lower parts of the Earth, defeating and conquering Satan, sickness, Hell and the grave. We on the other hand just have to receive His goodness and the gift of salvation that He has wonderfully provided. (If it is so simple, how come everyone is not saved?)

Fulfilling your destiny and dreams is another matter. It will require diligence, work and intensity. You will be challenged at every turn and curve on the road to your destiny.

Why? Because making Heaven is beneficial to me—it is *my* personal gain. Dreams being fulfilled always have a legacy attached to them that benefits others for *their* personal gain.

God put inside of me a dream to build and establish a daycare, pre-school, grammar school, high school and a ministry training school (our Bible Institute on the College level). Our vision in our ministry is, "from cradle to college." My hope is, with our godly, biblical influence and teaching from an infant attending our daycare all the way to our Bible Institute, people will graduate with a biblical worldview and do nothing short of engaging and changing their world!

I hope that the dream, which is all about legacy, will help children be transformed and make a difference. Isn't that what legacy is all about?

Make sure you make Heaven by turning your life over to Jesus, then dream—dream big. It will be your legacy that you leave behind for others!

Scripture Reading: Daniel 5, 6; 1 John 4

Trivia Question: What did Jesus say you would keep if you really love Him?

December 6

"Bad Apple"

Romans 16:17 — Now I beseech you, brethren, mark them, which cause divisions and offences contrary to the doctrine, which ye have learned; and avoid them.

We are called to love, pray for, and express compassion for everybody. We are NOT called to hang out with everybody.

There are some hard sayings of Jesus in the Bible and challenging exhortations and admonitions in the Word of God. Avoiding those whose agenda is divisive and speak contrary things to the orthodoxy of the Word of God is one of those warnings.

Paul said to "mark them." The term means to take aim at, take heed, or to watch. The Greek word, Skopeho, is where we get our English word scope. Paul says to scope out and watch for those that are causing schisms or divisions, and speaking things that are contrary to sound doctrine.

Paul said it this way to Titus, "A man (or woman) that is a heretic after the first and second warning, reject." (Titus 3:10) What is a heretic? It is a person who holds to a belief that is different from the truth found in God's Word. The New International Version says, "A divisive person…have nothing to do with him."

Those are strong words of Paul to the church. The early church leaders knew the importance of protecting the integrity of the Word of God. Who are you hanging around with? Who do you fellowship with regularly? Are there divisive people in your midst? Is there a heretic in your sphere of influence?

The saying, "one bad apple spoils the bunch" is true. Apples that are very ripe or ones that are bruised can often produce a gaseous hormone called ethylene, which can negatively affect other fruit or apples that surround it. To prevent a *bad apple* in the church from affecting the precious people of God, try to confront false doctrine. Stand tall to divisive people and attempt to correct contrary teaching that violates the Word of God. If people will not heed sound doctrine and godly counsel, avoid them!

Scripture Reading: Daniel 7, 8; 1 John 5

Trivia Question: When Paul was writing his last letter to Timothy, who did he say did him much evil?

December 7

"Cry Out"

Jeremiah 33:1-3 — Moreover the word of the Lord came unto Jeremiah the second time, while he was yet shut up in the court of the prison, saying, Thus saith the Lord the maker thereof, the Lord that formed it, to establish it; the Lord is his name; Call unto me, and I will answer thee, and show thee great and mighty things, which thou knowest not.

No matter what circumstance you face, or what condition you find yourself in, the Lord never gets weary of us calling out to Him in our time of need.

Daniel cried out to Him in the lion's den. Jonah cried out to Him from the belly of the whale. Jeremiah cried out to Him from prison. Paul and

Silas cried out to Him from a Philippian jail. Moses cried out to Him when facing a watery grave at the Red Sea. David cried out to Him when being hunted down like a wild animal by an angry, envious king.

No matter what valley you are enduring, health challenges you are confronted with, persecution that is pressuring you, or financial crisis that is trying to overtake you, you can cry out to Him whenever you need Him, anytime, even right now. He hears you, will answer you, will reveal Himself to you, and show you great and mighty things.

Scripture Reading: Daniel 9, 10; 2 John

Trivia Question: How does faith come?

December 8

"Hope Deferred"

Proverbs 13:12 — Hope deferred maketh the heart sick:
but when the desire cometh, it is a tree of life.

When your dreams and destiny are on hold, postponed, deferred or even derailed, you must make what I call *destiny statements*. A destiny statement is saying and more importantly doing something that gives substance to your faith and what you are believing for, even when your life is seemingly on hold or shelved.

I have had to make my destiny statements many times in life, especially when getting negative reports about my health, finances and areas of ministry. One example I will share with you is when I went through horrific health challenges after from my missions trip to Africa. The lies of the enemy relentlessly tried to convince me that my ministry influence and the raising of Christian leaders was coming to an end. My energy was zapped, my health failing and my ability to train leaders was waning.

I decided, in the midst of my difficulties, to make a destiny statement and to initiate the foundation of a ministry training school, called Abundant Life Bible Institute (ALBI). We have been teaching and imparting to Bible students now for many years as well as developing new campuses beyond our own location in New Jersey. Our four-fold objective in the school is information (knowledge of the Word), inspiration (anointing of God), impartation (deposit from our Bible school professors and instructors), and transformation (impacting our culture with our lives).

I had to make that a destiny statement before God and the kingdom of darkness. I was responding to the Lord and letting Him know I still believed Him and His promises. At the same time, I wanted to let the enemy know that "with God, all things are possible," (Matthew 19:26) and I would, by God's grace, fulfill God's assignment and destiny for my life.

Is the enemy trying to rob you of your dreams or destiny? Make a destiny statement today and stake your claim in God's promise to you!

Scripture Reading: Daniel 11, 12; 3 John

Trivia Question: Who doesn't listen to rebuke and correction?

December 9

"Do Not Make God Force You"

Psalm 23:1-2 — The Lord is my shepherd; I shall not want. He maketh me to lie down in green pastures: he leadeth me beside the still waters.

When reading this shepherd's psalm, the phrase, "he makes me lie down in green pastures," always caught my attention.

There was a time in my life, with the many ministry demands, people to counsel, sermons to preach, family to oversee and leaders to lead that I would find very little down time. Doesn't God want us busy anyway? Idle hands are the devil's playground, right? I believe we need to be active for Jesus, but the Lord wants us to have time to just feed, graze and rest in His green pastures. During very busy times, I must refocus and *graze*, lest God step in and "make me lie down."

The Lord is truly a gentleman, but He loves us so much that He will step in aggressively if we are about to do ourselves harm. The Hebrew word for shepherd in Psalm 23 is "rohi" which means to feed. God wants to lead and feed us as our shepherd. When we are running here, there and everywhere, even if it is for honorable and responsible tasks, we need to take time to feed, graze and rest in the green pastures of life that He has provided for us. If we disobey, He just might have to make us.

Scripture Reading: Hosea 1, 2, 3, 4; Jude

Trivia Question: Where did David say he wanted to dwell in forever?

December 10

"A Word in Season"

Isaiah 50:4 — The Lord God hath given me the tongue of the learned,
that I should know how to speak a word in season to him that is weary:
he wakeneth morning by morning, he wakeneth mine ear to hear as the learned.

It is the rhema, or tailor made word, that God personally gives you that protects you in the fire. It is that personal, powerful promise, a word in season that empowers you to trust Him in the trial. His Word is rich, immutable and will endure forever. The Word of God has and will always stand the test of opposition and attack. He wants to give you a word in season during your tests and trials. That word will also cause you to stand up against the opposition that comes against your life. That same word in season will sustain you until you see the victory.

Proverbs 25:11 says, "A word fitly spoken is like apples of gold in pictures of silver." May the promise God gives you during the fiery trial of your life *fit* perfectly to help you trust him more and more. His words will never fail. May you look to God today for a word in season. Even if it is a stormy, tumultuous season, He is faithful.

Scripture Reading: Hosea 5, 6, 7, 8; Revelation 1

Trivia Question: Solomon said that waters reflect the face, what did he say reflects the man?

December 11

"The Horse is Prepared for the Day of Battle"

Jeremiah 12:5 — If thou hast run with the footmen,
and they have wearied thee, then how canst thou contend with horses?
and if in the land of peace, wherein thou trustedst, they wearied thee,
then how wilt thou do in the swelling of Jordan?

We are living in a day of busyness. There is a lot going on in people's lives. In the Northeast of the country (where I am from), I observe the average family's busy lives. There is work for husband and wife, school for their children, soccer practice, cheerleading, PTA meetings, dance recitals, gymnastics, band practice, swim lessons, Cub Scouts, Girl Scouts, and the list goes on and on. Though these extracurricular activities are not wrong, many times it drains people of their energy, focus and drive for the things that really matter – the things of God.

Jeremiah says if we have run with the footmen and are wearied, how will we compete with horses? "The horse is prepared for the day of battle." (Proverbs 21:31) If we drain ourselves of all our energy running around with the so-called, "footmen" how will the rise up and fight in the day of battle?

The Christian life is likened to fighting in the military. "Put on the whole armour of God, that ye may be able to stand against the wiles of the devil." (Ephesians 6:11) "For we wrestle not against flesh and blood, but against principalities, against powers, against the rulers of the darkness of this world, against spiritual wickedness in high places. Wherefore take unto you the whole armour of God, that ye may be able to withstand in the evil day, and having done all, to stand. Stand therefore, having your loins girt about with truth, and having on the breastplate of righteousness; And your feet shod with the preparation of the gospel of peace; Above all, taking the shield of faith, wherewith ye shall be able to quench all the fiery darts of the wicked. And take the helmet of salvation, and the sword of the Spirit, which is the word of God." (Ephesians 6:12-17) "Thou therefore endure hardness, as a good soldier of Jesus Christ." (2 Timothy 2:3) "Fight the good fight of faith, lay hold on eternal life, whereunto thou art also called, and hast professed a good profession before many witnesses." (1 Timothy 6:12)

The day of battle is coming to you. It is inevitable that you will face some form of battle. It may be a financial, parental, marital, emotional, or health battle. Are you prepared? Are you up for the task? Do you have enough spiritual energy? We understand that the battle is the Lord's, but there will be some battles that God expects us to fight. We must compete with the horses in the day of battle. Set time every day to fill up the reservoir of your spirit with the Word of God. In all of your busyness, make time for prayer, daily devotions, Bible study and worship. When the battle comes, you will be well prepared!

Scripture Reading: Hosea 9, 10, 11; Revelation 2

Trivia Question: What does Paul call someone who does not provide for his family?

December 12

"Grow"

Ephesians 4:15 — But speaking the truth in love,
may grow up into him in all things, which is the head, even Christ.

In life there must be growth. Growth is a sign of progression, advancement, development and life itself. We grow in body, in mind, in our businesses, our children grow physically, socially and academically, and so on. Growth is essential in life. We watch the flowers grow. We watch trees grow. We even watch people grow old.

How about growing in God? The Bible exhorts us to grow in our faith. 2 Thessalonians 1:3 says, "We are bound to thank God always for you, brethren, as it is meet, because that your faith groweth exceedingly, and the charity of every one of you all toward each other aboundeth." Our faith always needs to be growing. We are charged to grow in grace and knowledge. 2 Peter 3:18 says, "But grow in grace, and in the knowledge of our Lord and Saviour Jesus Christ. To him be glory both now and forever." Are you growing in Bible knowledge and your understanding of the amazing grace of God? We are called to grow in the Word of God. (1 Peter 2:2) Are you developing and maturing as a result of God's Word? We are admonished to simply grow up in our relationship with the Lord. "But speaking the truth in love, may grow up into him in all things, which is the head, even Christ." (Ephesians 4:15)

Are you developing the love of God inside of you, speaking His Word and maturing as a Christian? God desires all of His children to grow. As you journey with Jesus may you be well-rounded as you grow in spirit, soul and body. Just as any parent would want their child to grow, so our heavenly Father is enthralled and blessed as He watches His children grow.

Scripture Reading: Hosea 12, 13, 14; Revelation 3

Trivia Question: According to Paul, how is the new man created?

December 13

"Baptism"

Hebrews 6:1-2 — Therefore leaving the principles of the doctrine of Christ, let us go on unto perfection; not laying again the foundation of repentance from dead works, and of faith toward God, Of the doctrine of baptisms, and of laying on of hands, and of resurrection of the dead, and of eternal judgment.

The English Standard Version (ESV) reads, "therefore we must progress beyond the elementary instructions about Christ and move on to maturity." The writer of Hebrews was not saying to forget about foundational truths, but to progress beyond them once we have learned and made them a staple in our lives. He talks about the doctrine (teaching) of baptisms. Notice the word *baptisms* is plural, denoting there is more than one teaching of baptism in the Word of God. First, we must understand in Bible language what baptism is. Baptism biblically denotes full immersion, submersion, or a full commitment. There is more than water baptism taught in the Scriptures. In every baptism teaching in the Bible, it is taught with the idea that the candidate would jump in completely with a full commitment to the cause.

In our next five days, I would like to share with you five different baptisms taught in the Word of God. They will be challenging, engaging and encouraging. Are you ready to be baptized the Bible way? Get ready to dive in all the way.

Scripture Reading: Joel 1, 2, 3; Revelation 4

Trivia Question: What do we have to labor to enter into?

December 14

"Connection"

Romans 6:3 — Know ye not, that so many of us as were baptized into Jesus Christ were baptized into his death?

What does being baptized into Jesus Christ mean? Paul is talking about the wonderful born again experience that Jesus taught in John 3:3-7. Scripture teaches us there is one way to God the Father and that is through His Son, Jesus Christ. John 14:6 says, "Jesus saith unto him, I am the way, the truth, and the life: no man cometh unto the Father, but by me." There is only one way to connect to the Father's goodness, mercy, forgiveness, pardon, power, love and favor; it is through Jesus. This reminds me of the old hymn I used to sing, "Oh, come to the Father through Jesus the Son and give Him the glory, great things He has done." The way humanity connects to the Father and all of Heaven's resources are through His Son.

God has no grandchildren. You cannot make Heaven because your parents were or are Christians. You must connect to God the Father through Jesus by personally being born again. "You must be born again." (John 3:7)

No one can do that for you. Others can share Christ with you and you can share Christ with others, but people must connect personally to the Father themselves. Are you baptized (committed all the way) into Jesus Christ? If not, get connected today. Ask Him to forgive your sins and to come into your heart and life. Confess Him now as your Savior and Lord. Connect with Him.

Scripture Reading: Amos 1, 2, 3; Revelation 5

Trivia Question: Who did Jesus say would be sent after His departure, that would teach all things and bring all things to remembrance?

December 15

"Church Community"

1 Corinthians 12:13-14 — For by one Spirit are we all baptized into one body, whether we be Jews or Gentiles, whether we be bond or free; and have been all made to drink into one Spirit. For the body is not one member, but many.

The church is not an edifice, structure or building. According to Jesus, the church is members of the Body of Christ. You do not build the church with brick and mortar. The church is not a place you step into. Jesus is the one who builds the church and steps into it Himself. Jesus said "I will build my church and the gates of hell shall not prevail against it." (Matthew 16:18)

The church is made up of a community of believers. Not perfect people, but a people who have the commonality of Jesus as the Lord of their lives. They purpose together to further the Gospel of Christ and advance His Kingdom. Being fully committed to the church community is essential for personal growth in God. When someone becomes born again, he/she becomes a member of the Church of Jesus Christ. It is expedient that one

337

is planted in a local church family with pastoral care and leadership, to be taught the Word, will and ways of God. This will help that person become well-balanced in all areas of life. Psalms 92:13 says, "Those that be planted in the house of the Lord shall flourish in the courts of our God."

The early church was engaged in the teaching of doctrine and enjoyed each other's fellowship. They ate meals, engaged in corporate prayer as well as congregational praise and worship to God together. Church community was vital and vibrant for the first century church.

Unfortunately, the times and culture has changed. People, even Christians, especially in the United States, do not see the importance and value anymore for the local church, church community, and joining arm to arm with other members of the Body of Christ. The American Church is probably the biggest offender of this. People that detach from the Body of Christ, at best, remain stagnant and stunted in their journey with Christ. At worst, they will digress and spiritually wither up like a tree branch detached from the trunk. Proverbs 21:16 says, "The man that wandereth out of the way of understanding shall remain in the congregation of the dead."

Do not wander away from church community; it could be your lifeline in times of crisis. Be fully immersed in church community. Ask God to plant you in a great Bible believing, Holy Spirit leading, sound doctrinal local church family. A place where your faith can grow as the Spirit of God baptizes you into the Body of Christ. May you truly be blessed in your local church community.

Scripture Reading: Amos 4, 5, 6; Revelation 6

Trivia Question: What fruit and force from God never fails?

December 16

"Commitment"

Matthew 28:19 — Go ye therefore, and teach all nations, baptizing them in the name of the Father, and of the Son, and of the Holy Spirit.

Another baptism taught in God's Word is baptism in water. We have learned that baptism speaks of full immersion or submersion. Baptism in water is probably one of the earliest acts of obedience by Christians. After we connect to God by baptism into Christ, and become a member of a church community through baptism into His body, we are certainly ready to give commitment to Christ through baptism in water.

We (church leadership) have made a mess and brought so much confusion to people because of our doctrinal pet peeves and denominational protocols. It has kept people from obeying this very simple act of obedience and public confession of Christ. Baptism in water is an outward depiction of an inward commitment to Christ that one should do publicly in front of family, friends and the world. What you are saying through water baptism is, "I'm committed to Christ and I am honored to be a Christian." Biblical baptism in water once again represents what the word baptism is all about – full immersion. (Matthew 3:16, Acts 8:35-39, Acts 10:44-48)

Express your commitment to Christ and get water baptized if you have not already. The only prerequisite to water baptism is repenting of sin. Acts 2:38 says, "Then Peter said unto them, Repent, and be baptized every one of you in the name of Jesus Christ for the remission of sins, and ye shall receive the gift of the Holy Spirit." Water baptism is so simple and easy to do as you publicly identify yourself with the death, burial and resurrection of Jesus. Death, when you go down into the water. Burial, when you go under the water. Resurrection, when you come up out of the water. This is the message of the Gospel of Christ exemplified through water baptism.

Scripture Reading: Amos 7, 8, 9; Revelation 7

Trivia Question: After Christ's resurrection, how many people saw Him at the same time at one occasion?

December 17

"Conviction"

Luke 3:16 — John answered, saying unto them all, I indeed baptize you with water; but one mightier than I cometh, the latchet of whose shoes I am not worthy to unloose: he shall baptize you with the Holy Spirit and with fire.

The baptism in the Holy Spirit is a gift for all believers. (Acts 2:38-39) This baptism will empower you to serve the Lord. When the manifested presence, power and purity of God dwell inside of you, it produces Christlike convictions. If you are born again, you have the Holy Spirit in you, but there is an experience subsequent to salvation called the baptism in the Holy Spirit. This baptism is not only about speaking in languages you've never learned; its main objective is to fill you with Christlikeness.

The reason the church lacks conviction is because we have thrown out the Holy Spirit from our midst. At very best, we have not welcomed Him in our fellowship, church gatherings, convocations and even our lives. We need the third person in the Holy Trinity to empower us and more importantly give us the convictions of Jesus. When you are fully immersed in the Holy Spirit, you will grow and develop godly, Christ like, holy convictions. The main purpose for the baptism in the Holy Spirit is to help you grow and become more like Jesus.

Scripture Reading: Obadiah; Revelation 8

Trivia Question: On the day of Pentecost the people that heard the 120 believers speaking in tongues thought they were what?

December 18

"Cleansing"

Matthew 3:11 — I indeed baptize you with water unto repentance.
But he that cometh after me is mightier than I, whose shoes I am not worthy
to bear: he shall baptize you with the Holy Spirit, and with fire.

The baptism in the Holy Spirit and baptism in fire, in my view, are different and distinct. The baptism in the Holy Spirit brings power, but the baptism in fire brings purity. Baptism with fire speaks of cleansing.

Fire purifies, purges, sanctifies, refines, washes and cleanses. The baptism of the fire of God helps us grow in sanctification (living a life of holiness and separate from sin), as His fire cleanses and purifies us. Our witness to the world must be very vivid and defined. Our declarations to the lost must be identified with the holiness of God. Jesus declared to be the Son of God with power, according to the spirit of holiness. (Romans 1:4) Purity fuels power. A church or body of believers that is baptized in the Holy Spirit, baptized in fire (purified) and growing in God, is visible, viable, dominant, influential, recognizable and culture engaging. We must embrace the baptism with fire to cleanse and burnout all the impediments and impurities of our lives. This is so we too can declare to be sons of God with power according to the spirit of holiness. (Romans 1:4) God has called us to be "vessels of honor, fit for His service." (2 Timothy 2:20-21)

May the fire of God burn out all the chaff and dross from our lives so that we can be those special vessels for God. "Take away the dross from the silver, and there shall come forth a vessel for the finer." (Proverbs 25:4)

If you need deeper cleansing from sin and impurity in your life, the good news is that Jesus will stoke the fire. Matthew 3:12 says, "Whose fan is in his hand, and he will throughly purge his floor, and gather his wheat into the garner; but he will burn up the chaff with unquenchable fire." He will purify, purge and cleanse you completely.

Scripture Reading: Jonah 1, 2, 3, 4; Revelation 9

Trivia Question: After God created sea monsters and all manner of birds, what did God command them to do?

December 19

"Jesus Loves the Church"

Ephesians 5:25-27 — Husbands, love your wives,
even as Christ also loved the church, and gave himself for it.
That he might sanctify and cleanse it with the washing of water by the word,
that he might present it to himself a glorious church, not having spot,
or wrinkle, or any such thing; but that it should be holy and without blemish.

There are three ways according to this text that Jesus showed His love for the church. Remember, the church is not an edifice but a people. The first way He showed His great love is, "He gave Himself for it (her)." Jesus did not agonize in the garden, endure the scourging, persevere through the ridicule and mocking, and resolve through the horrific cross to die for a building. He did that for you and I. Jesus showed His love for us by dying on the cross. (Romans 5:8)

The second way Jesus showed His love was He sanctified and cleansed the church by the washing of water by the Word. Jesus said, "Now ye are clean through the word which I have spoken unto you." (John 15:3) By Jesus' infinite love, He has sanctified and separated us by the Word of God.

Third, Jesus will present a glorious church to Himself, a body without spot or wrinkle, a holy and unblemished people. His blood has translated us from a ghastly people to a glorious church. What love our Savior has for us. Love in action, not only in Word. Jesus proved His love toward us, therefore may we in turn love Him and love others.

Scripture Reading: Micah 1, 2, 3; Revelation 10

December 20

"Close to the Heart"

Genesis 2:21-23 — And the Lord God caused a deep sleep to fall upon Adam, and he slept: and he took one of his ribs, and closed up the flesh instead thereof; And the rib, which the Lord God had taken from man, made he a woman, and brought her unto the man. And Adam said, This is now bone of my bones, and flesh of my flesh: she shall be called Woman, because she was taken out of Man.

It is interesting to note that woman was not created the same way that man was. Man was made out of dirt, and woman was taken out of what was already created. After God created the sun, moon, stars, land, sea, and animal life of all kinds, He beheld His creation and responded that, "it was good." God did a good work (He always does). After God created man, and saw that He was alone, He formed out of the ground every beast of the field and fowl of the air to be a helpmeet for Adam. Adam named them all, yet after all was said and done, there was still no compatible helpmeet suited for Adam. So man and the beasts of the field were formed out of the dirt but woman was created differently. (Genesis 2:18-22)

God caused Adam to go into a deep sleep and took one of his ribs in which He used to make woman. Then God presented her to the man Adam. I believe it is noteworthy that God did not take a part from Adam in his upper extremities or lower extremities. A woman is not to lord over a man, but a man is not to trample on a woman. She was taken from the center of his being; a rib which is in close proximity to his heart. That is God's design for marriage. The woman should be cherished, loved and remain close to the heart of her husband. Husbands should love their wives (keep them close in their hearts) as Christ loved the church and gave His life for her. (Ephesians 5:25)

I know there has been much attack on marriage in America and even in the overall church in these perilous times. In some areas over 50% of marriages are dissolving. Many have had to go through the great pain resulting from divorce. Marriage is still honorable and blessed by God for those who truly understand the marriage covenant. (Hebrews 13:4) Remember, woman was taken out of man, close to the heart of her husband. Man must always keep her there from the altar to "death do us part."

I have been so blessed to have a wonderful wife, a woman of God, a woman passionate for the things of God, a dedicated mother, grandmother and helpmeet. I married my high school sweetheart and we have been together for over 38 years. Debbi is close to my heart, and there she will stay.

Scripture Reading: Micah 4, 5; Revelations 11

Trivia Question: Was Paul married at the time of his writings?

December 21

"Honor your Father"

1 Corinthians 4:15 — For though ye have ten thousand instructors in Christ, yet have ye not many fathers: for in Christ Jesus I have begotten you through the Gospel.

I have been truly blessed in my life with wonderful fathers. Paul said, in this portion of Scripture, that we would have many teachers throughout our lives, but only a few fathers who would impart on a closer level.

My biological father is a great man. He has taught me work ethic, generosity and family values. My dad was married to my mom for over 60 years before she went home to be with Jesus. They exemplified the importance of holiness and sanctity in marriage, with no plan B. Dad taught me that hard work was essential. I witnessed his faithfulness and loyalty to my mom as well as his family. That impacted me to this day. I try to emulate his values in my life relationships with my wife, children and grandchildren. I love, honor and respect my dad. He truly is my hero.

My father-in-law was another wonderful man. In a difficult time in my life he became more than my girlfriend's father, he became my friend. He was kind, soft-spoken, a hard worker and a fun guy to be around. I had the honor to pray with him many times, especially towards the end of his natural life. I look forward to spending time with him in Heaven one day.

My spiritual father is a tremendous man of God. My first pastor is still my pastor. He has taught me countless truths concerning ministry. He saw something in me at 21 years old that I did not see in myself. My pastor took a risk and taught, trained and prayed for me in hopes that God would use my life for His glory. I am so thankful my pastor never gave up on me and I hope I have made him proud. I look forward to our days ahead together in ministry.

When my health was greatly attacked in 2006, I stood on the many healing Scriptures in the Bible that I had meditated on through the years. Coupled with that I stood on Ephesians 6:2-3, "Honour thy father and mother; which is the first commandment with promise; That it may be well with thee, and thou mayest live long on the earth." I told the devil that he could not end my life prematurely because I had honored the fathers in my life. God says, if you honor your father it will go well and you will live long. God did it, and I give Him all the glory. So I encourage you to honor the fathers that God has put in your life, so that it will go well with you!

Scripture Reading: Micah 6, 7; Revelation 12

Trivia Question: Why couldn't Jesus do mighty miracles in His hometown of Nazareth?

December 22

"A Resolved Heart"

Daniel 1:8 — But Daniel purposed in his heart that he would not defile himself with the portion of the king's meat, nor with the wine which he drank: therefore he requested of the prince of the eunuchs that he might not defile himself.

Daniel was a young, seventeen year old who was deported from his homeland and forced into a strange, heathen culture. He was chosen with other young people because of his intelligence and wit to serve the king, Nebuchadnezzar. Daniel and the other young people were to receive new names, be schooled in Babylon and prepared through diet and training to work for the king.

Daniel was brought up in the ways of the Lord, the true King. He strictly adhered to the Mosaic Law, which gave clear instruction on how to live, eat, act and do life. The Jewish dietary laws as outlined in the book of Leviticus 11, instructed God's people on what to eat and how to eat it – separating the clean from the unclean and holy from unholy. Daniel, along with others of his people taken captive in Babylon, was chosen personally by the king to serve. It was a heathen society that compromised the laws of Jehovah and the godly culture he was raised in. When Daniel was told he would have to eat the king's food that was offered to idols and was considered unclean (by Jewish law), he refused to indulge. Daniel purposed in his heart not to displease his God.

In some Christian circles, we have reduced a relationship with God, to rules and regulations, a list of do's and don'ts and overall legalism. The Bible is very clear how we should live and conduct ourselves. Our response cannot be out of self-righteousness, but a deep conviction rooted in the Word of God. We must purpose in our hearts, just as Daniel did to love the Lord through our actions. In the midst of extreme compromise in our culture and indifference to God, we must have a great love for His Word and deep conviction to make godly choices and biblical decisions. Have radical determination this day to live according to God's Word, but only out of deep love and relationship for the Redeemer and His incredible love for you.

Scripture Reading: Nahum; Revelation 13

Trivia Question: What were Daniel's friends' names that were given to them at birth?

December 23

"Arrows"

Psalm 127:3 — Lo, children are an heritage of the Lord: and the fruit of the womb is his reward.

Children are gifts from God to their parents. Scripture teaches parents to teach and train their children in the ways of God. "Train up a child in the way he should go: and when he is old, he will not depart from it." (Proverbs 22:6) Parents who train their children in biblical values, are raising up spiritual warriors who become weapons in the hands of a mighty God. Children become *arrows* that are developed by parents, forged by God and aimed at the enemies of the cross. They speak out against all forms of unrighteousness and injustice. For example, children who are taught in the ways of God, can become a voice for the unborn in the wombs of those who are contemplating abortion. They can also target the injustice, racism and bigotry of various cultures. "Happy is the man that hath his quiver full of them: they shall not be ashamed, but they shall speak with the enemies in the gate." (Psalm 127:5) Children left to worldly philosophies and ungodly influences cannot engage, impact or influence the culture for Christ and His Kingdom.

Personally, I thank God for my five children and five grandchildren who are making a difference in their world and culture. They all love God and the things of the Lord. They are all my loves and my legacy. They are mine and Debbi's *arrows*.

Scripture Reading: Habakkuk; Revelation 14

Trivia Question: Who should children obey in the Lord?

December 24

"Love Has Come"

1 John 4:14 — And we have seen and do testify that the Father sent the Son to be the Saviour of the world.

Saint John is known as the Apostle of love because of his revelation of God's love. In this epistle, he reveals to us that it was God's love that motivated Him to send His only Son to rescue us from spiritual death. All of us want to *see* God, but in 1 John 4:12, he says that no man has seen God. The good news and the all time best Christmas gift is that if we love each other (through God's love), God Himself will live in and stay with us forever. As verse 14 explains, we can now see Him and we even are a witness with our own undeniable testimony that our heavenly Father has sent His Son to be the Savior of the world. We may not have seen Him with our natural eyes, but because of God's love, we have seen Him, know Him and experience Him. Because of God's love gift, we have the promise of a merry life, not just a merry Christmas!

Scripture Reading: Zephaniah; Revelation 15

Trivia Question: What is the new commandment Jesus gave to His disciples?

December 25

"Behold Our Savior"

Luke 1:30-31 — And the angel said unto her, Fear not, Mary: for thou hast found favour with God. And, behold, thou shalt conceive in thy womb, and bring forth a son, and shalt call his name Jesus.

Luke 2:10-11 — And the angel said unto them, Fear not: for, behold, I bring you good tidings of great joy, which shall be to all people. For unto you

346

is born this day in the city of David a Saviour, which is Christ the Lord.

Luke's depiction of the birth of Christ is the most descriptive of all the Gospels. Each passage above begins with the angel of the Lord bringing peace and joyful tidings from God Himself. The angel begins each encounter stating, "do not be afraid," sending God's reassurance that all is well. You too can be reassured that all is well.

I can only imagine the awesome splendor of that moment when the angel of God came upon Mary as she accepted the ultimate gift of becoming the mother of our precious Lord and Savior, Jesus Christ. Because of Mary's servant heart, she was the perfect vessel for the Lord to perform His work through. Imagine the excitement of the shepherds as they heard the Word of God directing them to journey to the city of David to "find a babe wrapped in swaddling clothes, lying in a manger." (Luke 2:12) And finally, envision being there to behold the beautiful child who would be called, "Wonderful, Counselor, Mighty God, Everlasting Father, Prince of Peace." (Isaiah 9:6)

The same encounter that the shepherds experienced over 2,000 years ago is the same encounter we can experience in our daily lives as we seek Him. I encourage you to allow the Holy Spirit to penetrate your heart. As you receive His gift of salvation, you become His light so that you can be a witness enabling others to receive His gift of eternal life. As you keep your heart pure and stay humble, God will see a sweet, willing vessel, just as He found Mary, prepared to do His will.

Scripture Reading: Haggai; Revelation 16

Trivia Question: What was the heavenly host saying as they were praising God at the announcement of Jesus' birth?

December 26

"Unorthodox Miracles"

John 9:6 — When he had thus spoken, he spat on the ground, and made clay of the spittle, and he anointed the eyes of the blind man with the clay.

Jesus used various methods of ministering healing to the sick. The Bible is rich in stories of people receiving healing in unusual and unorthodox ways. In Mark 8:23, Jesus spit on a blind man's eyes. In Luke 17:14,

Jesus told ten lepers to show themselves to the priests while they were still leprous. As they went, they were healed. In Mark 3:5, Jesus told a man with a paralyzed hand, to "stretch it forth" and as he did, he was healed. In 2 Kings 5:10, God used the prophet Elisha to tell an army captain that was stricken with leprosy, to dip seven times in the Jordan River. He did it reluctantly, but as he did, he was healed.

There are countless, wonderful stories of extraordinary miracles in the Bible done by unusual methods. Though the method can vary, the message is constant. The message was, is and will forever be, faith in God. Do not put God in a box, or hold Him to your own standards. Let Him offer you His miracle, His way; you have the faith and just do the believing.

Scripture Reading: Zechariah 1, 2, 3; Revelation 17

Trivia Question: Where have we been seated with Christ?

December 27

"Jesus, My All in All"

Psalm 18:2 — The Lord is my rock, my fortress and my deliverer; my God is my rock, in whom I take refuge, my shield and the horn of my salvation, my stronghold. (NIV)

David expresses his relationship with the Lord in this Psalm. He displays how he draws from his intimate relationship with God.

"The Lord is my rock." David sees God as his stability and security when all seems volatile around him. He says, "The Lord is my fortress." A fortress is a military stronghold or a protected and impenetrable, safe place. David was a man of war, constantly engaged in battles with his enemies. In the midst of his life, he knew God as his personal fortress and stronghold. If you are facing a battle today of any type, know Jesus is your rock and fortress.

The Lord is, "in whom I will trust." Trust is difficult, unless you are convinced of one's love. David knew God loved him unconditionally, even through his mess-ups and mistakes. Because David had a revelation of God's love, he was able to trust in Him at all times, even in dangerous situations. The Lord loves you. You can put your total trust in Him because He will not fail you.

The Lord is, "my shield." A shield is used against blows, arrows or missiles. When the weaponry came against David, whether it was King Saul,

Goliath, the Amalekites or other enemies, David knew God was his shield. He was completely safe from the enemy's attack. Are there times when the enemy's blows or missiles are headed in your direction? The Lord is your shield and you can find safety behind Him.

The Lord is, "the horn of my salvation." The word horn is often used metaphorically to signify strength and honor. Horns are the chief weapons of some animals and are also used as a type of victory. David rejoiced because he knew his victory was in God. Jesus has given us salvation through His blood and finished work on the cross. We have victory through Him. "But thanks be to God, which giveth us the victory through our Lord Jesus Christ." (1 Corinthians 15:57)

The Lord is, "my high tower." A tower is truly a place of extreme safety while also a lookout for danger from the enemy. When imminent harm or danger was lurking, David remembered God was his high tower. He knew God would warn him of any potential harm while keeping him safe. The Lord is our high tower. The Holy Spirit will always, "show us things to come," (John 16:13), whether good or bad. God will show us of any danger and keep us safe. He will deliver us from evil and the evil one. (Matthew 6:13)

Scripture Reading: Zechariah 4, 5, 6; Revelation 18

Trivia Question: Who were the pillars in the first century church?

December 28

"The Power of Perseverance"

2 Timothy 2:1-2 — You therefore, my son, be strong in the grace that is in Christ Jesus. And the things that you have heard from me among many witnesses, commit these to faithful men who will be able to teach others also. (NKJV)

We all need perseverance in our lives. Perseverance is continuing to stay the course in spite of difficulty. Paul addressed his son in the faith, Timothy, and encouraged him to carry on even when Paul is no longer with him. This portion of Scripture is Paul's last letter he wrote before he went home to be with Jesus. In his letter, he charged Timothy as a son to be strong and continue persevering.

Paul exhorted Timothy with a challenge to teach others the same soundness of doctrine that Paul instilled in him. Paul imparted to Timothy,

Timothy will then impart to others and those will pass it down to those God brings into their lives. That is what legacy and leadership is all about. A true son (or daughter) in the faith should welcome from their mentor, compassion, correction, doctrine and discipline to help mold and prepare him (or her) to persevere in life. Too many individuals quit when life seems tough. We need more sons and daughters to continue in spite of difficulty. There is a generation under you that desperately needs your guidance and godliness, so they too can persevere.

Scripture Reading: Zechariah 7, 8, 9; Revelation 19

Trivia Question: What was Timothy's mother's name?

December 29

"The Persevering Soldier"

2 Timothy 2:3-4 — You therefore must endure hardship as a good soldier of Jesus Christ. No one engaged in warfare entangles himself with the affairs of this life, that he may please him who enlisted him as a soldier. (NKJV)

Life has a way of bringing pressure and opposition. It is during those seasons that we have to go into our military mode. Paul said to endure and persevere through difficulty and hardships as good soldiers. A good soldier can only endure the challenges of war if he is well prepared for battle. Proper preparation leads to the ability and strength to persevere. A good soldier is focused and resolute concerning the military mission and mandate. A soldier that perseveres through a battle cannot be double minded or have a split focus. "No one engaged in warfare entangles himself with the affairs of this life." This means when you are going through a battle, the preparation you have done through Bible study, prayer and building your spirit in God's promises, will bring you through, as long distractions in your life don't steal your focus.

Just like a good military soldier, prepare for life's challenges and you will persevere through to victory. Prepare to persevere.

Scripture Reading: Zechariah 10, 11, 12; Revelation 20

Trivia Question: Where did Jonah flee to instead of going to Ninevah?

December 30

"Increase"

Isaiah 54:2-3 — Enlarge the place of your tent, and let them stretch out the curtains of your dwellings; Do not spare; Lengthen your cords, and strengthen your stakes. For you shall expand to the right and to the left, and your descendants will inherit the nations, and make the desolate cities inhabited. (NKJV)

Was it a good year for you? Whether good, bad or indifferent, God says get ready for increase. It is time to enlarge, expand and break forth. Get ready to soar and fly again.

What area of your life needs to increase? Is it your finances, your marital integrity and happiness, your Bible knowledge? It is time to sing, rejoice and expect God to deliver what He has promised. It is time to break forth through numerous areas of your life, for your children to be blessed also and receive their God given, God promised inheritance. (Isaiah 54:3)

Purpose in your heart to go into the New Year with fresh determination, fresh expectation and fresh faith, so God can bring increase and blessing to you. "Sing, O barren, you *who* have not borne! Break forth into singing, and cry aloud, you *who* have not labored with child! For more *are* the children of the desolate than the children of the married woman, says the Lord." (Isaiah 54:1)

Can you sing even when you do not see the increase yet? You must sing in faith. God will see your faith and meet your need. God is going to bring increase to you in the New Year.

Scripture Reading: Zechariah 13, 14; Revelation 21

Trivia Question: What did God call Himself to the widows?

December 31

"Do Not Look in the Rear View Mirror"

Philippians 3:13 — Brethren, I do not count myself to have apprehended; but one thing I do, forgetting those things which are behind and reaching forward to those things which are ahead. (NKJV)

God has been faithful. In all of the challenges that you encountered this past year, He has brought you through. We must refuse to dwell on last year's pain and bring them with us into this New Year. We cannot look in the rear view mirror and progress effectively. Paul teaches us that we must do this one thing, forget that which is behind you, those things that have impeded, imposed or interrupted your life. Leave it in last year. Leave it in your past. It is a new day and we are embarking on a New Year with new vision and revived dreams. It is time to press forward into God's horizon and what He has for you in the future. Blessings and God's goodness await you in the New Year. Proceed with anticipation and leave behind those things that weighed you down and even stopped your journey. Go forward in God and His promises. The best is yet to come for you and all you put your hands to. Don't look in the rear view mirror; the road ahead is clear and bright. Look ahead, go forward and be blessed.

Scripture Reading: Malachi; Revelation 22

Trivia Question: What are we to *work out?*

Answers

Trivia Answers

JANUARY

1. Honor thy father and mother (Ephesians 6:2)
2. David (Psalms 56:8)
3. Adam (Genesis 3:12)
4. Habakkuk (Habakkuk 1:13)
5. The Pharisees (Luke 11:43)
6. Solomon (1 Chronicles 28:9)
7. Mary (Luke 1:38)
8. The things of the Spirit of God (1 Corinthians 2:14)
9. Enter His gates with thanksgiving (Psalm 100:4)
10. Saul (1 Samuel 10:11,12)
11. Mara or bitter (Ruth 1:20)
12. Three (Genesis 12:5 - Sarah; Genesis 16:3 - Hagar; Genesis 25:1 - Keturah)
13. Hobab (Numbers 10:29)
14. Methuselah (Genesis 5:27)
15. Jedidiah (2 Samuel 12:25)
16. Thirty-one (Joshua 12:24)
17. Eighty-five (Joshua 14:10)
18. Benjamin (Philippians 3:5)
19. Hananiah, Mishael, Azariah (Daniel 1:7)
20. A physician (Colossians 4:14)
21. Zebedee (Matthew 4:21)
22. One year and a half (Acts 18:11)
23. Two (Ephesians 1:15-23 and Ephesians 3:14-21)
24. Amram and Jochebed (Exodus 6:20)
25. Psalm 119

26. "Little girl, I say arise." (Mark 5:41)
27. Gershom and Eliezer (Exodus 18:3,4)
28. A tax collector for the Roman government (Matthew 9:9)
29. No fruit, fruit, more fruit, much fruit (John 15:2,8)
30. Shem, Ham, Japheth (Genesis 6:10)
31. Ten (Luke 17:12)

FEBRUARY

1. Gomer (Hosea 1:3)
2. Revelation (Revelation 3:12)
3. Will never prosper (Proverbs 28:13)
4. Bethany of Judea (John 11:1)
5. Twelve (Numbers 13:2-16)
6. Because many Jews believed on Jesus because of the miracle (John 12:11)
7. Bathsheba (2 Samuel 11:3)
8. Jairus (Mark 5:22)
9. Jesus (Revelation 1:18)
10. Amaziah (2 Chronicles 26:3,4)
11. Bethsaida of Galilee (John 12:21)
12. Christ Jesus (Hebrews 3:1)
13. Pride, fullness of bread, abundance of idleness, failure to care for the poor and needy (Ezekiel 16:49)
14. A man called Judas (Acts 9:11)
15. Fifteen years after he prayed (2 Kings 20:1-6)
16. To love the Lord and love your neighbor as yourself (Matthew 22:34-40)
17. Armageddon (Revelation 16:16)
18. Naaman (2 Kings 15:14)
19. Daniel (Daniel 6:3)
20. Josiah/8 yrs. old (2 Kings 22:1)
21. "My God, My God, why hast thou forsaken me?" (Matthew 27:46)
22. Six (Genesis 1:31-2:2)
23. Hezekiah (2 Chronicles 29:25-36)
24. Mary Magdalene (Luke 8:2)
25. James, Joseph, Judas, and Simon (Mark 6:3)

26. That they would serve the Lord (Joshua 24:15)
27. Tiller of the ground (a tiller who became a killer) (Genesis 4:2)
28. Jeremiah (Jeremiah 32:2,3)
29. Paul and Barnabas (Acts 15:36-40)

MARCH

1. Revelation (Revelation 13:8)
2. The tongue (James 3:8)
3. Song of Solomon (Song of Solomon 8:7)
4. The Fool (Psalms 53:1)
5. When he is drawn away of his own lust and enticed (James 1:14)
6. Jehoshaphat (2 Chronicles 18:1)
7. Jesus (Matthew 5:8)
8. The Philippian jailer and his family (Acts 16:27-34)
9. Jesus (Matthew 5:13)
10. 1,005 (1 Kings 4:32)
11. Cornelius (Acts 10:1)
12. "There is no respect of persons with God." (Romans 2:11)
13. Thirty-six (Joshua 7:5)
14. Every fifty years (Leviticus 25:10)
15. Belshazzar (Daniel 5:1-9)
16. Matthew (Matthew 21:5)
17. The sweet psalmist of Israel (2 Samuel 23:1)
18. Simon Peter (John 20:6)
19. Mary (Mark 16:9)
20. "The measure of the stature of the fullness of Christ." (Ephesians 4:13)
21. A stone (Genesis 28:11,18)
22. God (Haggai 2:8)
23. 180 years old (Genesis 35:28,29)
24. A marriage in Cana of Galilee (John 2:1)
25. Grace (Ephesians 4:7)
26. In the stern of the boat sleeping on a pillow (Mark 4:38)
27. Seven (Joshua 6:4,8)
28. From his birth (John 9:1)
29. Four (Cush, Mizraim, Put, and Canaan) (Genesis 10:6)
30. God comes down in human form / Pre-incarnate appearance of God

the Son (Daniel 3:25; Joshua 5:13-15; Genesis 12:7; Genesis 32:22-32)
31. Confusion (Genesis 11:1-9)

APRIL

1.　In Genesis 17:5 Abram's name was changed to Abraham
2.　With thanksgiving and praise (Psalm 100:4)
3.　Spirit, soul and body (1 Thessalonians 5:23)
4.　The chief butler and chief baker (Genesis 40:12)
5.　Thirty years old (Genesis 41:46)
6.　Two (Ephesians 1:17-23 and Ephesians 3:14-21)
7.　Apostles, Prophets, Evangelists, Pastors and Teachers (Ephesians 4:11)
8.　300 (Judges 7:6,8, 16)
9.　7 days (Exodus 7:25)
10. The plague of lice (Exodus 8:18,19)
11. Twelve (Exodus 1:1-3)
12. Run the ship a ground (Acts 27:41)
13. Envy (Proverbs 14:30)
14. He built an altar (Genesis 8:20)
15. Twelve years old (Mark 5:42)
16. Manna (Joshua 5:12)
17. Psalm 119
18. A contentious and angry woman (Proverbs 21:18)
19. The stormy waters (Mark 4:39)
20. Moses (Exodus 4:10)
21. Jeremiah (Jeremiah 20:9)
22. Joshua (Joshua 1:1, 2)
23. Pitch (Genesis 6:14)
24. Ezekiel (Ezekiel 37:1-2)
25. Noah got drunk (Genesis 9:21)
26. Herod (Acts 12:1, 2)
27. Simon of Cyrene (Matthew 27:32)
28. Saul (Acts 8:1)
29. Peter (Matthew 8:14-15)
30. The cock crowed twice (Mark 14:72)

MAY

1. Reuben (Genesis 37:20-22)
2. Goliath (1 Samuel 17:5)
3. Areopagus (Acts 17:18,19)
4. Two (Luke 15:11)
5. Holiness (Hebrews 12:14)
6. Zechariah (Zechariah 9:9)
7. Jupiter (Zeus and Mercurias (Hermes) Acts 14:12)
8. His birthright (Genesis 25:31-34)
9. Two (John 6:9)
10. 120 years old (Deuteronomy 34:7)
11. Prodigal son's brother (Luke 15:28)
12. Ten (Luke 17:12)
13. Uriah (2 Samuel 11:15)
14. Mary Magdelene (Luke 8:2)
15. Lot (Genesis 19:8)
16. Jael (Judges 4:21)
17. Ruth (Ruth 1:3-5)
18. Satan (Matthew 4:3)
19. Revelation (Revelation 16:21)
20. Uz (Job 1:1)
21. Absalom (1 Chronicles 3:2)
22. Silas (Acts 16:25)
23. Michal (1 Samuel 18:20)
24. Two years old (Matthew 2:16)
25. Three (2 Corinthians 12:8)
26. Two:Moses and Elijah (Matthew 17:23)
27. Two: Manasseh and Ephraim (Genesis 41:50-52)
28. Honor your father and mother (Exodus 20:12)
29. Adam (Genesis 3:10)
30. The Road to Damascus (Acts 9:8)
31. Because David was a man of war and shed blood (1 Chronicles 28:3)

JUNE

1. Blasphemy (Matthew 26:65)
2. To cut the child in half (1 Kings 3:23-36)

3. Ezekiel (Ezekiel 37:1)
4. Absalom (2 Samuel 14:25)
5. Shall direct our paths (Proverbs 3:6)
6. Palm branches (John 12:13)
7. David's song of deliverance (2 Samuel 22 and Psalm 18)
8. Thirty-eight years (John 5:5)
9. The book of 1 Thessalonians (1 Thessalonians 5:22)
10. More than 40 men (Acts 23:13)
11. The prodigal son (Luke 15:15, 16)
12. Twelve Oxen (1 Kings 19:19)
13. Two she-bears tore up 42 young people (2 Kings 2:23-24)
14. Three months (1 Chronicles 13:14)
15. Annas (John 18:13)
16. The hand of the Lord (Proverbs 21:1)
17. 120 (Daniel 6:1)
18. Mercy and truth (Proverbs 3:3, 4)
19. Sixth (Luke 1:26)
20. First and second warning (Titus 3:10)
21. His children are blessed after him (Proverbs 20:7)
22. Jerusalem, Judea, Samaria and uttermost part of the Earth (Acts 1:8)
23. Shimei (2 Samuel 16:5-10)
24. Elisha (2 Kings 2:23, 24)
25. 40 years (1 Chronicles 29:27)
26. David (1 Kings 2:1, 2)
27. Gibeon (1 Kings 3:5)
28. Ahaziah (2 Kings 1:2)
29. Ahithophel (2 Samuel 17:20-23)
30. They spoke with other tongues (Acts 2:1-4)

JULY

1. Peace (Isaiah 54:13)
2. 18 wives, 60 concubines (2 Chronicles 11:21)
3. Peter (Acts 5:29)
4. Like the feet of a deer (Psalm 18:33)
5. The grace of God that offers salvation (Titus 2:11)
6. Seven (Proverbs 9:1)

7. They become wiser (Proverbs 9:9)
8. That they who are approved may be made manifest among you. (1 Corinthians 11:19)
9. A gold ring in a pig's snout (Proverbs 11:22)
10. A man of understanding (Proverbs 20:5)
11. Adultery (Matthew 5:28)
12. Whatever you want men to do to you, do also to them (Matthew 7:12)
13. The man that wanders away from understanding (Proverbs 21:16)
14. The Lord (Proverbs 21:30)
15. Two (Proverbs 30:15)
16. Peace (1 Corinthians 14:33)
17. Idolaters, Fornicators, Tempting the Lord, Murmuring (1 Corinthians 10:7-10)
18. Blessed (Proverbs 3:13)
19. Ahithophel (2 Samuel 15:31)
20. Ramah (1 Samuel 1:19)
21. 3 sons and 2 daughters (1 Samuel 2:21)
22. Healed a government official's son from afar (John 4:52-54)
23. The ones that were sent to tell Jesus about Lazarus (John 11:2)
24. They were conspiring to kill Lazarus so they were afraid that they would be put to death also (John 12:9-11)
25. 1,000 (Judges 15:16)
26. Noah builds an altar and offers sacrifices (Genesis 8:20)
27. Edomites (Genesis 36:9)
28. After Pharaoh's horses and chariots were covered by the sea and the Israelites walked through on dry ground (Exodus 15:19-20)
29. Plague of Frogs (Exodus 8:1-15)
30. A young virgin (1 Kings 1:2)
31. Micah (Micah 5:1-2)

AUGUST

1. Two turtledoves or two young pigeons (Luke 2:24)
2. The crown of life (James 1:12)
3. The peacemakers (Matthew 5:9)
4. Paul the apostle (1 Corinthians 11:1)
5. Love (Romans 13:8, 10)

6. "will not hear me" (Psalm 66:18)
7. They are subject to corruption and thievery (Matthew 6:19)
8. Shiprah and Puah (Exodus 1:15)
9. He sold all he had and bought it (Matthew 13:45)
10. I have no need of you (1 Corinthians 12:21)
11. The Father, the Word and the Holy Ghost (1 John 5:7)
12. Judas (Mark 14:10, 11
13. Barnabas (Acts 13:2)
14. "sweet" sleep (Proverbs 3:24)
15. Peter (Acts 2:14)
16. 3,000 (Acts 2:41)
17. Seven (Proverbs 9:1)
18. Gave it to the one who invested and had 10 talents (Matthew 25:28
19. 5,000 men (John 6:10)
20. A donkey (Numbers 22:28)
21. Hilkiah the priest (2 Chronicles 34:14)
22. Tradition says 3 but scripture does not say how many (Matthew 2:2)
23. All things (Romans 8:28)
24. Cephas (John 1:42)
25. Putting your trust in the Lord (Psalm 71:1)
26. Babylon, Persia, Greece, Rome (Daniel 7:4-7)
27. Two (Titus 3:10)
28. That they might be saved (Romans 10:1)
29. The word (Jesus) (John 1:14)
30. Ananias and Sapphira (Acts 5:1-10)
31. Jesus Christ (Revelation 1:5)

SEPTEMBER

1. Jesus (Luke 10:18)
2. Lie (Hebrews 6:18)
3. Andrew (Matthew 10:2)
4. Our burden (Psalm 55:22)
5. Twelve (Matthew 10:2)
6. John (John 13:23)
7. 70 years (Jeremiah 29:10)
8. Epaphras (Colossians 1:7)

9. Sexual sin (1 Corinthians 5:1-13)
10. The Holy Spirit (Ephesians 5:18)
11. Your wrath (Ephesians 4:26)
12. John Mark (Acts 13:5)
13. Asia (Acts 16:6)
14. Blood (Hebrews 9:22) The Blood of Christ (Ephesians 1:7)
15. Son of Consolation (Acts 4:36)
16. Elizabeth (Luke 1:57-60
17. Nadab and Abihu (Leviticus 10:1)
18. Macedonia (Acts 16:9)
19. John the Apostle (1 John 4:1)
20. Euodia and Syntyche (Philippians 4:2)
21. Clean beasts and birds for food and sacrifice (Genesis 7:2, 3)
22. Tried to hide among the trees in the garden (Genesis 3:8)
23. Enoch (Genesis 5:24)
24. Pharaoh's daughter (Exodus 2:10)
25. 32,000 (Judges 7:3)
26. 66 (Isaiah 66)
27. Michael (Jude 9)
28. Honor your father and mother (Exodus 20:12)
29. Bathsheba (2 Samuel 12:24)
30. Jerusalem (2 Samuel 5:1-5)

OCTOBER

1. Samson pulled down the great pillar and thousands of Philistines died in the rubble with him (Judges 16:30)
2. Riches and honor (1 Kings 3:13)
3. Abram (Genesis 17:5)
4. Sodom (Genesis 18:20-22)
5. Thou shalt have no other gods before me (Exodus 20:3)
6. Rubies (Proverbs 31:10)
7. By interpreting Pharaoh's dream (Genesis 41:1-44)
8. Visiting the fatherless, and widows and keeping yourself pure (James 1:27)
9. Queen of Sheba (1 Kings 10:1-7)
10. Isaiah (more than others) (Isaiah 53:1-12

11. Jesus (John 1:3)
12. The Holy Spirit (Genesis 1:2)
13. Moon and Sun (Genesis 1:16)
14. Not good that man should be alone (Genesis 2:18)
15. A gardener (Genesis 2:15)
16. A farmer (Genesis 9:20)
17. Haran in Canaan (Genesis 11:31)
18. A famine (Genesis 12:10)
19. He was the son of his old age (Genesis 37:3)
20. Egypt (Genesis 37:28)
21. Said no (Genesis 39:7-10)
22. Now let me die, since I have seen your face (Genesis 46:30)
23. Because I drew him out of the water (Exodus 2:10)
24. Moses saw an Egyptian smiting a Hebrew (Exodus 2:11)
25. Slow of speech (Exodus 4:10)
26. She judged her brother unjustly and was a racist (Numbers 12:1)
27. Moses was standing on Holy Ground (Exodus 3:5)
28. Nun (Joshua 2:1)
29. Be strong and courageous (Joshua 1:6, 9)
30. Deborah (Judges 4:4)
31. Lord, lay not this sin to their charge (Acts 7:60)

NOVEMBER

1. James (James 1:8)
2. Jacob and Esau (Genesis 25:26)
3. Trumpet, pitchers and lamps (Judges 7:16)
4. 40 years (Deuteronomy 1:3)
5. Jethro (Moses's father in law) (Exodus 18:14-22)
6. There was a famine in the land (Ruth 1:1)
7. Their own power delivered them (Judges 7:2)
8. A woman who Jesus casts seven evil spirits out of (Luke 8:2)
9. The sword shall never depart from David's house (2 Samuel 12:10)
10. Cana of Galilee (John 4:46)
11. A Pharisee, a ruler of the Jews (John 3:1)
12. Archippus (Colossians 4:17)
13. Andrew his brother (John 1:40, 41)

14. God's Word (Psalm 119:89)
15. Cornelius (Acts 10:1-5)
16. 5,000 (Matthew 14:19-21)
17. Crown of life (James 1:12)
18. A lion (Proverbs 30:30)
19. King Cyrus of Persia (Ezra 1:1-3)
20. Peter, James and John (Mark 9:2)
21. Esther (Esther 4:15, 16)
22. Abigail (1 Samuel 25:18)
23. Zarephath (1 Kings 17:8, 9)
24. Ruth (Ruth 1:16, 17)
25. Rahab (Joshua 2:3,4)
26. If anyone speaks against Jehovah they will die (Daniel 3:29)
27. Jael (Judges 4:21)
28. In the synagogue in Nazareth on the Sabbath (Luke 4:18)
29. The Almighty has dealt bitterly with me (Ruth 1:20)
30. The law (Proverbs 1:8)

DECEMBER

1. A kiss (Matthew 26:48)
2. When he prayed for his friends (Job 42:10)
3. Grace (Ephesians 4:7)
4. A glorious church without spot or wrinkle, holy (Ephesians 5:27)
5. His commandments (John 14:15)
6. Alexander the coppersmith (2 Timothy 4:14)
7. By hearing the Word of God (Romans 10:17)
8. A scoffer (Proverbs 13:1)
9. The house of the Lord (Psalms 23:6)
10. His heart (Proverbs 27:19)
11. An infidel (1 Timothy 5:8)
12. Righteousness and true holiness (Ephesians 4:24)
13. Rest (Hebrews 4:11)
14. The comforter who is the Holy Spirit (John 14:26)
15. Love (1 Corinthians 13:8)
16. 500 (1 Corinthians 15:6)
17. Drunk with wine (Acts 2:13, 15)

18. Be fruitful and multiply and fill the sea and Earth (Genesis 1:22)
19. Because their deeds are evil (John 3:19)
20. No, he was not married (1 Corinthians 7:7-9)
21. Because of their unbelief (Mark 6:5-6)
22. Hananiah, Mishael, Azariah (Daniel 1:6)
23. Their parents (Ephesian 6:1)
24. That we love one another (John 13:35)
25. Glory to God in the highest, and on Earth peace, goodwill toward men (Luke 2:14)
26. Heavenly places (Ephesians 2:6)
27. James, Cephas, John (Galatians 2:9)
28. Eunice (2 Timothy 1:5)
29. Tarshish (Jonah 1:3)
30. Their husband (Isaiah 54:4-5)
31. Our salvation with fear and trembling (Philippians 2:12)

About the Author

Baseball player, major league try-out participant, power lifter, body builder, manager of one of the highest profit producing health spas in the country, Joe Arminio had it all. A prestigious job, money, fast cars, wild living and success—everything the culture says you need to be happy; but he still was void of peace, full of rage and empty on the inside. Until one Monday evening, February 23, 1978, driving his brown Firebird down the New Jersey Garden State Parkway, by exit 150 at 9:10 PM, Joe had an encounter that would change his life from that moment and forever. The light of Jesus Christ crashed into his darkness. He was introduced to the Son of God, radically transformed and instantly delivered from rage, riotous living and routine religion. Jesus Christ, ignited a fire in Joe and the journey began.

Today, Joe is the Senior Pastor and founder of Abundant Life Whippany in New Jersey, Executive Director and Overseer of Renovation House (a drug and alcohol rehabilitation for men), Executive Director of Renovation House for Women, Chancellor of Abundant Life Christian School (K4-12th Grade), Founder of Abundant Life Bible Institute Ministry Training Center, Founder and CEO of ROC (Recreational Outreach Center) Gym, Founder and CEO of Kings Kids Day Care Center for infant children to PreK3, Executive Overseer of Abundant Life Ministries International, church planter, author, husband, father and grandfather.

Only Jesus can transform someone from death to life, darkness to light, bondage to freedom. To God be all the glory, great things He has done.

CPSIA information can be obtained
at www.ICGtesting.com
Printed in the USA
FFHW020036090519
52352611-57736FF